PERSEUS 2.0

PERSEUS 2.0

Interactive Sources and Studies on Ancient Greece

User's Guide

Gregory Crane, editor in chief

Yale University Press New Haven and London

Designed by James J. Johnson and set in ITC Veljovic types.

The materials in the Perseus system have been created by Perseus Project editors, staff, and contributors. Kate Withey of Willow Design is responsible for the user interface to Perseus.

Robert Morris wrote the TextEdit, Convert, and SystemInfo XFCN using Symantec Corporation's Think C™.

ISBN 0-300-05935-3 user's guide
ISBN 0-300-05939-6 concise edition
ISBN 0-300-05936-1 comprehensive edition
ISBN 0-300-05928-0 supplement to the concise edition
ISBN 0-300-05938-8 videodisc

The paper in this book meets the guidelines for permanence and durability of the Committee on Production Guidelines for Book Longevity of the Council on Library Resources.

Printed in the United States of America.

10 9 8 7 6 5 4 3 2 1

CONTENTS

PERSEUS 2.0

CHAPTER 1: **INTRODUCTION**

Perseus 2.0 is an electronic database on Archaic and Classical Greece that was designed to expand the ways in which ancient Greek literature, history, art, and archaeology can be studied. This chapter of the User's Guide is intended to provide a brief introduction to the expectations and motivations for using Perseus, to show off new features built into Perseus, and to provide quick access to Perseus 2.0 for experienced users of version 1.0.

Newcomers to the Perseus environment will find all they need to know about equipment requirements and setup in chapter 2 and about using Online Help and the Guided Tours of Perseus in chapter 3. This guide is intended as more of a self-tutorial than a technical manual, and it is our hope that users will avail themselves of the many examples and illustrations herein.

1.1 WHAT IS PERSEUS?

Perseus 2.0 represents the completion of a plan, first outlined in 1985, to construct a large and heterogeneous database of materials—textual and visual—illustrating the Archaic and Classical Greek world. Primary support for Perseus 2.0 has come from the Annenberg/CPB Projects with additional support from Apple Computer, the Fund for the Improvement of Post-Secondary Education, the Getty Grant Program, the National Endowment for the Arts, the National Science Foundation, and the Xerox Corporation. Perseus is a collaborative enterprise to which individuals from dozens of institutions have contributed over the years. Originally centered at Harvard University, the Perseus Project moved to Tufts University in the fall of 1993.

Scale in such an enterprise is important: we knew that we could not, of course, include every piece of primary evidence about ancient Greece, but what we wanted to assemble was a "critical mass" of materials. We wanted the database to have enough overall depth to support wide-ranging study of many topics. For the general student of ancient Greece, Perseus 2.0 constitutes a compact digital library with many key materials: 24,000 images, with information on 1420 vases, 366 sculptures, 384 buildings, 179 sites, and 524 coins. Perseus 2.0 holds two-thirds of the surviving literature, up to the death of Alexander the Great, in Greek with English translation; the Liddell-Scott *Intermediate Greek-English Lexicon;* a color atlas of the Greek world; articles on ancient authors and archaeology; an overview of Greek history from Homer to the death of Alexander the Great; and a 2600-entry bibliography. Thus, Perseus contains a representative selection of primary data and a substantial amount of secondary documentation; however, it was not conceived as a replacement for the university library. Perseus 2.0 is, rather, a tool that complements traditional resources, and it may be compared to a bookshelf stocked with standard texts and references, with the ability inherent to the electronic medium to search and organize information quickly.

1.2 KEY GOALS

At the beginning of our work, we made two strategic decisions about the scope and design of this database. First, we had initially considered developing an "interactive curriculum" on ancient Greek culture—something like a unified book with a massive "appendix" of source materials. Such an approach would have had obvious advantages: we could have chosen several unifying themes and provided detailed materials on these, and such an electronic book could be packaged for a very wide audience. Students and scholars alike would have derived benefits from the predictability and homogeneity of such a design.

After considerable thought, however, we chose to build as general a tool as we could rather than a resource that covered one or more topics of ancient Greece in detail. In part, our decision reflected the prejudices of faculty who told us that they wanted better access to primary materials—texts, maps, pictures of art objects, site plans, searching aids, and other basic tools—so that they could construct their own arguments and narratives. At the same time, we sensed that neatly packaged electronic books were premature: all of us, in every field, are still learning how best to use interactive tools. We recognized early on that no one really understood how electronic editions of source texts should be designed or how catalog entries for museum objects should be organized so as to exploit the strengths of this new medium. We chose to concentrate on what we already, in 1986, called the "infrastructure" necessary to help people—from elementary school students to scholars—explore the ancient Greek world in ways that were not feasible with print tools.

Second, we were determined to build a database that would be accessible to the widest possible audience. It would, in some ways, have been much easier to build Perseus on a high-end workstation, but neither these high-end machines nor the expensive software components that we would need were widely accessible to our target audience. While we hoped to construct something of interest to computer scientists specializing in Hypertext systems, we wanted Perseus to extend, not restrict, the audience for ancient Greek culture. Our goal was to create a database for a hardware platform that cost less than $3,000. At present, the cost of a system to run Perseus—and run it well—is between $1,500 and $2,000. When in 1987 we began serious development, MS-DOS dominated the PC world and the Macintosh computer was the only feasible platform for our work. HyperCard (which we first encountered in May 1987 as beta software called WildCard), for all its limitations, provided a reasonable delivery environment. HyperCard is, however, slow, limited in its capabilities, and—worst of all—for all practical purposes restricted to the Macintosh environment. Perseus 2.0 is, in all probability, the last version of the database that will use HyperCard. Nevertheless, HyperCard has allowed us to provide a wide range of features on a relatively inexpensive hardware platform.

Our primary challenge, perhaps, has been reconciling the emphasis on infrastructure and the determination to reach the widest possible audience. Most of our efforts have gone into building a database that would not only serve a broad audience immediately but that could also grow more useful over time. As a result, there is a sharp distinction between Perseus 2.0—the monumental database that we can distribute inexpensively on CD-ROM (compact disc read-only memory)—and the "real" Perseus database, which consists of many applications and databases stored in a variety of formats, none of which is tied to any one application or operating system.

All texts, for example, have been stored in a general-purpose format called SGML (Standard Generalized Markup Language), which can facilitate sophisticated text analysis (for example, a comparison of the vocabularies of two different characters in a play, or a search for poetry quoted by Plato). HyperCard cannot support such work, however, and we have had to eliminate the SGML encoding from our texts before publishing them.

Likewise, when we began assembling pictures, videodiscs were the best medium for publishing images, and the infrastructure needed to support libraries of digital images was years away from our audience. We chose, however, to collect 35-mm slides, even though the film was vastly more expensive than videotape. The slides, when transferred to video, did not produce images as sharp as those based on 3/4 videotape. Now, however, as videodiscs have begun to disappear and digital images are common, our digitized slides are far clearer and more detailed than any video-based images could be, and we can, in future years, redigitize these slides to provide images of even greater quality. If we had used video images rather than slides to produce the best possible videodisc in 1992, we would have constructed a resource that was obsolete in 1995. The maps, linguistic databases, and other elements of Perseus each reflect self-standing projects that exploit or, in some cases, define standards. Perseus 2.0 is, in many ways, the tip of an iceberg. Even if we were not to add any more materials and were only to republish Perseus in newer software packages, its functionality could increase dramatically over the years.

1.3 GENERAL READERS AND SPECIALISTS

Although Perseus 2.0 has many things to offer a wide range of users, we have found that most people tend to fall into one of two groups.

First, those who are not specialists in ancient Greek culture have, in working with pre-release versions of Perseus 2.0, found it to be a handy and fairly comprehensive environment within which to explore aspects of ancient Greece. Thomas R. Martin's Overview of Classical Greek History has been expanded since Perseus 1.0 and now contains more than two thousand new links to other materials in the database. The Overview was designed to provide a succinct introduction both to many aspects of Greek history, literature, society, and culture and to the resources available in the database.

Second, Perseus 2.0 is one prototype for a digital library, but it was designed to augment, rather than replace, traditional tools. Perseus 2.0 offers to specialists a useful compendium of many source materials, but the individual pieces of Perseus 2.0 will probably be most useful for this group: the specialist will find in Perseus a series of interlinked individual tools, a collection of "books" rather than a comprehensive library. In Perseus 1.0, we were already able to offer a number of tools that constituted an advance on what had previously been published. The retrieval tools, for example, allowed users to search the texts included in Perseus 1.0 in ways that were not possible in any other system. Similarly, Perseus 1.0 included a substantial body of original visual materials commissioned by the project: the 1000 color pictures of 500 Greek coins from the Dewing Collection, the 450 images of the Aegina Pediments in Munich, and the 111 views of the Harvard Cleophrades Crater, to take only three examples, each could have constituted a separate publication that contributed to the study of Greek art and archaeology. Perseus 2.0 contains many more new resources for the specialist. The Philological Tools not only cover more authors but have themselves been refined and expanded. The coverage of art and archaeology has grown enormously—Perseus 2.0 contains, for example, information on more than ten times as many vases than did version 1.0. And where Perseus 1.0 contained only outline maps of ancient Greece, Perseus 2.0 contains roughly a thousand color satellite images and topographic maps.

1.4 NEW FEATURES IN PERSEUS 2.0

New additions to Perseus 2.0 fall into the areas of textual, geographical, and object data, on one hand, and electronic enhancements, on the other. As for data, there is more of almost everything, with a completely new Atlas containing about one thousand color maps derived from satellite data and the Digital Chart of the World. The following new features have been built into the software:

Online Help, keyed to the part of Perseus in which you are located

Search Tools for art and archaeology

the Browser and Lookup, designed to make it easier to find out what is in the databases the Search Saver, a means of storing and keeping at hand the results of an operation

new Philological Tools, which place at your disposal a sophisticated means of searching both Greek and English texts, and of processing and organizing philological data

With the exception of the Atlas (which has been completely rebuilt), no aspect of the Perseus database has grown more dramatically than the collection of vases. Perseus 2.0 contains information on 1420 vases illustrated with more than 14,500 images. A grant from the National Endowment for the Arts allowed us to commission six essays by experts in the field that introduce the styles of major Greek vase painters as well as the collection of vases included in Perseus 2.0. These essays, which total about 40,000 words (roughly 160 pages of double-spaced typescript), contain specific links to 428 separate illustrations, many of them new photographs taken by Maria Daniels, the Perseus Project photographer.

1.5 QUICK ENTRY FOR USERS OF PERSEUS 1.0

The basic operation of Perseus and its interface are substantially the same. Users of Perseus 1.0 will want to turn to the installation and startup procedure, which has been greatly simplified (section 2.3). New Guided Tours and Paths (section 3.2) highlight the new features built into Perseus. Online Help is available anywhere in Perseus by clicking the "?" icon on the Navigator Palette (this feature is described in section 3.3).

Of particular interest will be the chapters devoted to Search Tools (chapter 5), the Atlas (chapter 7), and Philological Tools (chapter 8).

Two issues concerning upgrading versions are covered: converting paths from version 1.0 to 2.0 (section 10.2.7), and the CD Swapper (section 10.4) built to accommodate this multi-CD version of Perseus.

1.6 THE CONCISE EDITION OF PERSEUS 2.0

Yale University Press has published Perseus 2.0 in two editions, the Comprehensive Edition and the Concise Edition. The former is a four-CD-ROM set, and the latter is a single CD-ROM. The Concise Edition corresponds to Perseus Disk 1 and contains all texts, tools, utilities, and thumbnail images that are in the Comprehensive Edition. Thus, the Concise Edition has the same textual contents, capabilities, and features as the Comprehensive Edition. It lacks most of the full-screen images.

Full-screen images in the Concise Edition include all pictures linked to the Historical Overview, to the Encyclopedia, to the Essays, to vases from the Boston Museum of Fine Arts cataloged by Caskey and Beazley, to more than nine hundred site or architecture images from the Large Site Plans, and to the Paths that are distributed with Perseus 2.0. In addition, all of the approximately 3600 sculpture images have been included. This brings the total to approximately 6100 full-screen images in the Concise Edition of Perseus.

These images are kept in five folders called Universal Images on the Perseus CD. To get a sense of what is there, you can browse through them with the Slide Shower (described in section 4.6.5).

For information on upgrading to the Comprehensive Edition of Perseus, contact Yale University Press, 203-432-7620 (phone), 203-432-2394 (fax), yupmkt@yalevm.cis.yale.edu (e-mail).

1.7 FUTURE DEVELOPMENTS

Perseus continues to develop on a number of fronts:

Perseus for Windows: Support from the Annenberg/CPB Projects has allowed us to begin work on a new platform-independent version of Perseus that will run both on the Macintosh and under the Windows operating system.

Perseus on the World Wide Web: Perhaps the most exciting development in recent years has been the rise of the Internet. We have established a Perseus World Wide Web site (http://www.perseus.tufts.edu), which contains a variety of useful tools and the latest developments in Perseus. The information at the Web site includes copies of documentation, a growing body of source materials (some of which are not in Perseus 2.0), reports on the use of Perseus in teaching and research, links to other relevant sites (such as the Perseus Atlas Project at Holy Cross), and various other services.

Perseus Atlas Project: The maps available in Perseus 2.0 were developed by Professor D. Neel Smith of Holy Cross. He continues to work with state-of-the-art Geographic Information Systems tools and such datasets as the satellite imagery and the Digital Chart of the World. One goal of the Perseus Atlas Project is to create an online service whereby this material could be accessed and analyzed directly over the Internet.

Evaluation of Perseus in Teaching and Learning: A grant from the Fund to Improve Post-Secondary Education has allowed us to study the impact of Perseus on teaching and learning at more than a dozen institutions. Results from this can be found on the World Wide Web site.

The Electronic Liddell-Scott-Jones Greek Lexicon: Grants from the National Endowment for the Humanities and the National Science Foundation have made it possible for us to begin creating an electronic version of the standard Greek lexicon as well as other more specialized lexicographic tools.

Ancient Science: Support from the National Science Foundation has allowed us to begin work on materials central to the history of science. This support will allow us to offer a complete version of Aristotle and of other key texts (such as Euclid's *Elements*).

CHAPTER 2: **EQUIPMENT REQUIREMENTS AND SETUP**

If you are...	then be sure to read...
Evaluating your equipment needs	Section 2.1 on hardware and software, and 2.2 on configurations
Installing Perseus for the first time	Section 2.4 on hardware installation and software installation
Installing Perseus 2.0 and are familiar with Perseus 1.0	Section 2.3 for quick installation and startup instructions
Optimizing your Perseus configuration	Section 2.2 on configurations
Changing your Perseus installation	Section 2.2 on configurations
Having trouble starting up Perseus	All of chapter 2, especially section 2.6 on troubleshooting
Having trouble opening images	Section 2.6 on troubleshooting

2.1 HARDWARE AND SOFTWARE REQUIREMENTS

Perseus requires certain hardware and software elements. To some extent, the requirements vary according to technical resources and the primary use of Perseus in your configuration.

Users of Macintosh computers belonging to the PowerPC family, please take note. In the most recent PowerPC machines—that is, those shipped as of fall 1995 with 8 MB of RAM installed—the system software eats up a tremendous amount of RAM, leaving only about 3.5 MB for Perseus. Because Perseus 2.0 requires 5 MB of RAM to run well, you will need to add more memory. See the discussion on SIMMs chips in section 2.2.

2.1.1 HARDWARE

Macintosh computer

Perseus runs on Macintosh computers and is distributed as a set of HyperCard stacks. HyperCard is a software foundation for building computer applications. As a sophisticated tool with a large database, Perseus is a high-end use of the HyperCard program. Formerly, Perseus required a fast computer to operate efficiently, but now you can achieve reasonable performance with almost any new Macintosh model.

Table 2.1 gives you a quick indication of the Macintosh models capable of running Perseus. You should also consult the more detailed technical requirements that follow.

Macintosh Models	Satisfactory Performance with Perseus	Optimal Performance with Perseus
Mac LC family	X	
Mac II family	X	
Mac LC-based Performa family	X	
Mac Quadra-based Performa family		X
Mac Centris family		X
Mac Quadra family		X
Mac PowerPC family		X

Table 2.1 Macintosh Models for Using Perseus

Smaller and older Macintosh computers, such as the Mac Plus, Mac SE, and Mac Classic, are not recommended for use with Perseus because of their 9-inch screens and their inability to display color digital images. The Macintosh Color Classic can display color images but is slow and has a small screen.

The Macintosh computer you select must meet certain minimum technical demands. An optimum configuration is one with a Macintosh Quadra, Centris, or PowerPC computer and 24-bit color display. Detailed requirements for Perseus are shown in table 2.2.

Specification	Minimum	Optimum
Microprocessor	68020	68040
Hard disk	7 MB minimum of free space available for hard disk files	7 MB minimum of free space available for hard disk files
RAM	5 MB allotted to Perseus Player	8 to 20 MB allotted to Perseus Player
Color display	8-bit color	24-bit color
Monitor size	13- or 14-inch color monitor	17-inch color monitor, or dual monitors (at least one color)

Table 2.2 Computer Specifications for Using Perseus

Hard disk size

Perseus requires at least 7 megabytes (MB) of free space available on your hard disk to run in the most basic configuration. This space is taken up by the Local Stacks folder, copied over from the CD-ROM during installation, which contains operating instructions for your computer. The remaining Perseus information is stored on the CD-ROMs, so relatively little other hard disk space is required.

You will need more hard disk space if you modify the primary configuration of Perseus by relocating CD-ROM information to the hard disk. This step speeds up the performance of Perseus, but it also substantially increases the required hard disk space (see section 2.2).

Computer monitor

You need a color monitor to use Perseus. (Perseus will also run on a black-and-white monitor, but this configuration will not allow the display of any color images.) Most Macintosh computers with color monitors are configured to display 16-bit or 8-bit color. The display mode of the monitor can be verified and reset through the Monitors Control Panel, available from the Apple menu (). Eight-bit mode displays 256 colors, 16-bit mode displays thousands of colors, and 24-bit mode displays millions of colors.

Color depth

Most color images in Perseus are 24-bit color images. Although the images look best when displayed in 24-bit color, they can be displayed in 8-bit and 16-bit color mode, with some corresponding degradation of image quality.

Many newer Macintosh models, such as the Performa 636, come with 16- or 24-bit color. Other recent Macintosh models use VRAM (video RAM) expansion kits to upgrade the display capability to 24-bit color. Older Macintosh models use display cards to upgrade the display capability to 24-bit color.

When you are evaluating the monitor and color display requirements for your Perseus configuration, consider the audience who will be using the program. If Perseus will be used mainly for its primary texts and philological tools, you may not need the ability to display images using millions of colors. If the main use is for art history or archaeological inquiry, you should probably have a configuration that provides for thousands or millions of colors (16-bit or 24-bit mode).

Monitor size

Although a 14-inch color monitor will work well with Perseus, large monitors (16–21 inches) offer several advantages: they allow many more windows to be simultaneously visible, and they are more convenient for the oversized images found in the Perseus Atlas and architectural site plans.

Another way to expand the available screen size is to use two monitors placed next to each other. The expanded screen size shows more windows and images simultaneously. In this configuration, one monitor can be color and one can be black and white. The computer treats the two monitors as one screen, where windows can be dragged from one screen to the other.

Apple-compatible CD-ROM drive

Both the Comprehensive and Concise Editions of Perseus 2.0 are CD-ROM-based programs, and a CD-ROM drive that is compatible with Apple Macintosh computers is necessary to read the Perseus compact discs. Various CD-ROM drives are available, including internal and external models. CD-ROM drives vary in their performance, which is measured by access speed (in milliseconds) and transfer rate (in kilobytes per second, or KBps). Some CD-ROM drives have achieved transfer rates greater than 300 KBps and average access times less than 300 milliseconds. The faster the drive, the better Perseus will perform. There are also ways to make your CD-ROM drive work faster by using software enhancements (see section 2.1.2).

Although the Comprehensive Edition is a four-CD set, you do not need multiple CD-ROM drives to use it. Instead, the Perseus software keeps track of requests for data located on CD-ROMs other than the one currently in the drive, and it will prompt you to swap CD-ROMs (see section 5.4). If you have more than one CD-ROM drive, however, you can use them to reduce the amount of CD-ROM swapping required. Multiple CD-ROM drives are "daisy-chained" together, with each one appearing as a separate drive on the Macintosh desktop.

To connect the CD-ROM drive to your computer, you need a SCSI (Small Computer System Interface) cable, which is normally provided with the CD-ROM drive. You may also need a SCSI terminator, if you do not already have a terminated SCSI device attached to your Macintosh. Consult the technical documentation for your CD-ROM drive for more information on connecting the drive to your computer. (See also "CD-ROM software drivers and accelerators," in the next section.)

Videodisc player and monitor (optional)

A videodisc player is needed only if you wish to use the Perseus videodisc instead of or in addition to the digitized images available on the Perseus CD-ROMs. The videodisc contains almost all the images available on the CD-ROM, as well as a short sequence of motion video and narration.

Possible options for the player include: Pioneer 4200, Pioneer 6000A, Pioneer 6010A, Sony LDP 1200, Sony 1500, Sony 2000, and Hitachi 9550. Any standard video or TV monitor will work, but models with video input jacks are much easier to use than models without such jacks.

You will need audiovisual cables to connect the videodisc player to the monitor and a computer interface cable to connect the player to the Macintosh. The player-to-monitor cable is a standard one if the monitor has built-in jacks, and the right connectors may be bought at any electronics store. The computer interface cable should be purchased with the player. Such cables can also be purchased from some specialized dealers.

Each player is different, and cables are not interchangeable. For example, a cable made for a Pioneer videodisc player will not work with a Sony videodisc player.

2.1.2 SOFTWARE

Perseus requires several software elements. Make sure you have each of these before you install Perseus.

System 7

Perseus 2.0 requires the Apple system software version 7.0 or later. Version 2.0 of Perseus takes advantage of features specifically offered by System 7, such as QuickTime.

Perseus Player, HyperCard, and HyperCard Player

It is no longer necessary to have the application HyperCard to run Perseus, because Perseus 2.0 is distributed along with a stand-alone Home stack, called Perseus Player. HyperCard 2.3 is still necessary for writing extensions to Perseus, and still must be used to run Perseus 1.0. In the past, Macintosh computers were distributed with the HyperCard application. More recently, they have been distributed with a limited version of HyperCard, called HyperCard Player. Stacks written as extensions of Perseus and Perseus 1.0 will not run under HyperCard Player, because it sets the user lever to Read Only. If HyperCard Player is on your Macintosh and you wish to run Perseus 1.0 or a Perseus extension, it is recommended that you archive or delete HyperCard Player and replace it with the full HyperCard 2.3 application. You can buy HyperCard from a software distributor.

The Perseus Installer software will automatically set the memory partition of Perseus Player to the minimum amount required for Perseus (see section 2.3).

SMK GreekKeys 7.0 (for typing accented Greek)

Perseus supports the SMK GreekKeys 7.0 character set for displaying Greek characters on the screen. You can read, copy, and paste Greek text in Perseus without GreekKeys 7.0, but to type accented Greek the character set must be installed in your system. This is strongly recommended, because the ability to type accented Greek is necessary for accurate searches of parsed Greek words.

GreekKeys 7.0 is a keyboard program, designed for the Macintosh, that enables you to type accented Greek letter fonts with a standard Macintosh keyboard. Greek letters are paired with keys on the keyboard, and diacritics are created by pressing the Option key in combination with a letter key.

Perseus does not hold any rights to SMK GreekKeys and therefore cannot distribute it. GreekKeys 7.0 may be purchased from Scholars Press Customer Services, P.O. Box 6996, Alpharetta, GA 30239-6996, 1-800-437-6692.

Section 8.4.1 includes a brief discussion on typing Greek. The Greek alphabet, its transliteration into Latin characters, and its GreekKeys equivalents may be found in Online Help under the stack topic "The Greek Alphabet."

CD-ROM software drivers and accelerators

Your computer needs a system software extension to read the CD-ROM drive. This software is normally provided with your CD-ROM drive.

System software enhancements can also be installed to accelerate the performance of the CD-ROM. These enhancements increase the access speed or transfer rate, or both, between the computer and the CD-ROM drive. Some enhancements can increase the speed by 50 percent or more. Investigate the availability of CD-ROM system enhancements through your system administrator or local software distributor.

The Perseus Project has not thoroughly tested these enhancements and does not guarantee their performance or reliability. Some software builds permanent files that must be discarded before upgrading from version 1.0.

QuickTime

QuickTime is an Apple system extension that comes with the Apple System 7 Software. It is a software architecture that defines ways in which digitized video is compressed, decompressed, and synchronized with sound. Perseus relies on QuickTime to display digitized images that have been compressed in the JPEG format. In most instances, QuickTime will already be installed in the Extensions folder of System 7. If QuickTime is not present in your Extensions folder, check your system diskettes for a copy and install it. The absence of QuickTime results in unusual image displays, showing the QuickTime symbol rather than the photograph. The current release of QuickTime is version 2.0.

2.2 CONFIGURATIONS FOR PERSEUS

Perseus is primarily meant to be used from the CD-ROMs on which it is published, but it can also be used in other system configurations, such as hard disks and networks. The factors that might influence your choice of Perseus configurations are the number of intended users, the resources available for hardware, and the technical skills available to set up alternate configurations. Some configurations and their strengths and limitations are listed in this section.

When you are using a single computer, there are several ways to optimize it for Perseus. The primary way is to select a fast computer (such as a Centris) and fast CD-ROM drive. The Apple CD-300S is a good choice for a CD-ROM drive, with an access speed of 300 KBps.

You can also add random-access memory (RAM) to the total available memory. More RAM will allow you to allocate a larger memory partition to Perseus Player, so that you can open more stacks and images at the same time. The preferred way to do this is to add Single Inline Memory Modules (SIMMs). Beyond 16 MB the computer will not run any faster; the advantage to expanding RAM above that level is the ability to run other applications simultaneously with Perseus. You can try using System 7's virtual memory facility to expand the total available RAM, although this method produces slower results than adding hardware RAM. The RAM partition of virtual memory cannot exceed the amount of free space on the computer's hard disk.

Another way to optimize your system is to place frequently used parts of Perseus on the hard disk, which allows faster access than the CD-ROM drive. The size of the hard disk will determine how much information can be relocated. For more information on this option, see section 2.3, "Quick Startup."

You may also use Perseus in a network configuration. The contents of the Perseus CD-ROMs or the CD-ROMs can be placed on dedicated file servers accessed through workstations linked to the network. If you plan a network configuration for Perseus, be sure to have enough disk space to accommodate the information on all the CD-ROMs of Perseus, about 2 gigabytes (GB).

Advantages of a network configuration are that several people can use Perseus at the same time, access time will likely be faster (depending on the network), and you might save money on hardware. (If you run Perseus on a network, you must have a network license. Contact Yale University Press for network licensing information.)

The information that follows provides some detail on alternative configurations for Perseus. The most effective way to use the information is to skim it for an overall understanding, then read it in greater detail when you have become familiar with Perseus. If you are a novice computer user or a first-time user of Perseus, you should also read the rest of this chapter for more complete information. If you are an experienced user of computers and Perseus, review this section for suggestions on ways to improve your configuration.

2.2.1 USING PERSEUS ON A SINGLE SYSTEM

No reconfiguration

The simplest configuration of Perseus is when individuals or groups use the program at a single computer using the Perseus CD-ROMs. The advantages are that a large amount of information is accessible via a single workstation, a relatively small amount of hard disk space is required, and the system need not be dedicated to Perseus. The disadvantages are that CD-ROM access can be slower than optimized access on a hard disk, and only one person or group can use Perseus at one time.

This configuration requires a computer, color monitor, and CD-ROM drive, at minimum. In a typical configuration, an individual runs Perseus by using the minimum required files from the hard disk (about 7 MB) and drawing all other information and images from the CD-ROMs.

If this is your configuration, you should consider adding CD-ROM accelerator software to speed up performance of the CD-ROM drive. These enhancements are described in section 2.1.2.

Moderate reconfiguration

Copying folders to the hard disk

You can improve the speed and performance of Perseus on a single computer by relocating some folders beyond the minimum required from the CD-ROMs to the local hard disk. The advantage is faster operation, because a hard disk can be accessed more quickly than a CD-ROM. The disadvantage of relocating folders is that a large amount of space on the hard disk will be occupied by Perseus.

The Installer automatically decides which folders to copy to your hard disk.

Using multiple CD-ROM drives

A different way to configure a single system is to use more than one CD-ROM drive. The advantage of adding drives is that you will spend less time swapping CD-ROMs, because more than one CD-ROM is available simultaneously. The disadvantages are continued slow access of the CD and the expense of adding another hardware item to your configuration. If your configuration uses multiple CD-ROM drives, consider adding the CD-acceleration utilities that speed up access to the CD-ROM (described in section 2.1.2).

Advanced reconfiguration—for system administrators

Caveat: The Perseus Installer software will not do this procedure for you. We advise you not to attempt this reconfiguration unless you are sure it is necessary.

An advanced reconfiguration of a Perseus system involves moving selected elements of Perseus to the hard disk based on the information that will be used most frequently. This step is like the previous suggestion for moderate reconfiguration, but it requires a more selective process of relocating Perseus elements and a firm understanding of search paths. The advantage is faster operation. The disadvantages are a more demanding installation procedure and the need to know which parts of Perseus you will use most often.

Perseus files consist of HyperCard stacks, drawings, photographic images, QuickTime movies, and database files. In the moderate reconfiguration described earlier, you move entire folders containing Perseus elements. In the advanced reconfiguration, you go through a more selective process to identify stacks, images, and database files to copy from the CD-ROM to the hard disk.

If you look at the same Perseus images repeatedly, you may want to copy some image folders to the hard disk. Images are grouped in folders according to their collection, and must be copied only one folder at a time. Section A.1 of the appendix contains a list of folder names and their contents. Identify the image folders you want to relocate and copy them to the hard disk. Copying folders from the CD-ROMs to the hard disk requires an adjustment to the Home stack to change the search paths. Read the next section in this chapter for information on the Home stack and search paths.

Folders containing images may be copied to the hard disk, but do not remove images from their folders or rename them, or else Perseus will be unable to find them.

If you use the same elements of Perseus repeatedly—for example, works by particular authors—you may want to move the pertinent database file from the Text Databases folder on the CD-ROM to the hard disk. This step will speed up access to the selected elements of Perseus. Just as you must change the Home stack search paths when you relocate an image folder, you must also change a special Perseus search path when you relocate a database file. Section 10.5.4, "Detailed Configuration," provides further information about the settings cards in the Gateway stack. This type of modification should be undertaken only after you are comfortable with file names, disk locations, and search paths.

These configuration strategies are best suited to the single-user, single-computer model. In many cases, particularly in instructional settings, more than one person or group will need to use Perseus at the same time. For solutions, read the network configuration descriptions in the next section.

2.2.2 USING PERSEUS ON A NETWORK

The purpose of a network is to share applications and data among several users at several workstations. File servers store the information, and local computers provide access to the shared information. Perseus can be used on a network to centralize access to the Perseus data and eliminate the need for redundant setups. Remember that network use of Perseus requires a network license from Yale University Press.

There are two main types of network protocols: LocalTalk and Ethernet. LocalTalk is an inexpensive network option, but it is slow. Ethernet is much faster, and many recent Macintosh models have built-in Ethernet capability, but it requires more expensive cabling. Ethernet can support many more simultaneous users than LocalTalk.

Several CD-ROM drives can be placed on a network as servers. This is an advantage only if you already own the CD-ROM drives. With the price of read-only memory (ROM) falling, it is cheaper and faster to copy the contents of the CD-ROMs onto large hard disks that will be file servers. (A 2.0 GB drive can be bought for around $500, a 4.0 GB drive for around $950.) You must have hard disk space for approximately 1.8 GB (2000 MB) of data from the CD-ROMs.

> A combination of CD-ROM drives and hard disks may be used. Just make sure that enough CD-ROM drives and hard disk space are available to provide access to all information in Perseus at the same time.

When you copy Perseus from the CD-ROMs to the file server disks, make sure the folders retain their original names. List the disk name and folder locations in the local Home stacks. All HyperCard stacks that are originally locked should remain locked.

The Home stack on each computer must list the image folders, the Atlas folder, and Local Stacks. Everything else is listed in the Gateway. The most efficient method of ensuring an accurate Home stack is to modify one Home stack with all the appropriate search paths for the file server folders. Copy that Home stack on each local computer, and make the appropriate changes to each local Home stack to reflect the name of the local hard drive.

A common challenge in network configurations is the security and stability of the data. Network administrators will be aware of software that protects the data from unintended modification and intentional tampering. For Perseus to work, however, it is essential that the stacks in the Local Stacks folder remain unlocked.

2.3 QUICK STARTUP

NOTE: Perseus users who are updating Perseus from version 1.0 to 2.0 should archive or delete all Perseus 1.0 files from the hard disk upon converting their version 1.0 Paths to version 2.0 (Path conversion is discussed in section 10.2.8). Some files have duplicate names. The version 1.0 files may create problems if they remain on the hard disk when you use version 2.0.

Follow these instructions to get Perseus 2.0 running right away. More detailed installation and startup instructions are given in section 2.4.

The following steps assume a familiarity with the Macintosh hardware and operating system. Also, these instructions apply only if you are using Perseus on a single system, not networked. If you are using a videodisc player, follow the hardware instructions in section 2.4.1 and the settings instructions in section 2.4.2.

➤ Switch on the CD-ROM drive (if it is an external one) and the videodisc player (if using one), start up the computer, and load the CD-ROM Perseus Disk 1 (or the Concise Edition Disk).

Be sure to turn on the CD-ROM drive and videodisc player before turning on the Macintosh.

NOTE: If you will be swapping CD-ROMs, be sure to turn off File Sharing in the Control Panels of your Macintosh. Otherwise the Macintosh will not eject the CD.

➤ When the Perseus Disk 1 icon appears on the desktop, open it.

➤ Double-click the application program Perseus Installer.

➤ When the Perseus Installer appears (figure 2.1), click the button appropriate to the amount of free space in your hard disk.

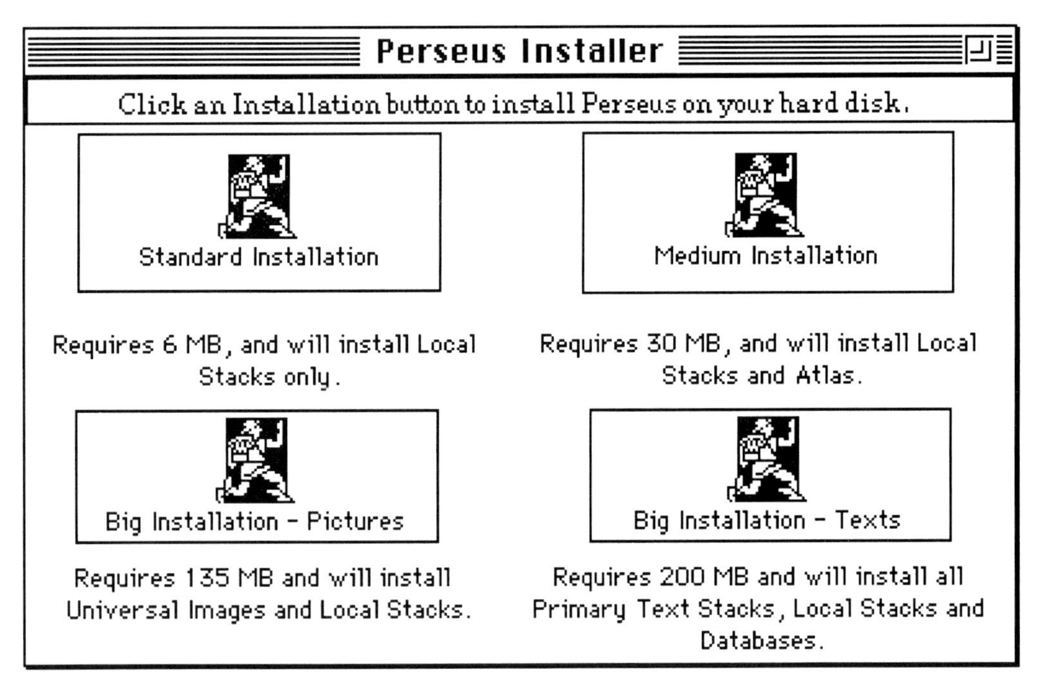

Figure 2.1 Perseus Installer

If you do not have enough ROM for the installation choice, the Installer will tell you.

The two Big Installations may take more than an hour, depending on your equipment.

➤ A dialog box appears, asking "Do you want to create a new folder for Perseus?" If you click Yes, you will be asked to type in a folder name after the next step. If you click No, the Installer will copy a folder called Local Stacks to your machine.

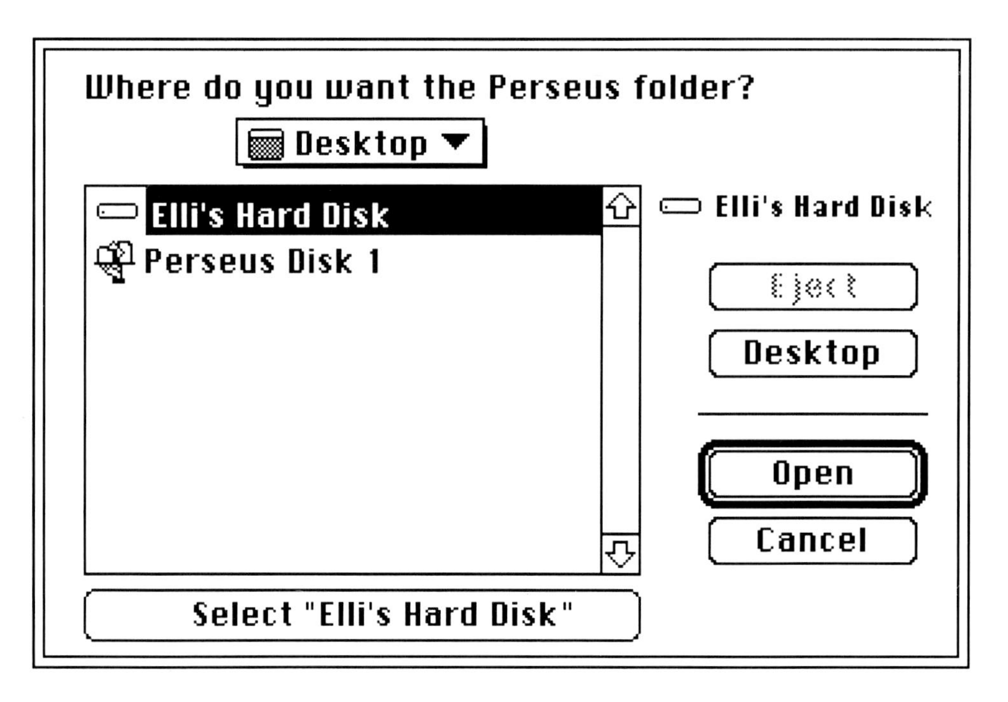

Figure 2.2 Installer dialog window

➤ A second dialog box appears, asking "Where do you want to install Perseus?" (figure 2.2). Choose your hard drive and click the button "Select [Your Hard Drive]" at the bottom.

➤ If you chose to create a new folder for Perseus, a third dialog box now appears, asking "Name of new folder." The default name is Perseus 2.0, or you can type in a name of your choice, then click OK.

➤ When the installation is complete, a dialog box will appear. Click Quit.

To start up Perseus 2.0, do the following:

➤ Open the folder you have designated for Perseus.

➤ Open the Local Stacks folder.

➤ Double-click the Perseus Player stack.

THIS PROCEDURE IS NEW FOR PERSEUS 2.0. DO NOT START UP BY DOUBLE-CLICKING THE PERSEUS GATEWAY.

After an interval, the Gateway and Navigator Palette will appear (figure 2.3).

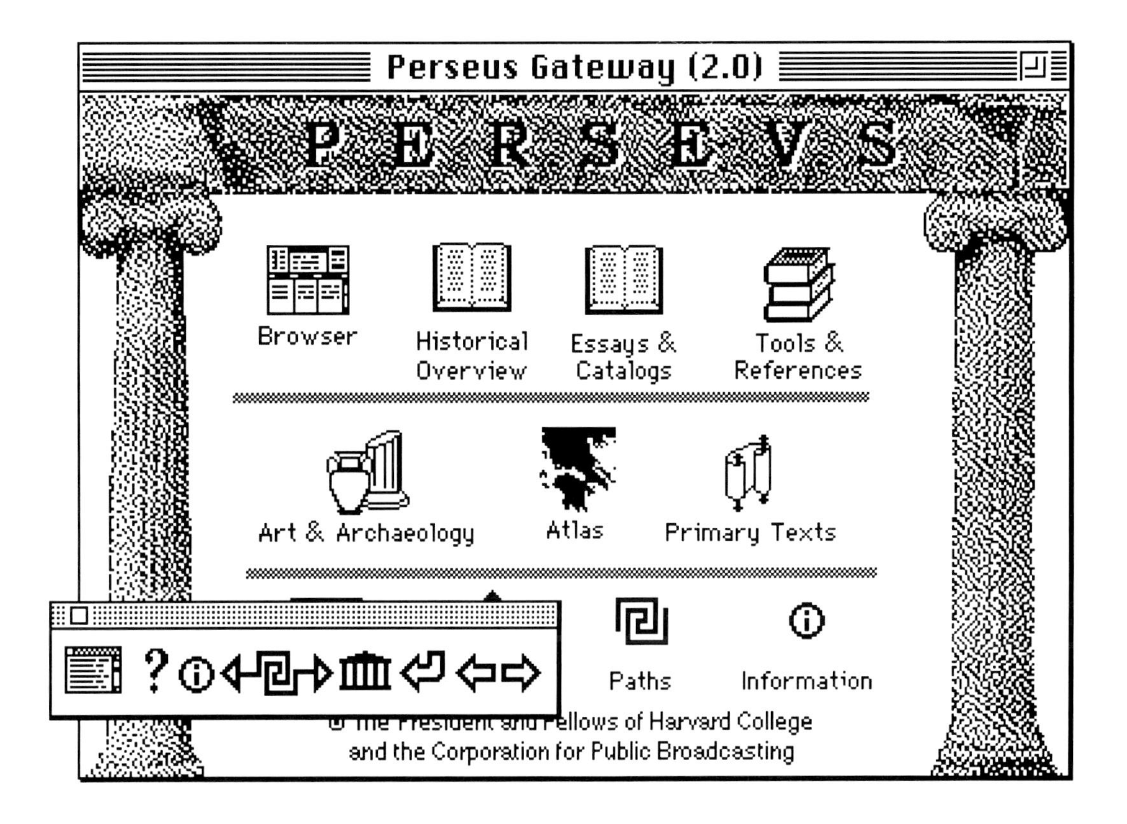

Figure 2.3 Perseus Gateway with Navigator Palette in lower left

While working in Perseus, you need only to single-click the mouse.

Perseus 2.0 is now ready to use. The Navigator Palette may be dragged out of the way. Remember that you can always return to the Gateway by clicking the Gateway (temple) icon on the Navigator Palette.

To quit Perseus, choose Quit from the File menu, or press the keys Command-q.

Here are two tasks you may want to complete before exploring Perseus 2.0.

➤ Duplicate the Paths, Notebook, and Perseus CD Swapper stacks and personalize them by renaming them, for example, "Elli's Paths" and "Elli's Notebook."

By renaming these stacks, you can distinguish your Paths and Notebooks from those of other users. When you start Perseus, you will need to identify the location of these stacks through the Settings option, available from the Gateway. More information on Settings is in section 2.4. Detailed descriptions of Path, Notebook, and Perseus CD Swapper procedures may be found in chapter 10, "Saving Your Work."

➤ Make an alias of the Perseus Player and keep it in a convenient place on your computer.

For more detailed instructions on installation of hardware and startup, read section 2.4.

2.4 DETAILED INSTALLATION AND STARTUP PROCEDURES

2.4.1 HARDWARE INSTALLATION

➤ Connect the CD-ROM drive to the Macintosh.

If your CD-ROM drive is external, it will be attached to the computer with a SCSI cable. A number of hardware devices (hard disk drives, scanners, and so on) may be linked together in a SCSI chain. One of the ports of the device at the end of the chain must have a terminator plugged into it. The CD-ROM drive documentation should describe proper cabling. In some cases the terminator must be plugged into the same port as the cable; in others, into the top or bottom port. If you have difficulties, consult your hardware documentation and try altering the configuration.

➤ Install the proper CD-ROM software drivers on your Macintosh system.

Your CD-ROM drive documentation should explain how to install this software.

CD-ROM drivers are not universal. If an Apple CD-ROM machine has been replaced with one built by another manufacturer, it will be necessary to install the proper driver software.

➤ Connect the videodisc player to the video monitor (if the videodisc is used).

If you are using a video monitor, this equipment is connected through audiovisual RCA cables. Other cable configurations are required for monitors without RCA input jacks.

When you put the videodisc into the player, you should see the color test bars on the monitor screen. If the player has front-panel controls, you should be able to check the connection by stepping through some images on the videodisc.

➤ Connect the videodisc player to the Macintosh (if the videodisc is used).

Use the correct cable to connect the communications port of the videodisc player to the appropriate port on the Macintosh. The appropriate cable is often provided with the videodisc player; if it is not, consult your local dealer. Check the baud rate setting on the videodisc player. The correct setting for computer interface should be specified in your videodisc player documentation.

2.4.2 STARTUP PROCEDURE

After setting up the hardware and installing the software, you are ready to start up Perseus. If you encounter any hardware or software problems, see section 2.6, "Troubleshooting."

NOTE: If you will be swapping CD-ROMs, be sure to turn off File Sharing in the Control Panels of your Macintosh. Otherwise the Macintosh will not eject the CD.

➤ Double-click the Perseus Player icon in the Perseus or Local Stacks folders you installed on your hard drive.

Never double-click the Perseus Gateway if you are starting up from the Perseus Player. Do not start up by clicking on another stack, or Perseus will not operate properly. If you encounter problems, start up by dragging the Gateway icon and dropping it onto the HyperCard 2.3 icon.

As Perseus initializes, the cursor changes to a watch, the Home card flashes on the screen, and the Perseus Gateway appears on your screen along with a small floating window, the Navigator Palette. Once the cursor becomes the hand or the arrow, Perseus is ready for use. You can move the Navigator Palette out of the way by holding the mouse down on its title bar and dragging it to a convenient part of the screen.

The Navigator Palette contains eight buttons that issue commands to help you make your way around the Perseus environment. Because the Navigator Palette is a floating window, it remains on the screen and active even though another window may also be active.

If the Navigator Palette disappears, you can select Navigator from the Perseus menu to reactivate it.

In addition to the menu bar items that normally appear in HyperCard (File, Edit, Go, Tools, Font, and Style), two new items appear in the menu bar, Links and Perseus. The resources and databases contained in Perseus are accessed both through the Gateway icons and through the Links menus.

You can always return to the Gateway by clicking the Gateway (temple) icon on the Navigator Palette.

To quit Perseus, choose Quit from the File menu, or press Command-q.

Videodisc instructions

With the videodisc hardware installed and switched on, and Perseus 2.0 running, click the Settings button on the lower left of the Gateway, and when the settings card appears (figure 2.4), perform these steps:

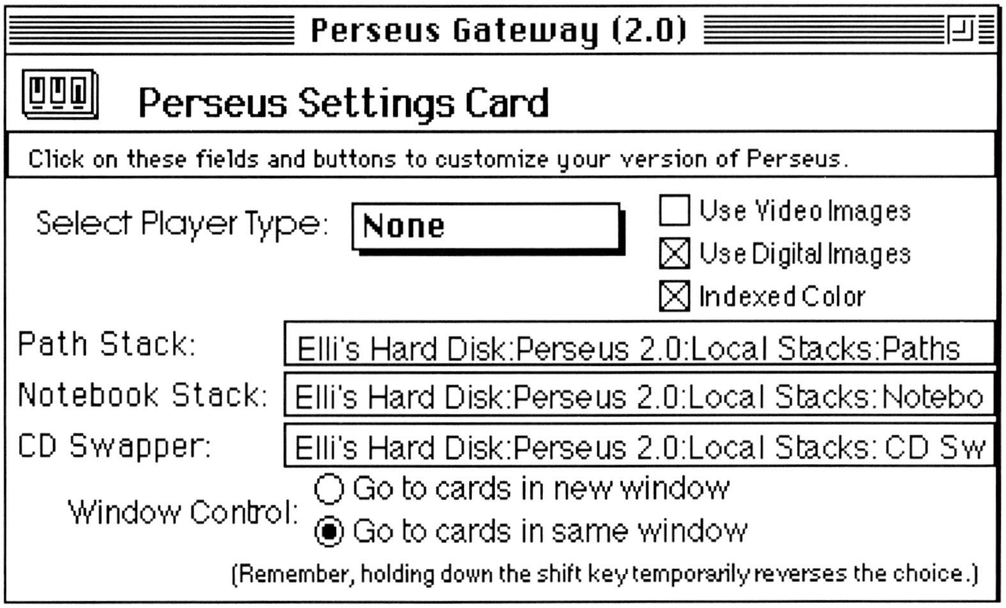

Perseus Gateway (2.0)

Perseus Settings Card

Click on these fields and buttons to customize your version of Perseus.

Select Player Type: None

Use Video Images

Use Digital Images

Indexed Color

Path Stack: Elli's Hard Disk:Perseus 2.0:Local Stacks:Paths

Notebook Stack: Elli's Hard Disk:Perseus 2.0:Local Stacks:Notebo

CD Swapper: Elli's Hard Disk:Perseus 2.0:Local Stacks: CD Sw

Window Control: Go to cards in new window

Go to cards in same window

(Remember, holding down the shift key temporarily reverses the choice.)

Figure 2.4 Settings card

- Select a player type by choosing the item in the pop-up menu corresponding to your model of videodisc player.
- Click the button Use Video Images, to the right.
- Return to the Gateway by clicking the Gateway (temple) icon on the Navigator Palette.

A general overview of Settings may be found in section 4.2.2. For detailed instructions on Settings, see section 10.5.

NOTE: We can recommend only the videodisc players listed in section 4.2.2 and on the settings card. Other models may not be compatible with Perseus.

To learn the basics of Perseus, turn to the next chapter, which includes a number of illustrative exercises in all facets of the database.

If you encounter problems in starting up Perseus, see the next section, on HyperCard issues, and section 2.6, "Troubleshooting."

2.4.3 CUSTOM INSTALLATION

Custom Installation is available on the second card of the Installer stack for system administrators who are putting all or some of Perseus on a server. All of Perseus requires 1.8 GB on a hard disk.

This procedure configures the Gateway to find the various Perseus resources. All copying from CD to hard disk must be done by the user.

- ➤ Make sure you have copied the Local Stacks folder from Perseus CD 1 to your hard drive.
- ➤ Click one of the eight fields for non-image resources at the top and choose the installation location from the dialog box.
- ➤ Click Choose, select the image folders you wish to copy, then choose the locations from the dialog box. Do not remove individual images from the folders.
- ➤ When you have finished relocating resources, click "Set up Gateway."
- ➤ Click Reset to return the settings to the CDs.
- ➤ Do not name any of the partitions Perseus Disk 1, and so on, because of software limitations.

2.5 USING HYPERCARD

This section is meant for users who are not familiar with HyperCard, or who are having problems related to the use of HyperCard and the Home stack.

The Perseus database is built on HyperCard, a Macintosh application that stores and accesses data through an interface analogous to a stack of note cards. HyperCard launches itself from the Home stack each time the application is opened. You need to know almost nothing further about HyperCard to use the Perseus program, but you might need to learn a few things to set up your configuration.

2.5.1 HYPERCARD ISSUES THAT AFFECT PERSEUS

To use Perseus 2.0, it is no longer necessary to have the HyperCard application installed on your computer, because Perseus 2.0 is distributed with a fully compiled, stand-alone Home stack called Perseus Player. Conflicts encountered between HyperCard and Perseus 1.0 have been eliminated in version 2.0.

Perseus Player should remain permanently in the Local Stacks folder on the hard disk. The Player stack does many things, but one of them is especially important for Perseus: establishing the search paths. The search paths make it possible for Perseus to locate specific pieces of information from the large universe of data, and they provide a prioritized structure for data searches. Thus, for example, search paths in the Perseus Player stack tell HyperCard where to find the image folders that contain the digitized photographs.

Do not place a HyperCard Home stack or stacks from Perseus 1.0 inside the Perseus Local Stacks folder. This will impair or prevent the successful use of Perseus, because Perseus may begin to use inappropriate search paths from the other Home stack.

The default memory partition of Perseus Player has been set at the minimum amount of memory required to use Perseus. If you have not already done so, go to the Finder, select Perseus Player (but don't double-click), then choose Get Info from the File menu. Check the memory partition of Perseus Player in the Get Info box and if necessary update it to at least 5 MB, if that much is available.

2.5.2 INCOMPATIBILITY OF HYPERCARD WITH OTHER APPLICATIONS

You may have HyperCard installed on your hard disk in order to run other applications or to write Perseus extensions. Problems encountered by beta testers of version 2.0 with the Audio Help stack have been resolved by the standalone Perseus Player software.

2.5.3 HYPERCARD SEARCH PATHS (FOR SYSTEM ADMINISTRATORS)

If you change the configuration of the system running Perseus 2.0—by relocating some image folders on a hard disk, for example—you must change the search paths manually by opening the Perseus Player stack in the folder Local Stacks. Similarly, if you change the configuration of your computer—by renaming the hard disk drive or placing Perseus within another folder, say—you must also change the search paths, because they specify device and folder names.

➤ Open the Perseus Player stack by double-clicking it. The stack contains six cards. You can go forward in the stack by clicking on the arrow in the lower right corner and backward by clicking on the arrow in the lower left. Click forward to the fifth card of the stack to see the search paths for documents (a button called Documents on this card will be highlighted).

➤ You will see a long list of Perseus image folder names listed in the document search paths. If you have changed your configuration, change the pertinent part of the search path here. Note that each line in the list of search paths ends with a colon. An example of this procedure follows, assuming that the Atlas and two image folders have been copied to a folder named Perseus 2.0 on a hard disk named Elli's Hard Disk:

Default search paths for documents:

Perseus Disk 1:Atlas:
Perseus Disk 2:1987.01.1s:
Perseus Disk 2:1987.01.1t:

Renamed search paths for documents:

Elli's Hard Disk:Perseus 2.0:Atlas:
Elli's Hard Disk:Perseus 2.0:1987.01.1s:
Elli's Hard Disk:Perseus 2.0:1987.01.1t:

The original search paths for documents can always be restored by repeating the installation procedure.

2.6 TROUBLESHOOTING

2.6.1 IDENTIFYING PROBLEMS

Table 2.3 summarizes troubles and their most common causes.

Symptom	Possible Cause
Startup messages about inability to find files, asking "Where is . . . " or error messages reporting "This operation has failed because an error has occurred."	Possible HyperCard conflict: try to start up by dropping the Gateway onto the Perseus Player or HyperCard application Multiple copies of Home stack exist on hard disk, and Perseus is using one with inappropriate search paths Home stack search paths are not listed correctly Computer configuration has been changed without updating the Home stack search paths Perseus 2.0 folder is missing necessary files
Path or Notebook is not accessible	Location of Path or Notebook stack has not yet been identified through the Settings option
Path stack is locked	Path stack is being used from the CD-ROM instead of from the hard disk
A message indicates insufficient memory, or the application quits spontaneously	HyperCard memory partition is set too low
No digital images are found	CD-ROM drive is not properly connected to computer Home stack does not have correct paths to images
CD will not eject	File Sharing has not been turned off
Quadra system crashes	Font problem
Greek font is very small or missing the lower dots	Font problem

Table 2.3 Troubleshooting

If you encounter problems as you set up Perseus, follow the recommendations in the remaining sections of this chapter.

2.6.2 MEMORY PARTITION OF PERSEUS PLAYER OR HYPERCARD

System 7 requires 3–3.5 MB of your computer's RAM to run. The remaining RAM is available for applications. Perseus needs at least 5 MB of memory to run properly. You must set the "application memory size" of Perseus Player to at least 5000. If you have more than 8 MB of RAM on your Macintosh, Perseus will perform even better if you allot increased memory to Perseus Player. Even if your computer has 20 MB of memory, Perseus Player will not capitalize on the excess memory until you set the application memory size to a higher setting. More memory allotted to Perseus Player means that more Perseus stacks and images can be opened simultaneously, and they will work more quickly.

➤ In the Perseus 2.0 folder, click the Perseus Player icon once while the application is not in use and choose Get Info from the File menu. The lower right-hand corner of the dialog box contains a number that reflects the current memory setting. Type "5000" into the box, or type a larger number if your computer has sufficient available RAM, as described above.

2.6.3 HARDWARE

If something is wrong with the CD-ROM drive, it may just spin, and the little indicator light either will stay lit and not flash or will flash constantly at regular intervals. If this continues for more than two minutes, press the button on the front of the CD-ROM drive, hold it for a few seconds, and then release. The disk should eject. Check all connections and software installations. Check SCSI terminators, and check that you have the correct CD-ROM drivers.

If the Perseus Disk 1 icon does not appear on your desktop, try restarting all hardware. Turn on the CD-ROM drive, *without* the disk in it, before you turn on the computer. When the computer has finished starting up, insert Perseus Disk 1 into the CD-ROM drive. If the icon still does not appear, try switching the places of the SCSI connector and the terminator in the CD-ROM ports. Finally, check the Extensions folder in your System folder to make sure that the Apple CD-ROM extension is there (for an Apple CD-ROM player), or that the appropriate extension is there (for another manufacturer's CD-ROM player).

If you are using a videodisc player and cannot display images from the videodisc, check the cable connections and confirm that you are using the appropriate cable. Also check the baud rate setting on your videodisc player (specified in the player documentation).

2.6.4 SOFTWARE

If extensions to Perseus are being used, check whether the hard disk contains versions of HyperCard earlier than 2.1; check whether other Home stacks and Perseus 1.0 stacks are in the Perseus 2.0 folder.

A related problem may be the existence of multiple copies of the Perseus Player stack. The Perseus Player is very important in using Perseus, because the Perseus Player stack specifies the location of files and instructs HyperCard where on your hard drive to look for Perseus data. Double-click the Perseus Player icon from the Macintosh desktop and move forward in this stack (by clicking the lower right-hand arrow) until you see the list of search paths for stacks, applications, and documents. Check that the search paths are specified correctly in relation to your software configuration.

If you see the error message "Cannot open MDB Index," check the path names in the correct version of the Perseus Player documents card.

If you are unable to type accented Greek, check that SMK GreekKeys 7.0 has been installed in your system. The Greek fonts Symbol and Super Greek are incompatible with GreekKeys and Perseus 2.0.

The first section of this chapter is intended as a general introduction to the contents and geography of the Perseus environment. Some users may want to start exploring Perseus right away, so section 3.1 provides quick-entry operating instructions with specific targets in the text, vase collection, atlas, and history portions of the Perseus database. These same targets are included in the Novice Tour of Perseus, described in section 3.2. Three additional Guided Tours are also presented in that section, with the intent of showing off both the new interface and the philological and archaeological features of version 2.0.

Both newcomers and users familiar with Perseus 1.0 will want to take advantage of the new Online Help (section 3.3). A detailed discussion of Macintosh and HyperCard techniques as they apply to Perseus will be found in chapter 4, "Tools for Navigating Perseus," and chapter 5, "Search Tools."

3.1 THE PERSEUS ENVIRONMENT: SOME BASIC TASKS

3.1.1 ACCESSING DATA IN PERSEUS

Please read section 2.4, "Detailed Installation and Startup Procedures," in which startup procedure, the Perseus Gateway, the Navigator Palette, and Settings are described.

Users unfamiliar with operating the Macintosh should read about buttons, pop-up menus, and pull-down menus in section 4.1.

The Perseus interface is what you see on the screen after you have started up Perseus on your computer; the interface contains the means by which you interact with the database (by clicking buttons or choosing menu items, for example); the interface also determines the particular format in which information (a text, or a picture of a vase, for example) appears on the screen.

You gain access to the Perseus databases by descending through several levels of the interface. The first or uppermost level is the Perseus Gateway (figure 3.1). By clicking an icon on the Gateway, you can enter one of the databases: the Historical Overview, Art & Archaeology, Primary Texts, and so on.

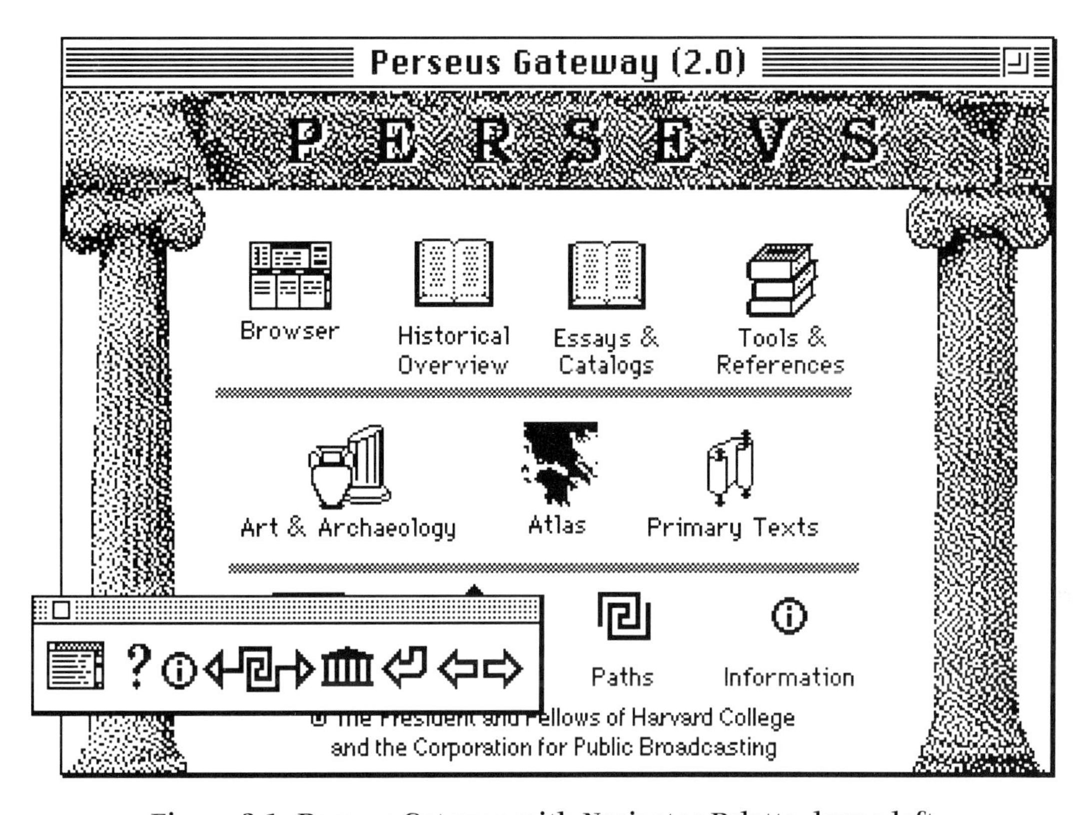

Figure 3.1 Perseus Gateway with Navigator Palette, lower left

Between the Gateway and the actual data is an intermediary level consisting of one or more Index cards, which further direct your search for information. From the Index level you can choose a work of a specific author, say, or a Catalog card with images of a specific vase. For example, the levels you descend when accessing vase images are illustrated in figure 3.2.

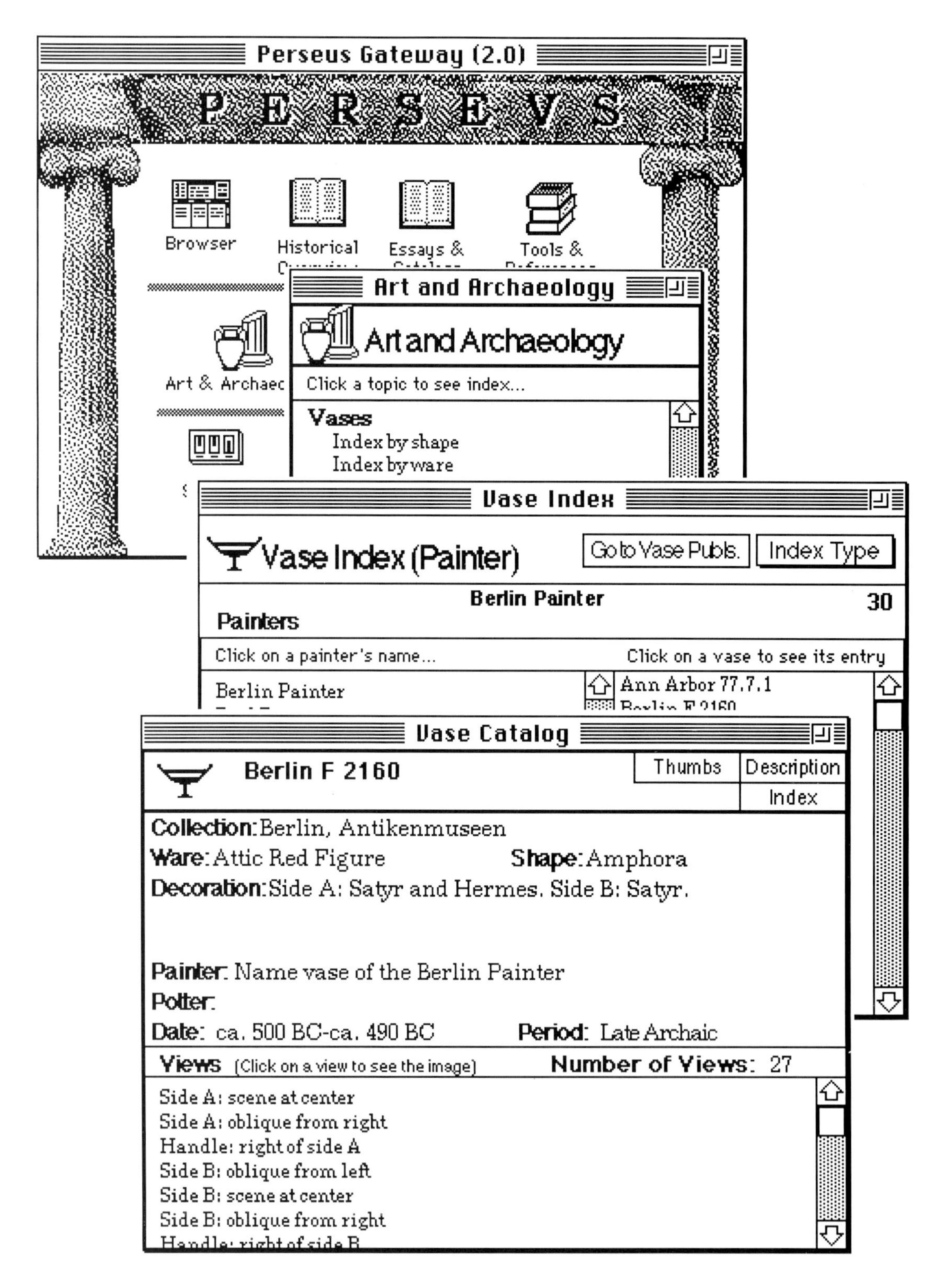

Figure 3.2 Interface levels from Gateway to Vase Catalog

In this case the route is as follows:

Perseus Gateway →
Art & Archaeology Index card →
Vase Index card →
Vase Catalog card (containing a list of images and the documentation for a particular vase) →
Image

If you were looking for Greek-English texts, the route would be:

Perseus Gateway →
Primary Text Index card →
Author →
Work

The following tasks have been designed to familiarize you with the Perseus environment. You will bring up the image of a famous vase painted by Douris, then explore links from "An Overview of Classical Greek History" by Thomas Martin. You will next access the text of Homer's *Iliad,* go to the passage describing Achilles' shield, analyze the verb form ἥατο, and search for Homeric uses of the word πόλις. The final task makes use of the Atlas to plot the site of Athens on a color map.

Perseus users often achieve good results working in groups. You may find that a cooperative effort works well here, with one person operating the computer controls and a partner reading from the User's Guide.

To bring up images of a Kylix painted by Douris (Berlin F 2285), perform the following steps:

➤ From the Gateway, click the Art & Archaeology icon. The Art & Archaeology Index card appears (figure 3.3). This card contains five topics: Sites, Architecture, Sculpture, Vases, and Coins.

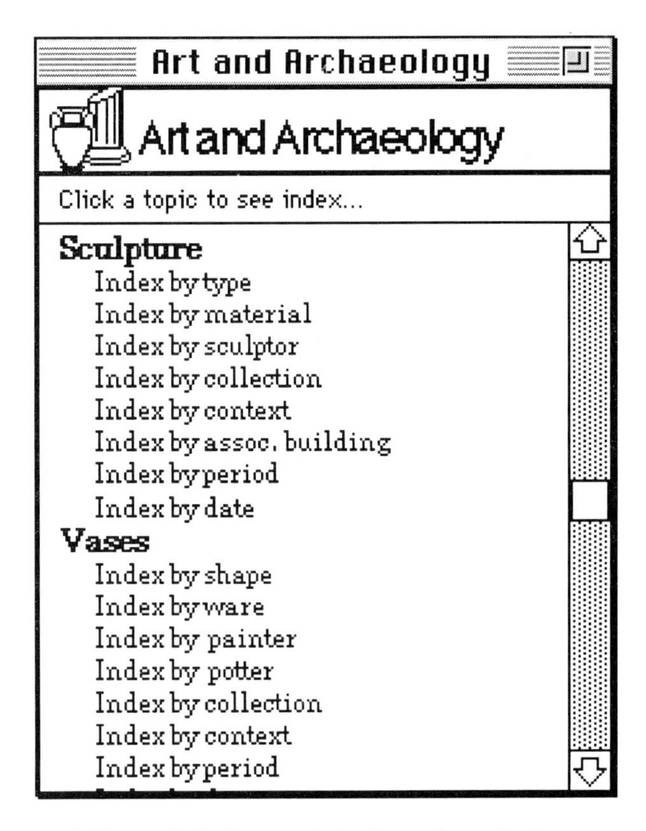

Figure 3.3 Art and Archaeology Index

➤ Scroll down to the Vases topic. Click "Index by painter." A new index card, Vase Index (Painter), appears with a list of painters in the field at the left. Scroll down and click Douris. A list of vases in Perseus 2.0 by Douris appears in the field at the right. Click "Berlin F 2285" and Perseus will take you to the Catalog card for this vase (figure 3.4). Click one of the nineteen views listed at the bottom to see an image of the vase.

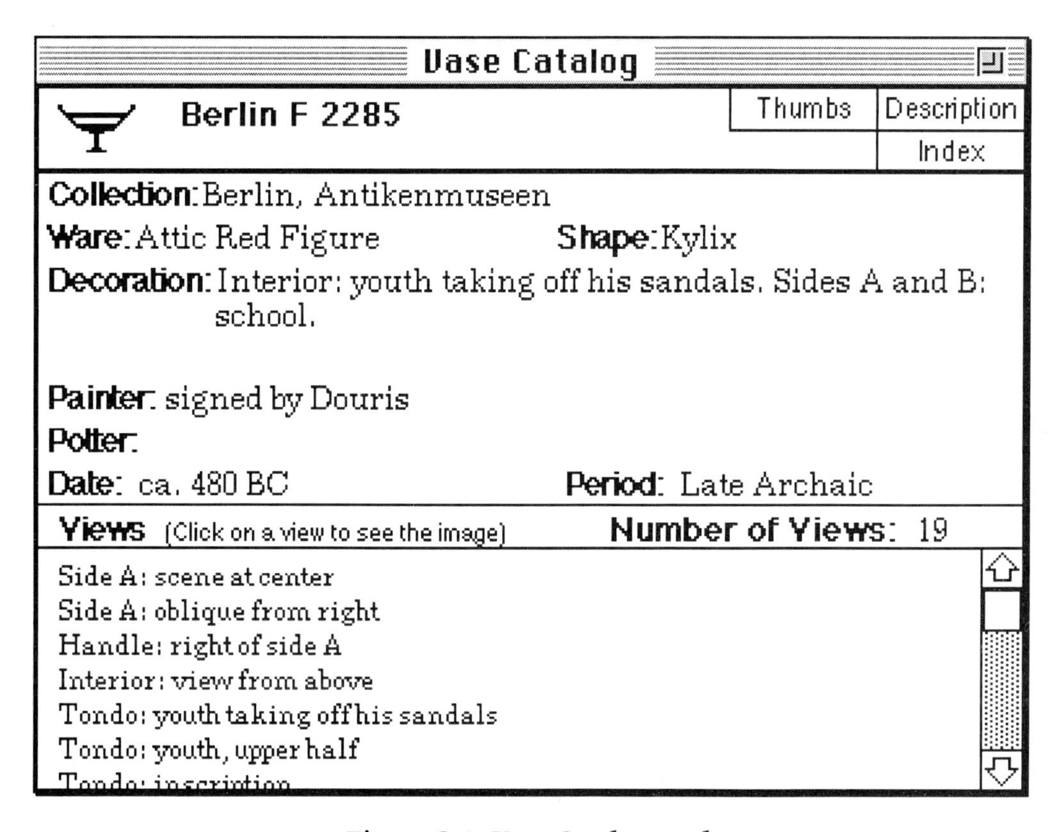

Figure 3.4 Vase Catalog card

You may find the view "Side A: teacher and student with writing tablet" of particular interest.

> One of Perseus's strengths is its ability to display objects in detail. Scroll down and click on the following images: Tondo: Staff; Side A: man on stool; Side B: teacher and student with stylus; Side B: school.

Along with the image, a floating window will appear with the photo credits. The credits window may be closed or dragged out of the way. You may wish to bring up other images of this vase. To do so, make the Vase Catalog card active by clicking it, then choose another view.

> You can look at several images at one time, but be aware that images consume memory. Perseus will remind you when your machine is getting low on RAM. Be sure to close the image before moving on.

To read a description of the vase, go to the upper right corner of the Vase Catalog card and click Description. To return to the Gateway, click the Gateway (temple) icon on the Navigator Palette.

> For further information on vases, see section 6.3.5.

To learn about Pericles' Acropolis from the Historical Overview, perform these steps:

➤ From the Gateway, click the Historical Overview icon. A card labeled Historical Overview TOC appears. Scroll down the outline and click item 9.4.4, "Pericles' Acropolis." Perseus will take you to the corresponding section of Martin's narrative history.

➤ The text contains links with other resources in the Perseus database; to see the links, click the button See Links/Lock Text in the upper right.

> This is a toggle button. Its name switches between the modes See Links/Lock Text and Hide Links/Unlock Text, depending on which mode it is set at. To select and copy text, you must use the Unlock Text setting.

➤ You will observe that several words or phrases in the text are now underlined. Move the pointer to the phrase "Athenian Acropolis" and hold down the mouse button. A pop-up menu appears, offering three choices (figure 3.5).

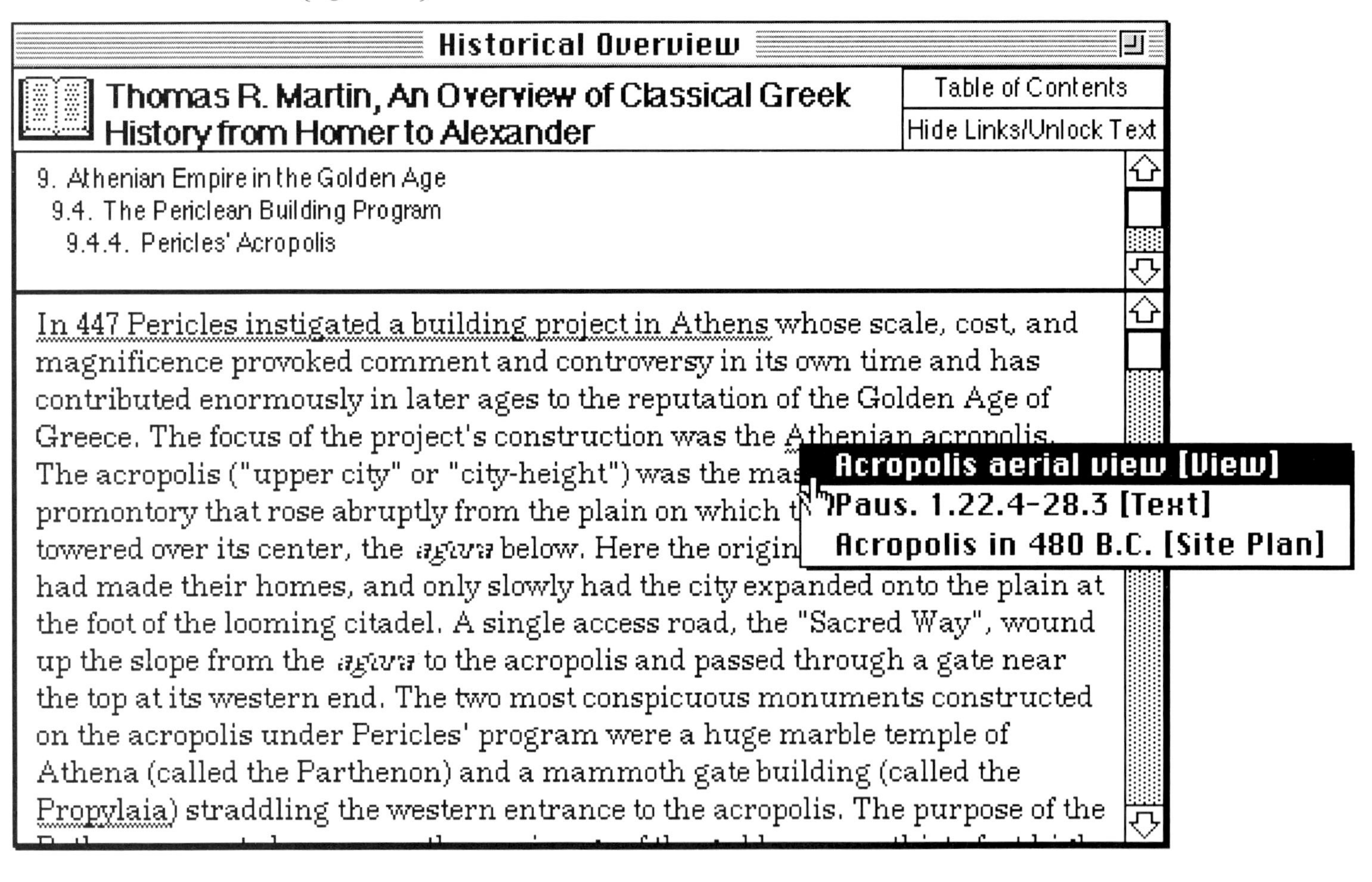

Figure 3.5 Historical Overview, showing link at Athenian Acropolis

➤ Choose the first possibility, Acropolis Aerial View [View]. Along with the image, Perseus will bring up a floating window with the photo credits. The credits window may be closed or dragged out of the way. To return to the Historical Overview, make it the active window by clicking it. Try the second choice from the Athenian Acropolis link, "Paus. 1.22.4-28.3 [Text]." Perseus will take you to the relevant passage in the Greek-English text of Pausanias Book 1. To return from Pausanias to the Historical Overview, click on the Go Back (bent) arrow on the Navigator Palette. To page forward and backward in the Overview, use the arrows on the right of the Navigator Palette. To return to the Gateway, click the Gateway (temple) icon on the Navigator Palette.

In the interest of saving space and memory, be sure to close any images before moving on.

For further information on the Historical Overview, see section 6.1.

In the following example you will bring up the text of Homer's *Iliad*.

➤ From the Gateway, click the Primary Texts icon. The Primary Text Index appears (figure 3.6), with a list of authors in the field to the left.

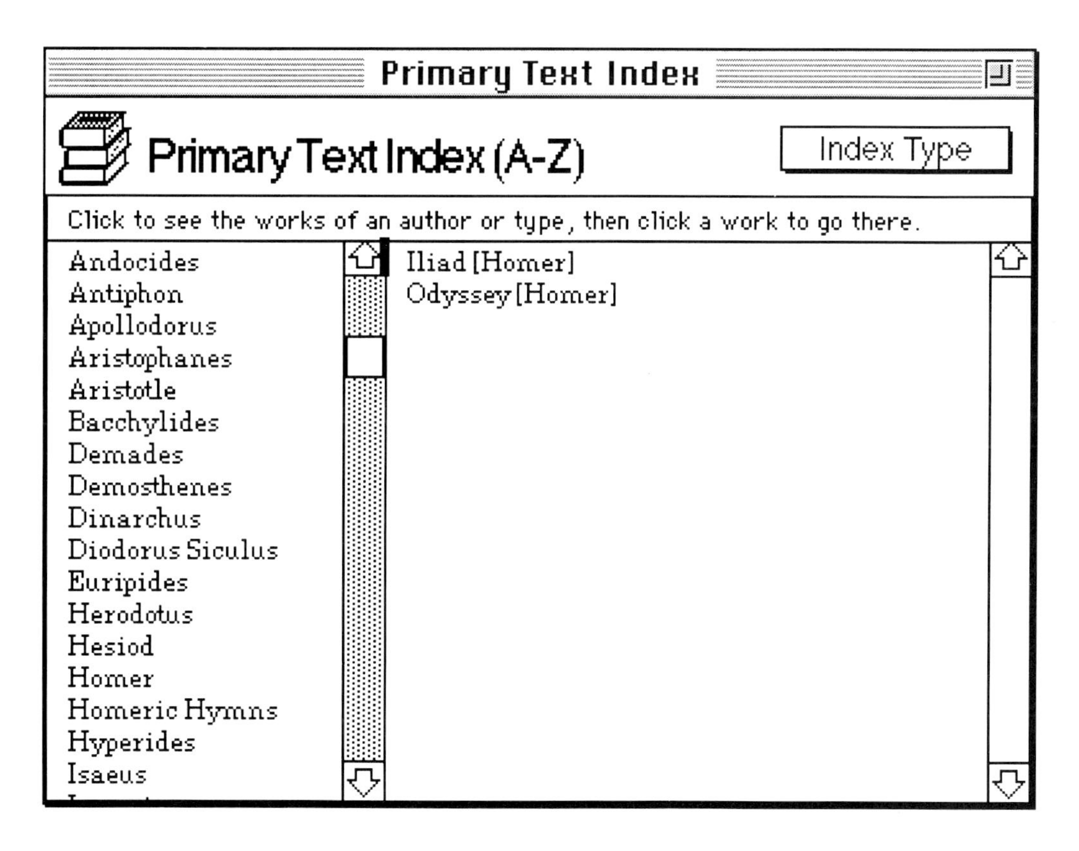

Figure 3.6 Primary Text Index

➤ Click Homer. The *Iliad* and *Odyssey* are now listed in the field to the right. Click Iliad. Perseus will take you to Hom. Il. 1.1. Page forward by clicking the right-pointing arrow on the far right of the Navigator Palette. Page backward by clicking on the left-pointing arrow next to it.

This example will continue with more illustrations from the text of the *Iliad;* or if you choose, you can return to the Gateway by clicking the Gateway (temple) icon on the Navigator Palette.

To go to *Iliad* 18, Achilles' Shield, perform the following steps.

➤ From within the text of the *Iliad,* click the button "Go to" (figure 3.7).

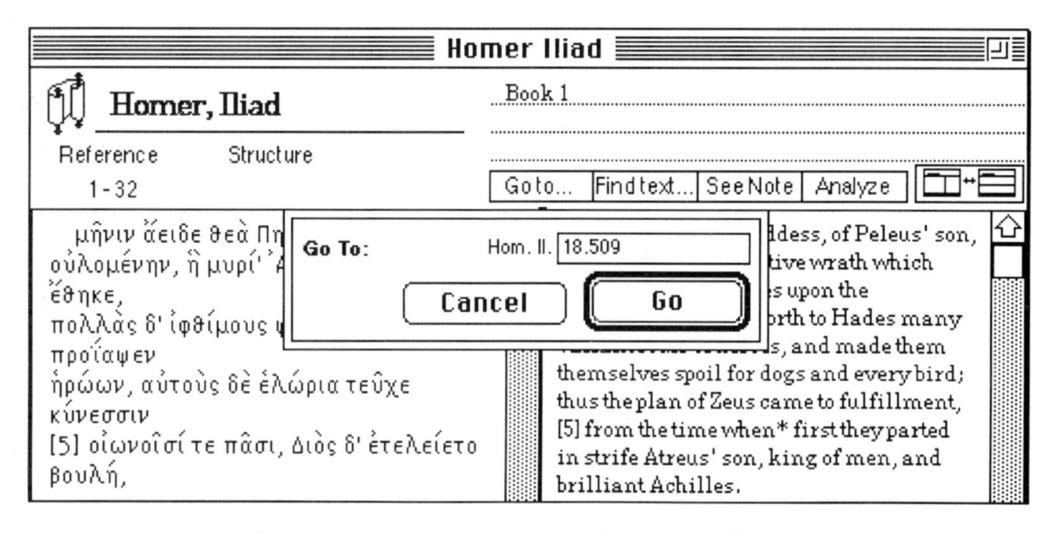

Figure 3.7 Primary Text with "Go to" feature

➤ Type 18.509 in the box and click Go (or press Return). Perseus will take you to the point in the passage where Homer describes the City at War. Note that the lines on this card (490-526) are listed under the heading "Reference." Scroll up or down in the Greek or English texts to see more of the passage.

Next, you will use the Morphological Analysis tool to parse the verb form ἥατο.

In this exercise, you will be opening new windows for the Morphological Analysis tool and the Lexicon. Be sure to hold down the shift key while opening new windows in order to retain the previous window.

➤ In line 509, highlight the word ἥατο. Click the button Analyze (figure 3.8).

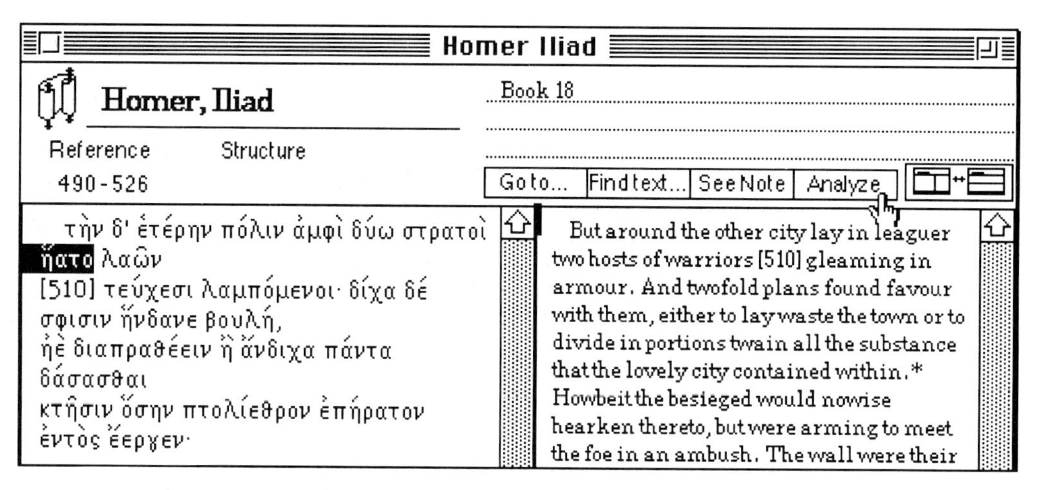

Figure 3.8 Primary Text with Morphological Analysis tool

Perseus's morphological database will analyze the form, as shown in figure 3.9.

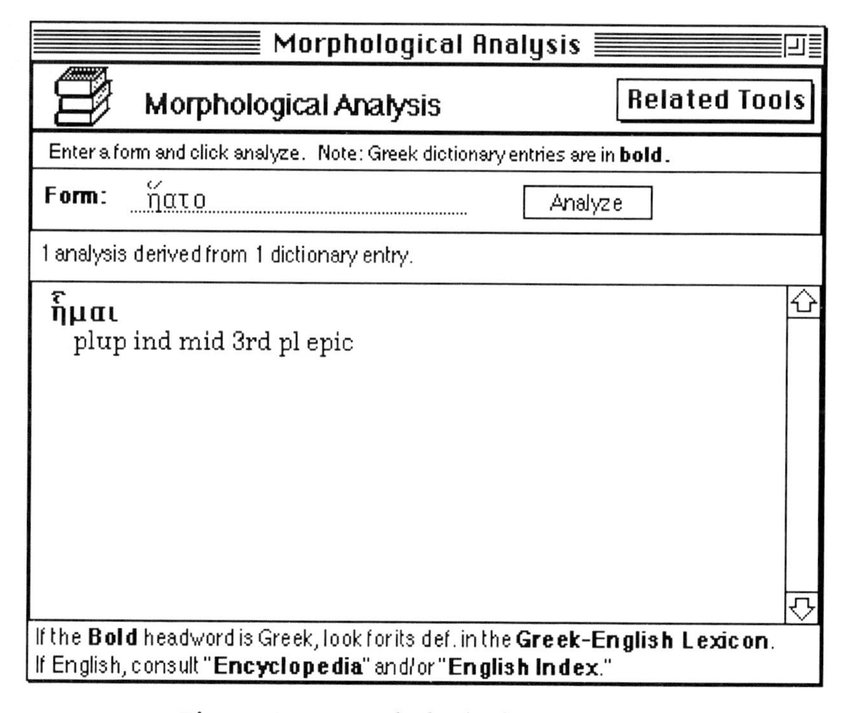

Figure 3.9 Morphological Analysis tool

➤ If you do not know the meaning of ἧμαι and do not have a Greek dictionary handy, highlight ἧμαι and choose Greek-English Lexicon from the pop-up menu Related Tools, in the upper right.

➤ To return to the text of the *Iliad,* slowly click the Go Back (bent) arrow on the Navigator Palette twice. (The first click takes you back to Morphological Analysis.)

In the following example, you will use the Greek Word Search tool to find occurrences of πόλις in Homer.

➤ It will be necessary to obtain the nominative form of this word in order to do the search. Follow the Morphological Analysis procedure given in the previous task: select the word πόλιν from line 509. Click the button Analyze. From the Morphological Analysis card, highlight πόλις and choose the item Greek Word Search from the pop-up menu Related Tools, in the upper right (figure 3.10).

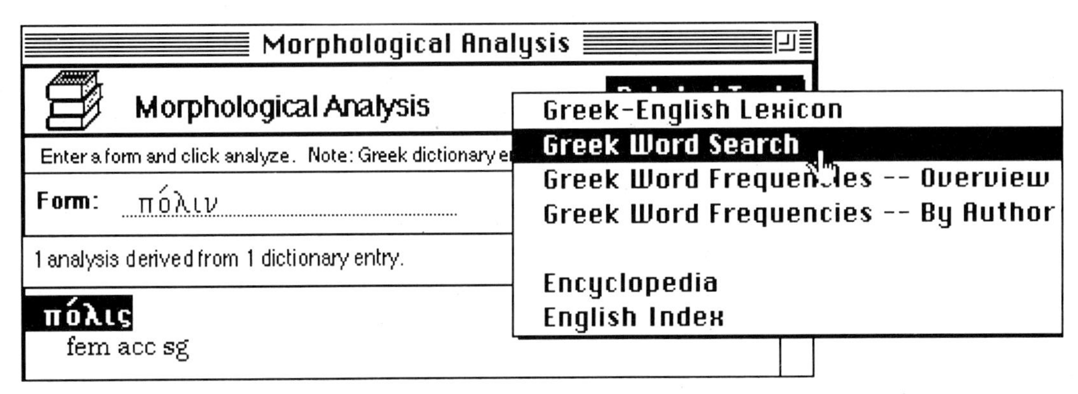

Figure 3.10 Morphological Analysis to Greek Word Search

With the Greek Word Search tool (figure 3.11), you can call up all occurrences of a Greek word in the works of an author in Perseus. You can then link directly to the text to see how the author uses the word.

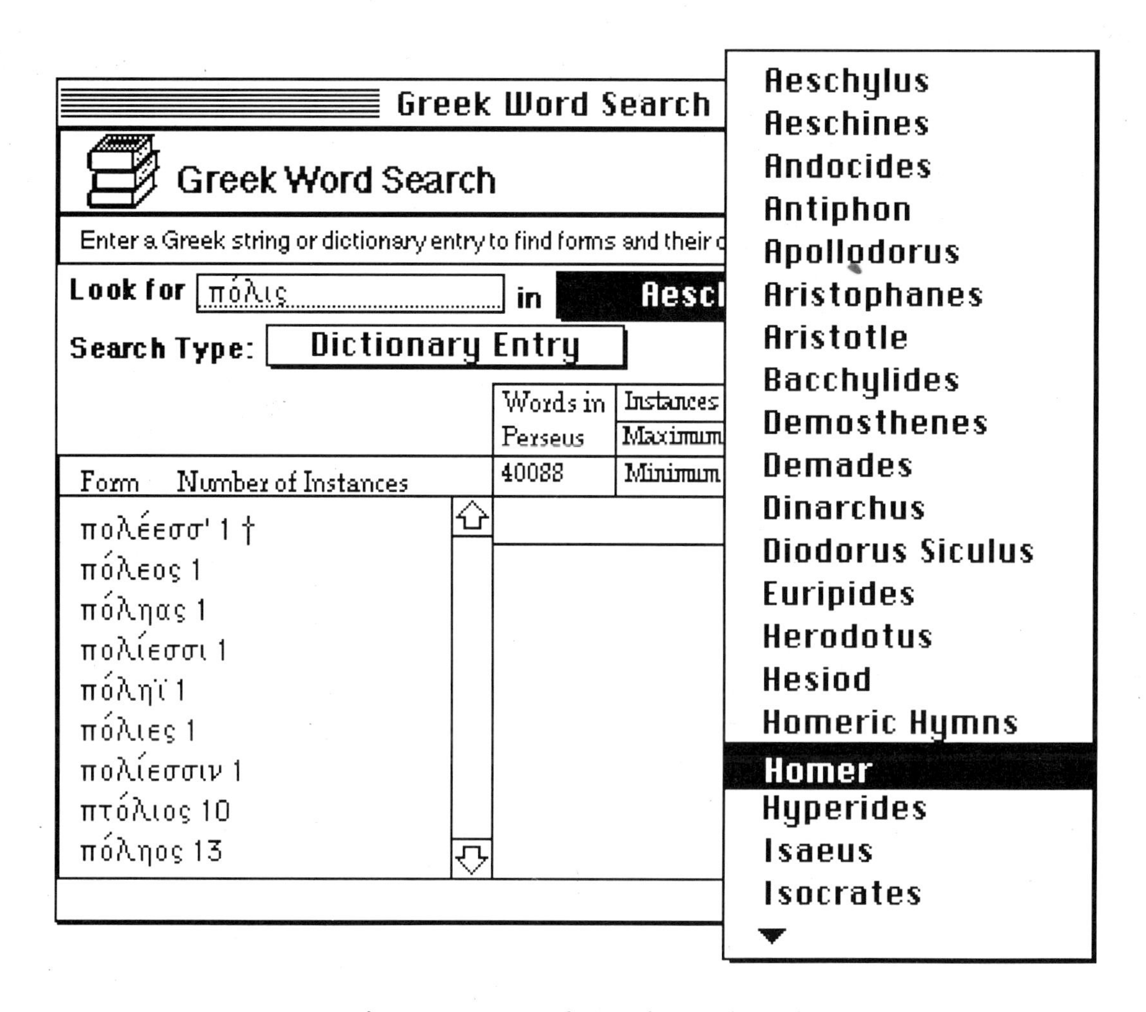

Figure 3.11 Greek Word Search tool

➤ Choose Homer from the pop-up menu of authors, and choose "All forms from a Dictionary Entry" from the Search Type pop-up menu.

> Although you have entered the nominative form, because you have chosen the search type "All forms from a Dictionary Entry," the oblique forms will also appear in the results.

➤ Click the Do Search button, and forms for πόλις will appear in the field in the lower left.

> Note that ambiguous forms are indicated with a dagger. In this case, πολ°εσσ' has a dagger next to it because it might come from πολύς.

➤ To get a list of all citations for πόλις in Homer, choose "Citations for All Forms" from the Options menu. To go to a cited passage, highlight the desired passage and click the "Go To Text" button. To return to Greek Word Search, click the Go Back arrow on the Navigator Palette.

Note that the results of your search will have been erased. You can click the Do Search button to redo the search, or you can save your work with the Search Saver, located on the left of the Navigator Palette. To read about the Search Saver, see section 4.3.

For further information on Primary Texts and Philological Tools, see chapter 8.

➤ To begin the following examples, return to the Perseus Gateway by clicking the Gateway (temple) icon on the Navigator Palette.

To plot Athens on a color map, perform the following steps.

➤ From the Gateway, click the Atlas icon, or choose Atlas from the Links menu. The entry point for the Atlas, the small outline map, appears along with a new floating window called the Atlas Tools Palette. Click the button "Graphic index of maps." The Graphic Map Index, a black-and-white outline map of the Greek world with active tiles, will appear (figure 3.12).

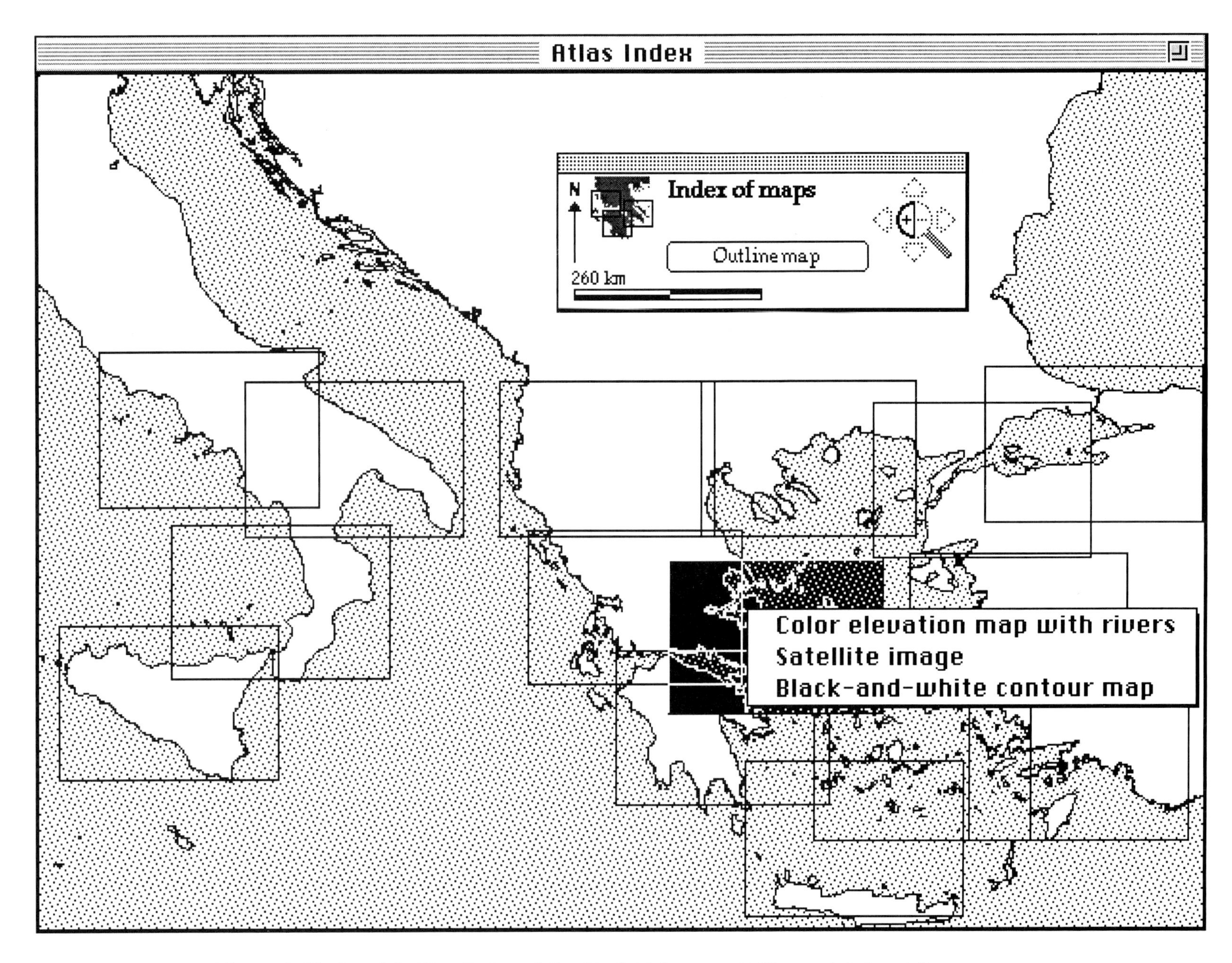

Figure 3.12 Graphic Map Index, Atlas Tools Palette, and tile containing Athens

➤ The fifteen tiles or rectangles superimposed on the map are actually pop-up menus. The rectangles become highlighted when the mouse is passed over them. Move the pointer to the rectangle containing Attica (second row from top, third rectangle from left). When you hold down the mouse, a pop-up menu appears, offering a variety of maps. Choose "Color elevation map with rivers," and Perseus will bring up a color map, "Atlas Elevation-Water 500 ms." Find the Show Tools toggle ( ) located in the lower right corner of the Atlas Tools Palette. Click to expand the selection of Atlas Tools.

➤ To plot the site of Athens, scroll down the field Select Site(s) and highlight Athens. Now click the button "Plot selected sites," middle right, and Perseus will plot the site (figure 3.13).

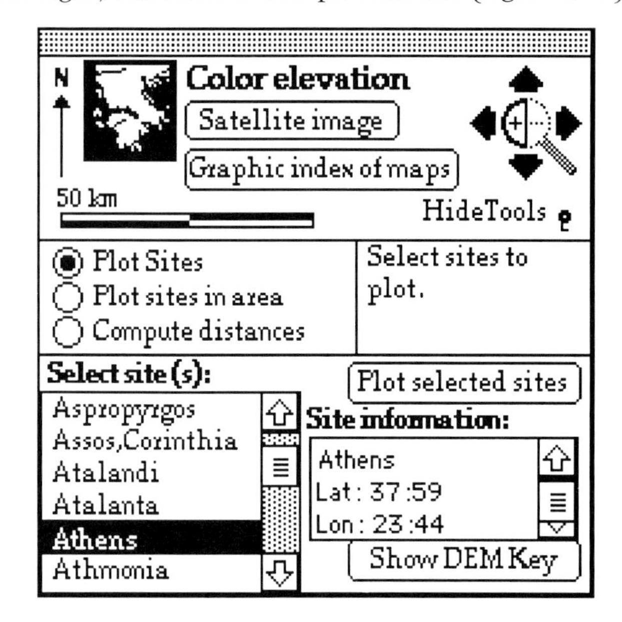

Figure 3.13 Atlas Tools Palette with toggle showing tools, and Athens selected from Select site(s)

To plot additional sites, repeat the above procedure. To return to the Gateway, click the Gateway (temple) icon on the Navigator Palette.

If the Navigator Palette disappears, you can select Navigator from the Perseus menu to reactivate it.

For further help with the Atlas, see chapter 7.

3.1.2 USING TOOLS TO SEARCH AND ORGANIZE DATA IN PERSEUS

First, you will use the Browser tool to explore the vase collection of University Museums, University of Mississippi.

The Browser may be described as an interactive catalog, a tool that enables you to access and sort information quickly from within the Perseus database. With the Browser tool it is possible to choose a database (Vases, Sculpture, Coins, Sites, or Architecture) and sort it based on a certain search context (Collection, Shape, Ware, Context, Painter, Potter, Period, Region, or Keywords). In this example, you will make a search of Vases in Perseus 2.0 organized by Collection.

You can search the Vases, Sculpture, and Coins databases for one of the 1437 Keywords linked with the text, such as "Athena," "spear," or "love-making." When you choose the Keywords search context, a further pop-up menu appears to its right with 22 categories of Keywords from which to search. Many users find not only that the Keywords feature provides the most fruitful starting point for investigations but that it is the part of Perseus that is the most fun to play with. A further exercise using the Keyword search topic is found in section 4.5.1.

➤ From the Gateway, click the Browser icon. Perseus brings up the Browser interface (figure 3.14), and in the upper left you will see a column of the five databases mentioned in the paragraph above (Vases, Sculpture, Coins, and so on).

Note that results obtained by other users may still be in the Browser, and the interface may not look exactly like figure 3.14 until you actually perform the search.

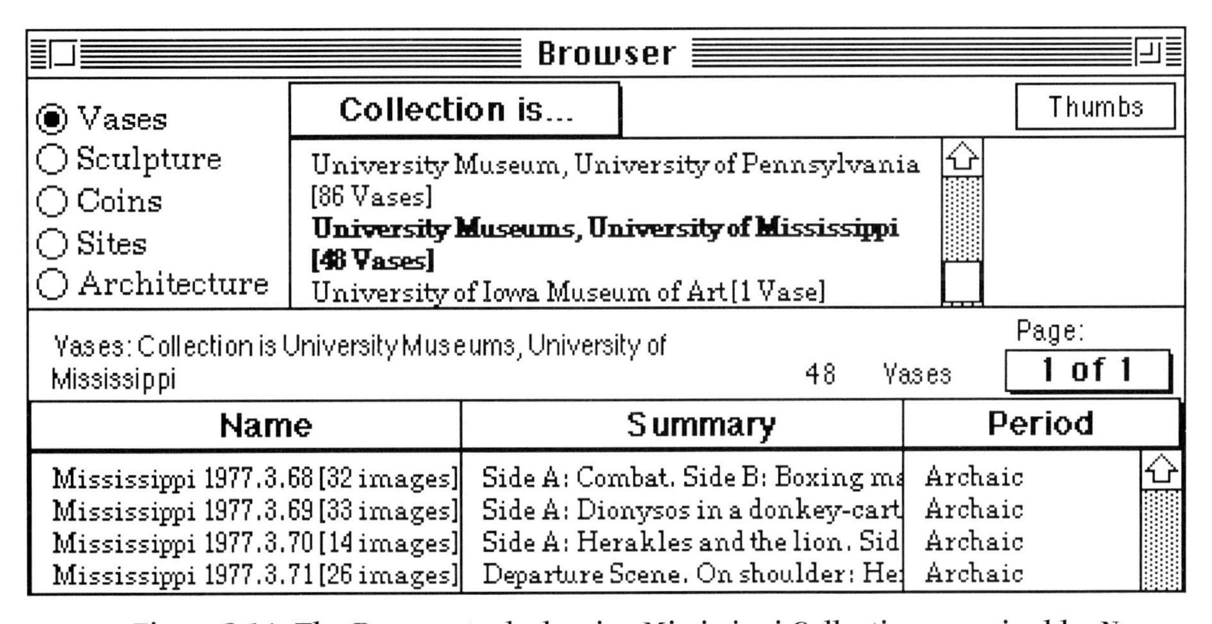

Figure 3.14 The Browser tool, showing Mississippi Collection organized by Name

➤ Click the button to the left of Vases. Now choose the item Collection from the pop-up menu, upper middle (see figure 3.14, in which the pop-up menu reads "Collection is"). Scroll down to "University Museums, University of Mississippi" and click anywhere on that line. Perseus will display the results of the search in the three columns below, sorted by Name. If you click a Vase Name in the left column, Perseus will take you to its Vase Catalog card.

➤ If the search result Name does not appear, select Name from the pop-up menu at the top of the left column. Each of the three columns is headed by a pop-up menu. You can customize the display of search results by selecting the desired result from the pop-up menus. Note that only the left column of Browser results is active.

If part of the vase's Name in the left column is cut off, change the width of a column by holding the cursor at the top of the vertical dividing line and dragging to change the column width; note that the cursor changes from the pointer to the field-expander mode (figure 3.15).

Figure 3.15 Expanding the Browser results column

➤ A good vase to start with might be Mississippi 1977.3.69, attributed to the Theseus Painter: a depiction of Dionysos in a donkey-cart preceded by a man and a goat. To go to the Catalog card for this vase, scroll down to Mississippi 1977.3.69 and click it. There are 33 views of this vase; to see a view, click it (users of the Concise Edition of Perseus will be able to see the view "Side A: oblique from left").

➤ To return to the Browser, click the Go Back (bent) arrow on the Navigator Palette. Your search will remain in the Browser until you make another search or quit Perseus.

You do not need to return to the Gateway when navigating from one place to another in Perseus. You can directly access the Browser, for example, by choosing Browser from the Links menu. The other Perseus databases and tools can be accessed directly from the Links menu as well.

For further information on the Browser, see section 5.1. To learn how to save the results of your search, see the discussion on the Search Saver tool in section 5.4.

In the next example, you will use the Lookup tool to locate information about Akragas contained in the various Perseus resources.

The Lookup tool, reached via the Links menu, is a quick way to access information in Perseus. Lookup often will be among the first tools you use to start an inquiry. It is certainly the easiest to use: just type in a word or lookup string, press Return, and Perseus will list a number of options; click an option and Perseus will take you there. (For a definition of lookup strings, see section 8.4.1.) The Lookup tool draws on a database consisting of all English words indexed in Perseus, a number in the tens of thousands. Built into the Lookup tool is a list of alternate spellings, such as Clytemnestra/Klytaimestra or Aegina/Aigina, to help you reach the desired target.

➤ From anywhere in Perseus, choose Lookup from the Links menu. A floating window appears (figure 3.16). The cursor should be on the left and blinking. Type Akragas and press Return.

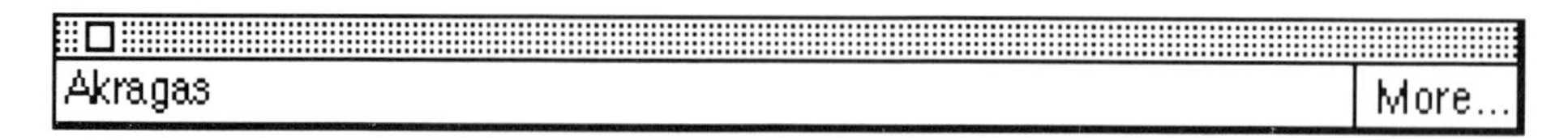

Figure 3.16 The Lookup tool

The Lookup window will now expand. Displayed on the left under "Could be" is "akragas," the canonical listing for this word in Perseus. Below the line are the various alternate spellings for

Akragas (figure 3.17). Databases containing Akragas are displayed on the right.

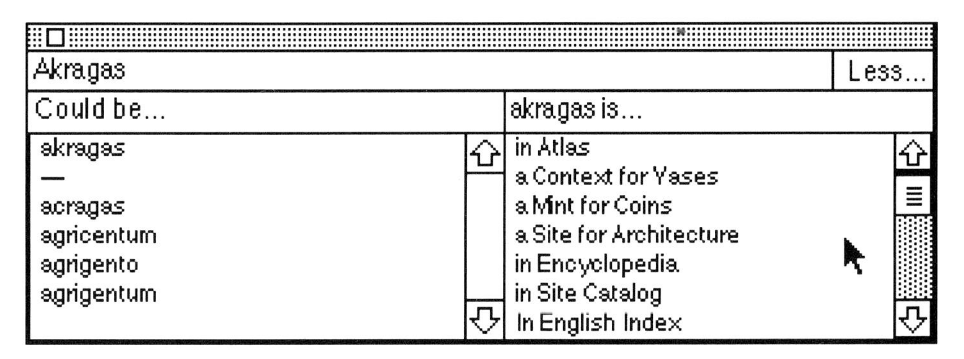

Figure 3.17 Lookup results

Note that Lookup is not case sensitive, that is, it is not necessary to distinguish uppercase from lowercase letters. However, you will need to be mindful of the canonical author abbreviations when looking up texts: "hom. od. 10.45" will work, but "homer od X 45" will not; see the appendix (section A.3) or the card "Canonical Abbreviations for Primary Texts" in Online Help.

➤ Click Site Catalog, on the right. Perseus will take you to the Akragas card of the Site Catalog. (The Lookup window may be dragged out of the way.) From the Site Catalog card you can bring up Views of Akragas by clicking one of the lines at the bottom (users of the Concise Edition of Perseus will be able to see the view "Quarries between Temple of Concord and Temple of Hera"). To bring up thumbnail images of the Akragas views, to see a description of the site, or to go to the Site Index, click one of the buttons in the upper right.

➤ Return to the Lookup window and try some of the other options Perseus has listed for Akragas. If it has disappeared, select Lookup from the Links menu, type in Akragas again, and press Return.

If you have a specific text or object in mind, you do not have to go through the various index levels to access it. Select Lookup from the Links menu. Type in what you want to find and press Return. Note that you must type in the name of the text or object according to the canonical list of Perseus contents found in section A.3 of the appendix. For further information on the Lookup tool, see section 4.5.1.

3.2 USING PATHS TO TAKE GUIDED TOURS OF PERSEUS

It is possible to record the locations you have visited in Perseus. Such a recording is called a Path, and each stop on the Path is called a Location. Perseus 2.0 comes with four prerecorded Paths that are tours intended to familiarize users, of various interests and levels of expertise, with the Perseus environment. Additional Paths show off Perseus's various strengths. For detailed information on creating, editing, and following Paths, see section 10.2.

For the following examples, it is assumed that you know how to start up Perseus and adjust the Settings. Please read about these procedures in section 2.4. To take the Guided Tours of Perseus 2.0, you only need to know how to use the Path Navigator (described below).

The Path Navigator is located on the Navigator Palette.

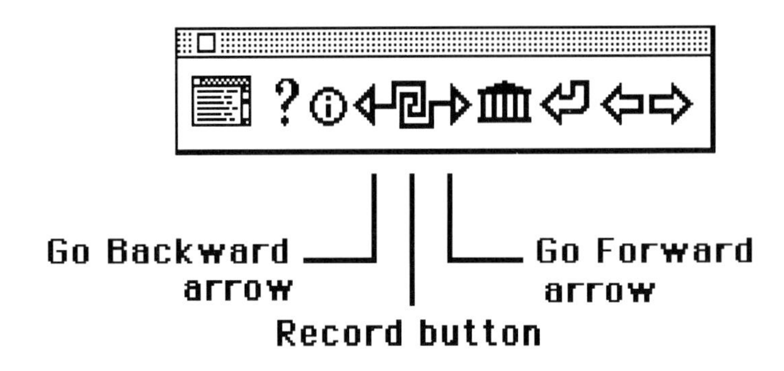

Figure 3.18 The Path Navigator on the Navigator Palette

To move to the next Location on a Path, click the Go Forward arrow. To move to the previous Location on a Path, click the Go Backward arrow. To record a Location on a Path, click the Record button.

The four Paths described here—the Novice Tour, the Expert Tour, the Philological Tour, and the Art and Archaeology Tour—were created so that users of the Concise Edition of Perseus would be able to view as many full-screen images as possible. The Paths "Grain" and "Women" were also created with these users in mind. The other Paths distributed with version 2.0, however, were selected from several Paths that have been used successfully with Perseus, and not all images will be available to users of the Concise Edition.

To begin a Path, read the following sections.

3.2.1 THE NOVICE TOUR

The Novice Tour explores some of the places in Perseus described in section 3.1.

NOTE: Both the Paths icon on the Gateway and the Path Index command in the Perseus menu will take you to the current Path stack, as identified on your Settings card. To take the Tours, be sure that the Paths stack included in the Perseus 2.0 Local Stacks folder is your current Path (see section 10.5).

➤ From the Gateway, click the Paths icon. The Path Index appears (figure 3.19).

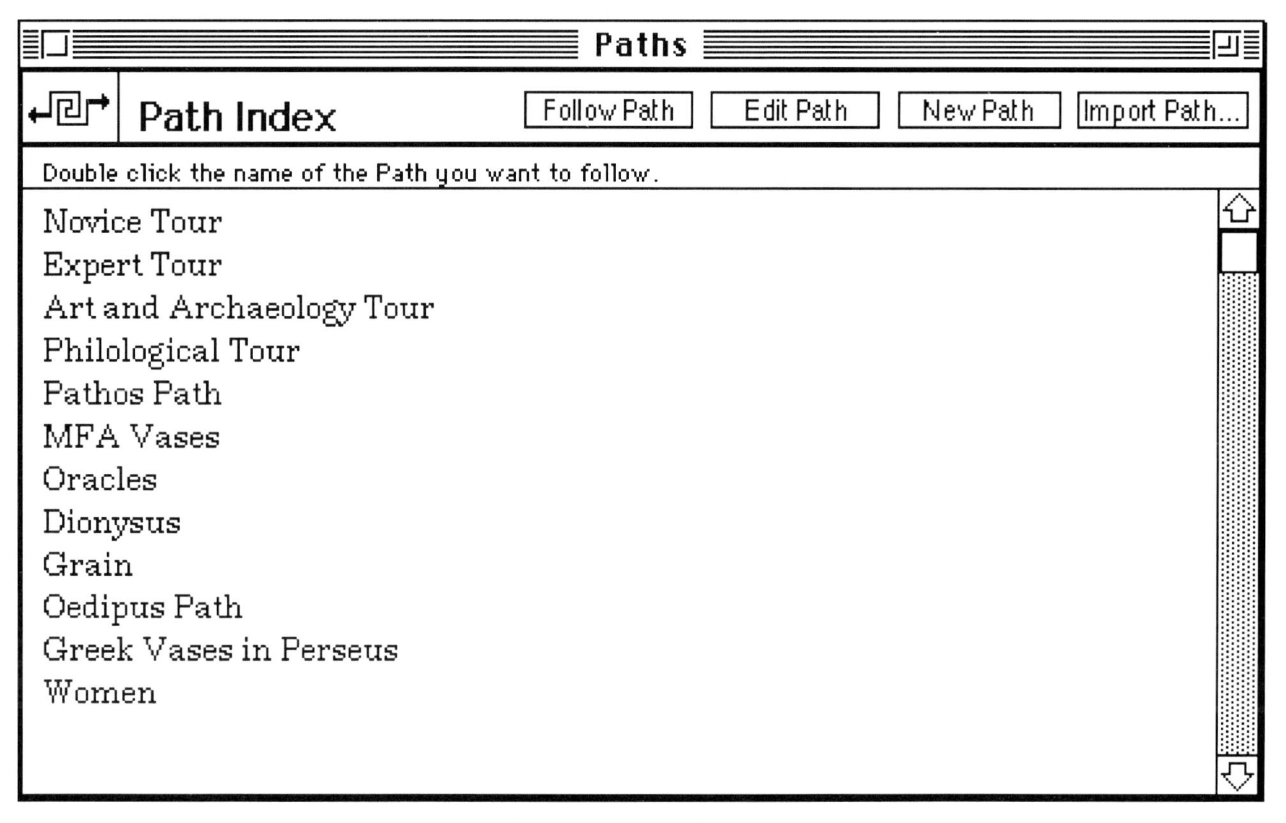

Figure 3.19 Path Index

➤ Click Novice Tour, then click Follow Path, and you are under way. Or begin the Path by double-clicking Novice Tour.

A new window called Path Note will appear, along with the first Location on the Path (figure 3.20). The Path Note window contains commentary or instructions concerning the Location. You may need to drag the top window out of the way in order to see the Path Note window.

Move the Path Note window to a location on the screen where it will not be obscured. Resize the Path Note window to accommodate the full text of the note.

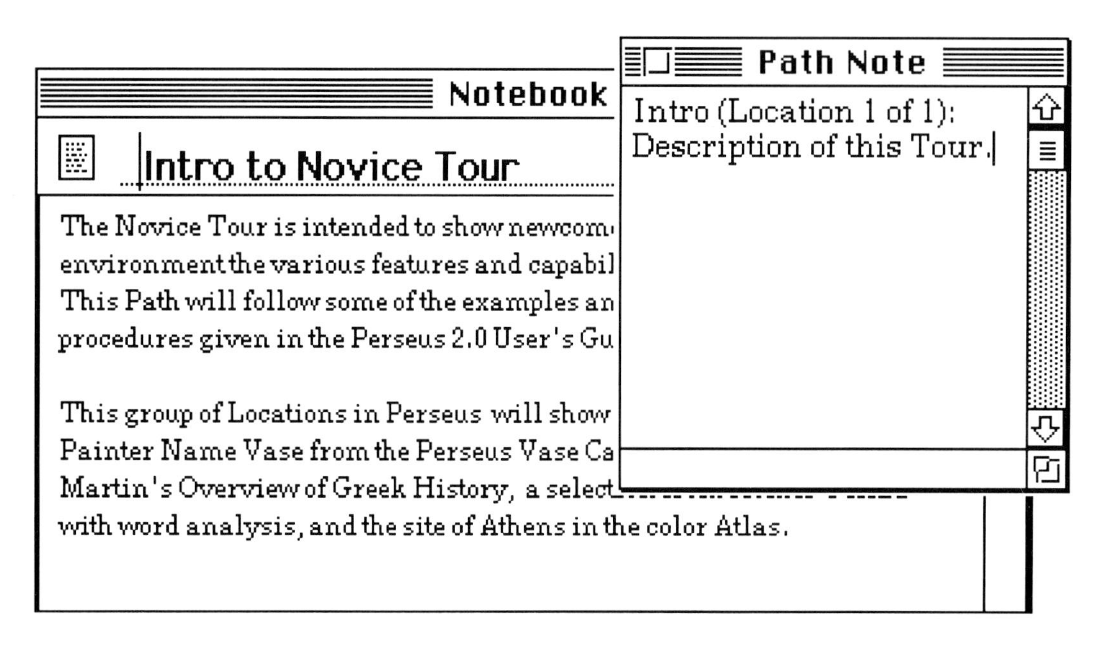

Figure 3.20 First Location on the Novice Tour, showing the Path Note window

To proceed to the next Location on the Path, click the Go Forward arrow on the Path Navigator on the Navigator Palette. To return to a previous Location on the Path, click the Go Backward arrow on the Path Navigator on the Navigator Palette.

Feel free to leave the Path at any time to explore the Perseus environment on your own. To rejoin the Path where you left it, choose Current Path Location from the Perseus menu. If you quit Perseus, however, you must again choose a Path to follow, according to the instructions in this section.

3.2.2 THE EXPERT TOUR

The Expert Tour is intended to familiarize both the veteran of version 1.0 and the eager novice with some of the newer and more advanced features of Perseus 2.0. Access the Path Index according to the directions in the previous section. Click Expert Tour, then click Follow Path, and you are under way. Or begin the Path by double-clicking Expert Tour.

To proceed along the Path, click the Go Forward arrow on the Path Navigator on the Navigator Palette.

For further information on customizing and creating your own Paths, and for instructions on how to convert Paths from version 1.0, see section 10.2.

3.2.3 THE PHILOLOGICAL TOUR

This tour surveys the capabilities of Perseus to collect and analyze philological data, focusing on both tools from Perseus 1.0 and tools newly developed for version 2.0. Access the Path Index according to the directions in section 3.2.1. Click Philological Tour, then click Follow Path, and you are under way. Or begin the Path by double-clicking Philological Tour. To proceed along the Path, click the Go Forward arrow on the Path Navigator on the Navigator Palette.

3.2.4 THE ART AND ARCHAEOLOGY TOUR

Perseus 2.0 contains more art objects and more effective ways to find and organize them than version 1.0. Some of these are shown in the Art and Archaeology Tour. Access the Path Index according to the directions in section 3.2.1. Click Art and Archaeology Tour, then click Follow Path, and you are under way. Or begin the Path by double-clicking Art and Archaeology Tour. To proceed along the Path, click the Go Forward arrow on the Path Navigator on the Navigator Palette.

3.3 ONLINE HELP

Online Help is available throughout Perseus by clicking the Help icon on the Navigator Palette or choosing Help from the Perseus menu. Help offers both general information on how to operate Perseus and context-related information about the current stack (that is, your present location inside Perseus). Topics in Online Help are cross-referenced with each other and referenced to this user's guide.

The term *stack* refers to the electronic place where data is stored in Perseus. *Stack* is the organizational metaphor for HyperCard, the software application on which Perseus is based. A stack is composed of a number of electronic "notecards."

➤ From the Gateway, click the Help (question mark) icon on the Navigator Palette.

When you request Help, information for the current stack appears (figure 3.21). Each icon on the Perseus Gateway represents a stack; help on the texts is given at the level of the Primary Text Index stack; help on Art & Archaeology is given at the level of the Catalog stack. The Help topic is shown at the top left, and the number of pages about this topic is shown at the top right.

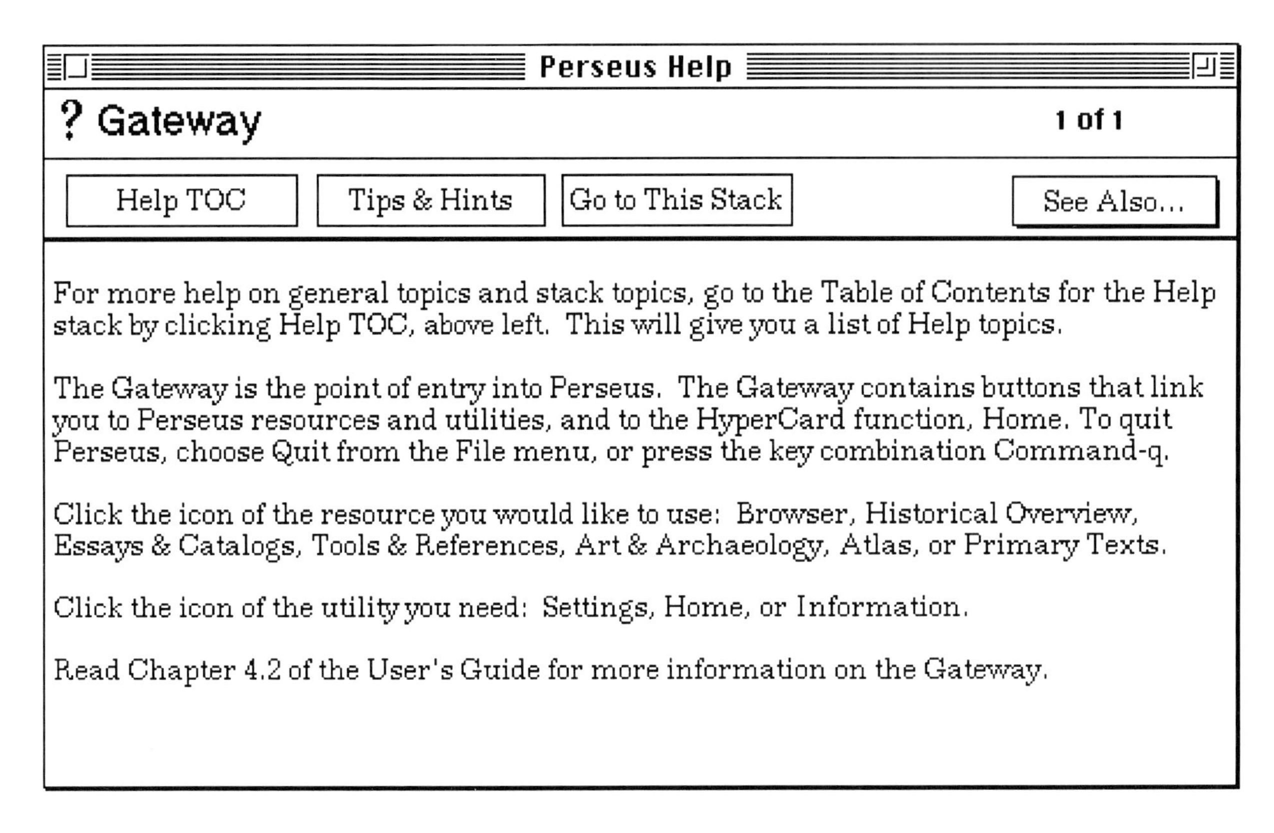

Figure 3.21 Online Help for the Gateway

➤ Click Tips & Hints for strategic information on this topic.

Tips & Hints is an additional element of the Help system that offers techniques and reminders for a particular topic. This information will help you save time, avoid mistakes, and use Perseus more efficiently.

From any Tips & Hints card, you can go to the Help TOC by clicking that button, or go directly to the stack being described by clicking "Go to This Stack." To return from the Tips & Hints card to the main Help, click the Go Back arrow at the top right.

The general Help topics include Getting Started, Perseus Basics, and Utilities. The stack Help topics are grouped by Browsing Tools and Indexes, Art & Archaeology, Atlas, Primary Texts, Philological Tools, Historical Overview, Essays & Catalogs, References, and Supporting Information. Use the arrows to page ahead and back when the topic offers more than one page of Help.

➤ Scroll down in the Stack Topics list, and click Small Site Plans under the Art & Archaeology category.

Some Help topics, such as the Small Site Plans topic shown in figure 3.22, display diagrams of the Perseus screen being described.

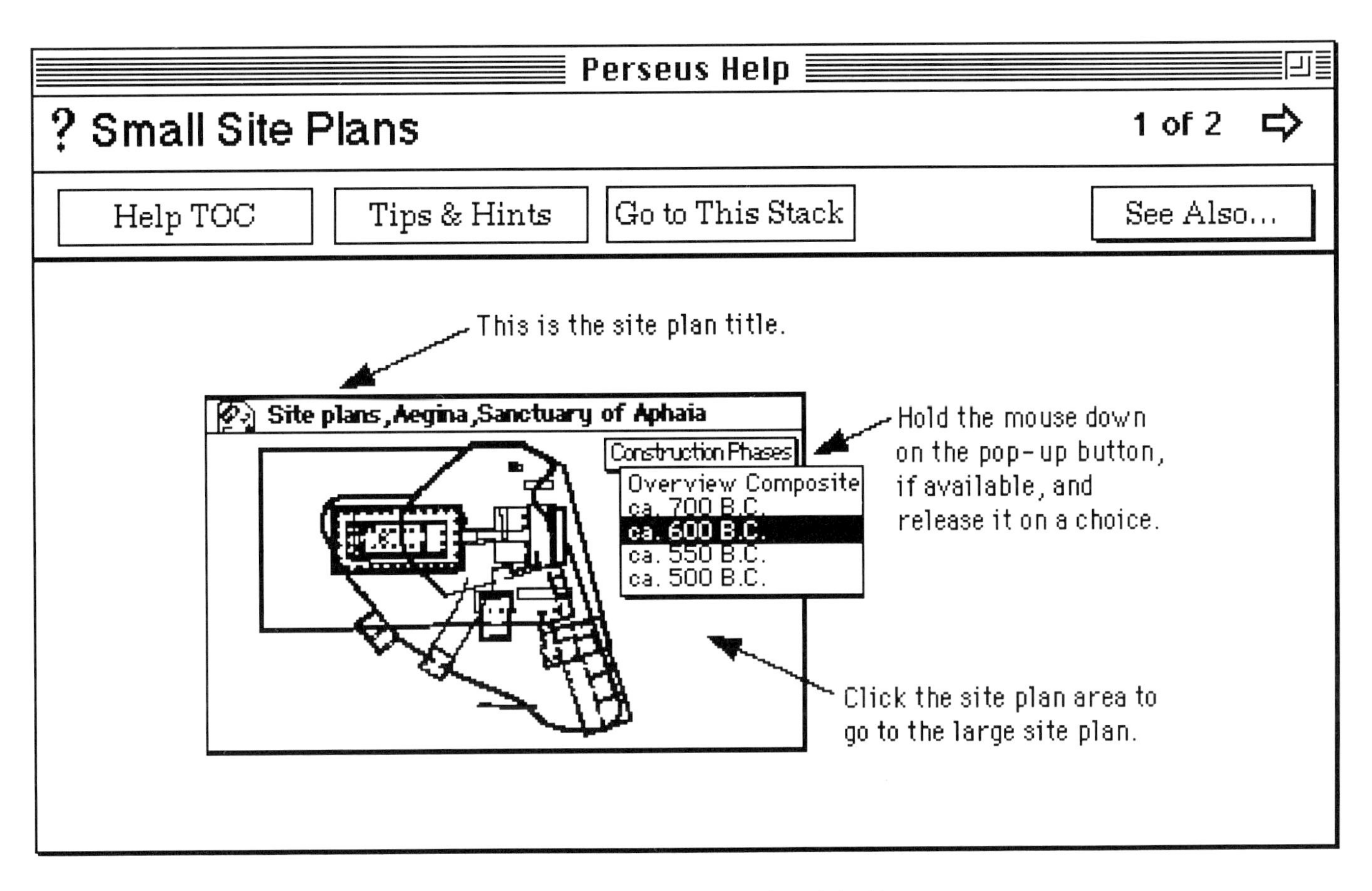

Figure 3.22 Help topic with diagram

➤ Click "Go to This Stack" to go to the Small Site Plans stack.

Any Help topic that describes a Perseus stack has a button that takes you directly to that stack from Help. General topics in Help do not have this button. A stack opened directly from Help opens in a new window instead of replacing the Help window, regardless of the setting registered on the Settings card.

➤ Close the stack you opened from Help (Small Site Plans).

➤ When you return to the Help topic for Small Site Plans, you may choose related help topics from the See Also menu.

In this example of the Small Site Plans, there are four See Also topics. Choose Large Site Plans to see the Help topic for that stack. You will go directly to the Help topic for Large Site Plans. Use the See Also menu to see the related topics there.

This chapter describes how to find your way through Perseus. It begins with the special ways that Perseus uses the various controls and buttons native to the Macintosh system and HyperCard and then explains the tools that were specially programmed for navigating through Perseus. This guide assumes that you are familiar with basic Macintosh vocabulary and standard Macintosh techniques, such as clicking and dragging with the mouse, using pop-up and pull-down menus, and so on. Basic Macintosh and HyperCard terminology is covered in section 4.1. Descriptions of Perseus-specific buttons, menus, and windows begin with section 4.2. If you need more help with the basics of the Macintosh system or a detailed description of HyperCard, consult the original disks and documentation for the Macintosh system and your copy of HyperCard.

4.1 BUTTONS, MENUS, AND WINDOWS

4.1.1 BUTTONS

Perseus uses several types of buttons to retrieve information. Three types of buttons are depicted in figure 4.1.

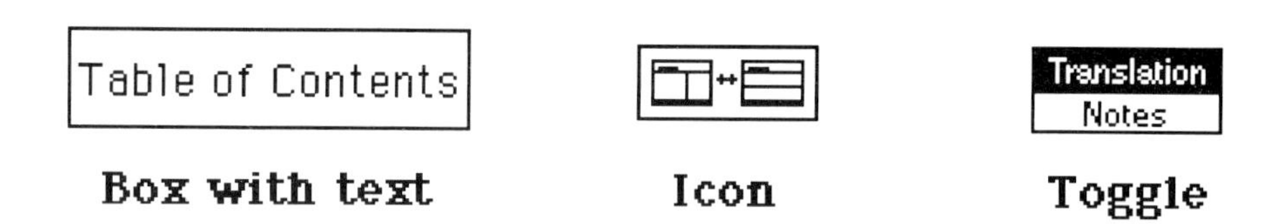

Figure 4.1 Types of buttons

Some buttons are toggles: clicking one turns a feature on or off, and the name on the button or the highlighted active area changes correspondingly. For example, clicking a button called Show Links reveals link areas in a text field. The name of the button then changes to Hide Links, which is the user's cue to click that button again to hide the link areas in the text field.

4.1.2 MENUS

Pop-up menus

Pop-up menus provide multiple choices from a button. Buttons that contain pop-up menus are shown as rectangles with shadows. To see the choices in a pop-up menu, move the pointer over the button and hold down the mouse button. While you hold down the mouse button, a list of choices pops up. Move the cursor over your choice and release the mouse. If you do not want to make a choice, move the cursor outside the boundary of the pop-up menu and release the mouse button.

The active choice in a pop-up menu is registered in one of three ways. The first way is that a check mark is placed next to the choice in the pop-up menu. The second is that the choice now appears as the name of the pop-up menu. The third is an action that occurs as soon as you release the mouse button. A pop-up menu from a button is depicted in figure 4.2. This menu allows you to set the type of videodisc player.

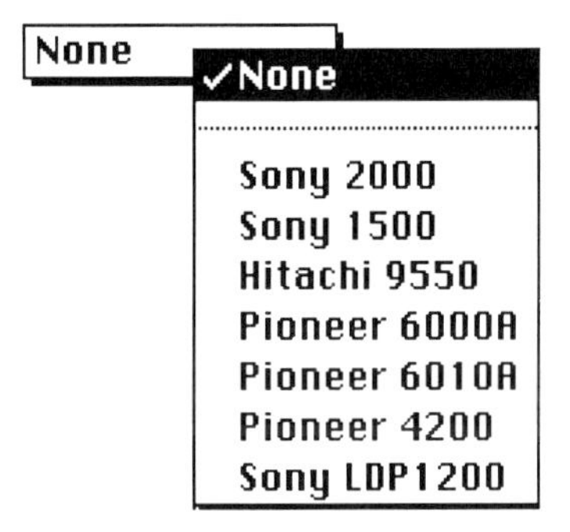

Figure 4.2 Pop-up menu

Pull-down menus

Pull-down menus provide choices from the menu bar. In addition to the menus regularly available through HyperCard, two menus are consistently available as you move through the Perseus resources. These two menus are Links and Perseus. The Links menu remains the same throughout Perseus. The items in the Perseus menu depend on your location and path within Perseus. The Perseus menu is depicted in figure 4.3.

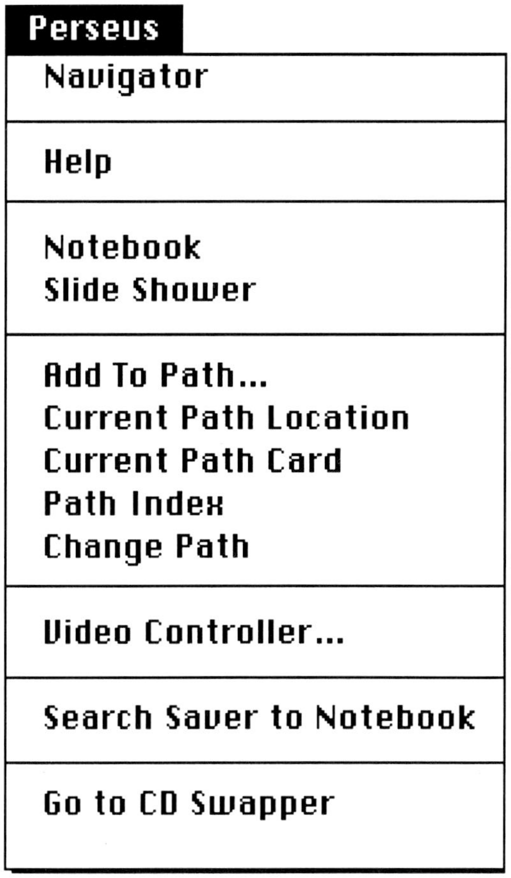

Perseus
Navigator
Help
Notebook
Slide Shower
Add To Path...
Current Path Location
Current Path Card
Path Index
Change Path
Video Controller...
Search Saver to Notebook
Go to CD Swapper

Figure 4.3 Perseus menu

Three specialized menus accompany some Perseus resources and appear on the right end of the menu bar when you open the resource. These menus provide tools, functions, and links designed to expand the power and flexibility of the Perseus resource. The Plan menu appears only when a Site Plan is on the screen, the Atlas menu appears when you go to the Atlas, and the Text menu is displayed when you select a Primary Text.

Detailed explanations of the Links and Perseus menus are offered in sections 4.5 and 4.6. Descriptions of specialized menus are included in the chapters describing the Perseus features that use them.

4.1.3 WINDOWS

Perseus uses the HyperCard features of multiple stack windows and a scroll window.

Open multiple windows

Perseus allows you to keep several windows open at the same time. If you choose, you may turn this function off in the Settings card. See section 4.2.2.

Perseus will warn you if your memory is running low because too many windows have been left open.

Open another stack window

When the Multiple Open Windows option is switched off, it can be manually applied. To keep a window open when you open a new one, hold down the Shift key while you click to go to a new card.

Only windows from different stacks can be seen at the same time; you cannot have two windows from the same stack open simultaneously.

Make a window active

➤ Click anywhere on a window to make it active.

Only one window is active at any time. The active window is shown on top of other windows and has a striped title bar. Inactive windows have plain white title bars. Although you can open several windows, available RAM restricts the number of windows that can be open at one time. If you open too many windows, you may see a warning message or, in extreme cases, the program may spontaneously quit.

Close windows

➤ Click the close box in the upper left-hand corner of the title bar.

Windows can accumulate on the screen and clutter the desktop. Close any windows you are not using. When only one Perseus window is open, its title bar does not have a close box.

Scroll windows

A scroll window (figure 4.4) is a tool for resizing windows and moving around windows that are bigger than the current screen (for example some Atlas drawings and the Large Site Plans). Scroll windows appear automatically when an image exceeds the screen size. The black rectangle in the middle of the scroll window outlines the region of the window currently displayed.

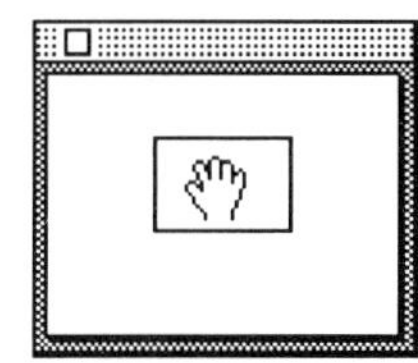

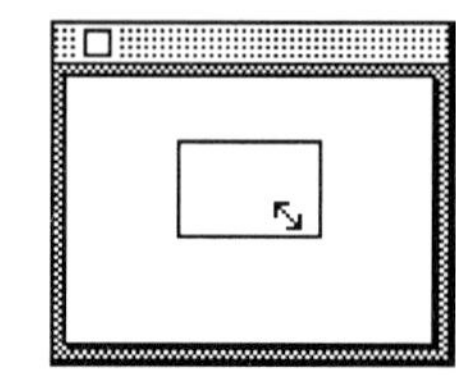

Figure 4.4 Scroll windows with Hand pointer and with Arrow pointer in the black rectangles

Move around the window

➤ Position the pointer in the middle of the black rectangle in the scroll window. The pointer becomes an open hand.

➤ Click the black rectangle with the hand and then drag it to show a different region of the map.

Resize the window

➤ Position the pointer near an edge or corner of the black rectangle. The pointer takes the shape of an arrow, facing in the direction in which you can change the dimension of the rectangle.

➤ Click the black rectangle with the arrow and then drag it to the desired size. The size of the window display changes, reflecting the change in dimension of the black rectangle.

NOTE: You can bring up the scrolling window by pressing the key combination Command-e, and put the scrolling window away again by again pressing Command-e.

Photograph and illustration windows

Many illustrations and all digitized photographs are not HyperCard stacks and therefore behave differently than the windows just described. In particular, you must click the close box to remove an illustration, because it will not be replaced or closed automatically by an action in Perseus. The window must be active for the close box to appear (the active window has a striped title bar). To make a window active, click in the title bar area. The close box should now appear.

If you use the Navigator Palette while a photograph or illustration window is open, you may not notice that the Palette is affecting the Perseus HyperCard resources. This is particularly true if you have opened a large photograph or illustration window that hides much of the screen behind it.

4.2 PERSEUS GATEWAY

The Gateway (figure 4.5) is the point of entry into Perseus. The Gateway contains buttons that link you to Perseus resources and utilities, and to the HyperCard Home stack. The Gateway also provides information about the Perseus Project and the Annenberg/CPB Project, which provided the major funding for Perseus.

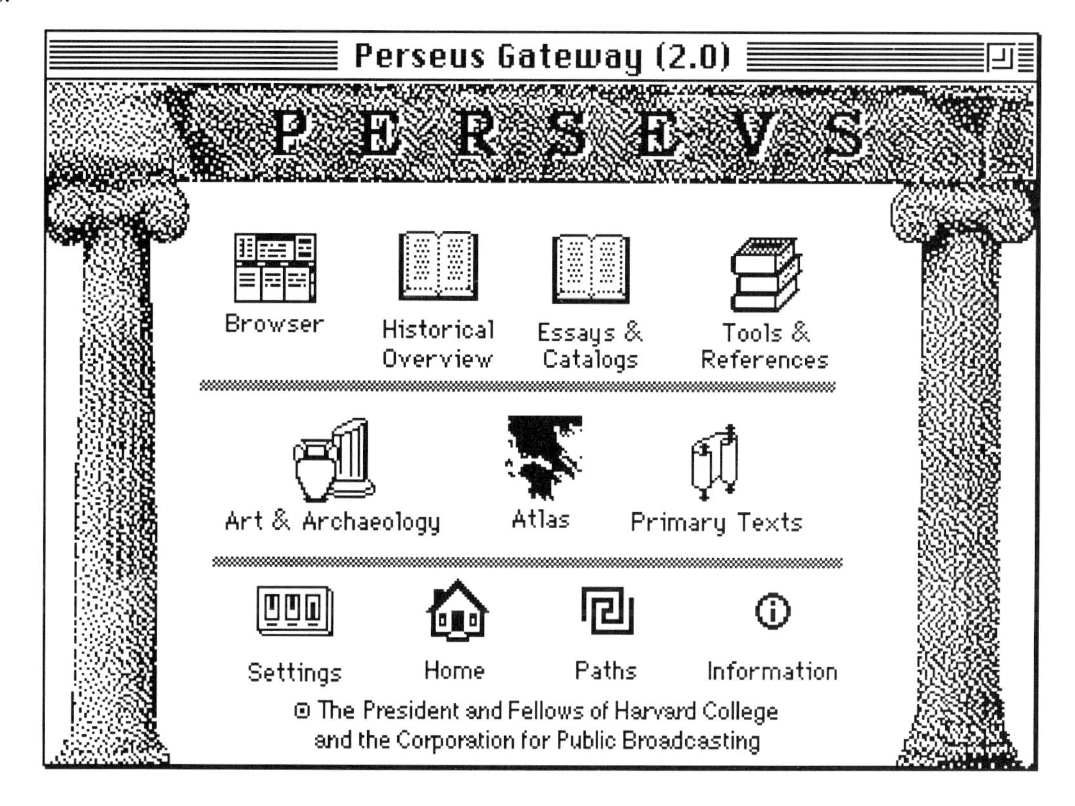

Figure 4.5 Perseus Gateway

The Browser, Historical Overview, Essays & Catalogs, Tools & References, Art & Archaeology, Atlas, and Primary Texts are the major resources of Perseus. Settings, Home, Paths, and Information are utilities.

4.2.1 PERSEUS RESOURCES

➤ Click the button of the resource you would like to use: Browser, Historical Overview, Essays & Catalogs, Tools & References, Art & Archaeology, Atlas, or Primary Texts. You will be taken to the Index level of the resource you have chosen.

4.2.2 SETTINGS

This section provides an overview of Settings. For detailed instructions, see section 10.5.

➤ Click the Settings icon to go to the Settings card.

Use the Settings function to customize your Perseus system. You can specify settings for a videodisc player, image displays, and the control of windows. For details on installation and setup procedures and information on how to run Perseus on a configuration other than the default (a single Macintosh and a single CD-ROM player), see sections 2.2 and 2.4.

➤ To identify the location of your personal Path, Notebook, and CD Swapper stacks, click one of the three buttons showing the Hard disk:Folder:File path. Select the desired Path, Notebook, or CD Swapper stack and click Save.

Videodisc players, CD-ROM digital images, and indexed color

If you will be running Perseus with a videodisc player, click the box Use Video Images, and choose the appropriate model from the Select Player Type pop-up menu.

NOTE: We can recommend only the videodisc players listed here and on the Settings card. These models are Hitachi 9550, Pioneer 4200, Pioneer 6000A, Pioneer 6010A, Sony LDP 1200, Sony 1500, and Sony 2000. Other models may not be compatible with Perseus.

If you will be displaying images only on the computer monitor, click the box Use Digital Images. It is possible to display images from both the videodisc and the CD-ROM at the same time. In this case, click both the Video Images and Digital Images boxes.

If your computer is running with an 8-bit color maximum, click the Indexed Color box. 8-bit color shows up as "256" in the field labeled "Settings of selected monitor" or "Characteristics of selected monitor" in the Monitors control panel in your system folder.

Window control

The button "Go to cards in new window" allows you to have more than one Perseus stack open on the desktop at one time. With this feature switched on, when you open a new stack, it will appear in an additional window, while the card from the old stack remains in an open window in the background of the screen. The advantage of opening stacks in new windows is the ability to view several resources at once.

The button "Go to cards in same window" allows you to open a new stack in the current window, with the new stack replacing the current stack. The advantage of opening stacks in the same window is that this option uses less RAM.

The Multiple Open Windows feature does not apply to image windows, which are a separate type of window that always open in addition to the stack window.

4.2.3 HOME (HYPERCARD FUNCTION)

➤ If you have HyperCard installed in your system, click the Home icon to go to the Home card.

You may wish to go directly to the Home card when you are finished using Perseus if you plan to use HyperCard in another application. You can also go to the Home card to review and adjust your search paths for Perseus. Refer to section 2.5 for information on HyperCard and the Home stack.

4.2.4 GO TO PATH INDEX

➤ Click the Paths icon to go directly to the Path Index. From the Path Index you may double-click any Path you wish to follow.

4.2.5 PERSEUS INFORMATION AND CREDITS

➤ Click this icon to learn about the Perseus Project, its funding, and other support.

An index lists entries for the Perseus Project and Annenberg/CPB Project, support information for using Perseus, and projects with topics related to Perseus.

4.2.6 QUIT (HYPERCARD FUNCTION)

➤ To quit Perseus 2.0, choose Quit from the File menu, or press Command-q.

The Quit icon (⌘Q) of version 1.0 has been replaced in version 2.0 with the Paths icon. When you choose Quit from the File menu, you will no longer see a dialog box asking you to confirm your choice to quit. You can also quit Perseus from anywhere in the program by pressing Command-q.

4.3 NAVIGATOR PALETTE

Users can navigate through the resources in Perseus by using the Navigator Palette (figure 4.6). The Navigator Palette is a small floating window that can be positioned anywhere on the screen and is always active, regardless of the number of windows open on the screen.

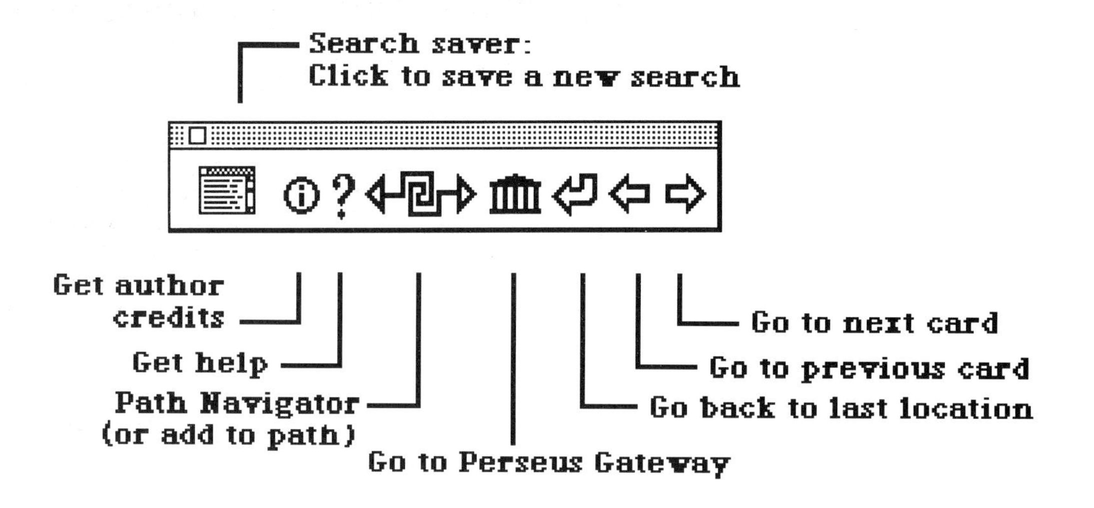

Figure 4.6 Navigator Palette

➤ Move the Navigator Palette by clicking the title bar and dragging the Palette to the desired place on the screen.

➤ Make the Navigator Palette reappear by choosing Navigator from the Perseus pull-down menu.

Use Search Saver

The Search Saver is a new feature of Perseus that lets you temporarily store the results of searches made with such tools as the Browser, the English Index, or the Philological Tools. The Search Saver icon on the Navigator Palette opens the Search Saver and stores the results of a new search. You can link to a citation in Perseus that is stored in the Search Saver by clicking it.

Because the Search Saver window remains active and on screen, there is no need to go back and forth between two Perseus resources when linking to search results, as had been necessary in version 1.0.

In this example, you will save the results of a search for the word πόλις in Homer.

➤ Follow the instructions for Greek Word Search given in section 3.1.1.

➤ Be sure that you have chosen "Citations for all forms" from the Options pop-up menu.

➤ Save the search by clicking the Search Saver icon on the Navigator Palette. The citations are saved to a new floating window, the Search Saver (figure 4.7).

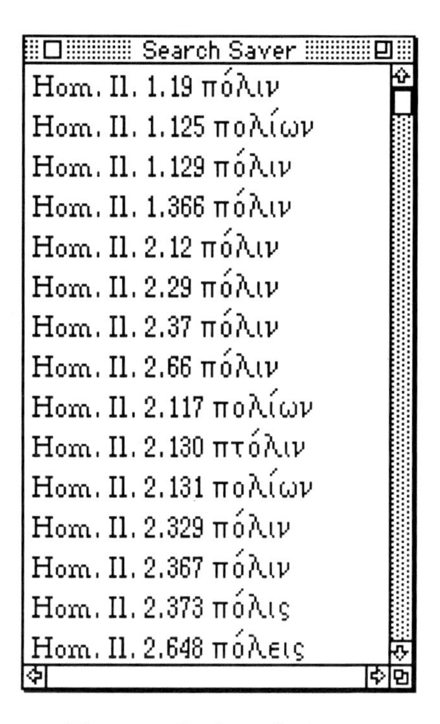

Figure 4.7 Search Saver

➤ Click a citation to link to it.

Results loaded into the Search Saver may be copied to a Perseus Notebook for later use. This task is automated by choosing "Search Saver to Notebook" from the Perseus pull-down menu. For more details on this feature, see section 4.6.8.

Get author credits

Use the Information icon to correctly cite material from Perseus used in a paper or publication.

Where applicable, author credits for articles, descriptions, and translations in Perseus are available by clicking the Information icon. If author credits are available, a card appears with information about the editions, sources, or author, as well as other information about the stack. To return to your original location, click the Go Back icon, described below.

Author credits are available for Primary Texts at the text level, for Art & Archaeology stacks at the catalog level, for the Encyclopedia at the article level, for the Atlas at the level of the small outline map, for the Essays at the level of the table of contents, and for the Historical Overview at the text level.

Note that the Information icon on the Gateway takes you to information about the Perseus Project.

Get help

Online Help is available in Perseus 2.0 when you click the Help icon on the Navigator Palette. It is also available from the Perseus menu. When you click Help, Perseus opens the Help stack and presents information related to the current stack. Section 3.3 addresses the Help system in greater detail.

Navigate a path

The Paths icon allows you to navigate a path. This icon is a square maze with an arrow at either side, suggesting a meander through Perseus. The meander has three active components: the left arrow, the meander center, and the right arrow.

The left and right arrows are Go Back and Go Forward along the Path, respectively. Click them to go to the previous and next Locations of the path you are following. The meander center is a Record button, which allows you to add a Location to the Path you are creating.

For instructions on following a prerecorded Path in Perseus, see section 3.2. For complete information on creating Paths, see section 10.2.

Go to Perseus Gateway

The Gateway icon places you at the main access point of Perseus, the Perseus Gateway. If you lose your bearings, you can always return to your starting point. From the Gateway, you can select any element of Perseus.

Go to previous card and go to next card

The left arrow on the Navigator Palette takes you to the previous card in a stack, moving you backward in a linear fashion. For example, if you are in the Architecture stack and the current card is "Olympia,Swimming Pool with Greek Baths," the left arrow will take you to the previous card of that stack, "Olympia,Stadium." (Because of programming requirements, commas in a catalog title are not followed by a space.)

It is, therefore, not necessary to return to the Index level in order to proceed through the cards of a stack.

The right arrow on the Navigator Palette takes you to the next card in a stack, moving you forward in a linear progression. For example, if you are examining the entry "Bell krater" in the Encyclopedia, the right arrow will take you to the next catalog entry in the Encyclopedia, "Bellerophon."

About cards and stacks: HyperCard organizes information electronically, analogous to a number of stacks of note cards. The sculpture data, for example, is stored in the cards of one stack, the text of Sophocles in the cards of another. The Go to Previous Card and Go to Next Card arrows take you to cards within the current stack. The Go Back arrow takes you to a location in a previous stack.

Go back to last location

The Go Back (bent) arrow returns you to a card in a previous location—most often to the stack you were in before you entered the current Perseus resource. If you click the Go Back arrow several times in succession, you will retrace your steps backward. This is not the same as the Go to Previous Card arrow, described above.

You should be aware of the limitations of the Go Back feature. Because Perseus is large and complex, the Go Back feature does not always take you where you might expect. An alternate method of retracing one's steps is to use the Go Recent feature of HyperCard. Choose Go Recent from the Go menu. A message window appears with thumbnail images of the windows previously accessed in the current HyperCard session. Click one of the thumbnails to return to that window.

4.4 AUTHOR/DRAWING CREDITS

When a Perseus screen or image has been created specially by an artist or photographer, the credit automatically appears in a floating window along with the screen or image. The floating window can be dragged across the desktop to any location and can be closed by clicking the upper left-hand corner of the box.

The display of credits is often a condition of the agreement negotiated with a museum, artist, or photographer to include a collection or work in Perseus. Accordingly, there is no provision for turning off the author credits.

4.5 LINKS PULL-DOWN MENU

The Links menu lists most of the Perseus resources that are available from the Gateway and from the main indexes, such as the Art & Archaeology Index and the Tools & References Index.

Perseus resources have several different types of links. Links are implemented through buttons, text, and the Links menu (figure 4.8). Using the Links menu, you can move among the Perseus resources without returning to the Gateway.

When you have selected text in any part of Perseus and you then use the Links menu to go to a new resource, Perseus tries to look up the selected text in the resource you have chosen from the Links menu.

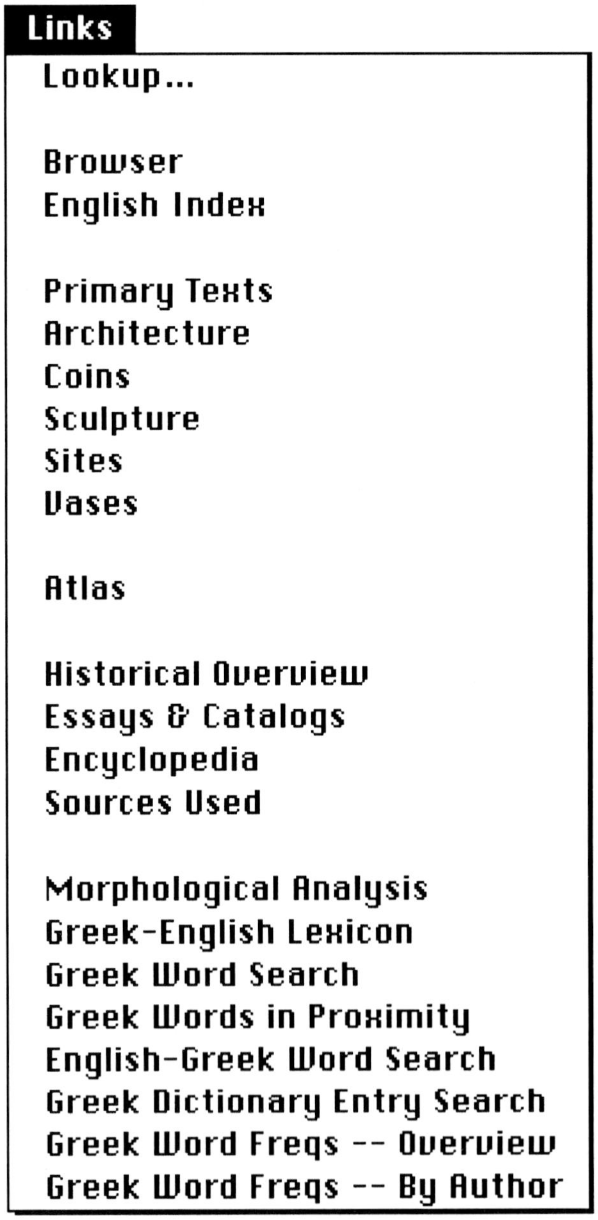

Links

Lookup...

Browser
English Index

Primary Texts
Architecture
Coins
Sculpture
Sites
Vases

Atlas

Historical Overview
Essays & Catalogs
Encyclopedia
Sources Used

Morphological Analysis
Greek-English Lexicon
Greek Word Search
Greek Words in Proximity
English-Greek Word Search
Greek Dictionary Entry Search
Greek Word Freqs -- Overview
Greek Word Freqs -- By Author

Figure 4.8 Links menu

4.5.1 LOOKUP TOOL

Lookup is a new tool in Perseus 2.0. The Lookup tool lets you make a global query of the Perseus databases with a single word or phrase. It resolves words or phrases into canonical Perseus references and associates conventional Perseus names with alternate versions of names. (Canonical Perseus references are the precise words or abbreviations used by the software program to locate information across all its resources.) Through this process, the Lookup tool identifies the resources in Perseus where the selected topic may be found. The Lookup tool also provides shortcuts for navigating the Perseus database when you know exactly the resource you want to see.

Using Lookup to query possible references

The Lookup tool does not identify all the instances of a particular word or phrase anywhere in the English text of Perseus; this task is performed by the English Index tool, also found under the Links menu. Instead, when you type in a particular word or phrase, Lookup points you to the Perseus resources containing the object of your query, or the attributes of the object.

If you want to search for all occurrences of a word or phrase anywhere in the English text of Perseus, use the English Index.

In the following example, you will use Lookup to find the Perseus resources for the query "Castor and Pollux" and to resolve this phrase into its canonical Perseus reference.

Use whole words or phrases, not starting characters, as search strings in Lookup. If you want to search by starting characters, use the English Index instead.

➤ Open the Lookup tool by choosing it from the Links menu. Type "Castor and Pollux" into the Lookup tool and press Return.

You will see "dioskouroi" in the left column (figure 4.9). "Dioskouroi" is the canonical Perseus reference derived from the query "Castor and Pollux"; the names below the line are names associated with "Castor and Pollux" that Lookup recognizes.

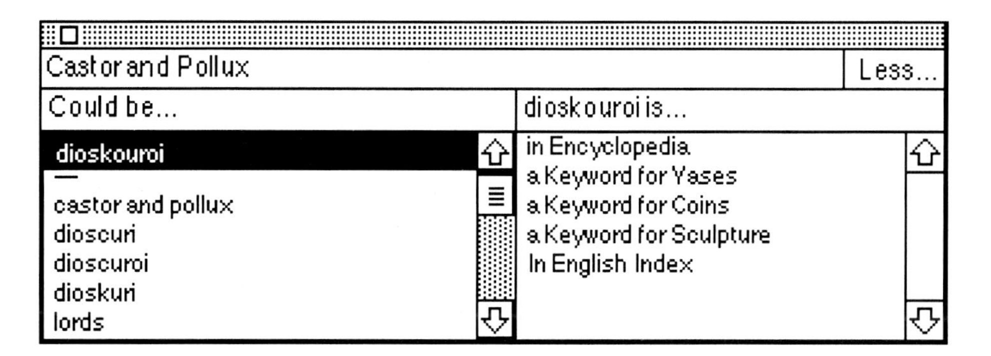

Figure 4.9 Lookup tool

The right column lists the resources in Perseus containing the canonical reference "dioskouroi," which is found, accordingly, as a Keyword for Sculpture and in the English Index. You can investigate each reference in turn by clicking one of the possible resources in the right column.

If the Lookup tool begins to fail or behave erratically, close it and reopen it from the Links menu.

Now you will use Lookup to undertake a more complex search, in which further canonical Perseus references are given, in this case to Hera and charioteer.

➤ Open the Lookup tool by choosing it from the Links menu. Type Hera into the Lookup tool and press Return. Seventeen possible links having to do with Hera appear in the left ("Could be") column (figure 4.10).

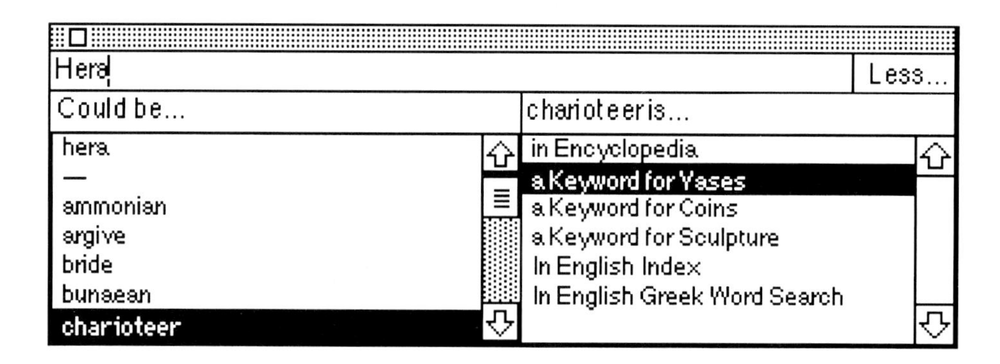

Figure 4.10 Lookup with results of clicking "charioteer" in left column

➤ To look for a connection between Hera and charioteer in Perseus vase painting data, click "charioteer," the fifth item below hera in the left column. A list of Perseus resources appears in the right column. To go to an associated Perseus resource, click a line in the right column. In this case, results for "charioteer" appear in four resources: in the Encyclopedia; as a Keyword in the Vases, Coins, and Sculpture Catalogs; in the English Index; and in the English-Greek Word Search.

➤ You may continue the Hera-charioteer search by clicking the line "Keyword for Vases" in the right column. This will take you to the Browser, which automatically makes the search for you (figure 4.11).

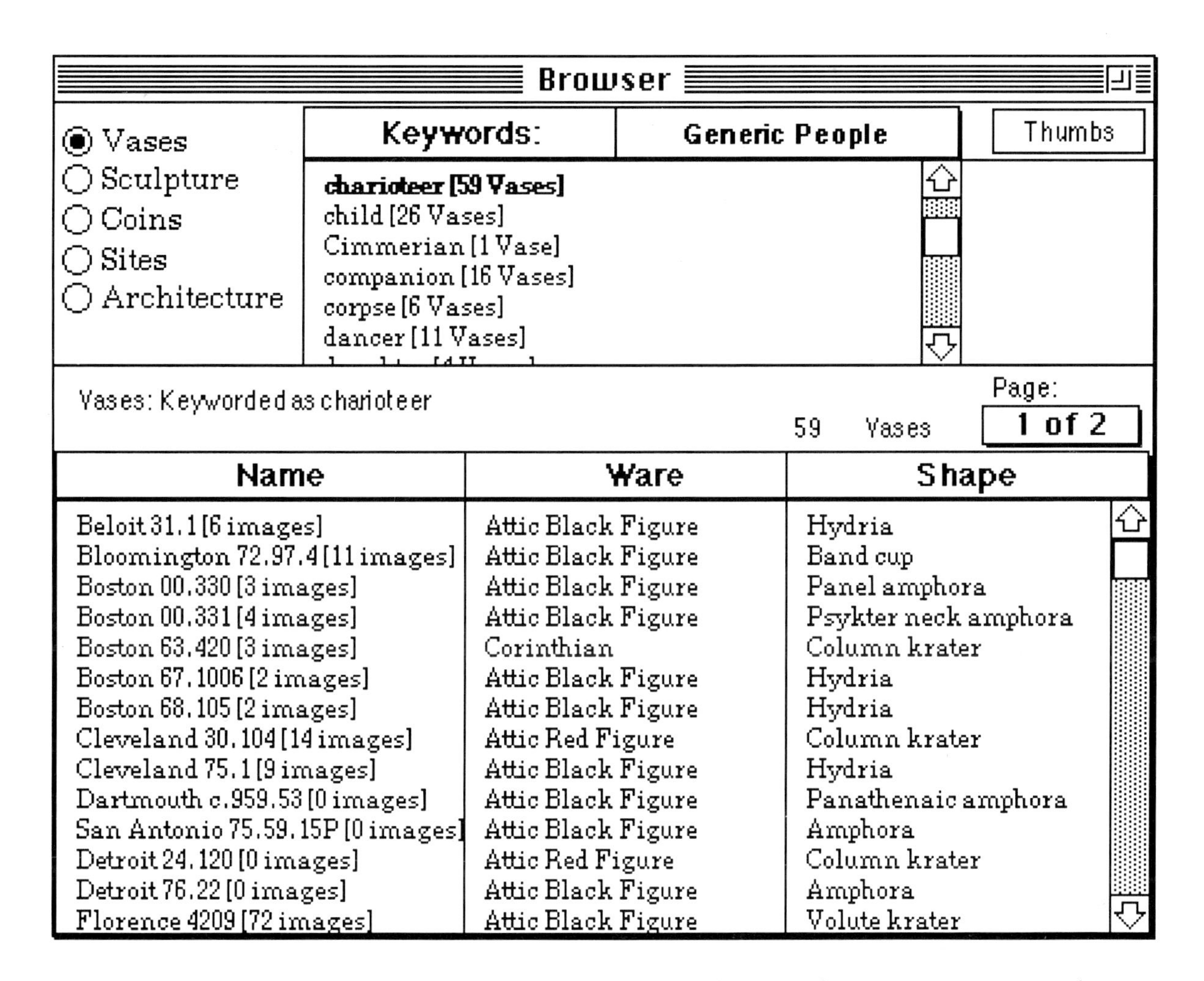

Figure 4.11 Clicking "Keyword for Vases" in Lookup produces a Browser search

The search produces a list of vases on two pages of Browser results. You will now compare this list of vases with a list produced by a Vase Keyword search for Divinities, specifically, Hera.

➤ Save the results for "charioteer" in the Search Saver by clicking the Search Saver icon on the Navigator Palette. To make a Keyword Search for Hera, find the pop-up menu of search topics at the top of the Browser and choose Keywords (figure 4.12). A pop-up menu of Keyword search topics is at the right; choose Divinities.

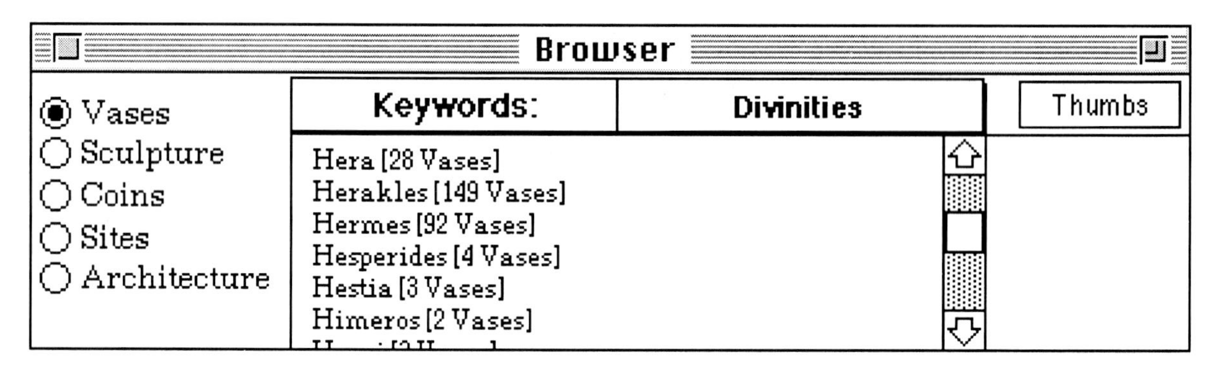

Figure 4.12 Vase Keyword Search for Hera

➤ Scroll down and select Hera. A new set of Browser data will be displayed.

➤ Compare the list of charioteer vases stored in the Search Saver with the Hera vases in the Browser. Vases that appear in both lists are Cleveland 30.104, Florence 4209, and Munich 1437. You can go to the Catalog card for any of the vases by clicking on its name, in either the Browser or the Search Saver.

Use Lookup to go directly to a known Primary Text destination

If you have a specific citation in the Primary Texts in mind, you can use the Lookup tool for quickest access to it. Type in the canonical Perseus name or abbreviation and press Return. This is a feature you will probably use only after you have become familiar with Perseus and only if you frequently use the same resources in Perseus.

The direct Lookup feature does not apply to Perseus resources other than Primary Texts.

➤ To go to line 250 of Euripides' *Medea*, choose Lookup from the Links menu. A small floating window appears. Type "Eur. Med. 250" and press Return.

NOTE: When you use the Lookup tool as a shortcut to Primary Texts, you must use specific abbreviations and formats for author's name, work, and references to book, chapter, section, or line. These are known as canonical Perseus references, and complete lists are found in the appendix of this User's Guide and in Online Help under the topic "Canonical Abbreviations for Primary Texts."

Use Lookup to go to a known resource

If you know specific catalog and article titles, you can use Lookup to go to these resources quickly. This procedure involves one more step than the procedure for finding Primary Texts, described above.

➤ To go to the card for the Doric Treasury at Delphi in the Architecture Catalog, choose Lookup from the Links menu. A small floating window appears. Type "Delphi,Doric Treasury," and press Return. Do not leave any spaces between Delphi, the comma, and Doric. Now click Architecture Catalog in the right column.

Note that when you use Lookup as a shortcut to a particular building, coin, sculpture, site, or vase, you must use the exact title of the catalog entry, and you must perform the extra step of clicking the desired item in the right column.

4.5.2 GO TO A NEW PERSEUS RESOURCE OR TOOL

A Perseus resource is a database of primary or secondary information. These are the resources found in the Links menu and the locations of their descriptions in this User's Guide:

Primary Texts (8.1)
Architecture (6.3.3)
Coins (6.3.6)
Sculpture (6.3.4)
Sites (6.3.2)
Vases (6.3.5)
Atlas (7)
Historical Overview (6.1)
Encyclopedia (9.2)
Essays & Catalogs (6.2)
Sources Used (9.3.1)
Greek-English Lexicon (8.4.7)

A Perseus tool is a software program written to access or organize the information in a resource. The tools found under the Links menu are:

Lookup (4.5.1)
Browser (5.1)
English Index (5.3)
Morphological Analysis (8.4.6)
Greek Word Search (8.4.8)
Greek Words in Proximity (8.4.9)
English-Greek Word Search (8.4.10)
Greek Dictionary Entry Search (8.4.11)
Greek Word Freqs—Overview (8.4.12)
Greek Word Freqs—By Author (8.4.12)

➤ Choose any resource or tool from the Links menu.

Using the Links menu to go to Perseus resources and tools is a shortcut for returning to the Gateway and clicking an icon.

If you know the exact form of a Perseus Catalog title or Catalog number, you can link with its card by highlighting the text containing the title or number, and choosing the appropriate resource from the Links menu. Perseus will look up the selected text in the resource you have chosen.

In this example, you will link with the Sculpture Catalog card for Kleobis and Biton from the Stewart essays on Greek sculpture.

➤ Go to the Essays by clicking the Essays & Catalogs icon on the Gateway or by choosing Essays & Catalogs from the Links menu. Click "One Hundred Greek Sculptors: Their Careers and Extant Works." A table of contents for the Stewart essays appears. Click "4.2.4.2 Hageladas of Argos." Highlight Kleobis and Biton from the second line of text. Choose Sculpture from the Links menu. Perseus will take you to the Catalog card for Kleobis and Biton.

This is an advanced technique, and it will work only if the selected text is identical to the Perseus Catalog card title or number.

4.5.3 OPEN A LINKS MENU ITEM IN A NEW WINDOW

➤ Hold the Shift key down while choosing an item from the Links menu.

As described in section 4.1.3, holding the shift key down during a navigational action will temporarily reverse the default setting for opening windows. When you press the Shift key as you choose a Links menu item, the new stack appears in an additional window, if the default setting is to open windows as replacements of the current window. If the default setting is the opposite selection (to open in a new window rather than replace one), the new stack will now replace the current window.

4.6 PERSEUS MENU

The Perseus menu is always available from the menu bar in Perseus. The Perseus menu allows you to control Perseus tools and facilitates navigation and Paths. The item Current Assignment and the items showing the current open windows change or disappear altogether, depending on your Settings and on your location inside Perseus. Figure 4.13 reflects the Sculpture Index as the current open stack.

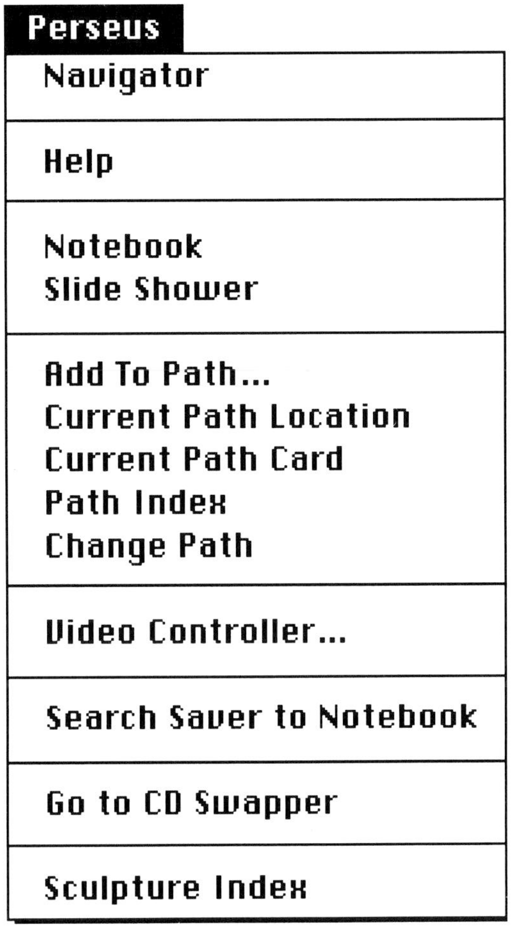

Perseus

Navigator

Help

Notebook
Slide Shower

Add To Path...
Current Path Location
Current Path Card
Path Index
Change Path

Video Controller...

Search Saver to Notebook

Go to CD Swapper

Sculpture Index

Figure 4.13 Perseus menu

4.6.1 NAVIGATOR

➤ Choose Navigator to make the Navigator Palette reappear, if it has been closed. The operation of the Navigator Palette is described in section 4.3.

4.6.2 CURRENT ASSIGNMENT

➤ Choose Current Assignment to activate a personal stack attached to Perseus.

The Current Assignment item will not appear on the Perseus pull-down menu unless you have created a new stack that you have named Current Assignment.

See section 10.6 to find out more about implementing the Current Assignment feature.

4.6.3 HELP

Online Help is available in Perseus 2.0 by choosing Help from the Perseus menu. It is also available by clicking the Help icon on the Navigator Palette. When you click Help, Perseus opens the Help stack and presents information related to the current stack. Section 3.3 addresses the Help system in greater detail.

4.6.4 NOTEBOOK

➤ Choose Notebook to see the Notebook Index.

You first must identify the hard disk location of the Notebook stack by using the Settings feature from the Gateway. This procedure is described briefly in section 4.2.2. See section 10.3 for detailed instructions in the use of the Notebook.

4.6.5 SLIDE SHOWER

You can assemble any number of Perseus images in a list by archive number, and display them with the Slide Shower (figure 4.14).

Figure 4.14 Slide Shower

Add Slide

➤ With a Perseus image displayed on the screen, click the button Add Slide to import it into your list of slides. A dialog box will ask you to confirm your choice. If you click Add Image, the Perseus acquisition number will be listed in the field at the left.

Clear List

➤ Click the button Clear List to delete a list of slides.

Save List...

➤ If you have assembled a list of slides, you may save it by clicking the button Save List.

A dialog box will appear, asking you to name your list (figure 4.15).

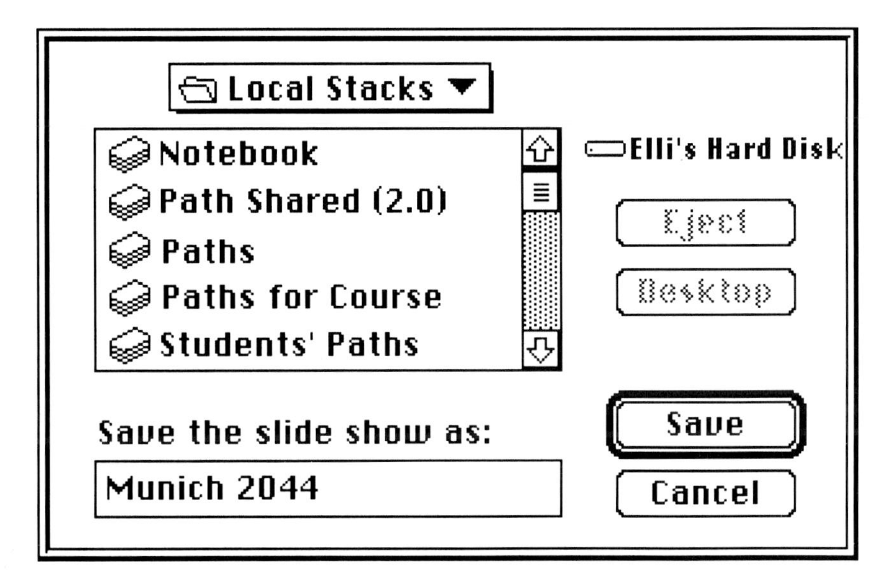

Figure 4.15 Save List dialog box

We suggest that you save the list to a folder on your hard disk.

Load List...

➤ To load a previously saved list of slides, click the button Load List. Select the list you wish to display and click Open.

Settings...

Two options are offered when you click the Settings button: "Show images in a new window," and "Include non-Perseus images."

➤ Click the Go Back button to return to the Slide Shower controls.

Slide Shower buttons

The buttons at the top control the slide show.

➤ Click Auto to begin the show at the top of the list. Click Next to show the next slide. Click Prev. to show the previous slide.

4.6.6 PATH MENU ITEMS

Five items on the Perseus pull-down menu operate Paths. The following overview describes how to add a Location, or stop, to a Path, how to see the current Path Card, how to see a Path Index, how to rejoin a Path, and how to change a Path. For complete information about using Paths in Perseus, see chapter 10, "Saving Your Work." Before you use Paths, you first must identify the location of your Path stack on the hard disk by using the Settings feature from the Gateway. This procedure is described in section 4.2, and in greater detail in section 10.5.

Any number of Paths may be stored in a personal Path stack. The card listing the Paths kept in the stack is called the Path Index. The Current Path is that Path presently loaded into Perseus, the one that you have chosen to follow. The Current Path card contains a series of icons representing the various Stops on the Path.

Add to Path

➤ Choose "Add to Path" to add your current location in Perseus to your Current Path.

This menu item is the same as clicking the center of the Path Navigator on the Navigator Palette.

Current Path Location

➤ Choose Current Path Location to rejoin a Path that you had left.

If you had been following a Path but had left it to explore Perseus on your own, you can rejoin the Path where you left it by choosing this item.

Current Path Card

➤ Choose "Current Path Card" to see the Path card (if any) for your Current Path.

If there is no Current Path, Perseus will put up a message window telling you so. Choose a Path to follow from the Path Index.

Path Index

➤ Choose Path Index to see a list of all paths (if any) in your version of Perseus.

This is the electronic location where you choose or edit the Current Path. Alternatively, you may use the Change Path feature, described below.

Change Path

➤ Choose Change Path to select a different path.

A dialog box appears, listing all paths (if any) in your version of Perseus. Click on the Path you wish to follow.

4.6.7 VIDEO CONTROLLER

Archive display

➤ Choose Video Controller to gain direct access to the videodisc player.

NOTE: Be sure that the player is attached via your computer's modem port.

A small window with controls for the videodisc player appears (figure 4.16). Use the window to test connections to the player, if one is being used, to bring up a desired image, or to move forward and backward in the videodisc. This window also enables you to display the digital images on the CD-ROMs.

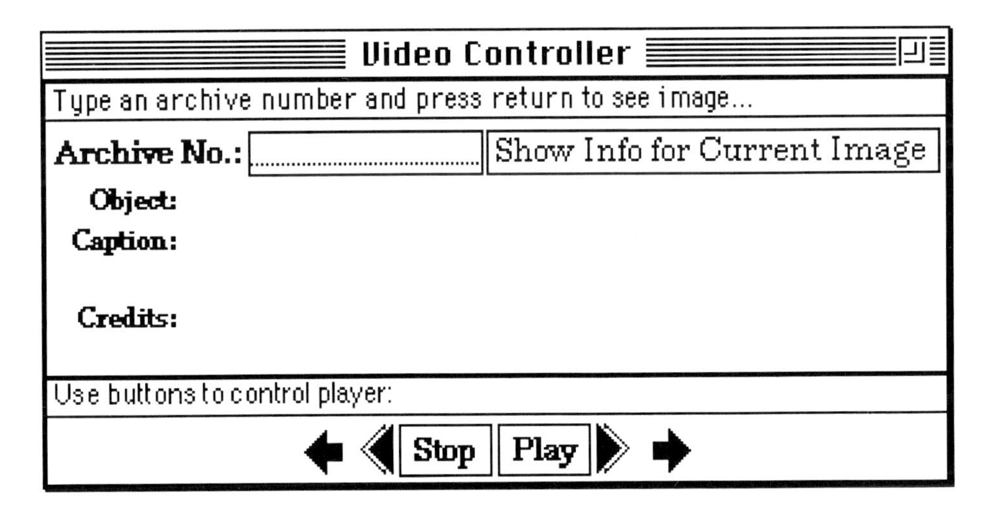

Figure 4.16 Video Controller

➤ To display an image of waterbirds on a piece of Protoattic ware, position the pointer in the field "Archive No." and type the Perseus archive number "1990.01.0003." Press Return.

All Perseus images have an archive number. The archive number for videodisc images is found in the catalog that comes along with your videodisc. For images stored on the CD-ROMs, the archive number appears in the title bar of the image. The caption and credits (if applicable) are shown for the current image.

NOTE: Perseus archive numbers are not the same as the frame numbers of images on the videodisc. Perseus archive numbers are permanent, but videodisc frame numbers change from one version of Perseus to another.

➤ Click "Show Info for Current Image" to obtain the Perseus archive number for the image displayed on the video monitor.

Player control buttons

The videodisc player can be controlled from the computer by using these buttons. From left to right, their functions are Step Reverse, Scan Reverse, Stop, Play, Scan Forward, and Step Forward (figure 4.17).

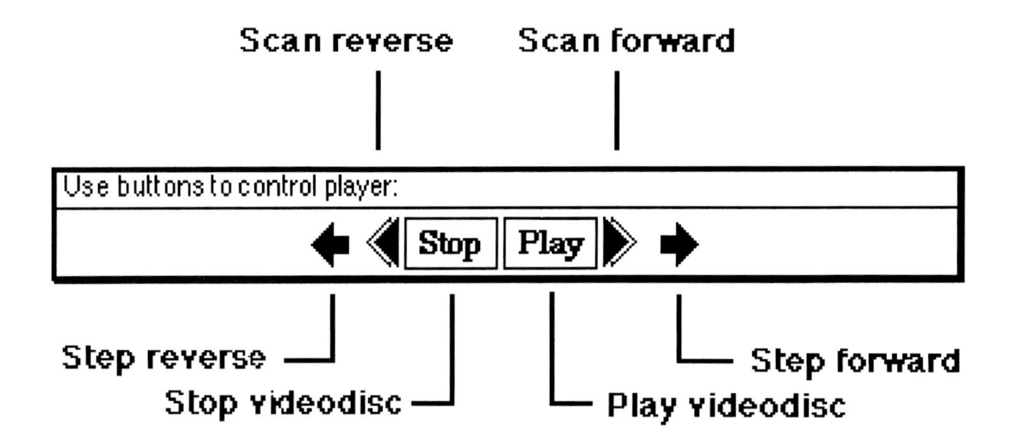

Figure 4.17 Videodisc Controller buttons

➤ Click Stop and Play to stop and play the videodisc, respectively.

➤ Use the Step and Scan buttons to continue a step or scan action.

4.6.8 SEARCH SAVER TO NOTEBOOK

➤ Choose "Search Saver to Notebook" from the Perseus menu to store the results of a search captured by the Search Saver.

Your search results are saved in a Perseus Notebook. This is a somewhat more permanent record of your work than the Search Saver, which is cleared whenever you make a new search or when you quit Perseus. Read about the Notebook in section 10.3 (the "Search Saver to Notebook" option is discussed more thoroughly in section 10.3.3).

4.6.9 GO TO CD SWAPPER

➤ Click "Go to CD Swapper" to go to your personalized CD Swapper stack.

The use of the CD Swapper is covered in section 10.4.

4.6.10 STACKS CURRENTLY OPEN

At the bottom of the Perseus menu is a list of all open Perseus stacks, if any stacks other than the Gateway are open. (Figure 4.13 shows that the stack Sculpture Index was open at the time.) Choosing a stack from this list brings it to the forefront of the windows.

➤ Choose the name of an open stack from the Perseus menu to go to that stack.

This menu feature is especially useful if you are using Perseus on a system that has a small monitor, or if you keep many stacks open at the same time.

Because of the large scope of data in Perseus, specialized tools are needed to give you control of the data and access to it. The searching tools described in this chapter help you find information quickly and make your search methods strategic and efficient. With the searching tools you can

find specific objects (a particular vase, a text reference, an image);

find classes of objects (plays by Sophocles, vases by Euphronios, sculpture of the Archaic period, coins keyworded with "Scylla");

see textual and visual summaries of objects before going to the more detailed sources of information; and

store search requests until the appropriate CD-ROM is on line.

The basic tools for searching the Perseus database are the Browser, Thumbnail Browser, English Index, and Search Saver. The Browser and Thumbnail Browser, in particular, help you target information for detailed study and spend less time following false leads. A fifth tool, the CD Swapper, is used to store requests for information on another CD-ROM.

The Lookup tool, explained in the previous chapter, performs some limited searching features, but it is primarily a navigation tool for going directly to resources in Perseus.

5.1 BROWSER

The Browser offers a centralized way of finding and viewing data in Perseus. It provides a way to search through the catalogs for vases, sculpture, coins, sites, and architecture, looking for various attributes and keywords. You can choose the Browser from the Gateway or the Links menu (figure 5.1).

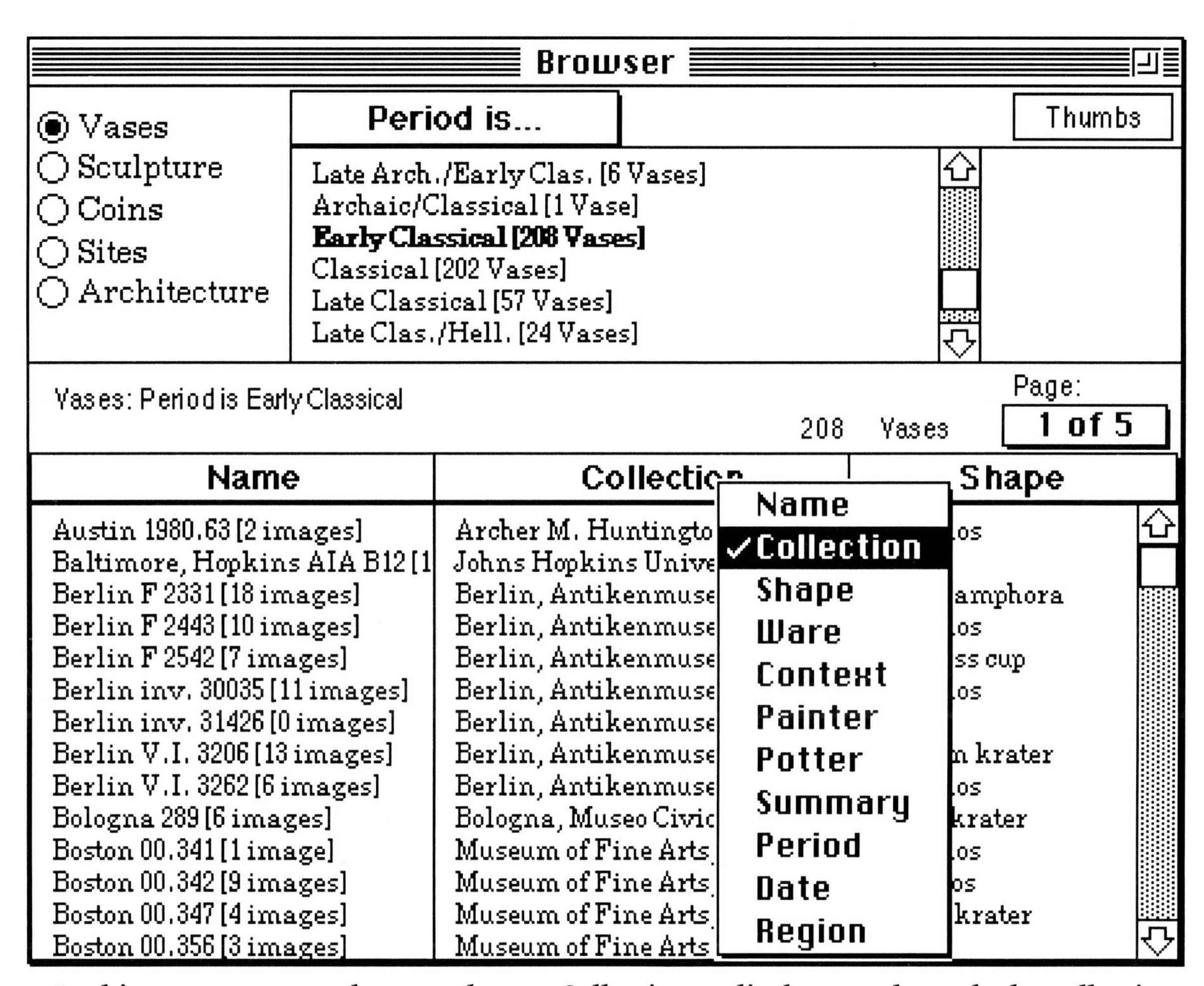

Figure 5.1 Browser. In this pop-up menu, the user chooses Collection to display search results by collection.

To search for vases in Perseus from the Early Classical period, follow these steps.

➤ From the Gateway, click the Browser icon, or, from anywhere in Perseus, choose Browser from the Links menu.

➤ Click the Vases button in the upper left (◉ Vases). Immediately to the right of the Vases button is a pop-up menu containing search topics. Choose Period from this menu. A list of attributes appears in the field below. In this case, it is a list of chronological periods.

> Many objects in the Perseus database have been linked to the Browser by keyword, an item in the search topic pop-up menu. If you choose the item Keywords, a second pop-up menu appears for you to select a category of keywords. The Keyword search feature does not work for texts, however. The Browser searches texts by author, title, genre, form, period, and region. You can use the English Index, described in section 5.3, to search texts for the appearance of any English word.

➤ Scroll down and click Early Classical in the list of attributes. Your selection is indicated by the boldface type. As soon as you click a line in the attribute list, the Browser conducts the search and puts the results into three columns.

The parameters of your search are recorded in the horizontal field below the list of object types and the attribute list (figure 5.2). This information indicates the object database, search topic, the number of objects identified with those parameters, and the number of pages of results listed in the three columns.

Figure 5.2 Search parameters

In the example used here, the search for vases of the Early Classical period yields 208 vases. The page indicator shows page 1 of 5. A "page" in this context means a list of 50 or fewer objects. If a search yields more than 50 objects, the Browser shows the first 50 objects on page 1 of the results and the remainder on page 2 (or more). To go to a different page of results, choose a new page from the Page pop-up menu. Note that when you hold the mouse down on this pop-up menu, the information that appears includes a brief description of the search and the corresponding page number.

Use the scroll bar on the far right to scroll through the three-column list. Each of the three columns may contain information for any of the available attributes. Change the attribute viewed in a column by using the pop-up menu at the top of the column. Change the width of a column by holding the cursor at the top of the vertical dividing line and dragging to change the column width; note that the cursor changes from the pointer to the field-expander mode (figure 5.3).

By default, the object's name always appears in the left column. In this example, the first vase listed is from the Archer M. Huntington Art Gallery, University of Texas at Austin, identified as such by the attribute Collection. Its catalog Name is Austin 1980.63, and its Shape is Lekythos (see figure 5.3).

If attributes other than Name, Collection, and Shape appear at the top of the three columns, they have been reset by a previous user.

➤ Change the type of information shown in the middle column by choosing Summary from the pop-up menu at the top of the column. Now you can read that this vase shows "Flying Nike with kithara and phiale."

If there is not sufficient room in the field to read its contents, click on the border between the two field titles. The pointer will change to field-expander mode. Drag to the right or left to expand or contract the field (see figure 5.3).

Name	Collection	Shape
Austin 1980.63 [2 images]	Archer M. Huntington Art Gal	Lekythos
Baltimore, Hopkins AIA B12 [	Johns Hopkins University Mus	Kylix
Berlin F 2331 [18 images]	Berlin, Antikenmuseen	Nolan amphora
Berlin F 2443 [10 images]	Berlin, Antikenmuseen	Lekythos

Figure 5.3 Pop-up menus with the cursor in field-expander mode

➤ Click any line item in the left column to go to its Catalog card.

The images and descriptions are stored on the Catalog cards. Return to the Browser by clicking the Go Back arrow on the Navigator Palette.

Note that you must always link to an object by clicking on a line in the left column; the left will remain active, regardless of its attribute setting.

➤ To save the results of your search, click the Search Saver icon on the Navigator Palette.

A description of the Search Saver is given in section 4.3.

The Browser sorts object databases alphabetically only within the attribute appearing by default at the left. The default settings for the five object databases are, left to right:

Vases: Name, Collection, and Shape
Sculpture: Collection, Title, and Type
Coins: Name, Collection, and Material
Sites: Name, Type, and Summary
Architecture: Name, Type, and Site

5.2 THUMBNAIL BROWSER

The Thumbnail Browser is a new browsing tool in Perseus 2.0, used to survey and select images. It gives you a quick and comprehensive visual overview of a single object or group of objects. The Thumbnail Browser displays a series of postage-stamp size images ("thumbnails") in a single full-color window (figure 5.4). You can page and browse through hundreds of thumbnails without having to call up the full-size images.

The Thumbnail Browser displays images from three databases: Vases, Sculpture, and Coins. It also comes in two sizes, small and large, to accommodate different amounts of available memory. The Thumbnail Browser is an image-based tool and requires large amounts of free memory—a setting of at least 5 MB of application memory is recommended. The small Thumbnail Browser shows a two-by-two array of thumbnail images, or a total of four per page. The large Thumbnail Browser shows a two-by-three array of thumbnail images, or a total of six per page.

Perseus is set to use the small Thumbnail Browser by default. You may change the default by going to the Thumbnail Browser Settings card, described below.

The Thumbnail Browser is most useful when you want to survey a large group of images without having to call up each full-size image. It is not as useful for surveying only a few images.

Once you have stored visual data in the Thumbnail Browser, you can leave it open and return to it as you continue your work. If you no longer need the Thumbnail Browser, close it to free up memory.

> Note that all three Thumbnail Browser windows (Vases, Sculpture, Coins) can be left open simultaneously. You may want to close one or more windows to free up memory.

The Thumbnail Browser is opened from the Browser and the Catalog summary cards by clicking the Thumbs button. The following example continues the search for all vases of the Early Classical period described in the previous section.

➤ Click the Thumbs button on the Browser after the search results have appeared.

The Thumbnail Browser for vases will appear (figure 5.4). (Depending on the speed of your system, this may take a moment.) The thumbnail images that appear represent one to three canonical images of each vase found in the search. The Thumbnail Browser displays images for only one page of Browser results at a time. You must return to the Browser and choose a new page of results before you can obtain Thumbnail images for the new page.

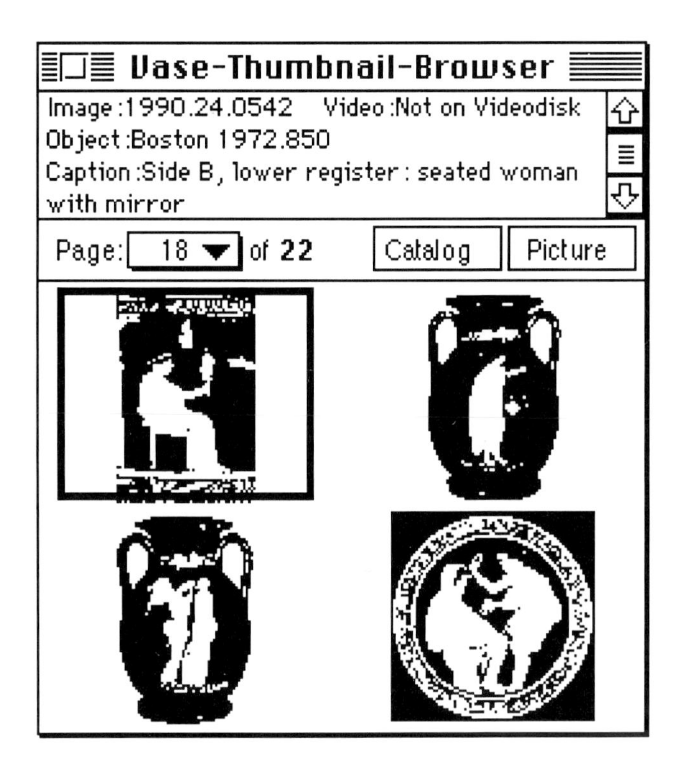

Figure 5.4 Thumbnail Browser, small, showing page 18 of 22 of Early Classical vases

Note that when the Thumbnail Browser is accessed from the Browser, it does not show all possible images for each vase but, rather, the canonical images, usually two. When you use the Thumbnail Browser from the Catalog summary cards, all possible images for the object are shown as thumbnails.

A black box around an image indicates that this image is selected and that its caption appears in the Object Information field, above the image.

➤ Click other images on this page of the Thumbnail Browser to select different images and see their Object Information fields.

Information in this field includes the image number, videodisc frame (if applicable), Perseus object reference, caption, and credits. The last line is a short description of the image.

NOTE: Do not double-click the thumbnail images. To see the full-size image of a thumbnail, select it by clicking it once, then click the button Picture, in the upper right. (If you double-click a thumbnail image, it will change to a different image not necessarily related to the images previously selected.)

➤ The Thumbnail Browser indicates how many pages of thumbnail images are available and the current page number. Choose a different page from the Page pop-up menu.

➤ Click Picture to view the full-size image of the thumbnail currently selected (the one surrounded by a black box).

- Click Catalog to open the catalog summary of the object depicted by the current thumbnail. (Hold the shift key down to open the catalog in a new window.)

To change the default from small to large Thumbnail Browser, follow these steps.

- From the Gateway, select the Settings icon. The Perseus Settings card appears. Go to the next card, Perseus Movie Settings, by clicking once on the Go to Next Card (right) arrow on the Navigator Palette.
- Unlock the card by selecting Edit Settings. A dialog box appears, asking if you are sure you want to make the change. If so, click Yes. If you are not sure that your computer has adequate memory for the large Thumbnail Browser, click the Advise button. Click the button Large Thumbnail Browsers. Be sure to click the Lock Settings button before leaving the card.

To change the movie locations, follow these steps. (For network administrators.)

- From the Gateway, select the Settings icon. The Perseus Settings card appears. Go to the next card, Perseus Movie Settings, by clicking once on the Go to Next Card (right) arrow on the Navigator Palette.
- Unlock the card by clicking the button Edit Settings. A dialog box appears, asking if you are sure you want to make the change. If so, click Yes.
- Type the file path for the movie location in the field provided. Don't forget to click the Lock Settings button before leaving the card.

5.3 ENGLISH INDEX

With the English Index tool, you can perform word searches in English throughout the entire range of Perseus databases and link with the results of your search. The English Index is accessed from the Links menu.

The English Index (figure 5.5) is an index of all English words in Perseus occurring in the translation of all the Primary Texts or the works of a selected author and in the Atlas, Encyclopedia, Historical Overview, and Art & Archaeology catalogs. You can use this tool to search for locations of an English word or for a string of letters at the beginning, middle, or end of a word.

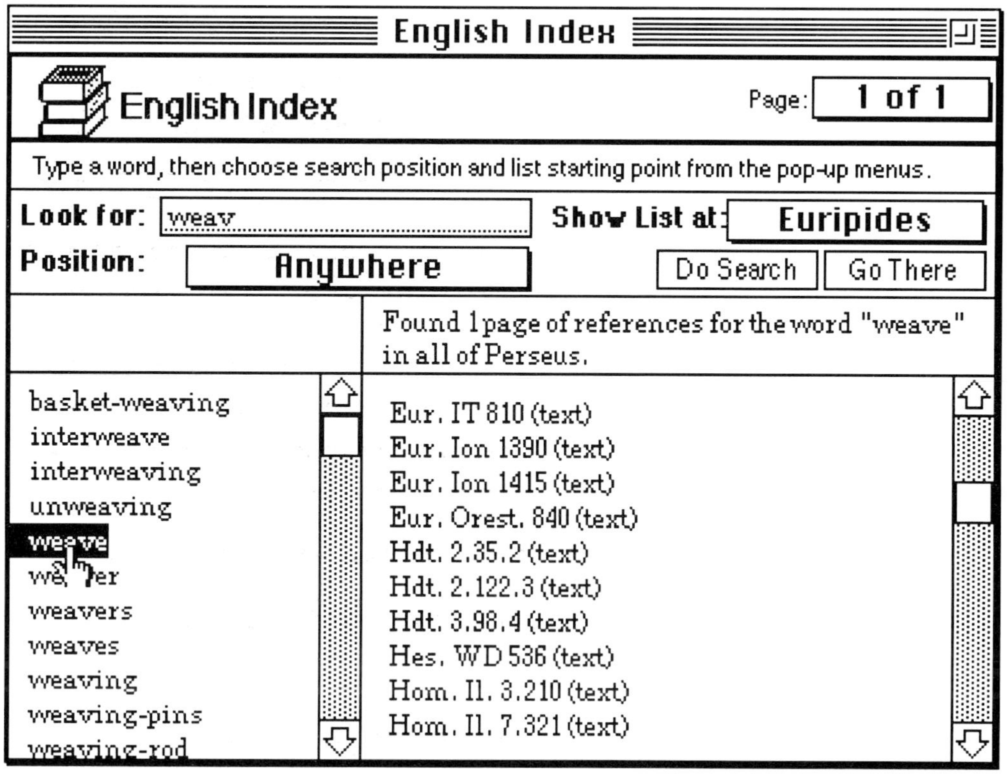

Figure 5.5 English Index. Note that the search has been made for the string "weav" occurring anywhere in the word, and that the list of results has been made to start at Euripides.

In the following example, you will look for the string "weav" occurring anywhere in a word in all of Perseus. The string "weav" was chosen because the search will produce results not only for "weave," but for "unweave," "weaving-pins," and so on.

➤ Choose English Index from the Links menu. Click the "Look for" field to make the insertion point appear. Type in "weav."

➤ Choose "Top of List" from the "Show List at" pop-up menu.

You can narrow your search by choosing a designated search area (for example, All Text for all Primary Text works, a selected author, the Atlas, or the Encyclopedia).

➤ Choose the type of search from the Position pop-up menu (Exact Match for a complete word, Anywhere for a string of characters anywhere within a word, Starting Characters for a string of characters at the beginning of a word, or Ending Characters for a string at the end of a word). In this case, choose Anywhere.

➤ Click Do Search to activate the word search. The results of the search will be reported on the left. Select any word to bring up its citation.

You can save the list of citations by clicking the Search Saver icon on the Navigator Palette. Use of the Search Saver is described more thoroughly in section 5.4.

➤ To go immediately to a citation, scroll down and highlight the citation you wish to link with. Click the Go There button to go directly to a reference within Perseus.

Note that two Macintosh techniques are involved in operating the English Index. First, you can select a word from the list by clicking it. Second, to go to a citation, you must highlight it, and then click Go There.

To return from a reference to the English Index, click the Go Back arrow on the Navigator Palette.

5.4 SEARCH SAVER

The Search Saver is a tool designed to store the search results obtained during a Perseus session. This tool is accessed from the Search Saver icon on the Navigator Palette, and it lives in a floating window. It stores a list of object citations found in a search that may be linked with the objects inside Perseus to which they refer. Each citation can be clicked to go to the full entry. For example, when you use the Browser to search for Early Classical vases, you can use the Search Saver to avoid returning to the Browser each time you want to link with a new vase summary on its Catalog card.

The contents of the Search Saver are automatically erased when you save a new search, when you close the Search Saver by clicking the box in the upper left, and when you end your Perseus session. The procedure for permanently saving your searches is explained in section 5.4.3.

5.4.1 SAVING SEARCHES FROM THE BROWSER

As you use Perseus to investigate a topic, you can temporarily store the results of searches produced by the database tools, such as the Browser and Philological Tools, in the Search Saver. Your results are kept in a floating window that remains open until you close it (figure 5.6). Once you have stored a search in the Search Saver window, you can continue working in the same tool or resource, or you can go to a new part of Perseus while the results of the stored search remain accessible.

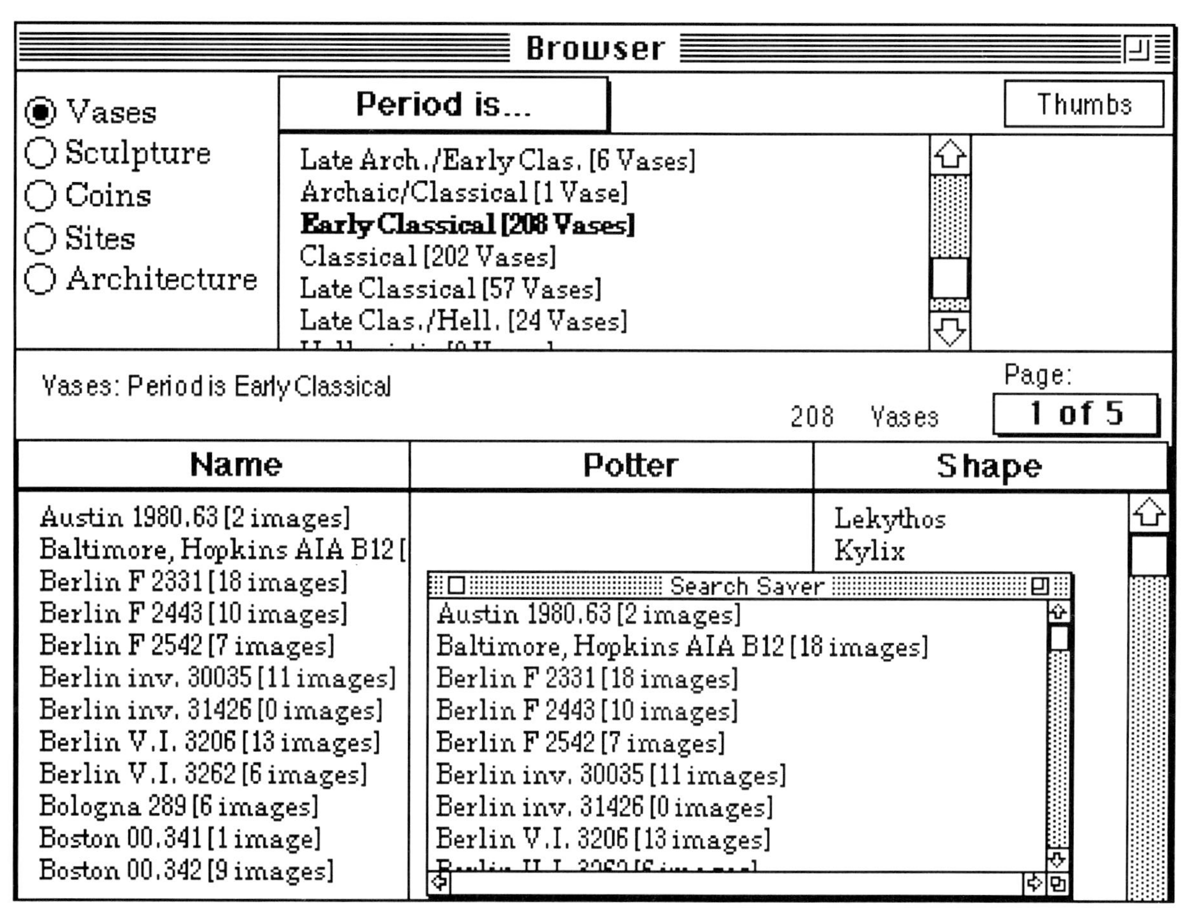

Figure 5.6 Search Saver appearing as a floating window over the Browser. Note that only the results from the left column of the Browser are saved.

The following example continues the search for all vases of the Early Classical period, described in section 5.1.

➤ To save the results of a search, click the Search Saver icon on the Navigator Palette.

The Search Saver window appears, with the results of the current search copied into it—in this case, the contents of the far left column of the Browser. If you change the attribute displayed in the left column of the Browser and click the Search Saver icon again, the Search Saver will list the search results using the new attribute.

By default, vases are listed by name, collection, and shape. If you would like to save a more descriptive list of Early Classical vases, you can change the attribute of the left column to Summary by choosing that item from the pop-up menu (figure 5.7). Then click the Search Saver icon. The Search Saver lists the vases found in your search by summary, the attribute selected for display in the left column.

Summary	Collection	Shape
Flying Nike with kithara and phia	Archer M. Huntington Art G	Lekythos
Dionysiac scenes	Johns Hopkins University M	Kylix
Fight. Side A: Greek. Side B: Pers	Berlin, Antikenmuseen	Nolan amphora
Mother seated, and maid with baby	Berlin, Antikenmuseen	Lekythos
Potter at work.	Berlin, Antikenmuseen	Stemless cup
Herakles & Pirithoos in Hades	Berlin, Antikenmuseen	Lekythos
Interior: youth and woman. Side A	Berlin, Antikenmuseen	Cup
Side A: youth at herm. Side B: Nak	Berlin, Antikenmuseen	Column krater
Woman and youth at a tomb.	Berlin, Antikenmuseen	Lekythos
Amazonomachy.	Bologna, Museo Civico	Calyx krater
Eros.	Museum of Fine Arts, Boston	Lekythos
Gigantomachy. A: Dionysos and	Museum of Fine Arts, Boston	Stamnos
A: Apollo. B: priestess and woman	Museum of Fine Arts, Boston	Volute krater
Cover: Apollo and a Muse. A and B	Museum of Fine Arts, Boston	Kylix

Figure 5.7 Browser with Summary in left column of results

Try to store searches with descriptive or varying information, such as catalog number, name, or summary. This will create a more useful list than a list with 28 entries for "kylix."

➤ Select a line in the Search Saver window.

To continue the example of vases of the Early Classical period, click the top line in the Search Saver window ("Flying Nike with kithara and phiale," if results are listed by Summary [figure 5.8], or "Austin 1980.63," if results are listed by Name). Perseus will display the Catalog card containing the summary of this vase. When you want to see another vase from the search, click another line in the Search Saver window.

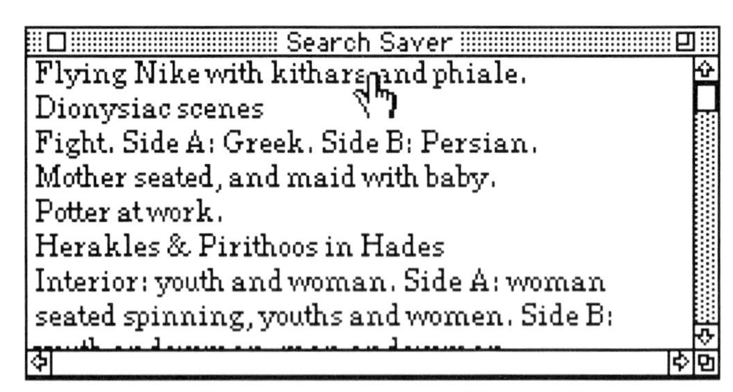

Figure 5.8 Click a line in the Search Saver to link with its Perseus Catalog card

The Search Saver window retains the current search results as long as it is open. Clicking the Search Saver icon to save a new search will replace the current search results. Clicking the close box of the

Search Saver window will close the Search Saver and will erase the current search results.

If the results of your search are more than one page long, the Search Saver will store only the current page. Thus, to save an entire search of more than one page, you will need to use the "Search Saver to Notebook" feature, described in section 5.4.3.

5.4.2 SAVING SEARCHES FROM OTHER PERSEUS DATABASES

The Search Saver can be used to store a search from any list of data references inside Perseus. These areas include the English Index, Philological Tools, Indexes, and Catalog card image lists.

With the English Index, the Search Saver always stores the Perseus canonical references. Canonical references can be typed or copied into the Lookup tool in the Links menu to go directly to a reference.

When you use the Philological Tools to conduct searches, you can also use the Search Saver to store the results. In this case, the Search Saver stores the results applicable to the particular tool (citations for "Greek Words in Proximity," words and their locations for the Greek Word Search, and so on).

➤ To save the results of a Greek Word Search for ἀλκή in Euripides, choose Greek Word Search from the Links menu. Type ἀλκή (courage) into the "Look for" field if GreekKeys is installed in your system.

> If you do not have SMK GreekKeys installed, you will need to copy and paste the word in. Go to Euripides Phoenissae 274 (by typing Eur. Phoen. 274 into the Lookup tool and pressing Return), copy ἀλκή from the text, and paste it into the "Look for" field in Greek Word Search. Further information on GreekKeys and typing in Greek characters is given in sections 2.1.2 and 8.4.1.

➤ Choose Euripides from the pop-up menu on the right. Click the Do Search button.

The results appearing in the lower left are nine forms derived from ἀλκή.

➤ Choose "Citations for All Forms" from the Options pop-up menu.

➤ Save these citations by clicking the Search Saver icon on the Navigator Palette (figure 5.9).

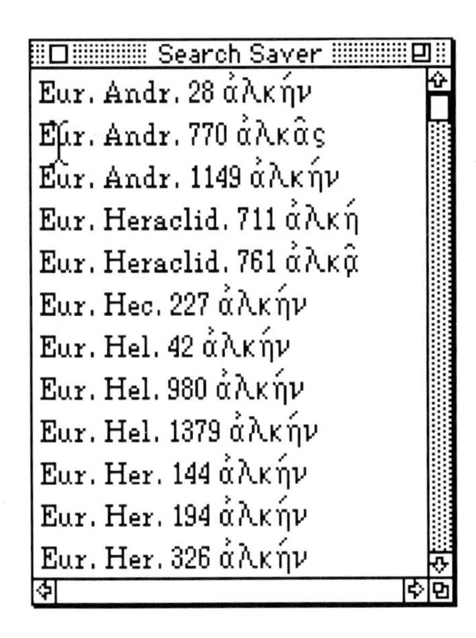

Figure 5.9 Results of Greek Word Search in Search Saver

➤ Go to a citation by selecting it in the Search Saver.

The Search Saver can also be used to compare the results of one search with the results of another search. After you have saved the results of a search in the Search Saver, perform a second search with different parameters. One set of results appears in the Search Saver window, and the second is in the current tool.

5.4.3 USE THE SEARCH SAVER TO NOTEBOOK FEATURE

➤ Maintain a permanent record of your search by choosing "Search Saver to Notebook" from the Perseus menu. A Notebook card will appear (figure 5.10).

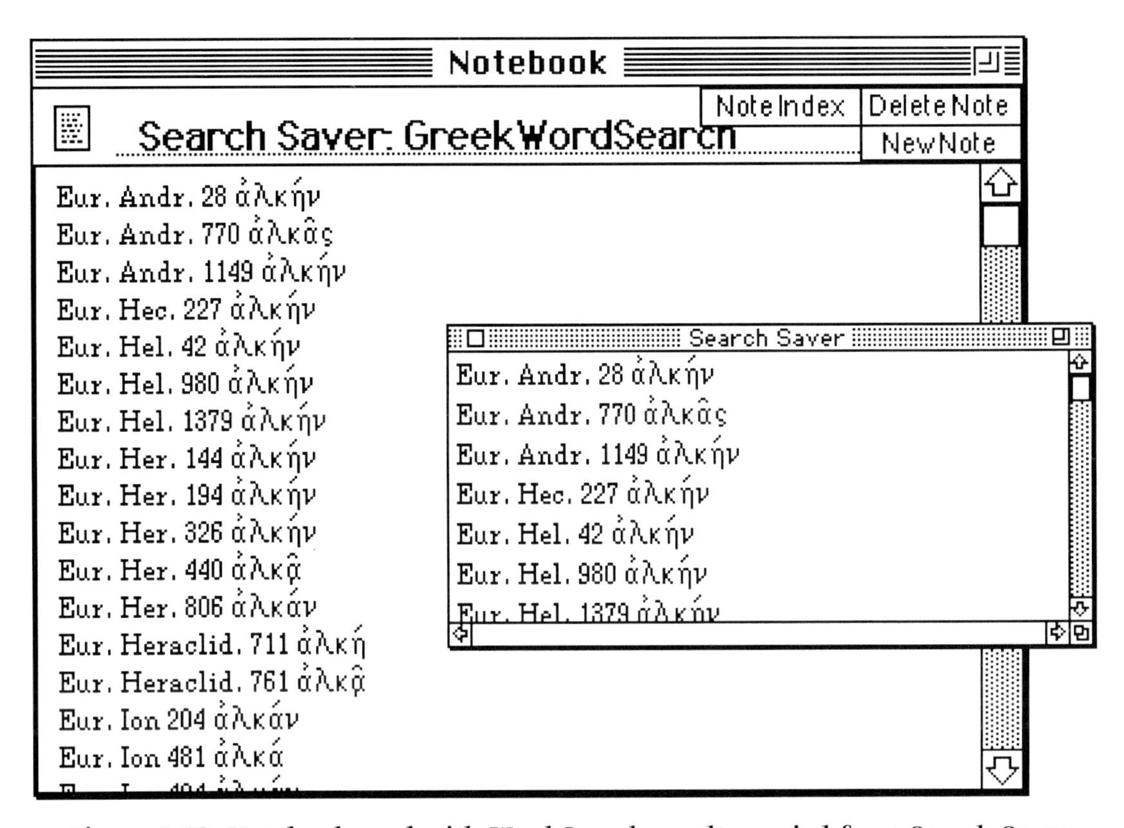

Figure 5.10 Notebook card with Word Search results copied from Search Saver

➤ Give the Notebook card a new title by typing one into the field at the top.

The Note will be stored permanently in the Notebook Index and will be available to you in any future Perseus session.

More information on the Notebook feature may be found in section 10.3.

The content of Perseus—its resources, such as the Historical Overview, and its databases, such as Art & Archaeology—is described in this chapter.

6.1 HISTORICAL OVERVIEW

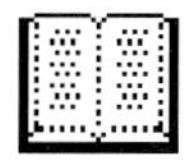

"An Overview of Classical Greek History" was commissioned by the Perseus Project. Written by Professor Thomas R. Martin, this Overview is a narrative history of ancient Greece with emphasis on the Golden Age of Athens in the fifth century B.C.

The Historical Overview has two parts, a table of contents and a narrative section. Within the narrative, words and phrases in the text are linked to the primary texts, images, maps, and plans that compose Perseus. A link may have more than one possible destination, indicated by a pop-up menu.

Use the Historical Overview to investigate interrelated items from a historical context.

To open this resource, click the Historical Overview icon on the Gateway or choose Historical Overview from the Links menu.

6.1.1 TABLE OF CONTENTS

The Historical Overview is divided into sixteen major sections:

1. Introduction to the Historical Overview in Perseus
2. Geographical and Historical Introduction
3. The Early Greek Dark Age and Revival in the Near East
4. Remaking Greek Civilization
5. The Archaic Age
6. The Late Archaic City-State
7. Introduction to the Golden Age of Athens
8. Clash Between Greeks and Persians
9. Athenian Empire in the Golden Age
10. Athenian Religious and Cultural Life in the Golden Age
11. Continuity and Change in Athenian Social and Intellectual History
12. The Peloponnesian War and Athenian Life
13. Introduction to the History of the Fourth Century
14. The Aftermath of the Peloponnesian War
15. New Directions in Philosophy and Education
16. The Creation of Macedonian Power

The Table of Contents (figure 6.1) shows the organization of topics within each section in outline form.

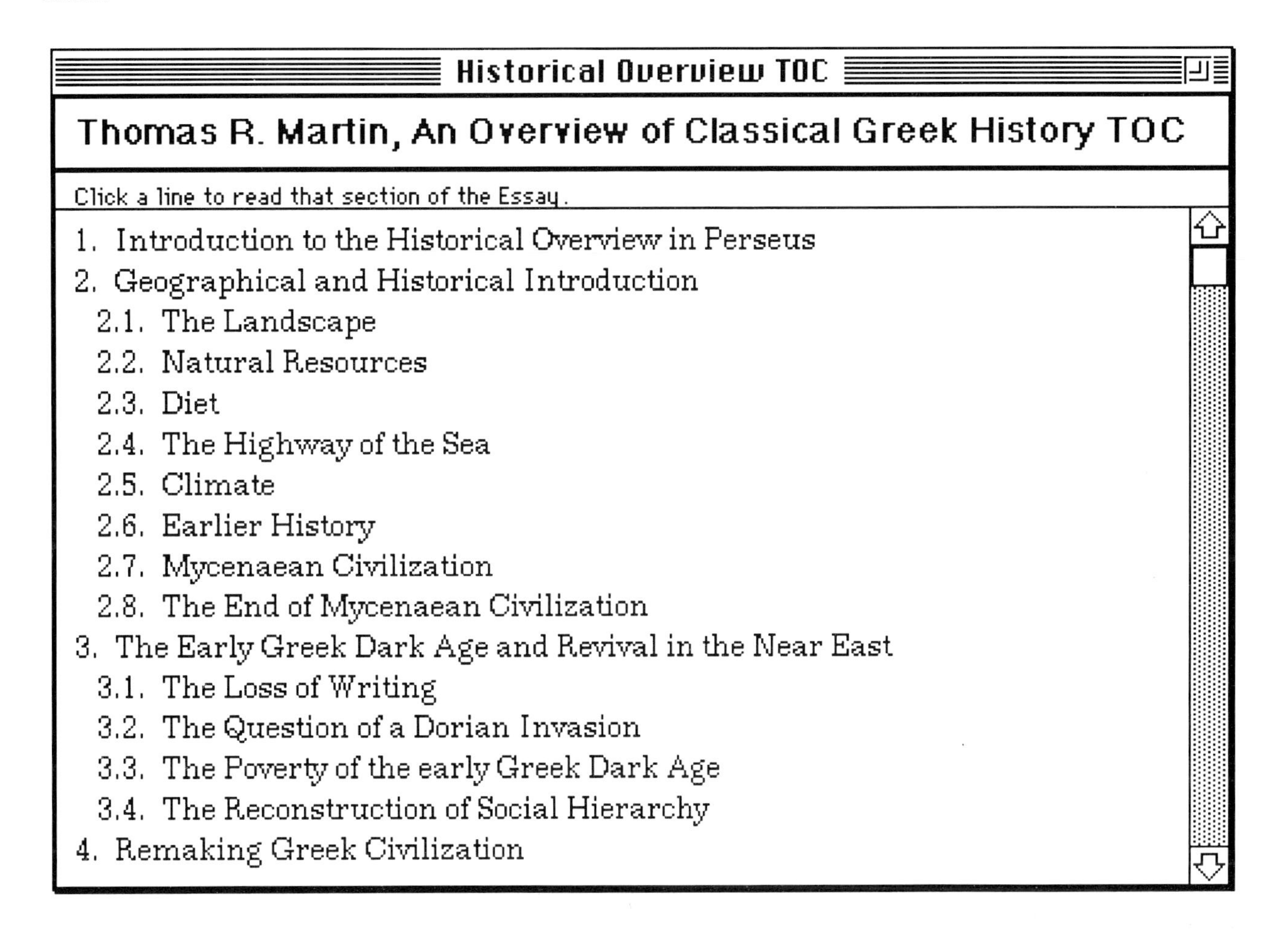

Figure 6.1 Table of Contents for the Historical Overview

➤ Select a heading in the Table of Contents to read that topic.

To follow along with the example described in this guide, scroll down and select topic 9.1.5, "The Rebellion of Thasos."

6.1.2 TOPICS

Each topic in the Historical Overview appears on a separate card. Topic 9.1.5, "The Rebellion of Thasos," is depicted in figure 6.2.

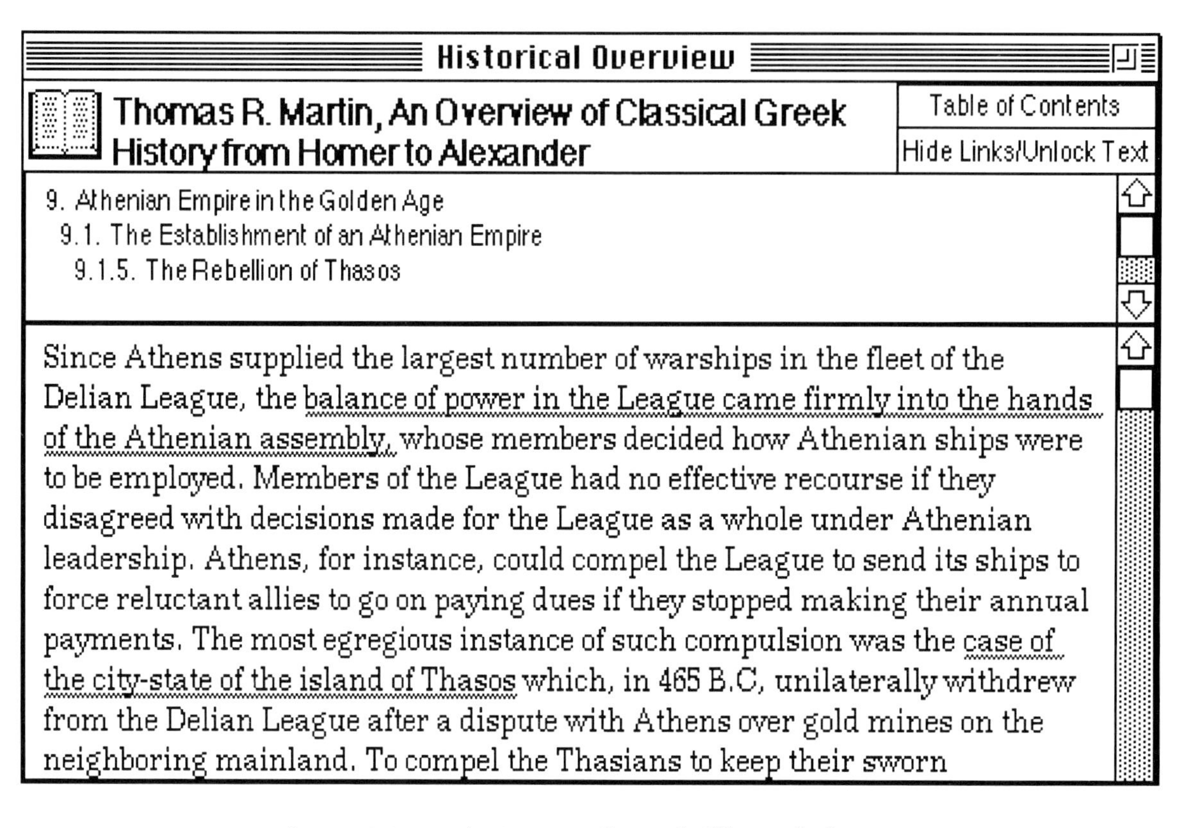

Figure 6.2 **Topic 9.1.5, "The Rebellion of Thasos"**

Each topic card is titled "Thomas R. Martin, An Overview of Classical Greek History from Homer to Alexander." The topic's location in the outline is shown above the narrative; this area is active, meaning that you can click there to move from the current topic up to a section or subsection. Below the main title bar are two buttons, used to return to the Table of Contents and to perform the action Hide Links/Unlock Text.

➤ Click the right and left arrows on the Navigator Palette to move forward and backward in the Historical Overview.

Linked Text and Locked Text

A toggle button changes the state of the text between shown and hidden links and between locked and unlocked text. This button is named Hide Links/Unlock Text or Show Links/Lock Text, depending on the state of the toggle.

Narrative in the Historical Overview is linked thematically to other Perseus resources. Linked text is underlined in gray and appears when the text field is locked. Text may also be unlocked so that you can use the text select tool (indicated by the I-beam pointer) to select text. After selecting text, you can use the Links menu to find connections in other resources, or you can use the Perseus menu to add the card to a Perseus path with selected text. For more information, see section 4.5 on the Links menu and section 10.2 on Paths.

➤ Click Hide Links/Unlock Text to disable the links to other Perseus resources.

Note that the name of the button changes (toggles). When text is unlocked, you can change as well as select the text on the screen. These changes are not permanent, and they disappear when you leave the card.

➤ Click Show Links/Lock Text to enable the links.

In figure 6.2, the phrase "case of the city-state of the island of Thasos" is linked to other parts of Perseus.

Use an existing link

➤ Click an underlined phrase to see a pop-up menu of the links from that word.

To follow the example here, click the phrase "case of the city-state of the island of Thasos."

Links in the Historical Overview are coded according to category. Links to other parts of Perseus include the Atlas, site plans, texts, and views. Links to Primary Texts are indicated by the standard or Perseus canonical system of abbreviations, which includes the author, work, and references to the book, chapter, and line, as applicable. Section A.3 of the appendix contains the standard system of abbreviations used in the Historical Overview links.

A pop-up menu for the linked text is depicted in figure 6.3. The phrase in this figure is linked to a Primary Text, the Atlas, two Views, a Site, and the Browser Tool.

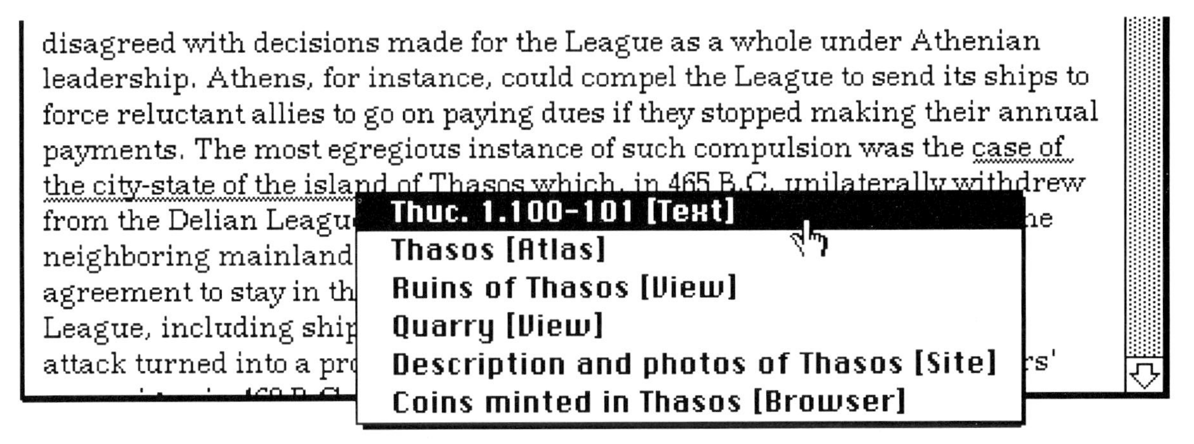

Figure 6.3 Pop-up menu for linked text

- Choose a link from the pop-up menu.

Try each available link in this example. To keep the Overview window open while linking with a resource, hold the shift key down while releasing the mouse. Remember to close the recently opened window before moving on.

- Click the Go Back icon on the Navigator Palette to return to the Historical Overview card from Primary Text or the Atlas. Close an image by clicking the box in the upper-left corner.

Try your own link

As with almost all Perseus resources, you can explore the relations of narrative, primary texts, maps, and images by using the Lookup tool.

- Click Hide Links/Unlock Text on the same topic described in the previous example (9.1.5, "The Rebellion of Thasos") so that you can select text. Highlight the word "Thasos" in the ninth line of text.
- From the Links menu, choose Lookup.

Because you have activated this choice on the Links menu while a word was selected in your current location, Perseus has entered the selected text into the Lookup tool.

- Press Return, and in a few seconds you will see a list of links for Thasos within Perseus (figure 6.4). Select a line to go to its link.

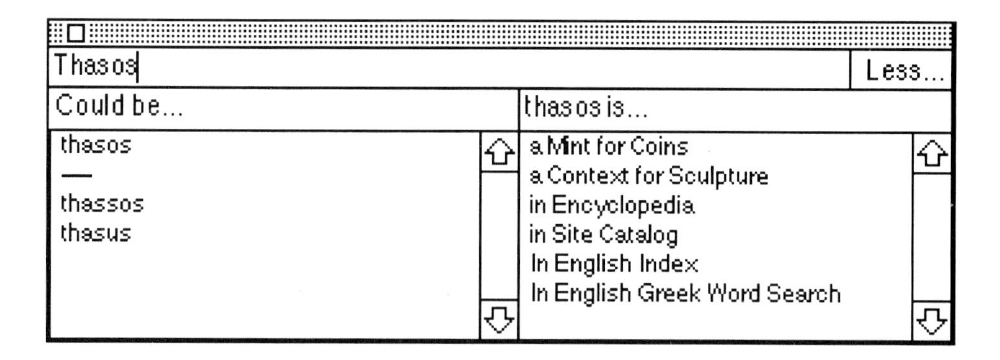

Figure 6.4 Lookup tool showing possible links for "Thasos"

For more information on the Lookup tool, see section 4.5.1. Click the Go Back arrow on the Navigator Palette to return to your place in the Historical Overview. You may need to click several times, slowly.

Another way to make a link is with the English Index. Again, highlight Thasos from the text of the Historical Overview. Choose English Index from the Links menu. The English Index will make the search for you. Link to an item from the results field by selecting it and clicking the Go There button. For more information on the English Index, see section 5.3.

6.2 ESSAYS & CATALOGS

Perseus includes several essays on art, archaeology, the Athenian court system, biographies, music, and regions of Greece. Some of the essays were commissioned by the Perseus Project and written by scholars with a particular area of expertise. Others were prepared independently of Perseus for publication in other sources. All the scholarly works have integral ties to the Perseus resources, such as text citations and object descriptions.

Each essay consists of two parts, a table of contents and a narrative section. Within the narrative, underlined words indicate a direct link to another part of Perseus. You can select the underlined words and choose a menu item from the Links menu to go directly to the reference. Advance from page to page in the Essays by clicking the right arrow on the Navigator Palette.

In the Historical Overview links are made from a pop-up menu; in the Essays & Catalogs, links to other Perseus resources are made by clicking an illustration or selecting text.

To open this resource, click the Essays & Catalogs icon on the Gateway or choose Essays & Catalogs from the Links menu.

6.2.1 GREEK VASE PAINTERS

The six vase painter essays share an identical interface. Links and buttons in the Kleophrades Painter essay are described below; the other essays behave similarly.

Kleophrades Painter

The Kleophrades Painter essay was written by Michael Padgett. Like the Historical Overview, the other essays in Perseus are indexed by a table of contents. Figure 6.5 shows the Table of Contents for the Kleophrades Painter essay.

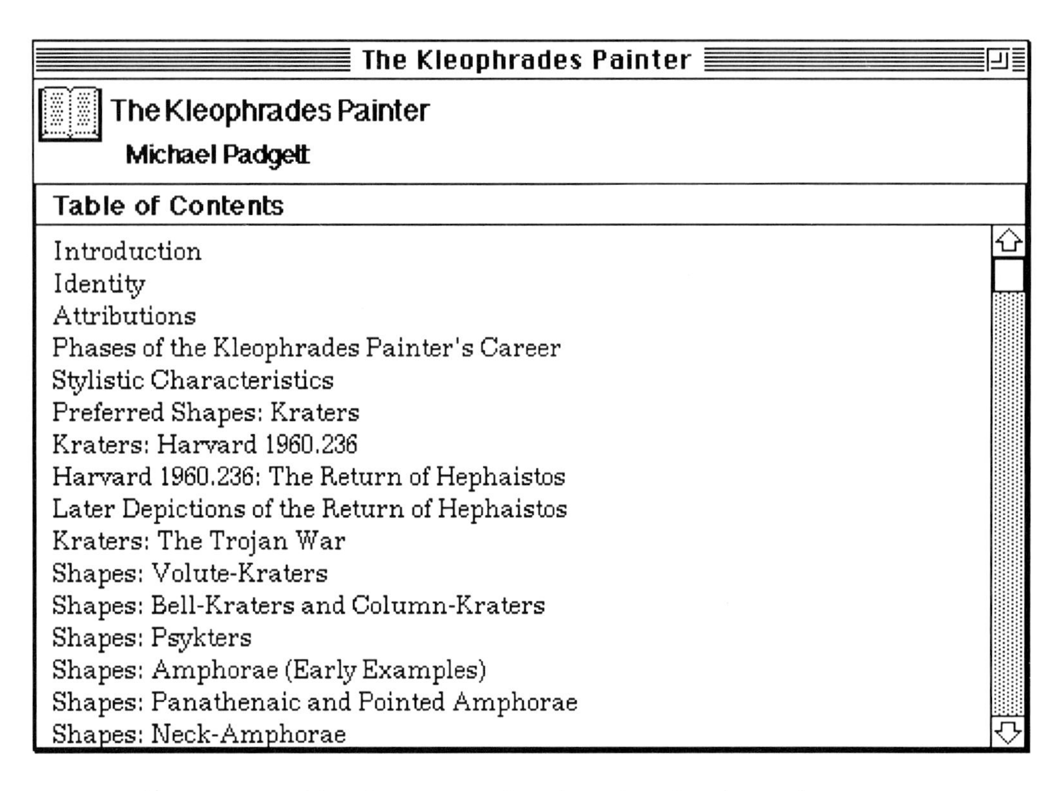

Figure 6.5 Table of Contents for the Kleophrades Painter essay

➤ Select an item in the Table of Contents to see that topic.

To follow the example here, select Stylistic Characteristics from the Table of Contents. The essay topic appears (figure 6.6). Note the three buttons in the upper right: Table of Contents, Hide Illustrations, and Find Text. Clicking "Table of Contents" returns you to the Table of Contents of the essay. To return to the Essays & Catalogs Index, choose Essays & Catalogs from the Links menu.

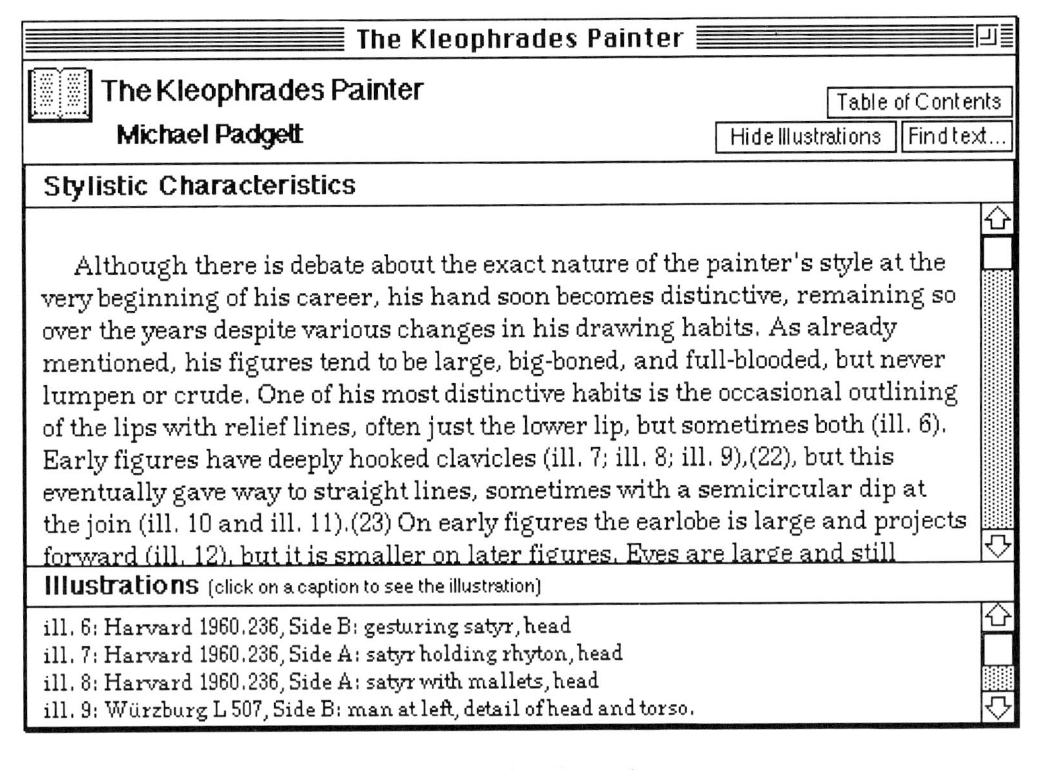

Figure 6.6 Kleophrades Painter essay

The button Hide Illustrations toggles to Show Illustrations when you click it. This button either hides or shows the illustrations field at the bottom of the card. The illustrations are indicated in the text by "ill. 7," "ill. 8," and so on, and correspond to the illustration numbers in the field at the bottom. Note that the accession number and a short description of each illustration are also given.

➤ To see an illustration, click its name. You can put away the credits window and the image window by clicking the box in the upper left of each window.

Note that the illustrations field will be empty if no illustrations are mentioned in the text.

Find Text is a utility for finding a word or phrase in the body of the essay.

➤ Click the button Find Text and enter a word or phrase. Click Search, and Perseus will find the first instance of the word or phrase. Click Cancel if you change your mind.

There are many other references in the essay to vases and secondary sources. Underlined phrases indicate links within Perseus to specific vases and to the Sources Used stack. You can recognize vases because their references begin with the collection name, such as Boston, Munich, and so on. To see one of these reference links, select it, then choose Lookup from the Links menu.

Other essays in Perseus concerning vase painting

Other essays in Perseus concerning vase painting include "The Harrow Painter, with a Note on the Geras Painter," written by Michael Padgett; the Douris essay, written by Diana Buitron-Oliver; the Phintias and Euthymides essay, written by Jenifer Neils; the Achilles Painter essay, written by John Oakley; and "Polygnotos and His Group," written by Susan Matheson.

These essays have the same structure as the Kleophrades Painter essay. They are indexed by a table of contents. Click illustrations in the field at the bottom to see them. Other links are also available to the Vase Catalog and the Sources Used stack.

6.2.2 CASKEY-BEAZLEY VASE CATALOGS

In 1931–63, L. D. Caskey and J. D. Beazley published catalogs describing Attic vase paintings in the Museum of Fine Arts, Boston. This work has remained a valuable reference for any study of Greek vase painting. All of the 176 vases described by Caskey and Beazley are in the Perseus Vase Catalog.

The first card in this stack is the Table of Contents (figure 6.7). Select a vase from this list by scrolling down to locate the vase you want, then clicking once on the line describing it. The program will search for that vase and take you to the card where its description starts.

➤ Click "2 PLATE. TWO ATHLETES. (Plate I)" to go to the card describing this plate.

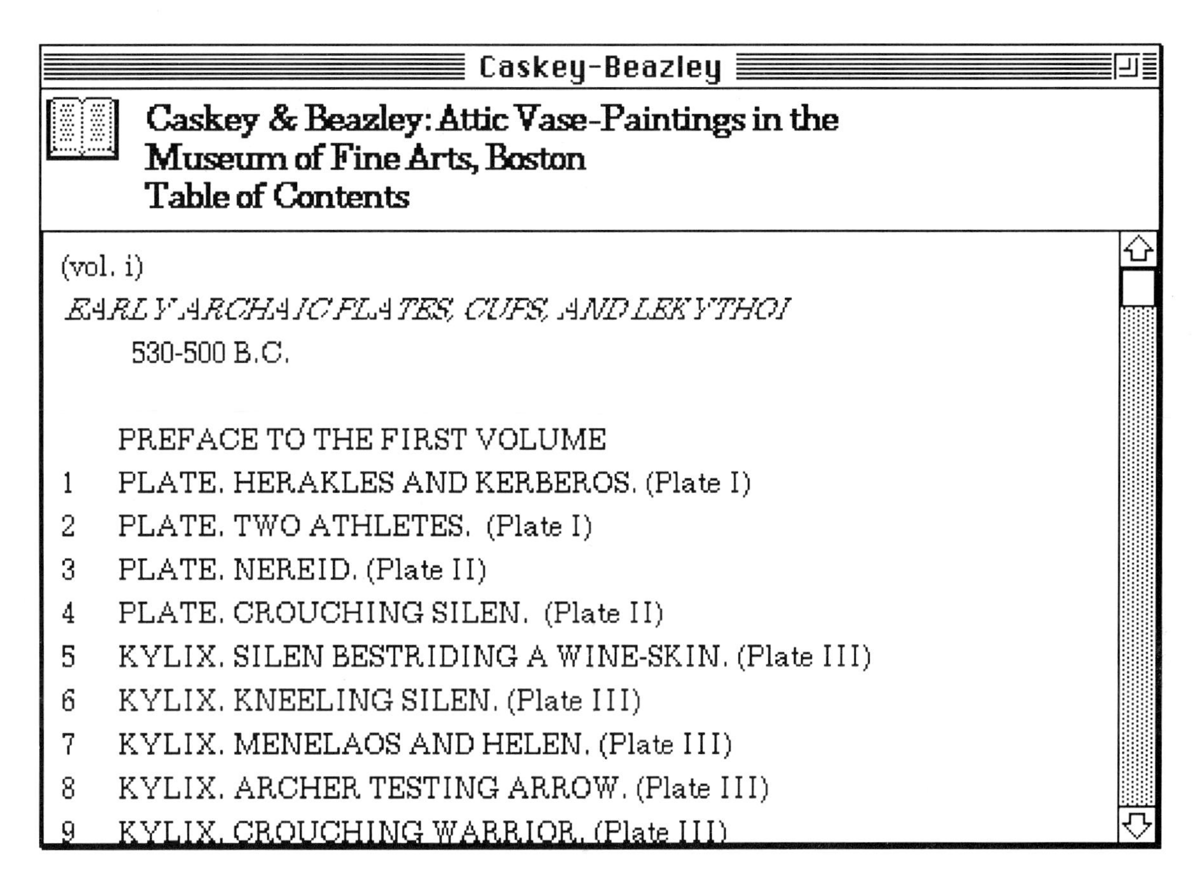

Figure 6.7 Caskey & Beazley Table of Contents

The catalog cards contain five buttons in the upper right, and are divided into three parts: a top area containing navigation and display tools, a central area where the catalog text is displayed, and a bottom area listing the available views of the vase (figure 6.8). This bottom part can be hidden or displayed by clicking once on the Hide Views/Show Views button.

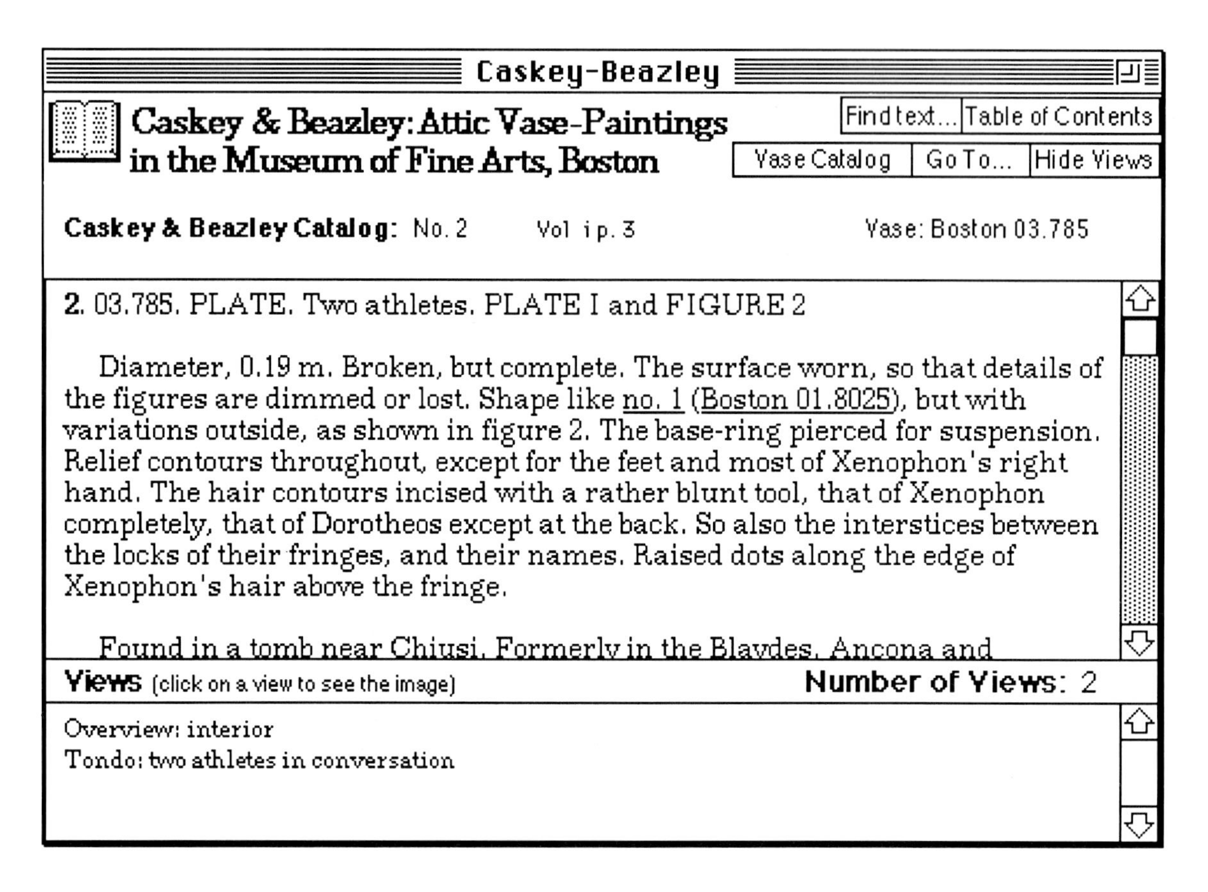

Figure 6.8 Caskey-Beazley catalog. Note that the Hide Views/Show Views button is toggled to Show Views.

Clicking the "Table of Contents" button returns you to the Table of Contents.

The Vase Catalog button provides a link to the full Perseus Vase Catalog (of which Views is the bottom part).

➤ To go to the Vase Catalog card, select an underlined vase reference (such as Boston 01.8025) and click the Vase Catalog button.

Bibliographical references contained in the Perseus Bibliography are usually cited in an abbreviated form and underlined. Examples may be seen in the next card of the Caskey-Beazley catalog, "Additional Bibliography."

➤ To look up any underlined bibliographic references, select the reference where it appears in the catalog (for example, Buitron 1972), then choose Sources Used from the Links menu.

Finally, it is possible to move around the Caskey-Beazley catalog by typing one of three possible citation systems into the dialog window brought up by the Go To button.

➤ To go to the Caskey-Beazley card containing the Kneeling Silen, click the Go To button and type in the Caskey-Beazley number (No. 6), the Caskey-Beazley volume number and page number (Vol. i p. 6), or the accession number (Boston 10.212).

6.2.3 SCULPTURE ESSAY

"One Hundred Greek Sculptors: Their Careers and Extant Works" is excerpted from Andrew S. Stewart's *Greek Sculpture, an Exploration,* volume 1 (Yale University Press, 1990).

The Stewart sculpture essay is indexed by a table of contents.

➤ From the Table of Contents, click topic 2, "THE LITERARY SOURCES," to follow the example below (figure 6.9).

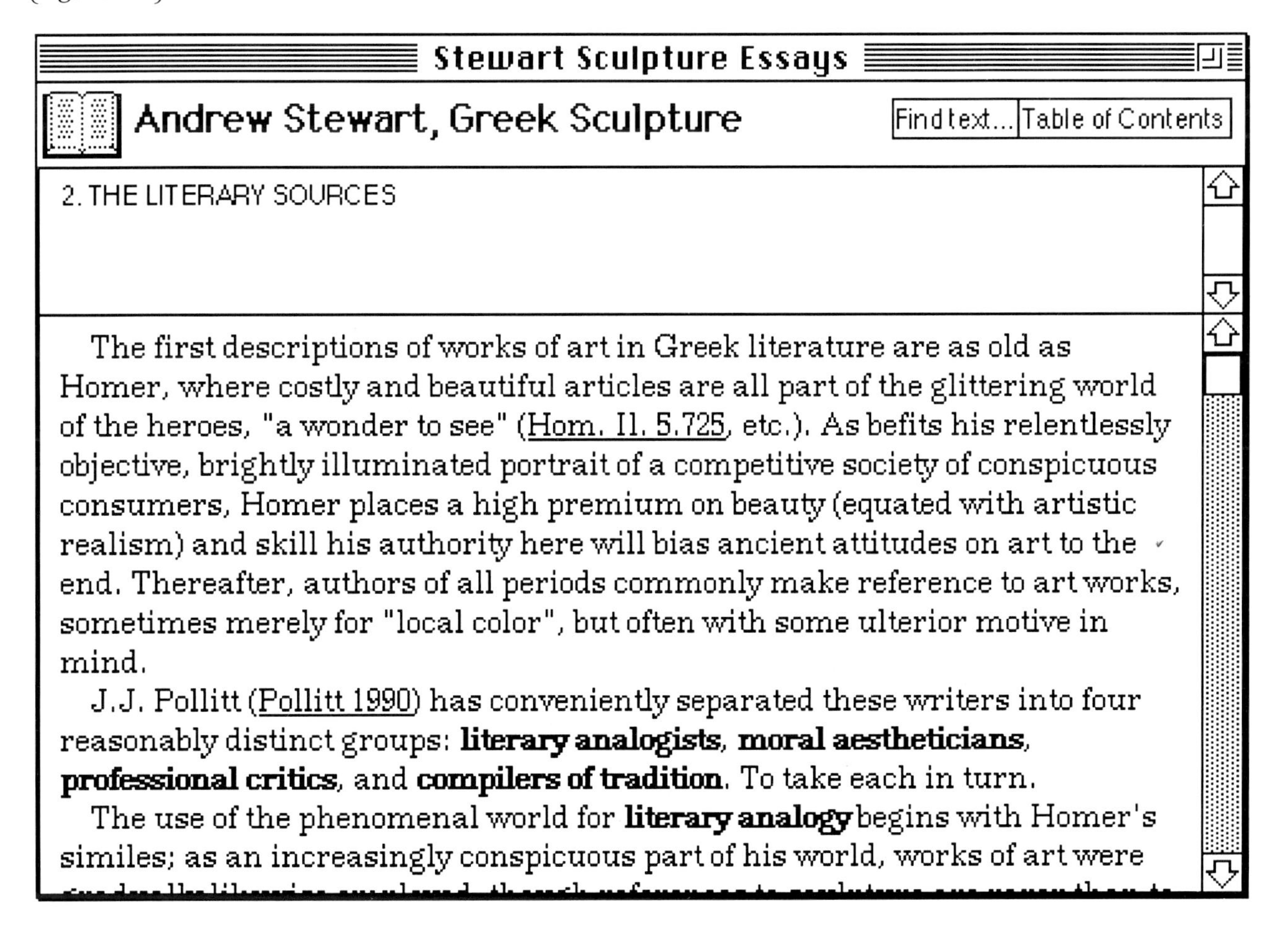

Figure 6.9 Stewart sculpture essay

Two buttons appear in the upper right. To return to the Table of Contents for the essay, click "Table of Contents." Find Text is a utility for finding a word or phrase in the body of the essay. Click the button Find Text and enter a word or phrase. Click Search, and Perseus will find the first instance of the word or phrase. Click Cancel if you change your mind.

Available links within Perseus are to the Sculpture Catalog, Primary Texts, and Sources Used. The links are indicated by underlined references in the text, which you must select. Then choose the appropriate item from the Links menu—that is, Primary Texts, Sculpture, or Sources Used.

Advance or turn back from page to page using the right and left arrows on the Navigator Palette.

6.2.4 HISTORICAL ESSAY

The historical essay "Three Court Days" was written by Alan Boegehold. The essay is substantially a chapter (without the footnotes) in *The Athenian Agora,* volume 28, *The Lawcourts at Athens: Sites, Buildings, Equipment, Procedure, and Testimonia,* by Alan Boegehold with contributions by John M. Camp II, Margaret Crosby, Mabel Lang, David R. Jordan, and Rhys F. Townsend (American School of Classical Studies at Athens, 1995). The essay provides three accounts of the way a trial may have occurred on three separate occasions in a span of 140 years. The days fall within the periods 460 B.C. to 410 B.C. (roughly), 409 B.C. to 340 B.C., and 340 B.C. (roughly) to 322 B.C.

"Three Court Days" works in the same way as essays on vase painting. It is indexed by a table of contents. Click topic lines to see the body of the essay. Within the body of the essay, paragraphs are shown on separate cards. They are titled by paragraph number within each of the six sections. For example, Paragraph 4.13 is the thirteenth paragraph within section 4. To go to the next paragraph within a section, use the right arrow on the Navigator Palette. To go to the beginning of the section, click its title in the field above the text. Click the "Table of Contents" button in the upper right to return to the topic list.

References to texts in Perseus are underlined (figure 6.10). To go directly to a text reference, highlight the text, then choose Lookup from the Links menu and press Return. Remember that you can open the text reference in a new window by holding the shift key down while choosing an item from the Links menu. (The Settings option lets you specify whether windows will be opened as an addition or a replacement to the current window. Holding the shift key down while you click temporarily reverses this choice.)

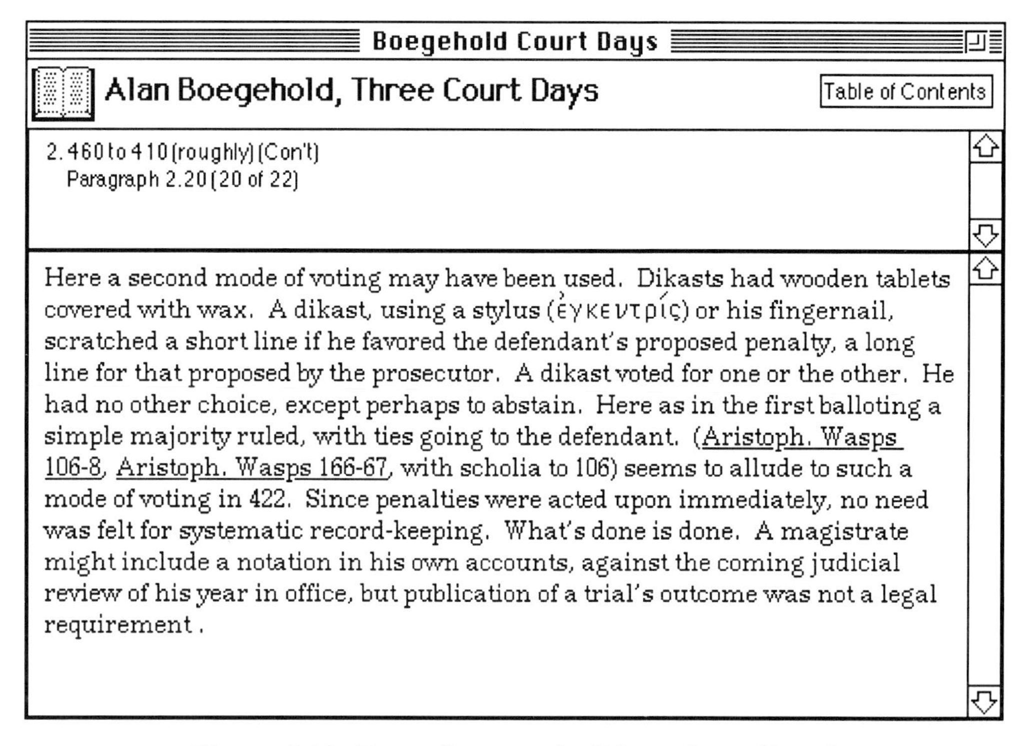

Figure 6.10 Text references in "Three Court Days"

6.3 ART & ARCHAEOLOGY

Perseus contains information, illustrations, and images about the art and archaeology of ancient Greece. The Art & Archaeology resource is the main repository for this information, although relevant entries are also found in the Essays, the Encyclopedia, and other resources in Perseus. Information is contained in five catalogs: Sites, Architecture, Sculpture, Vases, and Coins. Each catalog is organized according to a structure based on the particular characteristics of its objects. For example, Architecture is indexed by site, building type, period, and date, while Coins are indexed by mint, metal, region, issuing authority, denomination, collection, period, and date.

All objects in the Art & Archaeology catalogs are documented in text and visual formats, according to the best information available. Not all characteristics are known for all objects, however, and so there are sometimes blanks. Dates identified for archaeological objects are approximate. Each entry is accompanied by color photographs and illustrated site plans, as applicable. The catalogs are also linked with one another. For example, the Sculpture Catalog indicates the building on which a sculpture is located, and the Architecture Catalog indicates the site at which the building is located.

The Browser (described in section 5.1) provides a primary point of entry to the Art & Archaeology catalogs. The Browser searches for objects by attribute or keyword and summarizes the results of the search in textual and visual formats. From the Browser you can investigate individual objects in detail by opening the Art & Archaeology catalogs. You may also use the catalog indexes and the Links menu to open the Art & Archaeology catalogs.

6.3.1 ART & ARCHAEOLOGY INDEX

The Art & Archaeology Index is accessible by clicking the Art & Archaeology icon on the Perseus Gateway. The catalogs and indexes of Art & Archaeology are presented in a scrolling text field (figure 6.11).

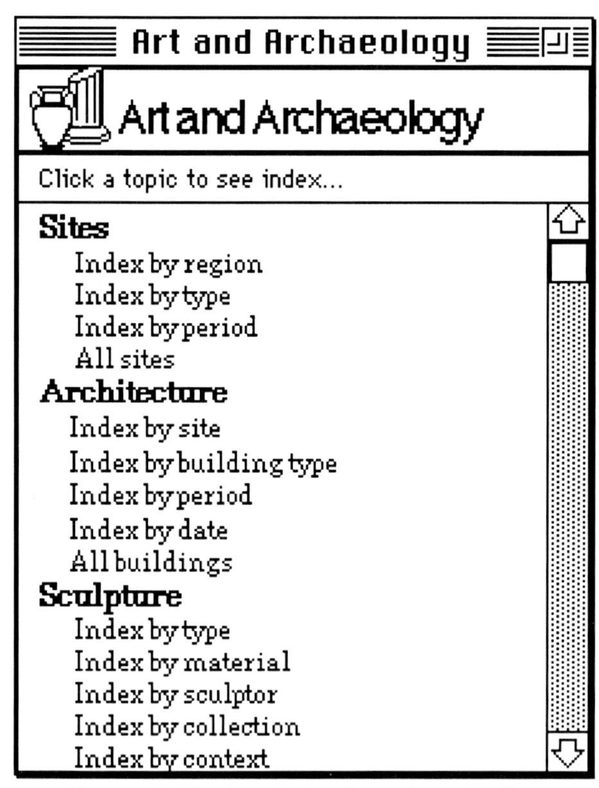

Figure 6.11 Art & Archaeology Index

➤ Click an index name under one of the Art & Archaeology catalogs.

Perseus displays a detailed index of the resources available for the selected category. For example, if you click "Index by region" under the category Sites, a detailed index of sites sorted by region appears.

6.3.2 SITES

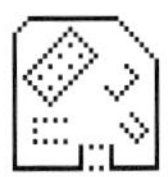

Site indexes

Sites are indexed in three ways: by region, type, and period. All sites are also listed alphabetically. The description here uses the index by region as an example. Regions encompass cities or sites that may have belonged to different political units at different times. Assignment of cities and sites to regions follows accepted conventions for the classical period.

➤ From the Gateway, click the Art & Archaeology icon, then click "Index by region" under the topic Sites. Or choose Sites from the Links menu, then choose the item Region from the Index Type pop-up menu.

Perseus displays a more detailed index that shows the list of sites in the left column. On any of the detailed index displays, the list in the left column is based on the type of index selected, which is indicated by the icon and title at the top of the display. The detailed index for sites listed by region is depicted in figure 6.12.

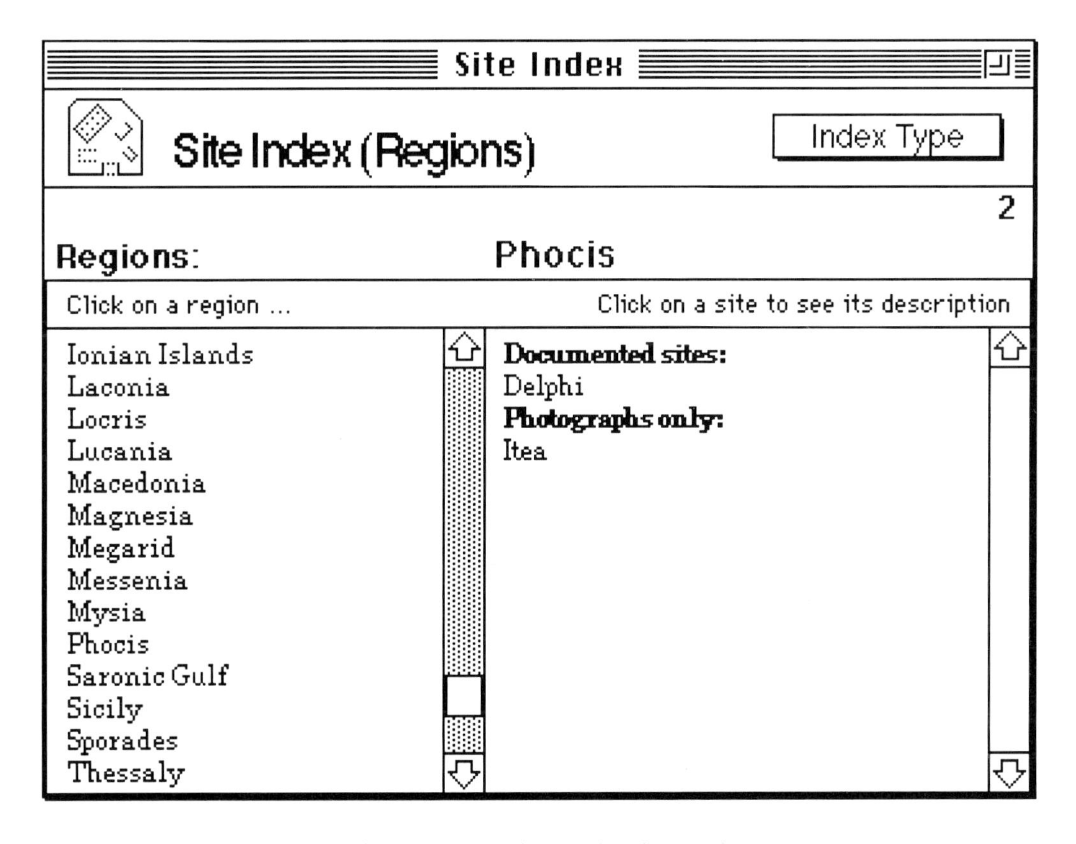

Figure 6.12 Site Index by region

➤ Choose a different index from the Index Type pop-up menu.

Try the other three indexes. Return to the index by region to follow the rest of this description, which will use the site at Delphi by way of example.

➤ Scroll down and click Phocis under the region list in the left column.

The left column lists regions. The right column lists the sites in the selected region, Phocis. The name of the selected region appears above the right column.

The sites are listed in two categories: Documented Sites and Photographs Only. Documented Sites means that the site has a full catalog entry. Photographs Only means that the catalog entry has only a Site Summary, blank except for region information. Undocumented sites are included to provide access to Perseus images of these sites.

➤ Click Delphi under the site list in the right column.

For Documented Sites, the full catalog entry consists of a Site Summary and a Site Description.

Site Summary

Perseus displays a Summary of the selected site.

The Site Summary for Delphi is depicted in figure 6.13. The name of this site is displayed above the site information.

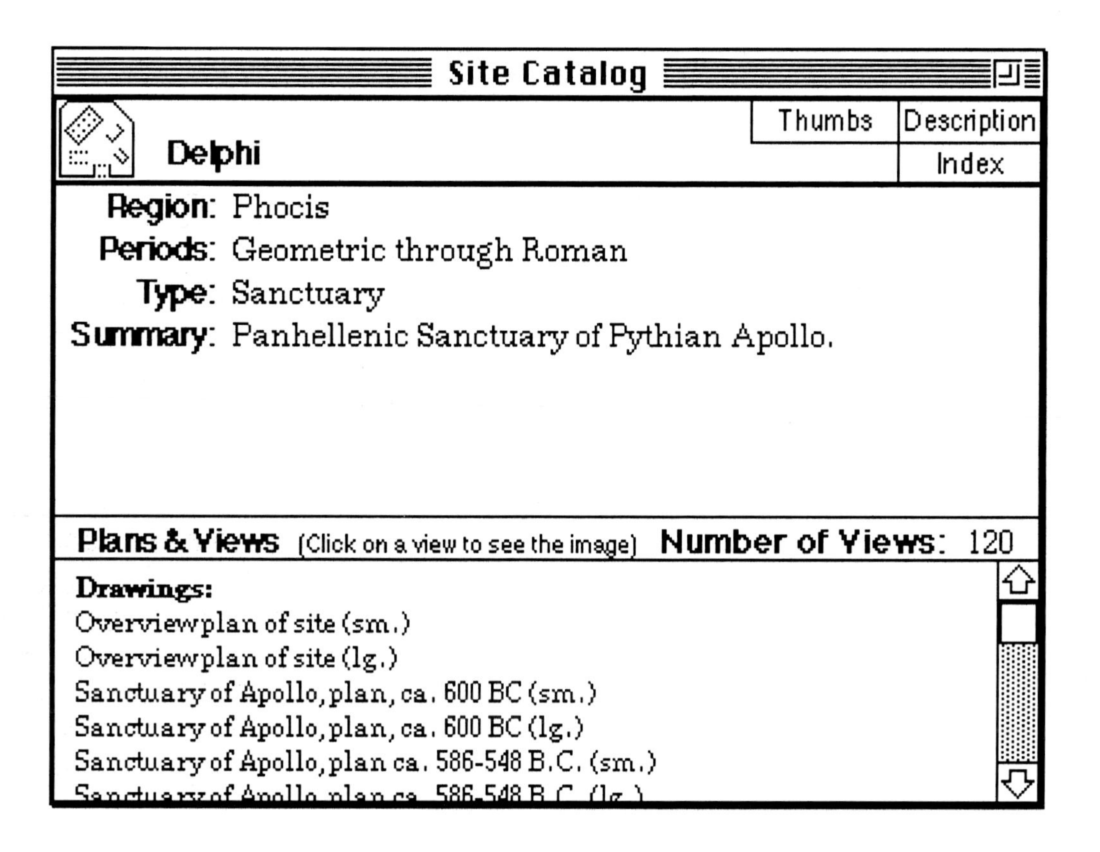

Figure 6.13 Site Catalog card containing Summary for Delphi

Plans and views

Site plans and photographic views accompany the sites. Large and small composite site plans are described later in this section. Views are described below.

The views are digitized images or videodisc still-frames, depending on your Perseus Settings and your equipment. The views available for the selected site are listed alphabetically below the site information. The number of views available is also displayed.

➤ Click a view to see a digitized or videodisc image.

Your Perseus Settings (available from the Gateway) control the display of digitized images, videodisc images, or both. Image credits appear in a floating window that can be closed or repositioned on the screen. Settings are described in general in section 4.2.2 and in detail in section 10.5.

➤ Click the close box of the image, in the upper left, if you are using digitized images.

NOTE: The images are not stored in HyperCard and therefore their treatment should be different from that of other Perseus elements. In particular, you must click the close box to remove an image.

If the window is not active, click the title bar. If you use the Navigator while an image window is open, Perseus will respond, but you will be unable to see the response if the image window is covering the active HyperCard window.

Thumbs

➤ Click Thumbs, in the upper right, to see the visual summary of views available for Delphi.

One hundred twenty views are available for Delphi. The Thumbnail Browser shows miniature images of the available views. The Thumbnail Browser is described in section 5.2.

Description

➤ Click Description to see a more detailed article for this site (figure 6.14).

When Perseus displays the article, the name of this button changes to Summary. Click Summary to return to the Summary on the Site Catalog card. Clicking Index returns you to the Site Index.

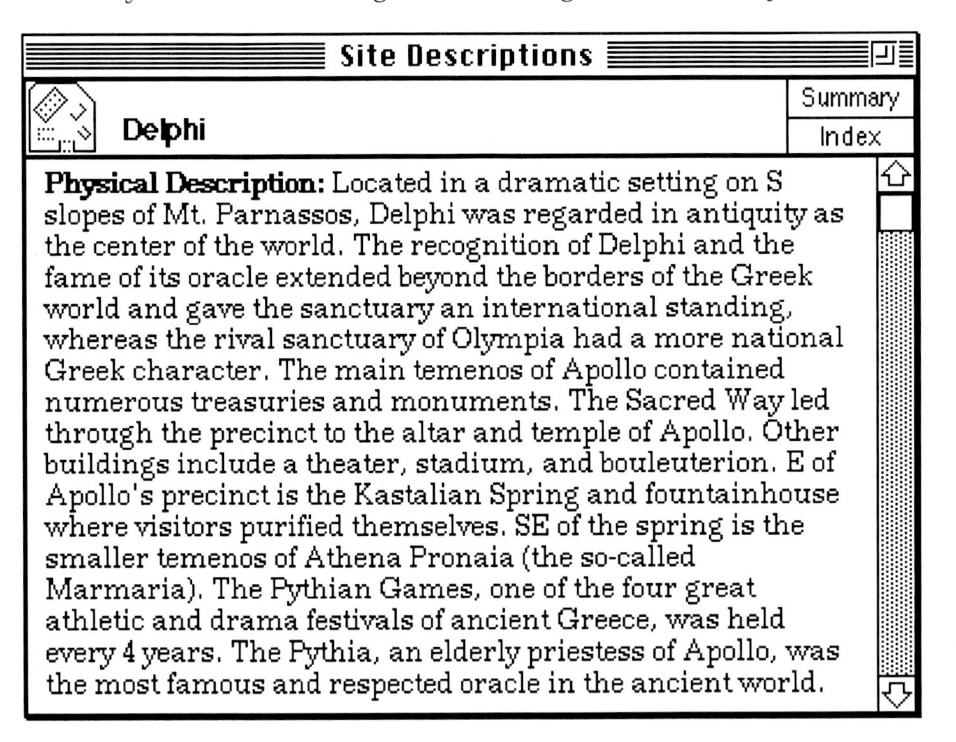

Figure 6.14 Site Description for Delphi

The name of the site is displayed above the description. The description of the site includes, as applicable, information on its physical characteristics, history, and excavation. Sources and general bibliographic information are included, as applicable.

Direct links to other Perseus material are indicated in the description by underlined references. Many references are to Primary Texts, showing the author's name and the abbreviated text citation.

Other references are to Sources Cited.

To use these links, select the underlined reference, choose the Lookup tool from the Links menu and press Return. References to Primary Texts will go directly to the text. For other Perseus resources (for example, the reference to Leekley and Efstratiou 1980), highlight the text, choose Lookup from the Links menu, press Return and click the results in the right column.

Index

- ➤ Click Index to return to the Site Index.
- ➤ Click the Go Back arrow on the Navigator Palette to return to the Site Summary for Delphi.

SMALL SITE PLAN

The list of plans and views may include a small site plan for the selected site. Some small site plans show the evolution of the site through different phases. The following example assumes that you are starting at the Site Summary for Delphi.

- ➤ Click "Overview plan of site (sm.)" in the list of Plans & Views to see a small-scale overview plan of Delphi.

The small site plan for Delphi is depicted in figure 6.15. Drawing credits appear in a floating window that can be closed or repositioned on the screen.

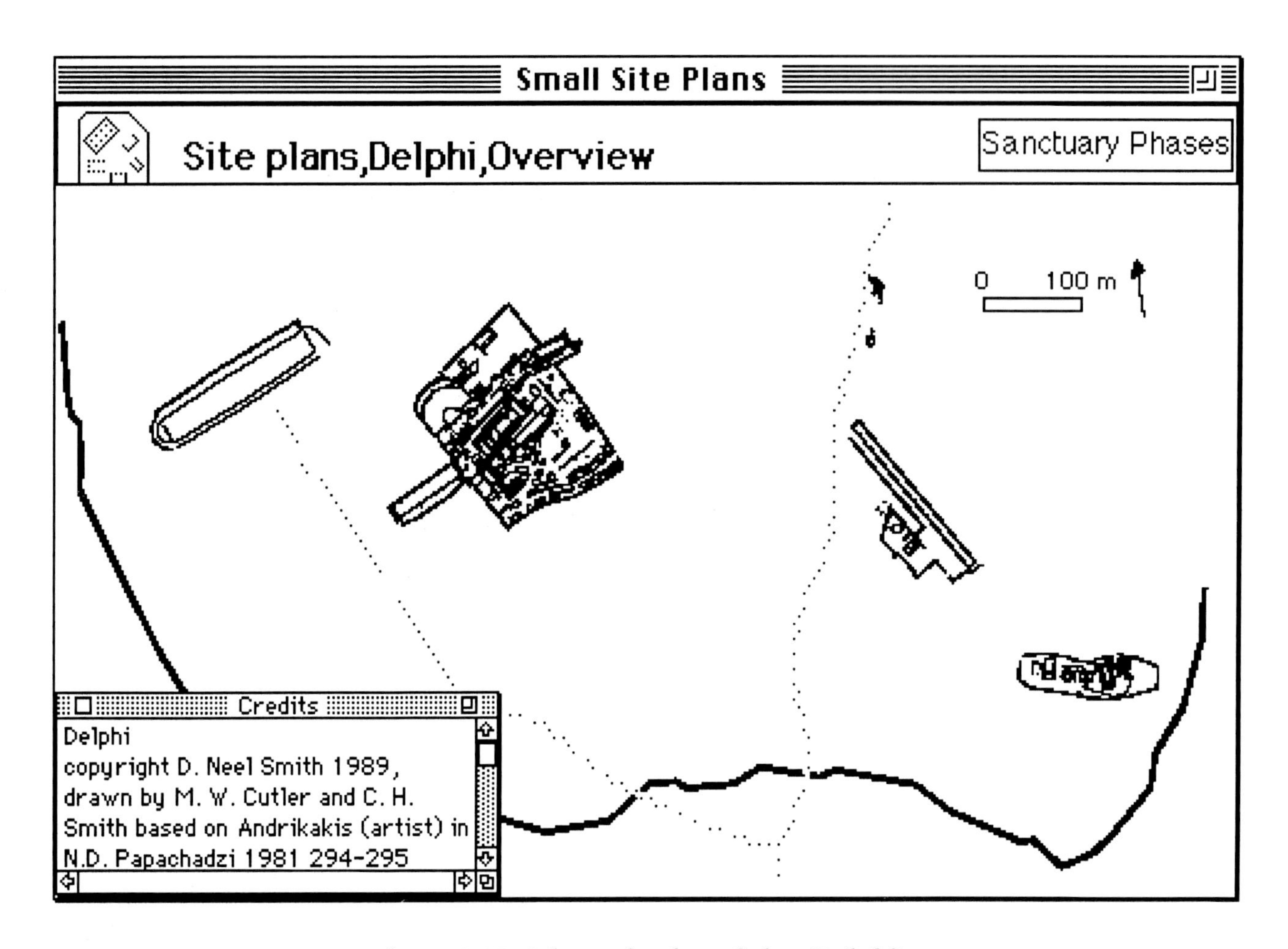

Figure 6.15 Schematic plan of site (Delphi)

Plan menu

The Plan menu appears in the menu bar, to the right of the Links and Perseus menus, when you are looking at a small plan. The Plan menu for the small site plan has one option.

➤ Choose Site Catalog from the Plan menu to see the Site Summary.

➤ Click the Go Back arrow on the Navigator Palette to return to the small site plan.

Construction Phases

On some site plans, a button appears that links to views showing the evolution of the site through maps of different phases of construction. (Some sites, such as Athens, may have more than one such button.)

➤ Click the button Sanctuary Phases to bring up a small site plan. Now choose one of the items from the pop-up menu Construction Phases. The plan shows the layout of the site during the selected phase (figure 6.16).

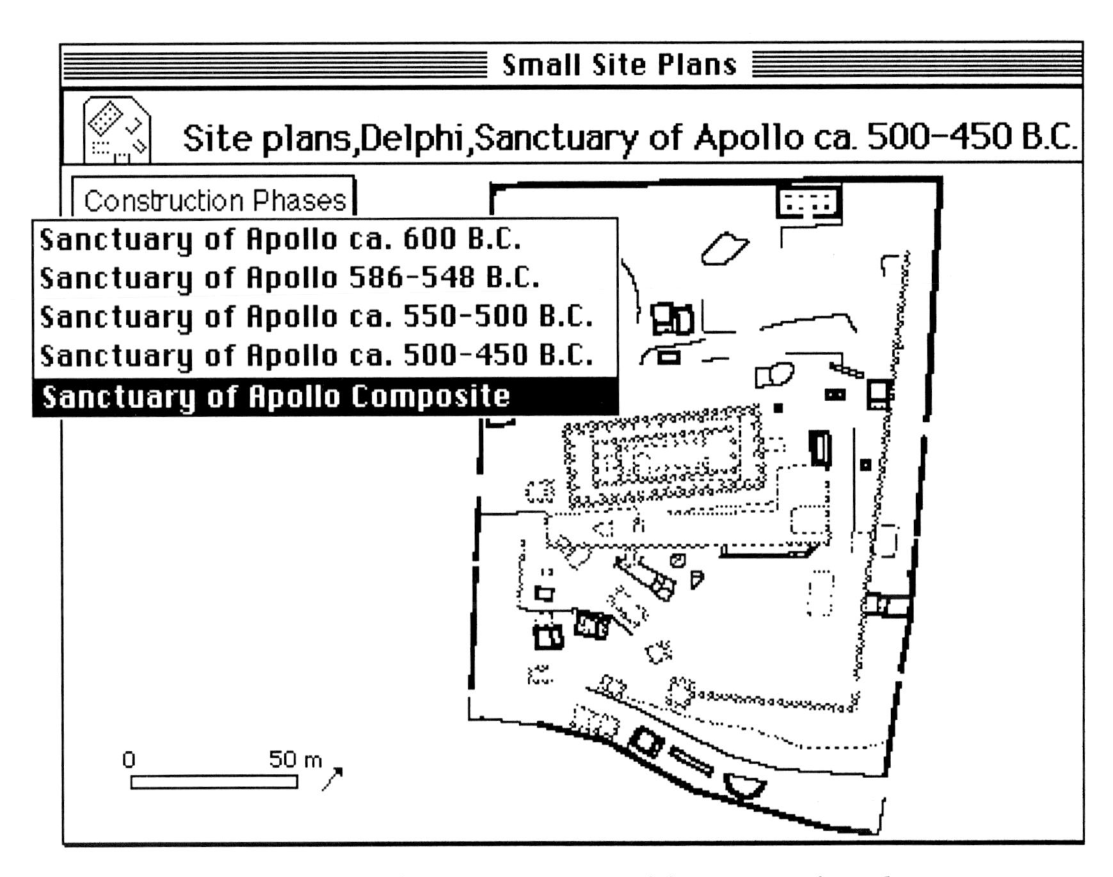

Figure 6.16 Site plan of Delphi ca. 500-450 B.C. with Construction Phase pop-up menu

LARGE SITE PLAN

A large site plan for the selected site may be available from the list of Plans & Views.

Return to the Site Catalog card for Delphi by choosing Site Catalog from the Plan menu. From the Site Catalog card click "Overview of site (lg.)."

The large site plan is a large, detailed plan. It features a scroll window, a Plan menu, and active areas on the plan that can be clicked for more information. The large site plan for Delphi is depicted in figure 6.17.

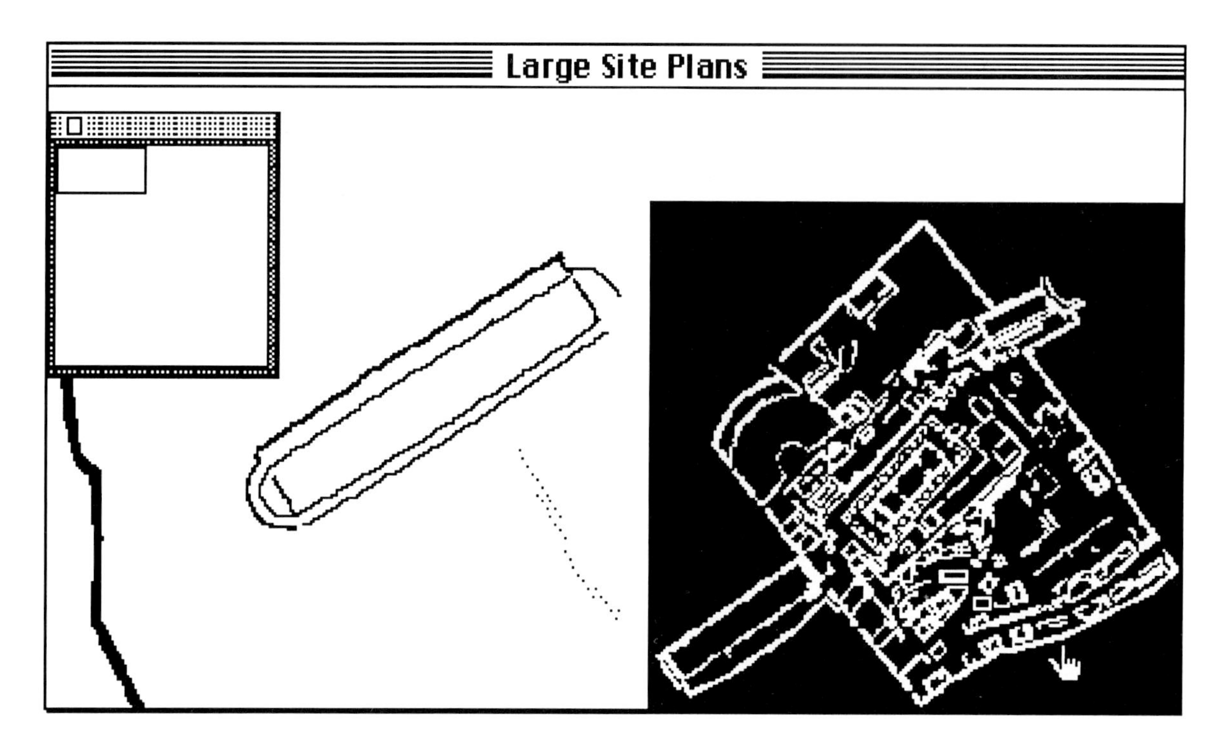

Figure 6.17 Large site plan for Delphi showing scrolling window and "active" sanctuary of Apollo (see "Identify Architecture on Site Plan," later in this section)

A caption appears in a floating window that can be closed or repositioned on the screen.

Scroll window

A second floating window, the scroll window, appears with a small rectangle that indicates the relation of the current screen to the full size of the large site plan.

➤ Move the rectangle to see a different portion of the full map window. (Place the pointer in the center of the rectangle and drag it to a new location.)

➤ Resize the rectangle to increase or decrease the map size. (Place the cursor near an edge or corner of the rectangle and drag it to resize the rectangle.)

If necessary, review the information in section 4.1.3 about the scroll window.

Plan menu

The Plan menu appears in the menu bar, to the right of the Links and Perseus menus, when you are viewing a site plan. The Plan menu for the large site plan has four items.

Show Image Buttons/Hide Image Buttons

Image buttons can be displayed on a dimmed image of the site plan to indicate views. These image buttons correspond to particular vantage points in the site plan that are captured in digitized or videodisc images. The direction of the arrow on the image buttons indicates the perspective from which the original photograph was made.

The first item is Show Image Buttons (or "Go to Plan with Image Buttons," depending on whether image buttons are available for the current site plan). This item toggles to Hide Image Buttons, which you can use if you want to put the image buttons away.

➤ Choose Show Image Buttons from the Plan menu.

Image credits appear in a floating window that can be closed or repositioned on the screen. If you are viewing a digitized image, you must click the close box to remove the image.

Small Site Plan

➤ Choose Small Site Plan from the Plan menu to go directly to a small plan of the site.

Site Description

➤ Choose Site Catalog from the Plan Menu to go directly to the Summary on the Site Catalog card.

Show Scroll Window

The final menu item is Show Scroll Window, which will recall the scroll window if it is not there.

➤ Choose Show Scroll Window from the Plan Menu to make the scroll window appear.

Identify Architecture on Site Plan

The site plans are closely linked to the Architecture resources in Perseus.

➤ Move the mouse over a building in the large site plan you wish to explore. If the building is active, that is, if there are links to an architectural plan and description, the building will become highlighted (see figure 6.17). Click the building to bring up the further information.

If the image buttons are showing, this feature will be inoperative. Choose Hide Image Buttons from the Plan menu.

If the building is in the Perseus Architecture Catalog, a dialog box appears, showing the name of the building and site, with the choices to see a plan for that building, see a catalog article for the building, or cancel. Not every building at a site is cataloged.

6.3.3 ARCHITECTURE

Architecture is indexed in five ways: all buildings, and by site, building type, period, and date. The description here uses the index by building type as an example.

Architecture Index

➤ From the Gateway, click the Art & Archaeology icon, then click "Index by building type" under the topic Architecture. Or choose Architecture from the Links menu, then choose the item Type from the Index Type pop-up menu.

Perseus displays an alphabetical list of building types in the left column. The detailed index for architecture listed by building types is depicted below (figure 6.18).

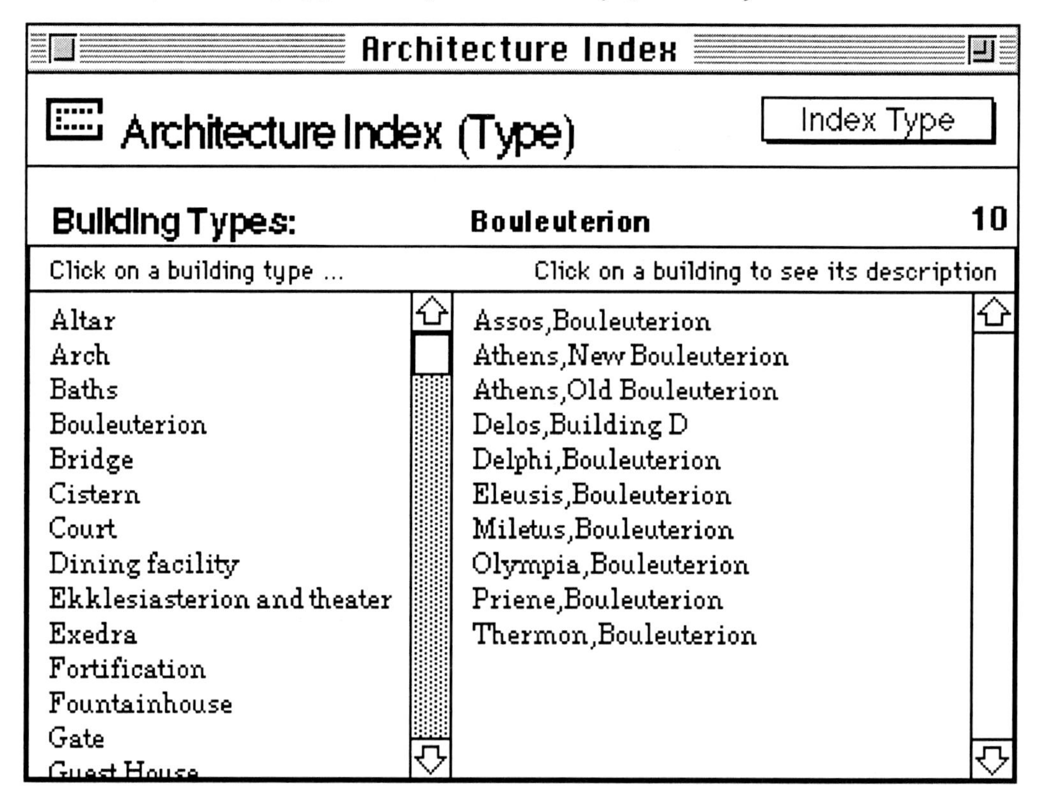

Figure 6.18 Detailed index for architecture listed by building types

➤ Choose a different index from the Index Type pop-up menu.

Try the other index types to see their detailed indexes. Return the selection to the index by building type to follow the rest of this description.

The left column lists building types. When a building type is selected, the right column lists the sites at which this type of building is located. The number of buildings of the selected type is also displayed.

➤ Click Bouleuterion under the list of building types in the left column.

Ten sites with bouleuteria are listed in the right column.

➤ Click "Olympia,Bouleuterion" under the list of buildings in the right column.

The full catalog entry consists of an Architecture Catalog card with an Architecture Summary, and an Architecture Description.

Architecture Summary

The Architecture Summary is in a format similar to the Site Summary. The title of the article is displayed next to the Architecture icon. The Thumbs button displays the available views in the Thumbnail Browser. The Description button allows you to move from the Architecture Summary to the Architecture Description. The Index button returns you to the Architecture Index.

Architectural information for the selected building includes, as applicable, the site, date, period, and type. A summary of the building is also displayed.

Locate Building

➤ Click the button "Locate Bldg." in the upper right to see the building in a site plan.

Perseus displays a site plan and indicates the building by flashing its location.

➤ Click the building to see a more detailed building plan. A dialog box appears, asking if you wish to see the Plan, return to the Catalog, or Cancel your request. To go to the building plan, click Plan.

➤ Put the Plan away by clicking the close box, in the upper left. Click the Go Back arrow on the Navigator Palette to return to the catalog description for the Bouleuterion in Olympia.

Plans and views

Some sites are accompanied by digitized images or videodisc still-frames, depending on your Perseus Settings and your equipment. The views available for the selected site are listed alphabetically below the site information. The number of views is also displayed.

➤ Click a view to see an image.

Image credits appear in a floating window that can be closed or repositioned on the screen.

➤ Click the close box of the image, if you are using digitized images.

NOTE: The images are not stored in HyperCard. You must click the close box to remove an image. If the window is not active, click the title bar. If you use the Navigator while an image window is open, Perseus will respond, but you will be unable to see the response if the image window is covering the active HyperCard window.

Architecture Description

The Architecture Description is in a format similar to the Site Description. The Description button displays the narrative part of the architecture article. The Index button returns you to the Architecture Index.

The description of the building includes, as applicable, information on its plan, history, construction, and dimensions. Sources and general bibliographic information are included, as applicable. Related entries in the sculpture catalog are listed under "See also."

The description may have underlined references that indicate a link elsewhere in Perseus. Many of the references are from the Sources Used stack. Others are literary references to Primary Texts. To use these links, select the underlined reference, choose the Lookup tool from the Links menu, and press Return. References to Primary Texts will go directly to the text (for example, Paus. 5.10.3). For other Perseus resources (for example, the reference to Mallwitz 1972), highlight the text, choose the Lookup tool, press Return, and click the results in the right column.

6.3.4 SCULPTURE

Sculpture is indexed in eight ways: by type, material, sculptor, collection, context, associated building, period, and date. Because available information varies with each sculpture, not all sculptures appear on each index. It is possible to choose an index type and not see all sculptures included in Perseus. The description here uses the index by type as an example.

Sculpture Index

➤ To go to the Sculpture Index from the Gateway, click the Art & Archaeology icon, then click "Index by type" under the topic Sculpture. Or from anywhere within Perseus, choose Sculpture from the Links menu, then choose the item Type from the Index Type pop-up menu.

Perseus displays an alphabetical list of sculpture types in the left column.

There are two ways to identify sculptures in Perseus: by title and by collection name. In many instances, figures are better known by their collection name. A Title/Catalog toggle button enables you to see sculptures listed by their title or by their catalog identification.

The detailed index for sculpture listed by sculpture types is depicted in figure 6.19.

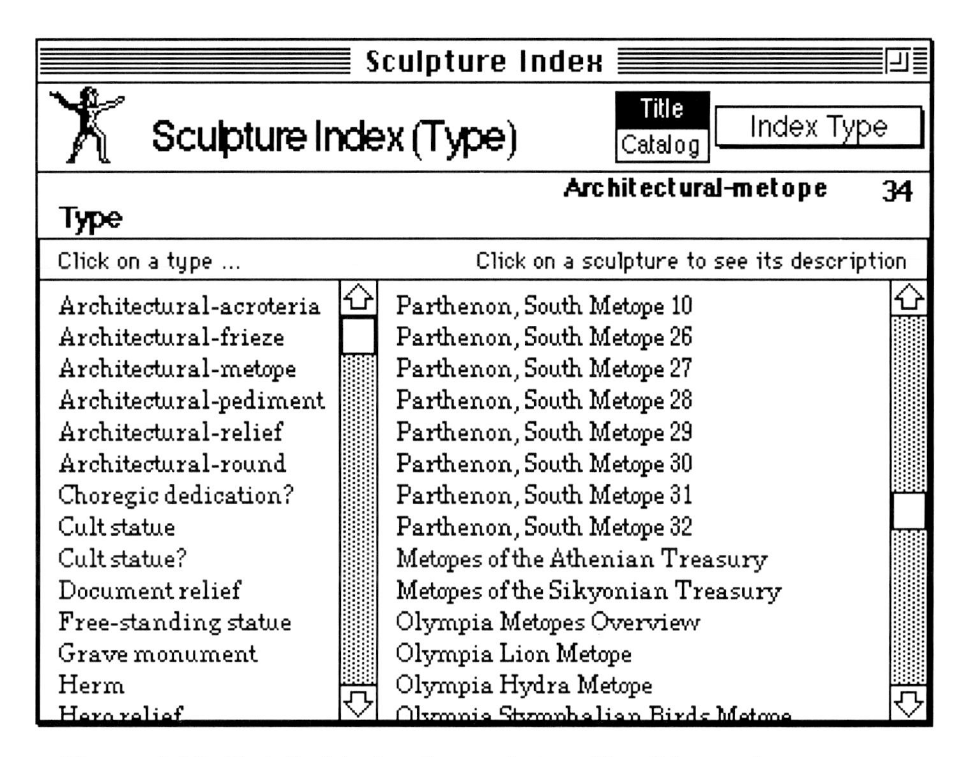

Figure 6.19 Detailed index for sculpture listed by sculpture types

➤ Choose a different index from the Index Type pop-up menu.

Try the other index types to see their detailed indexes. Return to the index of sculptures by type to follow the rest of this description.

The left column lists sculpture types. When a sculpture type is selected, the right column lists the sculptures. The number of sculptures of the selected type is also displayed above the list of sculptures.

➤ Click Architectural-metope under the list of sculpture types in the left column.

Thirty-four sculptures are listed in the right column.

➤ Click Olympia Metopes Overview under the list of sculptures in the right column.

The full catalog entry consists of a Sculpture Catalog card with a Sculpture Summary, and a Sculpture Description.

Sculpture Summary

The Sculpture Summary is in a format similar to the Site Summary. The title of the article is displayed next to the Sculpture icon. The Thumbs button displays the available views in the Thumbnail Browser. The Description button allows you to move from the Sculpture Summary to the Sculpture Description. The Index button returns you to the Sculpture Index.

Information for the selected sculpture includes the catalog number, collection, subject, material, sculptor, type, context, date, and period, as applicable.

Views

All sculptures are accompanied by digitized images or videodisc still-frames, depending on your Perseus Settings and your equipment. The views available for the selected sculpture are listed alphabetically below the sculpture information. The number of views available is also displayed at the top of the Views list.

➤ Click a view to see an image.

Image credits appear in a floating window that can be closed or repositioned on the screen.

➤ Click the close box of the image, if you are using digitized images.

NOTE: The images are not stored in HyperCard. You must click the close box to remove an image. If the window is not active, click the title bar. If you use the Navigator while an image window is open, Perseus will respond, but you will be unable to see the response if the image window is covering the active HyperCard window.

Sculpture Description

The Sculpture Description is in a format similar to the Site Description. The Description button displays the narrative part of the sculpture article. The Index button returns you to the Sculpture Index.

The description of the sculpture includes, as applicable, information on its scale, dimensions, and collection history. Sources and general bibliographic information are also included, as applicable. Related entries in the architecture catalog are listed under "See also."

The description may have underlined references that indicate a link elsewhere in Perseus. Many of the references are from the Sources Used stack. Others are literary references to Primary Texts. To use these links, select the underlined reference, choose the Lookup tool from the Links menu, and press Return. References to Primary Texts will go directly to the text (for example, Paus. 5.10.9). For other Perseus resources (for example, the reference to Robertson 1975), highlight the text, choose

Lookup from the Links menu, press Return and click the results in the right column.

6.3.5 VASES

Vases are indexed in eight ways: by shape, ware, painter, potter, collection, context, period, and date before and after 500 B.C. In addition to the Caskey-Beazley catalog of the vase collection of the Boston Museum of Fine Arts, additional published indexes have been incorporated into Perseus 2.0, including regional U.S. indexes by Buitron-Oliver, Moon, Shapiro, and Williams; Beazley's ABV and ARV2 indexes; and the Furtwängler and Reichhold index. These special indexes are described in this section. Because the information known about each vase varies, not all vases appear in each index.

Vase Index

The description here uses the index by painter as an example.

➤ To go to the Vase Index from the Gateway, click the Art & Archaeology icon, then click "Index by painter" under the topic Vases. Or from anywhere within Perseus, choose Vases from the Links menu, then choose Painter from the Index Type pop-up menu.

Perseus displays an alphabetical list of painters in the left column. The detailed index for vases listed by painter is depicted in figure 6.20.

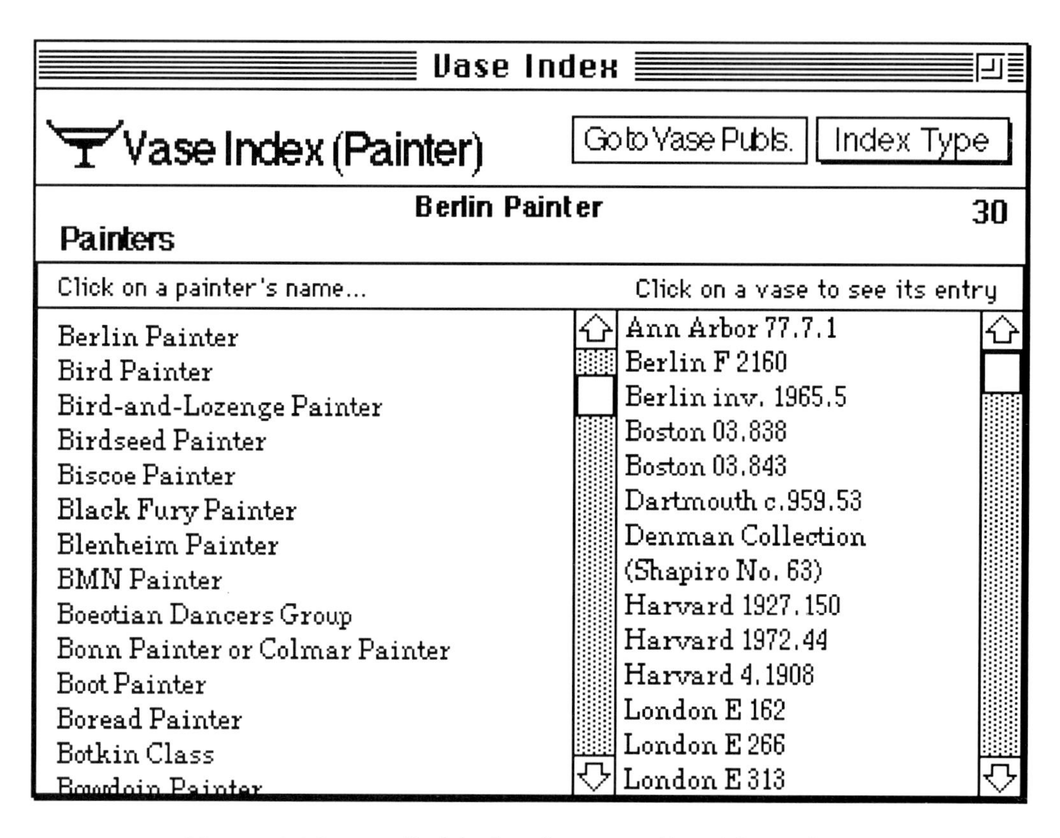

Figure 6.20 Detailed index for vases listed by painter

There are two controls in the upper right. Click the button "Go to Vase Publs." to go to an index of specialized vase publications. Click the pop-up menu Index Type for a menu of Vase Index types.

➤ Choose a different index from the Index Type pop-up menu.

Try the other index types to see their detailed indexes. Return to the index of vases by painters to follow the rest of this description.

The left column lists painters. When a painter is selected, the right column lists vases by that painter. The number of vases of the selected type is also displayed above the list of vases.

➤ Click Achilles Painter under the list of painters in the left column.

Eighteen vases painted by Achilles Painter are listed in the right column.

➤ Click London D48 under the list of vases in the right column.

The full catalog entry consists of a Vase Catalog card with a Vase Summary, and a Vase Description (figure 6.21).

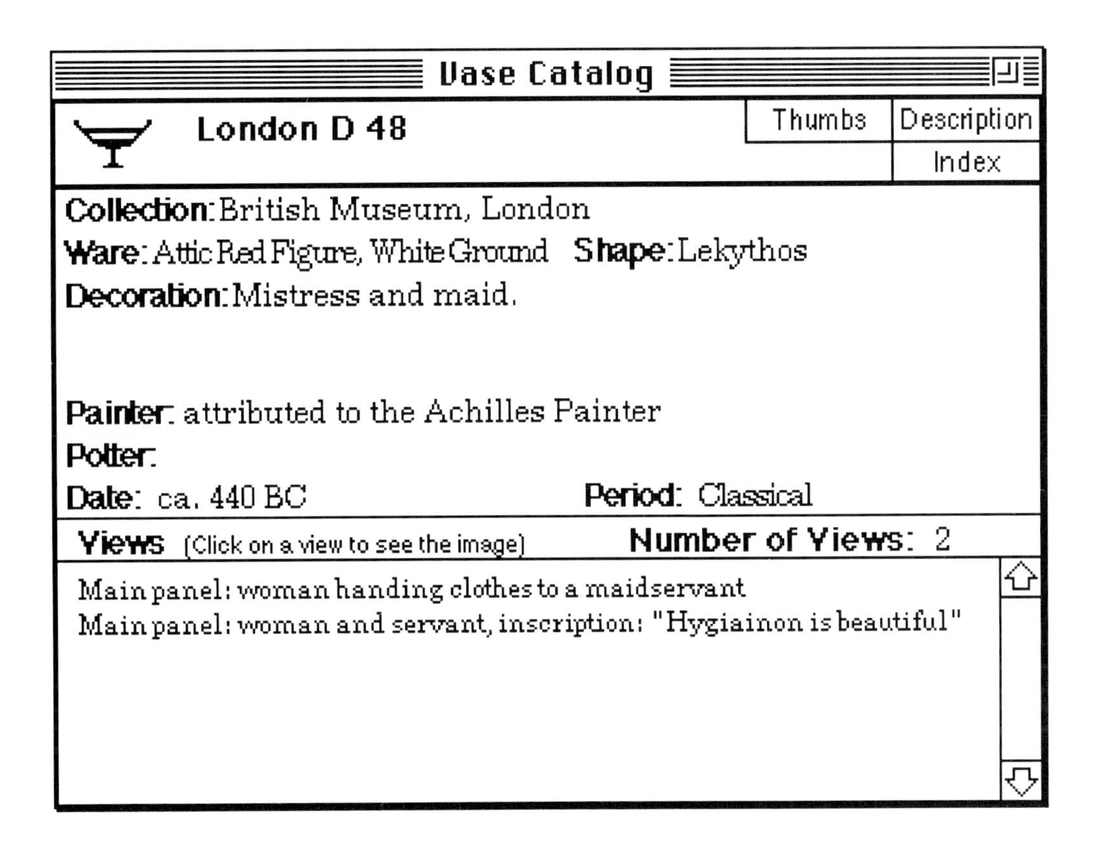

Figure 6.21 Vase Catalog card

Vase Summary

The Vase Summary is in a format similar to the Site Summary. The title of the article is displayed next to the Vase icon. The Thumbs button displays the available views in the Thumbnail Browser. The Description button allows you to move from the Vase Summary to the Vase Description. The Index button returns you to the Vase Index.

Information for the selected vase includes the catalog number, collection, ware, shape, decoration, painter, potter, date, and period, as applicable.

Views

All vases are accompanied by digitized images or videodisc still-frames, depending on your Perseus Settings and your equipment. The views available for the selected vase are listed alphabetically below the information given in the summary. The number of views available is also displayed at the top of the Views list.

➤ Click a view to see an image.

Image credits appear in a floating window that can be closed or repositioned on the screen.

➤ Click the close box of the image, if you are using digitized images.

NOTE: The images are not stored in HyperCard. You must click the close box to remove an image. If the window is not active, click the title bar. If you use the Navigator while an image window is open, Perseus will respond, but you will be unable to see the response if the image window is covering the active HyperCard window.

Vase Description

The Vase Description is in a format similar to the Site Description. The Description button displays the narrative part of the vase article. The Index button returns you to the Vase Index.

The description of the vase includes, as applicable, information on catalog number, decoration, ceramic phase, shape, fabric description, inscriptions, graffiti, dimensions, preservation, condition, parallels, date, collection history, primary citation, sources used, and vase description author.

The description may have underlined references that indicate a link elsewhere in Perseus. The Vase Descriptions have several links to the Caskey-Beazley essay. Many other references are to the Sources Used stack and to Primary Texts. To use these links, select the underlined reference, choose the Lookup tool from the Links menu, and press Return. References (if any) to Primary Texts will go directly to the text. For other Perseus resources (for example, the reference to ARV2), highlight the text, choose Lookup from the Links menu, press Return, and click the results in the right column.

Specialized vase publications

Perseus 2.0 contains selections from the following specialized vase publications:

J. D. Beazley, Attic Red-Figure Vase-Painters (contents)

J. D. Beazley, Attic Black-Figure Vase-Painters (page references)

J. D. Beazley, Attic Black-Figure Vase-Painters 2, Paralipomena and Addenda (page references)

U.S. regional catalogs compiled by Buitron-Oliver, Moon, Shapiro, and Williams

Furtwängler and Reichhold index

The specialized vase publications may be reached from the Gateway by clicking the Art & Archaeology icon, then clicking Vase Publications Index under the topic Vases. Or, from anywhere within Perseus, choose Vases from the Links menu, then click the button "Go to Vase Publs."

Perseus will bring up the Vase Publications Index (figure 6.22).

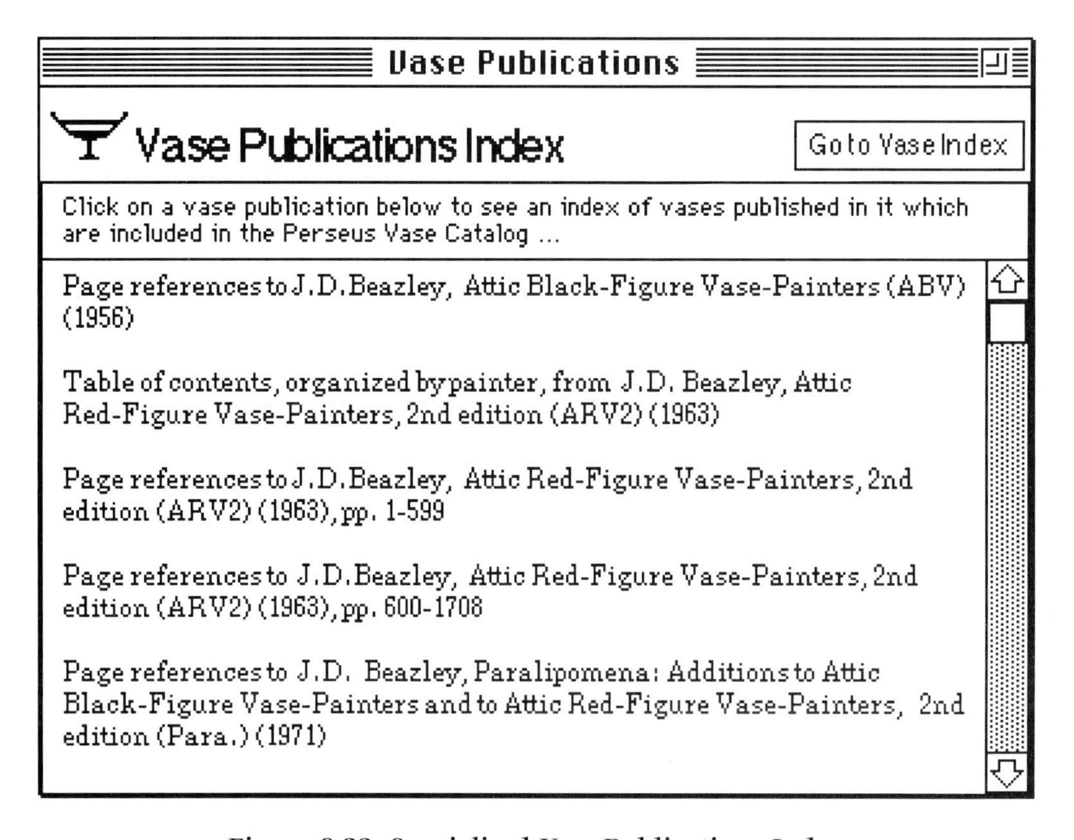

Figure 6.22 Specialized Vase Publications Index

➤ Click a heading in the Vase Publications Index to go to a table of contents for that topic.

➤ Click the button "Table of Contents" to return to the Vase Index.

Beazley, ARV2 contents

This is a special index for the Perseus Vase Catalog that allows you to access a listing of vases according to Beazley's *Attic Red-Figure Vase-Painters*.

➤ To see the index, click "Table of contents, organized by painter . . ." (figure 6.23).

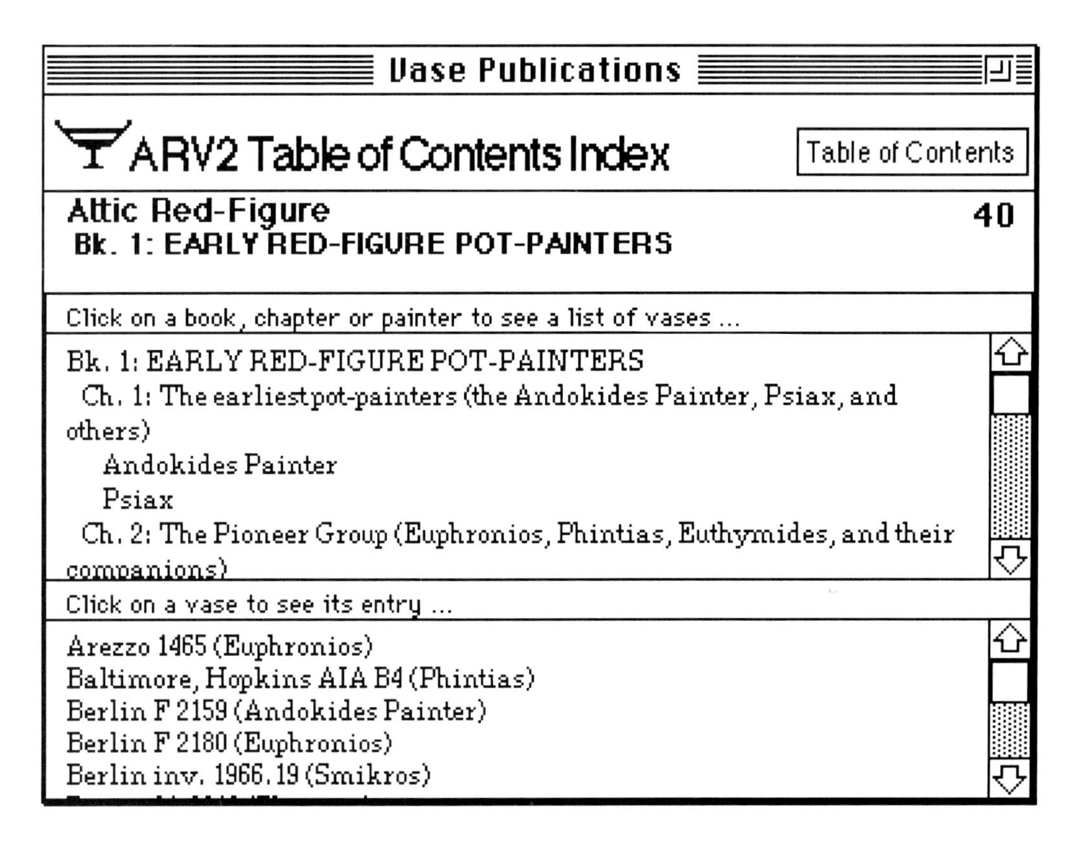

Figure 6.23 Vase Index using Beazley ARV2

The Perseus ARV2 Catalog displays vases by book, chapter, and painter. The following example will look in turn for vases in book 1, in chapter 1, and by the Andokides Painter.

The ARV2 Catalog as it appears in Perseus has been edited. It contains only those vases that are also in Perseus 2.0.

- ➤ To see a list of vases contained in Perseus and described in an ARV2 book, scroll up or down the central field to see displayed all 20 books of ARV2. Click Book 1, and a list of all 40 painters in Perseus covered by Beazley in book 1 will appear in the field at the bottom. The book number and title will be displayed in the field above (see figure 6.23).
- ➤ Click a vase catalog number in the lower field to go to the Perseus Vase Catalog card for that vase.
- ➤ To see a list of vases contained in Perseus and described in an ARV2 chapter, scroll up or down until you come to the desired chapter. Click Chapter 1, and a list of all 10 painters in Perseus covered by Beazley in chapter 1 will appear in the field at the bottom. The field at the top will reflect your choice.
- ➤ To see a list of vases contained in Perseus and described in an ARV2 painter article, scroll up or down

until you come to the desired painter. Click Andokides Painter, and a list of the four vases in Perseus covered by Beazley in this article will appear in the field at the bottom. The field at the top will reflect your choice.

Beazley ABV page references

This is a special index for the Perseus Vase Catalog that you can access from a listing of vases according to Beazley's *Attic Black-Figure Vase-Painters*. Figure 6.24 shows the index.

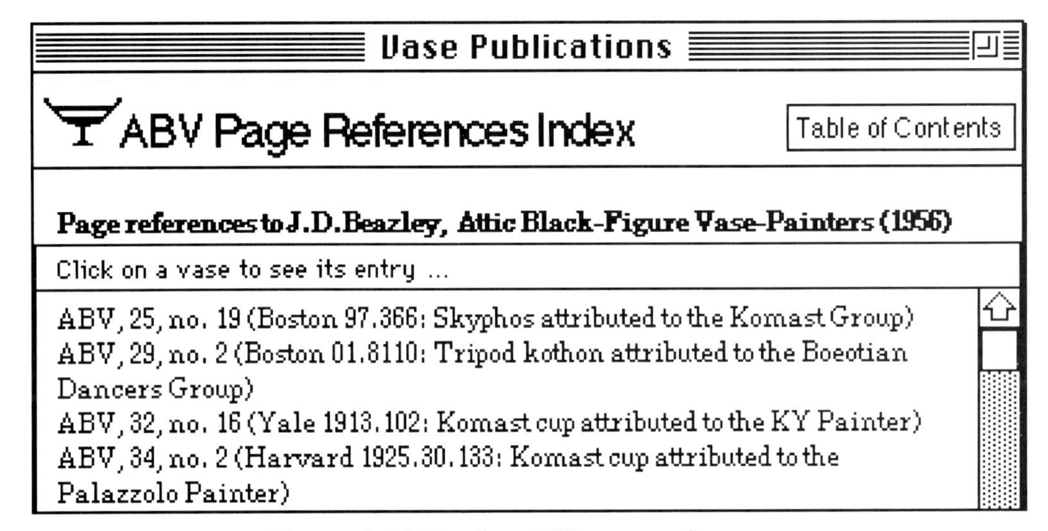

Figure 6.24 Beazley ABV page references

The ABV Catalog as it appears in Perseus has been edited. It contains only those vases that are also in Perseus 2.0.

➤ Click an ABV page reference to go to its Vase Catalog card in Perseus.

Beazley ARV2 page references, Paralipomena page references, and Addenda page references

These special indexes have been edited for Perseus, and they behave in the same way as the ABV Index.

U.S. regional catalogs

Perseus contains four catalogs documenting regional collections in the United States. They are Diana Buitron-Oliver, *Attic Vase Painting in New England Collections;* Warren Moon, *Greek Vase Painting in Midwestern Collections;* E. R. Williams, *The Archaeological Collection of the Johns Hopkins University;* and H. A. Shapiro, *Art, Myth, and Culture: Greek Vases from Southern Collections*.

These indexes have been edited for Perseus, and they behave in the same way as the ABV Index.

Furtwängler and Reichhold Index

This index is organized according to the plates from *Griechische Vasenmalerei*. You can click a plate to see the Perseus Vase Catalog card for the associated vase (figure 6.25).

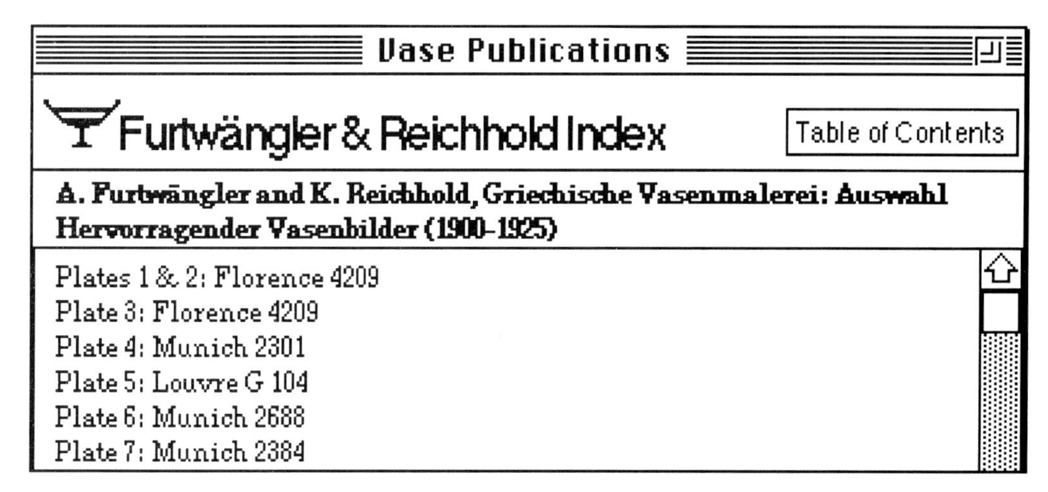

Figure 6.25 Furtwängler and Reichhold Index

The Furtwängler and Reichhold Index has been edited for Perseus, and it behaves in the same way as the ABV Index.

6.3.6 COINS

Coins are indexed in eight ways: by mint, metal, region, issuing authority, denomination, collection, period, and date. Issuing authority is the ruler under whose authority the coin was issued. In contrast, mint is the place where the coin was minted. If the coin was issued by an autonomous city rather than a ruler, then no issuing authority is listed (it is the same as the mint).

The description here uses the index by mint as an example.

Coin Index

➤ To go to the Coin Index from the Gateway, click the Art & Archaeology icon, then click "Index by mint" under the topic Coins. Or from anywhere within Perseus, choose Coins from the Links menu, then choose the item "Index by mint" from the Index Type pop-up menu.

Perseus displays an alphabetical list of mints in the left column. The detailed index for coins listed by mint is depicted in figure 6.26.

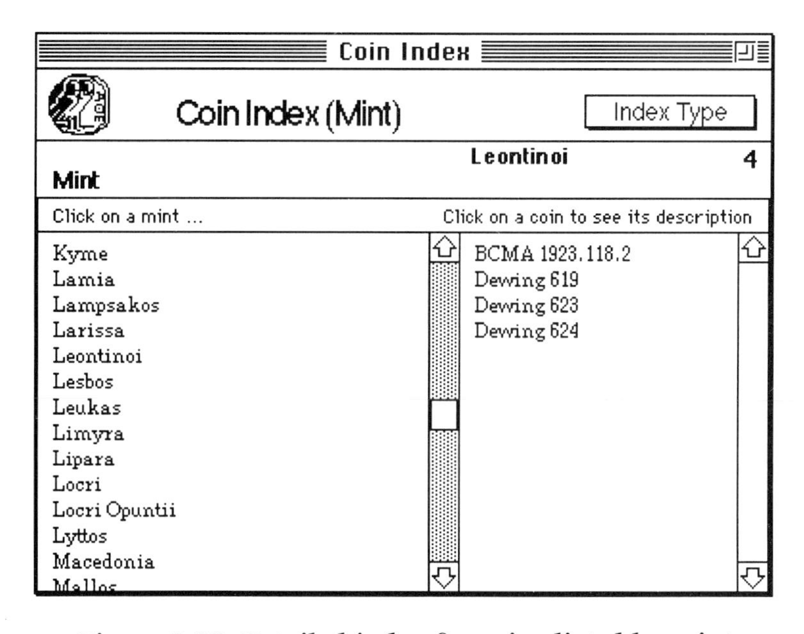

Figure 6.26 Detailed index for coins listed by mint

➤ Choose a different index from the Index Type pop-up menu.

Try the other index types to see their detailed indexes. Return to the index by mint to follow the rest of this description.

The left column lists mints. When a mint is selected, the right column lists the coins issued by that mint. The number of coins of the selected type is also displayed.

➤ Scroll down and click Leontinoi under the list of mints in the left column.

The four coins in Perseus issued by Leontinoi are listed in the right column according to the catalog label.

➤ Click Dewing 624 in the right column.

The full coin description consists of a Coin Catalog card with a Coin Summary, and a Coin Description.

Coin Summary

The Summary on the Coin Catalog card is in a format similar to that on the Site Catalog card. The catalog label of the coin is displayed next to the Coin icon. The Thumbs button displays the available views in the Thumbnail Browser. The Description button allows you to toggle between the Coin Summary and the Coin Description. The Index button returns you to the Coin Index.

Information for the selected coin includes the collection, metal, denomination, weight, die axis, mint, and issuing authority, as applicable. Summaries of the obverse and reverse sides and the date and period are also displayed.

Views

All coins are accompanied by digitized images or videodisc still-frames, depending on your Perseus Settings and your equipment. Most coins have two views: the obverse and reverse of the coin. In this example, users of the Concise Edition of Perseus will be able to see the view of the reverse.

➤ Click a view to see an image.

Image credits appear in a floating window that can be closed or repositioned on the screen.

Each white or black bar on the scale at the left of the image represents actual size of one centimeter.

➤ Click the close box of the image, if you are using digitized images.

NOTE: The images are not stored in HyperCard. You must click the close box to remove an image. If the window is not active, click the title bar. If you use the Navigator while an image window is open, Perseus will respond, but you will be unable to see the response if the image window is covering the active HyperCard window.

Coin Description

The Coin Description is in a format similar to the Site Description. Unlike the descriptions of other archaeological objects, coin descriptions tend to be very brief. The Description button displays the descriptive part of the coin article. The Index button returns you to the Coin Index.

The Atlas is an interactive tool for investigating the geography of the Greek world and the surrounding Mediterranean region. The Atlas contains graphic drawings, digital elevation models, satellite images, and three-dimensional topography views. Various functions in the Atlas allow you to locate and plot sites, compute distances between sites, identify sites within a region, examine elevation and drainage, and zoom in and out to see maps of different scales. As a geographic reference, the Atlas can be used in traditional ways, but its content and design encourage more complex and interactive uses.

7.1 INTRODUCTION TO THE ATLAS

7.1.1 A DEFINITION OF TERMS

The Atlas is a complex tool with several unique features. Here are some terms used to describe the Atlas.

"Projection" refers to the system used to translate locations on a (nearly) spherical earth into the plane of a map. The large-scale longitude-latitude (lon-lat) map uses a Plate Carrée projection. The other maps use the Universal Transverse Mercator (UTM) projection system.

"Coordinate system" refers to the system by which points on the current map are located. In Perseus, all geographic data are recorded in longitude and latitude coordinates, expressed in degrees (minutes, seconds) east of Greenwich, England, and north of the Equator. The large-scale lon-lat map works directly with these coordinates in a Plate Carrée projection. The other maps use the UTM coordinate system expressed in integers in a UTM projection.

"Graphic Map Index" refers to the black-and-white line drawings that serve as pointers and gateways to detailed maps. Typically, a map index shows a line drawing of the Greek world overlaid with numerous rectangles. The rectangles are active areas that, when clicked, open the respective detailed map in the selected scale and theme (defined below).

"Scale" refers to the meters-per-pixel ratio of the maps. Depending on the map, the scale may be 1300, 1000, 500, 250, 125, or 60 meters per pixel. (A pixel is the unit of measure for a computer monitor.)

"Theme" refers to the type of map selected, such as a color topography map. The map themes are defined in the next section.

"Detailed maps" are the color maps and the black-and-white topography maps.

7.1.2 MAP THEMES

Four map themes are used in the Atlas.

Outline maps: Large- and small-scale black-and-white line drawings show the coastline of the Greek world from Sicily and Magna Graecia to Asia Minor.

Black-and-white topography: This black-and-white line drawing shows elevation, and resembles a standard paper topographic map, with contour lines showing 1000-foot intervals in elevation.

Satellite images: These maps show a conventional, false-color representation of satellite data and cover the Greek mainland. The three bands of satellite data are shown in red, green, and blue.

Color elevation maps with rivers: These maps have been created from digital information on land elevation. A range of colors, from yellow to dark brown, is used to describe elevation. These maps show streams and lakes overlaid on topography.

7.1.3 COLOR ATLAS: OVERVIEW OF FEATURES

The Graphic Map Index of the Greek world is the gateway to all color Atlas features. The Graphic Map Index contains active rectangles superimposed on the map of the Greek world. Each rectangle represents the size and location of a map in the selected theme and scale. Procedures for navigating the Atlas are described in section 7.2.

A summary of features found in the color maps is shown in the following table:

Map Theme	Scales (meters per pixel)	Plot Sites	Plot Sites in Region	Compute Distances
False-color infrared	500, 250, 125, 60	Yes	No	Yes
Color topography and hydrography	500, 250, 125	Yes	Yes	Yes

The coverage of the Greek world in Perseus 2.0, which is derived from several sources, is shown in figure 7.1.

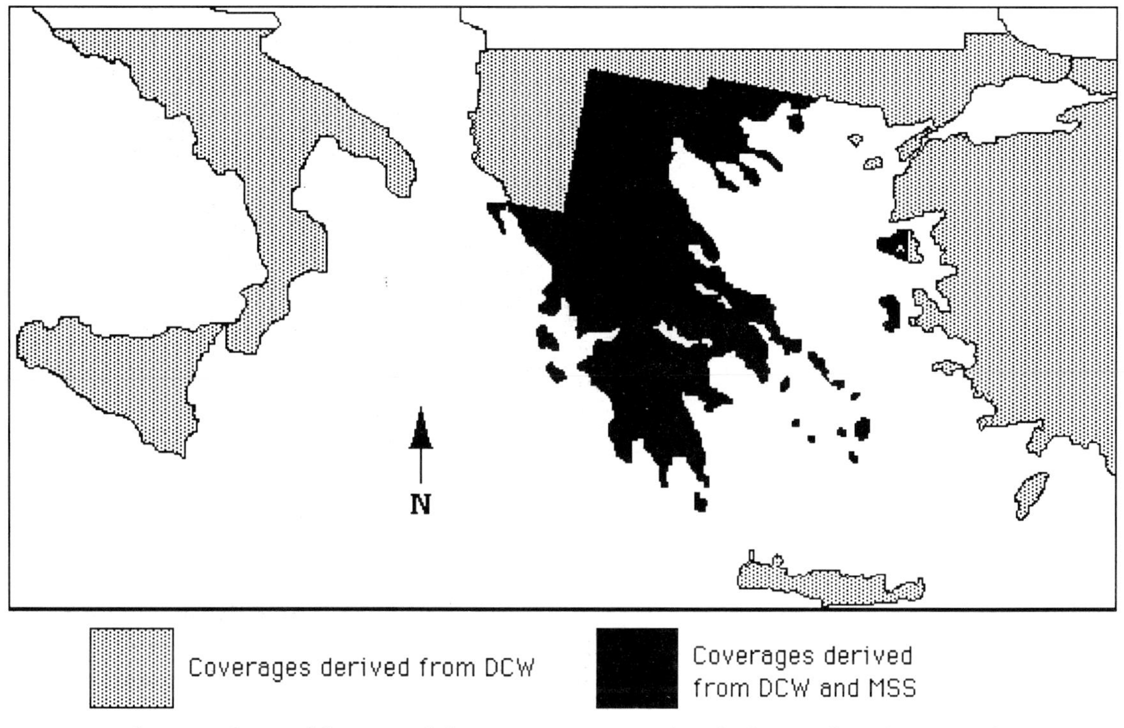

Figure 7.1 The Greek world covered in Perseus 2.0, using information from various sources. DCW = Digital Chart of the World; MSS = the Landsat Multispectral Scanner.

Satellite images (false-color infrared)

The satellite photographs, shown as false-color infrared maps, cover the Greek mainland and are available in four scales: 500, 250, 125, and 60 meters per pixel. The maps show a standard coloration of three bands of satellite data: red, green, and blue. Bright red areas reflect heavy vegetation, and blue to gray areas indicate heavy urbanization.

The false-color infrared maps are based on five regions in mainland Greece:

Epirus (Albania/Illyria)
NW Greece (Acarnania, Phocis, Aetolia, and so on)
SE Greece (Attica, Boeotia, Euboea, Thessaly, and so on)
Peloponnese, including Attica
Macedonia/Thrace

Color elevation maps with rivers

These color topography maps are based on the fifteen regions used to divide the black-and-white topography maps. The maps are digital elevation models that use color to indicate topography. Topographic data in the black-and-white topographic maps were used to interpolate values for the areas between the contour lines, so that every point on the map has an elevation value.

The key used to read elevations from the color elevation maps is available by clicking Show DEM Key on the Atlas Tools Palette, in the lower right. A small floating window with the color key and elevation scale appears. Hide the window by clicking the close button on the key.

The color topography maps are available in three scales: 500, 250, and 125 meters per pixel.

Sources for Atlas images

The Atlas includes information from three kinds of sources: the Digital Chart of the World (DCW), the Landsat Multispectral Scanner (MSS), and printed materials of varying quality.

The DCW offers worldwide coverage of a variety of themes represented as vectors in the Vector Product Format. For the Perseus Atlas, the most important themes are topography and hydrography. The published accuracy of the DCW is roughly 1:1 million, but according to the developers of the DCW, the accuracy will be substantially better in many parts of the world.

The Landsat MSS sensors measure electromagnetic radiation at four different points in the spectrum: 0.5–0.6 micrometers (blue), 0.6–0.7 μm (green), 0.7–0.8 μm (infrared), and 0.8–1.1 μm (infrared). Because different materials reflect and absorb radiation in characteristic ways, these data provide evidence of land cover.

The Atlas includes a database of approximately 1900 sites, based on maps published by the Greek Statistical Service, and on printed gazetteers. The Greek maps can be used reliably to within 30 seconds of longitude or latitude. (At 39 degrees of latitude, near the center of our core area, 30 seconds of longitude represents about 720 meters on the ground.)

7.2 NAVIGATING THE ATLAS

The Atlas comprises more than a thousand map images. This section provides information on how to navigate among them and find the ones most useful to you.

Briefly, to see a map, choose an item from one of the pop-up tiles on the Graphic Map Index. To return to the Index, click "Graphic index of maps" on the Atlas Tools Palette. To move to an adjacent topography map to the north, south, east, or west, click the directional arrows around the magnifying glass icon. To move to the map of the next highest scale in a theme, click one of the map's quadrants. To move to the map of the next lowest scale in a theme, click the minus sign inside the magnifying glass icon. Detailed procedures are given in the following sections.

7.2.1 GRAPHIC MAPS AND GRAPHIC MAP INDEXES

In broad terms, the Atlas maps can be categorized in three ways: as graphic outline maps, Graphic Map Indexes, and detailed maps. There are two graphic outline maps, the large- and small-scale lon-lat maps of the Greek world. Sites can be plotted on both maps.

The Graphic Map Indexes are gateways to detailed maps; they are analogous to the map keys found in traditional print atlases (figure 7.2). The detailed maps—color elevation, satellite image, and black-and-white contour maps—are available in up to four scales. You choose which scale you want from the Graphic Map Index, described later in this section.

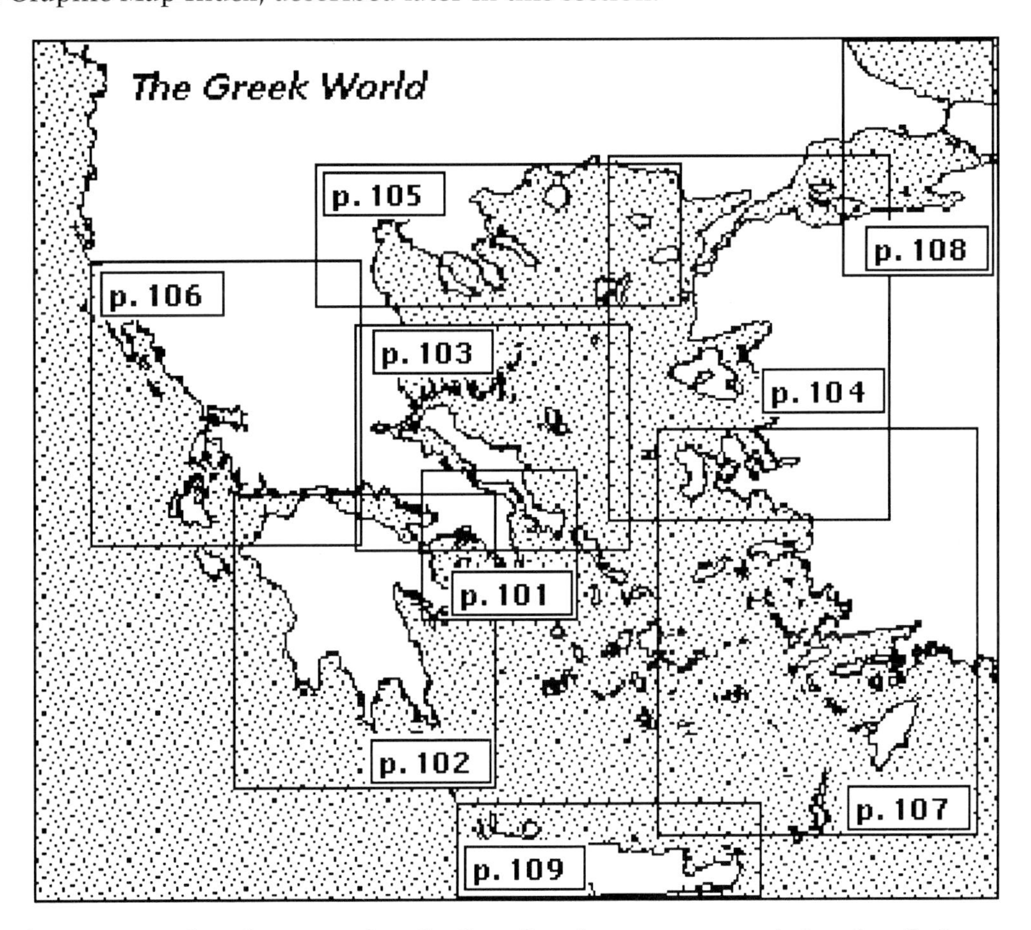

Figure 7.2 A key from a printed atlas, showing pages containing detailed maps

Use of a map key in a printed atlas is intuitive; you find the tile corresponding to the part of the world you want to see in detail, and then turn to the page indicated by the number in the corner of the appropriate tile. Similarly, each tile in the Perseus Graphic Map Index takes you to a detailed map, but instead of turning pages, you choose the desired item from a pop-up menu.

The following examples are arranged to show first how to display the various map themes, then how to use the specialized map tools.

➤ To enter the Perseus Atlas environment from the Gateway, click the Atlas icon. Or from anywhere in Perseus, choose Atlas from the Links menu. Your point of entry into the Atlas is the small outline map of the Greek world (figure 7.3).

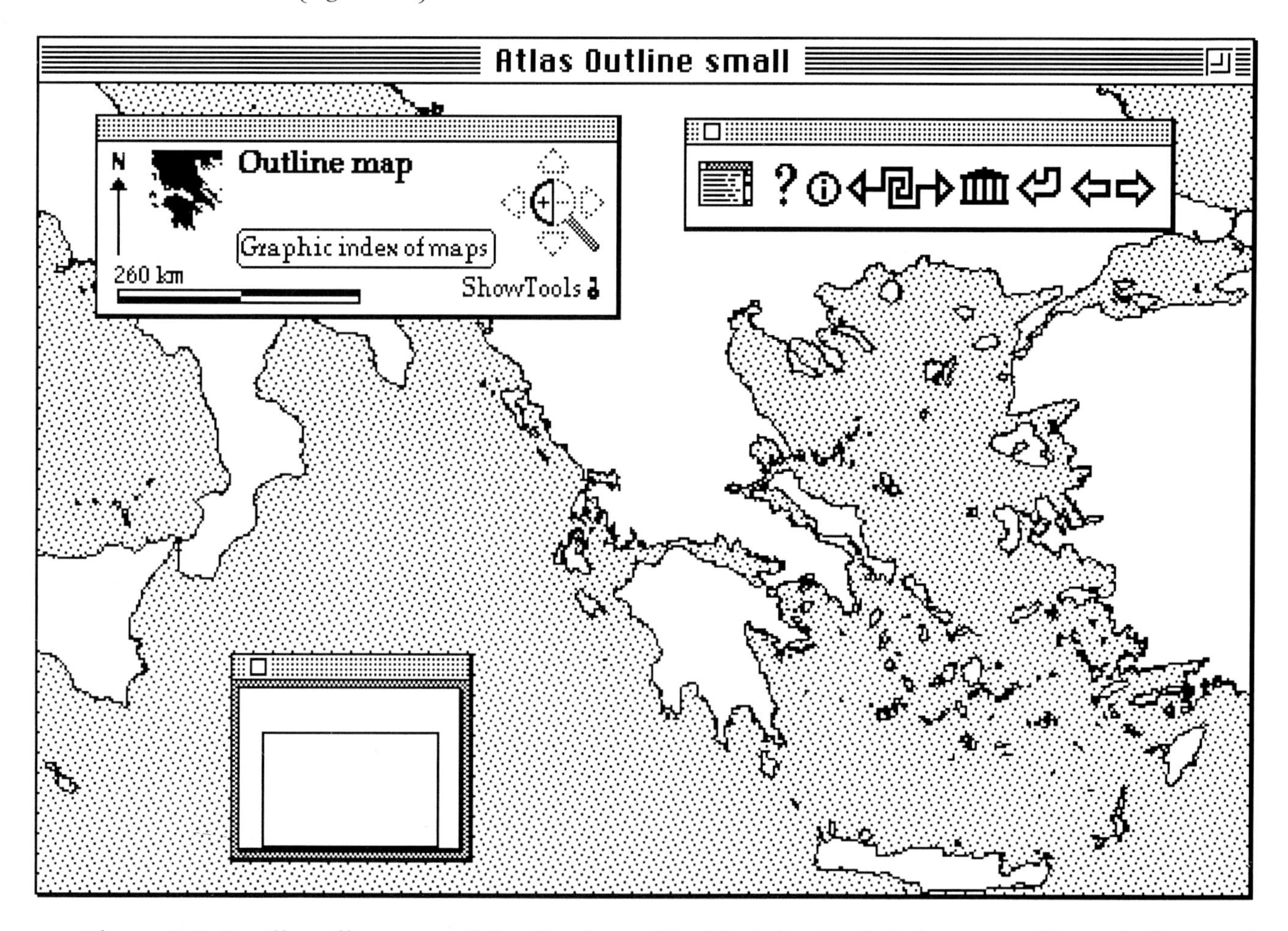

Figure 7.3 Small outline map of the Greek world with Atlas Tools Palette, scrolling window, and Navigator Palette

Notice that a new floating window appears, the Atlas Tools Palette (see figure 7.3), and that a new menu, Atlas, appears on the menu bar. On the Atlas Tools Palette is a magnifying glass, with plus and minus signs in the lens.

➤ To view the large outline map of the Greek world, click the plus sign on the magnifying glass icon. You can toggle from small to large outline maps by clicking the plus and minus signs.

Next you will go to the Graphic Map Indexes.

➤ From either the small or the large outline map of the Greek world, click the button "Graphic index of maps" on the Atlas Tools Palette. An outline map appears with active rectangles, or tiles, overlaid on it (figure 7.4). The title field of the Atlas Tools Palette now reads "Index of maps." Note that the tiles become highlighted as you move the mouse over them.

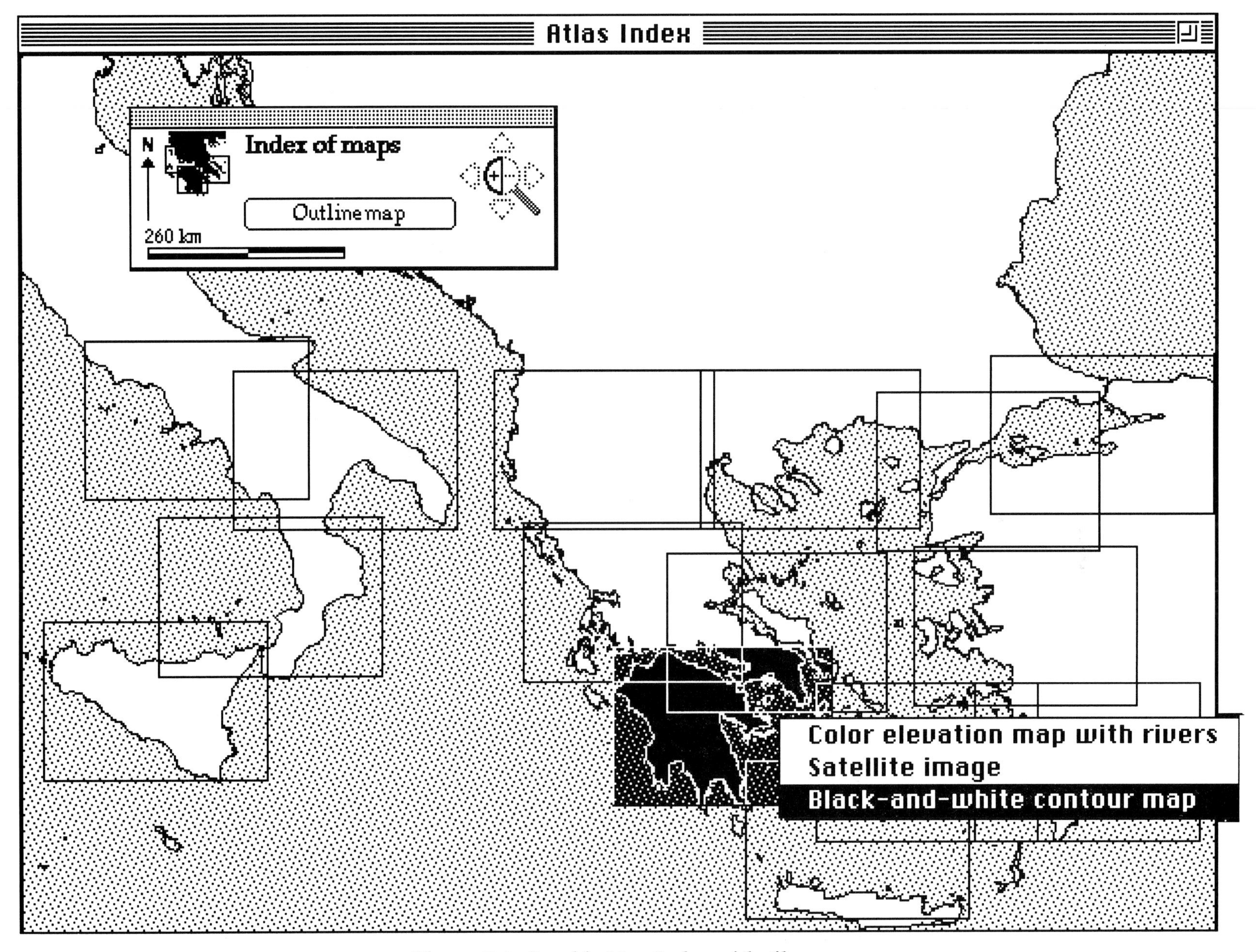

Figure 7.4 Graphic Map Index with tile pop-up menu

To go to the detailed maps, follow these steps:

➤ Move the mouse to the tile over the Attic peninsula (middle row, third from left). Hold the mouse down to bring up a pop-up menu. To see a detailed map, choose one of the pop-up menu items. The items available are "Color elevation map with rivers," "Satellite image," and "Black-and-white contour map." The interpretation of the satellite images and the color elevation maps is explained earlier, in section 7.1.3.

You can toggle between satellite image maps and color elevation maps by clicking the button on the Atlas Tools Palette. This action will preserve sites plotted on one of the color maps. To go to a black-and-white contour map, however, you must return to the Graphic Map Index. Any plotted sites will be lost unless you first save them by clicking the Search Saver icon on the Navigator Palette. To replot the sites, choose "Plot Sites in Search Saver" from the Atlas menu. To return to the Graphic Map Index, click the button "Graphic index of maps" on the Atlas Tools Palette (figure 7.5).

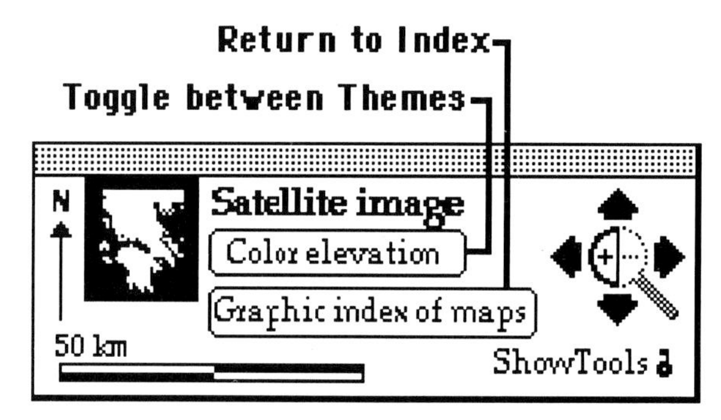

Figure 7.5 Toggle buttons on the Atlas Tools Palette

Note that some tiles do not have satellite image maps.

7.2.2 ATLAS TOOLS

The Atlas has unique tools for navigating among the themes, scales, and maps. The tool set consists of the Atlas Tools Palette, with its special tools, and the Atlas menu, which includes the Atlas Browser and the various customizing settings.

Atlas Tools Palette

The Atlas Tools Palette (figure 7.6) is a floating window that provides controls to navigate the Atlas. It also reports sites for the current map, their coordinates, and distance computation between sites (described later in this section).

The scale bar shows the distance taken up by one hundred pixels of the monitor's screen. The distance represented by the scale is shown above it in kilometers and changes depending on the scale of the map.

At the top of the Atlas Tools Palette is an information field that reports the theme of the map you are viewing, and below it is a button that links directly with the Graphic Map Index.

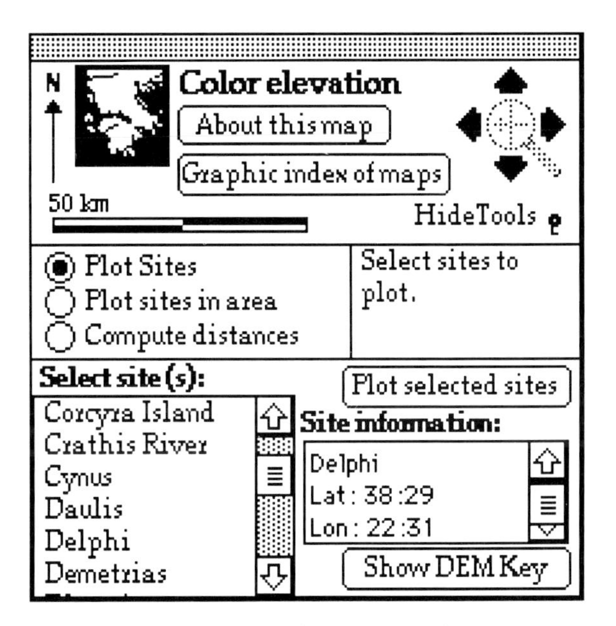

Figure 7.6 Atlas Tools Palette

The directional reference on the map is indicated by the arrow labeled "N" for north. This orientation is constant.

The small magnifying glass surrounded by directional arrows is a tool for moving among maps in the current theme. To change the scale of a map within a theme, click the plus sign (+) in the magnifying glass and you will zoom in to the next larger scale of the current map, if one is available. Click the minus sign (-) and you will zoom out to the next smaller scale of the current map, if one is available.

The detailed maps come in four scales: 500 meters per pixel, 250 meters per pixel, 125 meters per pixel, and 60 meters per pixel. A pixel is a dot on the monitor of your computer. Because monitors vary from workstation to workstation, the representation of a geographical distance will also vary.

You can readily get a sense of distance in the Atlas from the kilometer scale on the Atlas Tools Palette; its length is always 100 pixels, and the equivalent of 100 pixels in kilometers is displayed above the scale for each map.

Not every theme is available in each of the four scales. Satellite images are the only theme available in the 60-meters-per-pixel resolution.

To see the four map scales available from the Graphic Map Index, follow these steps.

➤ Enter the Graphic Map Index. There will be 15 tiles imposed on regions covered by detailed maps. By default the scale displayed is the smallest, 500 meters per pixel, shown on the title bar (and on Atlas Tools Palette) when the detailed map is displayed. The figure 260 km, which you see currently displayed on the Atlas Tools Palette, is the scale for the entire outline map.

➤ Increase the scale by clicking the plus sign of the magnifying glass icon on the Atlas Tools Palette. There will now be 56 tiles imposed on regions covered by detailed maps. Each tile represents a detailed map at a scale of 250 meters per pixel.

Note that each of the former tiles is now subdivided into four tiles, with the exception of the tile over the upper Bosphoros (250-meters-per-pixel resolution is not available for that region).

➤ Increase the scale to 125, then to 60, meters per pixel by clicking the plus sign of the magnifying glass icon. Note that the number of tiles on the Graphic Map Index again increases by a factor of four each time.

You can decrease the scale back to 125, 250, and 500 meters per pixel by clicking the minus sign on the magnifying glass.

To see detailed maps in the four available scales, perform the following steps. This example will use the satellite image theme and will zoom in on the Isthmus of Corinth.

Not all themes are available for each scale. The pop-up menu for each tile of the Graphic Map Index displays the themes available.

➤ From the Graphic Map Index at the scale of 500 meters per pixel, move the mouse to the tile over the Corinthiad (second row from top, third tile from left). Choose "Satellite image" from the pop-up menu. The satellite image will appear. The Isthmus of Corinth is the neck of land in the lower left quadrant connecting the Attic peninsula above with the Peloponnesus below.

➤ To zoom in to the 250-meters-per-pixel scale, click the plus sign on the magnifying glass icon on the Atlas Tools Palette. The cursor will now change to a magnifying glass. Now move the cursor over the Isthmus of Corinth and click it. The 250-meters-per-pixel satellite image will appear, with the Isthmus of Corinth in the lower right quadrant.

➤ Zoom in to 125 meters per pixel by clicking the Isthmus; click the Isthmus again to reach the 60-meters-per-pixel map.

You can decrease the scale by clicking the minus sign in the magnifying glass on the Atlas Tools Palette.

➤ Use the directional arrows on the Atlas Tools Palette to go to adjacent maps in the same theme.

Four arrows at 90-degree intervals surround the magnifying glass. These directional arrows, when clicked, move you to an adjacent map in the current scale (north, south, east, and west, respectively, for up, down, right, and left). By using the directional arrows, you can skip the step of returning to the index to see an adjacent map.

Show Tools/Hide Tools toggle

For the following examples, use the small outline map of the Greek world. If you are already inside the Atlas, click the button "Graphic index of maps" on the Atlas Tools Palette, then click the button "Outline map." Otherwise, from the Gateway, click the Atlas icon; from anywhere in Perseus, choose Atlas from the Links menu.

The Show Tools/Hide Tools toggle alternately shows and hides three additional map tools: "Plot Sites," "Plot sites in area," and "Compute distances." These tools appear in the interface as round buttons. When the map tools are showing, they are attached to the lower part of the Atlas Tools Palette.

➤ Click the Show Tools toggle on the Atlas Tools Palette.

The Palette will expand to show the three buttons that operate the tools (see figure 7.6).

Plot Sites

Maps in Perseus appear without political boundaries or other indications of human settlement. The Plot Sites tool allows you to plot sites on a map by selecting sites from the scrolling field "Select sites," in the lower left. The "Select site" list shows in alphabetical order the sites that can be plotted on the current map. The list of sites ranges from more than 2000 sites that can be plotted on the large-scale lon-lat map to 2 or 3 sites on some detailed maps of sparsely populated areas.

In the following example, you will plot the site of Delphi.

➤ Make sure that the Atlas Tools Palette is toggled to Show Tools, and click the button Plot Sites.

The scroll bar at the right side of the "Select sites" list provides a quick way to move through the list. (Remember that you can drag the scroll indicator up or down to move quickly in a list, rather than moving line by line.)

➤ Click Delphi in the "Select site" list, then click the button "Plot selected sites." The site is marked with a dot; the site name may be dragged to another location on the map. You may need to drag the Atlas Tools Palette out of the way in order to see the plotted sites.

If you want to plot a number of sites, either shift-click (click while holding down the Shift key) to select a continuous range of sites, or command-click (click while holding down the Command key) to select a discontinuous range of sites. When your selection is ready, click the button "Plot selected sites."

As many as 50 sites may be displayed at one time.

The site coordinates appear in the scrolling field on the right and are given either in lon-lat degrees or in UTM (explained in the "Settings" portion of section 7.2.3).

Plot sites in area

This feature plots all known sites within a rectangular region that you define.

In the next example, you will define an area in Thrace for the Atlas to plot sites.

> If you receive the error message "Not enough memory to use printing tools," you will need to increase the amount of RAM allotted to the Perseus Player. See section 7.4, "The Atlas and Memory Issues."

➤ If you have been following the previous example, first clear old sites from the map by choosing "Clear plotted sites on this map" from the Atlas menu. Be sure that the Atlas Tools Palette is toggled to Show Tools.

➤ Click the button "Plot sites in area."

Three changes now take place in the Atlas Tools Palette: the scrolling field in the lower left becomes "Sites in this area"; a new array of buttons appears in the lower right; and a message appears to the right of the radio buttons prompting you to click the button "Define area" (figure 7.7).

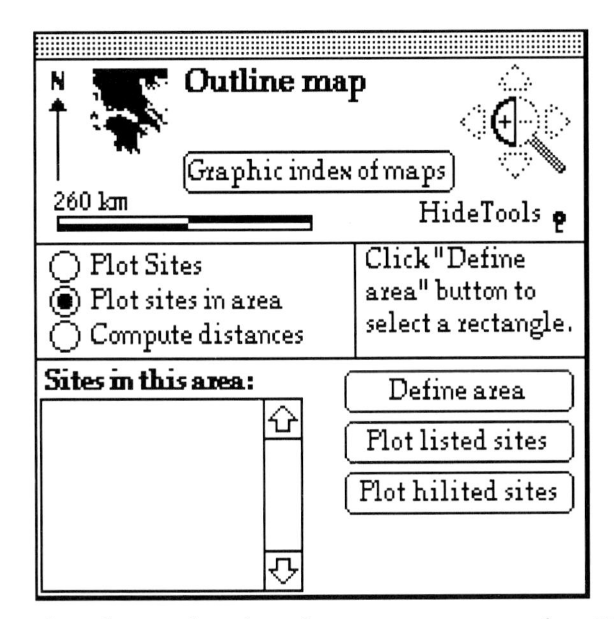

Figure 7.7 Atlas Tools Palette, showing changes accompanying "Plot sites in area"

➤ Click the button "Define area." You will now receive the prompt "Click and drag on map to define an area."

For this exercise, a sparsely populated region was chosen because on a small-scale map the plotted sites tend to get overcrowded. For best results, therefore, use the "Plot sites in area" feature on a large-scale map, and be careful not to choose too big or too densely populated an area, because the maximum number of sites that the Atlas can plot is 50.

➤ Select approximately the area shown in figure 7.8.

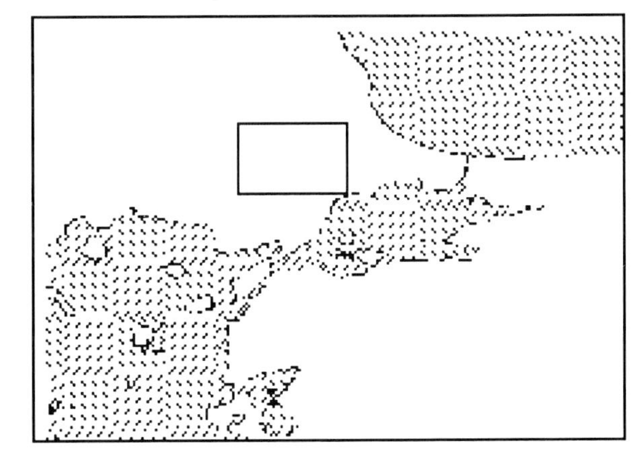

Figure 7.8 Thrace with area selected

When you release the mouse button, the "Sites in this area" field, in the lower left, lists the sites in the area (figure 7.9).

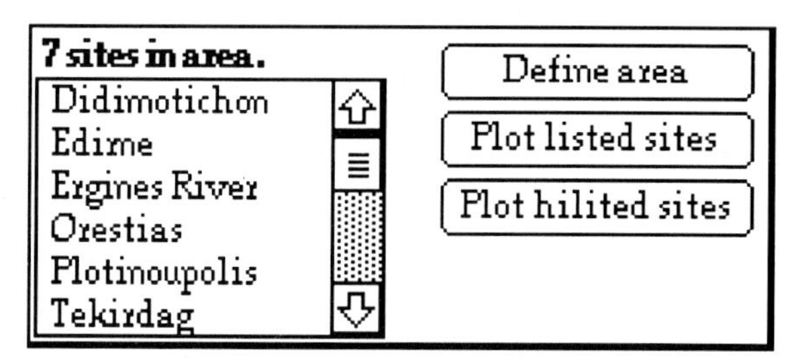

Figure 7.9 Sites in the area around Thrace

➤ To plot the entire list of sites, click "Plot listed sites." To plot a particular site, click a site on the list, then click "Plot hilited sites."

> KNOWN BUG: You cannot use the scroll bar in the "Sites in area" field, although you can scroll down the list of sites by holding down the mouse button in the top or bottom of the field itself.

Compute distances

This feature allows you to compute the distance in straight lines between two or more points on a map. It is available on both the black-and-white and the color maps.

In the following example, you will compute the distance of the paraplous from Iapygeum to Syracuse, via Kroton, Locri, and Rhegion.

➤ From the small outline map, plot the sites Iapygeum, Kroton, Locri, Rhegion, and Syracuse according to the instructions above (figure 7.10).

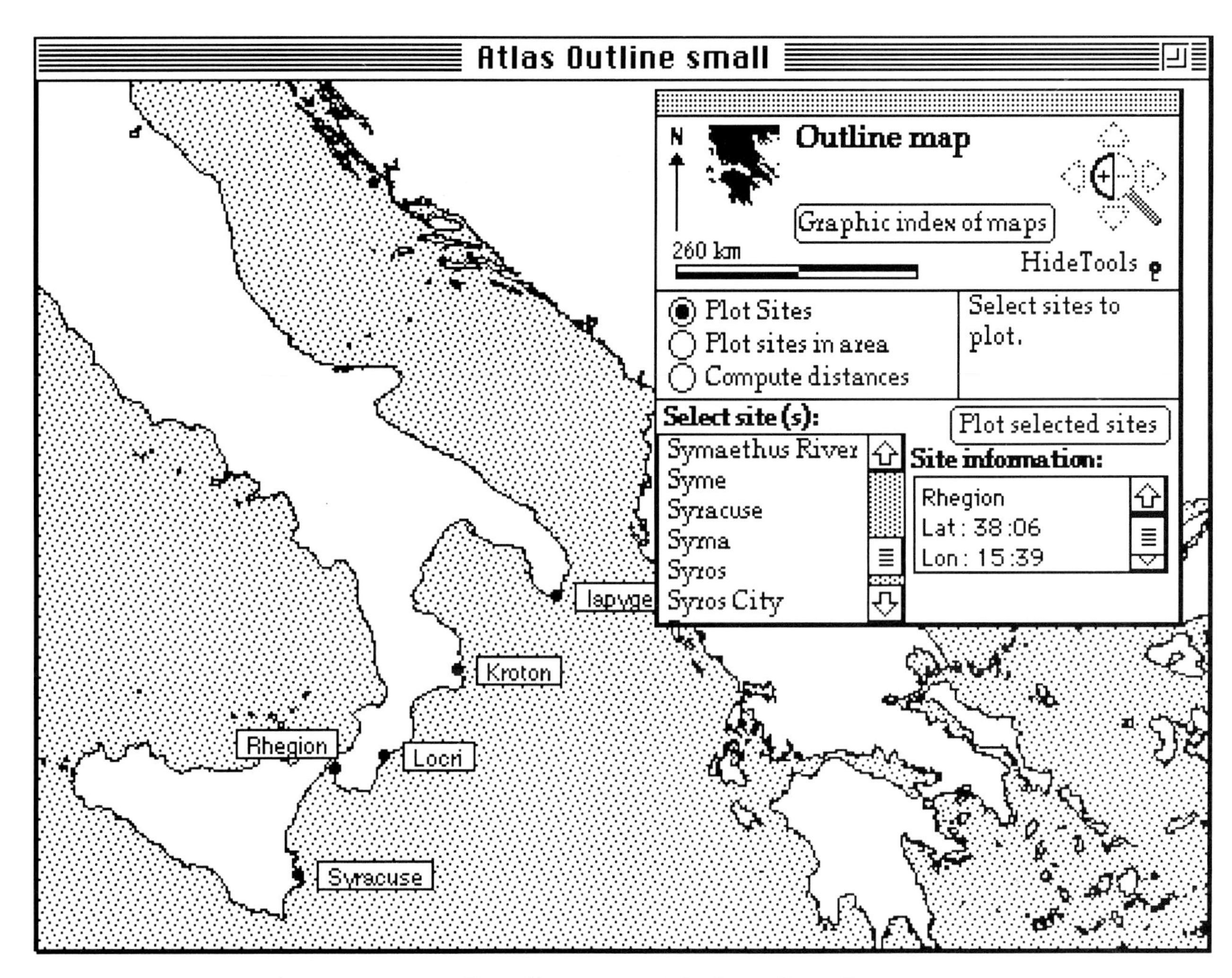

Figure 7.10 Small outline map with sites plotted

➤ Click the button "Compute distances."

Three changes now take place in the Atlas Tools Palette: the scrolling field in the lower left becomes "Travel log," a new array of buttons appears in the lower right, and a message appears to the right of the buttons prompting you to click the button "Start route" (figure 7.11).

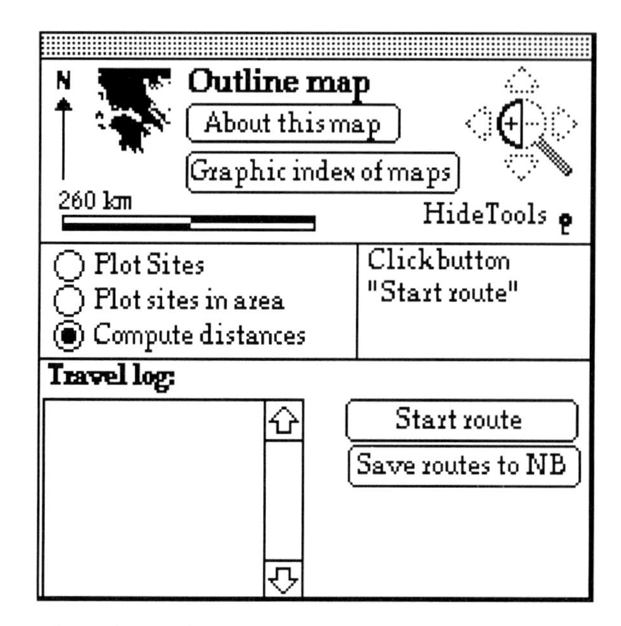

Figure 7.11 Atlas Tools Palette showing changes accompanying "Compute distances"

When you click "Start route," you are enabling a distance computation feature that measures the distance along a series of points. These points are wherever you click the mouse, whether plotted sites or white space.

If you receive the error message "Not enough memory to use printing tools," you will need to increase the amount of RAM allotted to the Perseus Player. See section 7.4, "The Atlas and Memory Issues."

➤ Click "Start route." The first point you click on the map will be the starting point. Click the site of Iapygeum; it is now marked with an X.

➤ Now click the site of Kroton, and the new leg will be connected with a straight line. Repeat for each site along the journey, making a dogleg around the toe of Italy, until you are ready to end the route.

A running total showing the distance of each leg of the journey appears in the field in the middle right.

➤ When you have reached Syracuse, click the button "Stop route" to end the trip. The total distance, in this case 437 km, is computed for each trip in the "Travel log" field, on the left (figure 7.12).

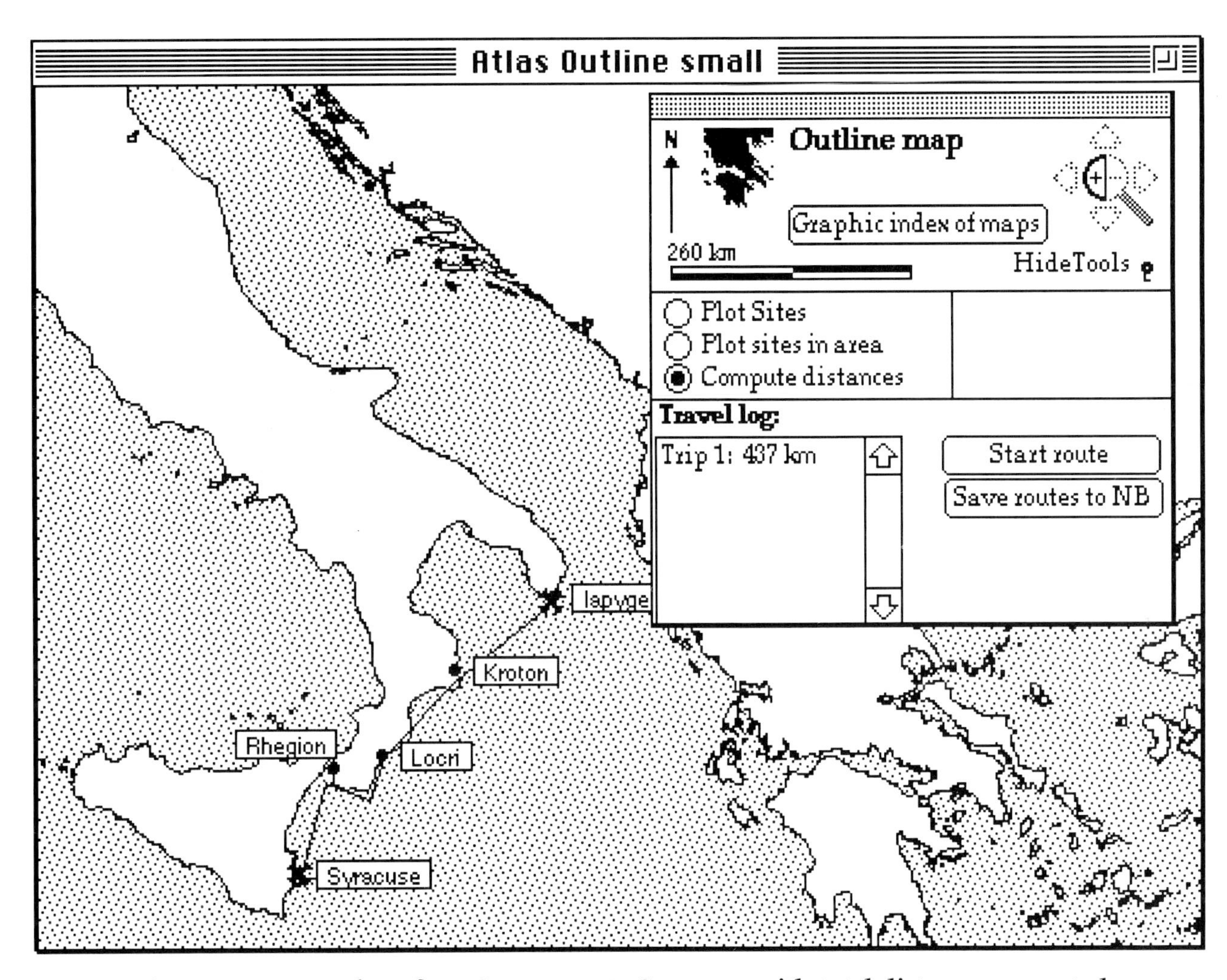

Figure 7.12 Paraplous from Iapygeum to Syracuse, with total distance computed

You can compute the distance of a journey with any number of legs, limited only by the amount of available memory.

➤ Save the results in your Travel Log to a Perseus Notebook page by clicking the button "Save routes to NB." For information about Notebooks, see section 10.3.

NOTE: If the distance computation feature is enabled, you cannot interrupt it to choose a map from a map index or plot sites from the site list.

Show DEM Key

This feature appears in the Atlas Tools Palette with the color elevation (color topography and hydrography) maps. The Digital Elevation Model (DEM) Key shows the range of colors used in these maps and their associated values of elevation. Click the button Show DEM Key, in the lower right, to show a floating window with a color bar corresponding to elevations in the color elevation maps. Click the close button on the DEM Key to hide it.

7.2.3 ATLAS MENU

The Atlas menu has six items, which become active or inactive depending on the part of the Atlas you are using. Menu items that are shown in light gray type are inactive, while those shown in black type are active.

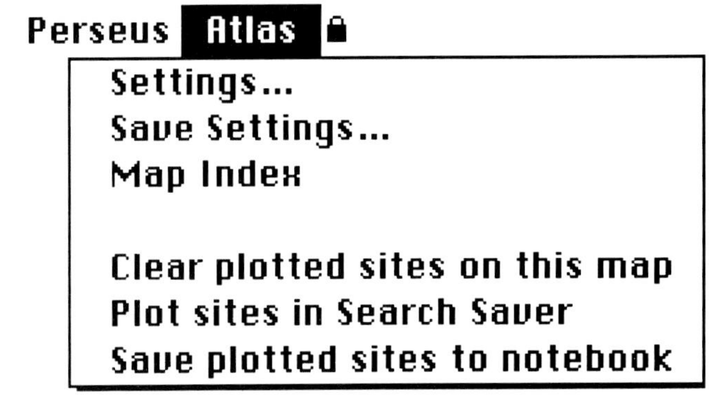

Figure 7.13 Atlas menu

Settings

Choose Settings from the Atlas menu to customize the environment of the Perseus Atlas. A dialog window with Current Atlas Settings appears (figure 7.14).

There are four map display options. The "Show site names" box is turned on (indicated with an X) by default. This instructs Perseus to display the name of the selected site. To make the site names disappear, click the "Show site names" box to erase the X. A dot will remain on the map, indicating the location of the plotted site.

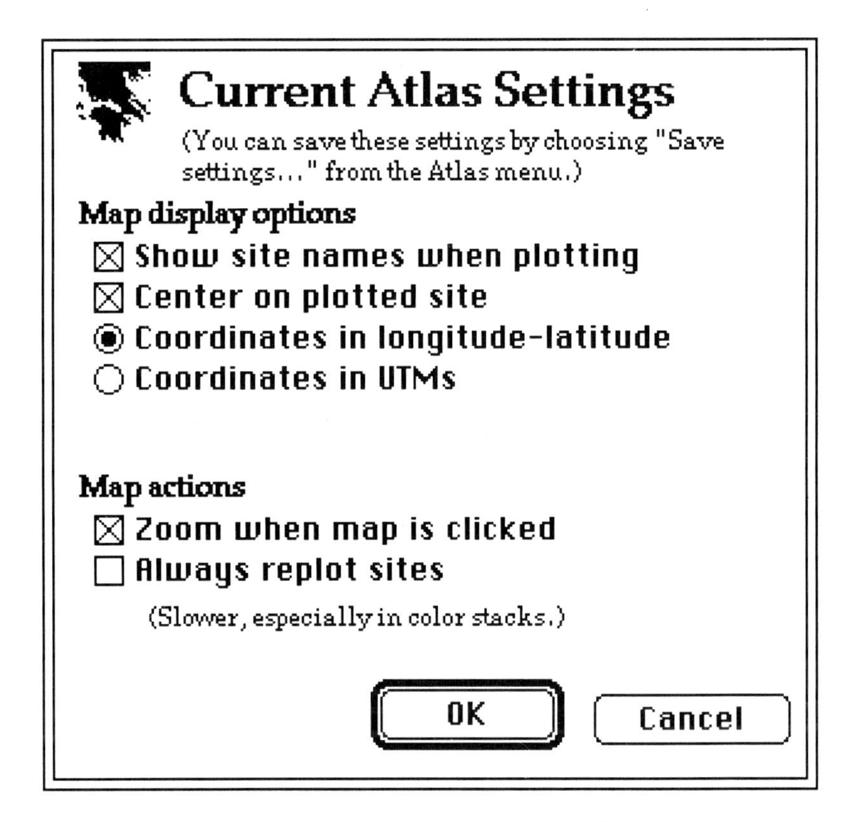

Figure 7.14 Atlas Settings options

Click the "Center on plotted site" box to make Perseus center the Atlas around a site that is off-screen. This feature applies to black-and-white maps only.

Click the "Coordinates in longitude-latitude" button to display site coordinates in degrees of latitude and longitude in the "Site information" field on the Atlas Tools Palette. Alternately, click the "Coordinates in UTMs" button to display the site location in Universal Transverse Mercator coordinates.

There are two options concerning map actions. With the "Zoom when map is clicked" box selected, you can zoom in on a map by clicking it.

The "Always replot sites" feature saves sites you have plotted while you go to another stack in Perseus. The sites will not be saved after you quit Perseus, however. Note also that this option will slow down the operation of Perseus.

Save Settings

You can save your Atlas Settings for the next Perseus session by choosing Save Settings from the Atlas menu, and selecting the desired settings as described in the previous section.

Map Index (By Site and By Region)

This tool finds all maps in Perseus containing a given site, and then goes to the desired map. It also plots all sites in the Perseus database associated with a given region. Choose Map Index from the Atlas menu to go to it.

Map Index (By Site)

To plot a site, choose Site from the pop-up menu Index Type, in the upper right (figure 7.15). Type the name of the site you wish to locate in the field "Look for" and click Do Search. Or click the site in the scrolling field, in the lower left.

Figure 7.15 shows the results of an inquiry for Phaleron. Select a theme at the right to go to that map.

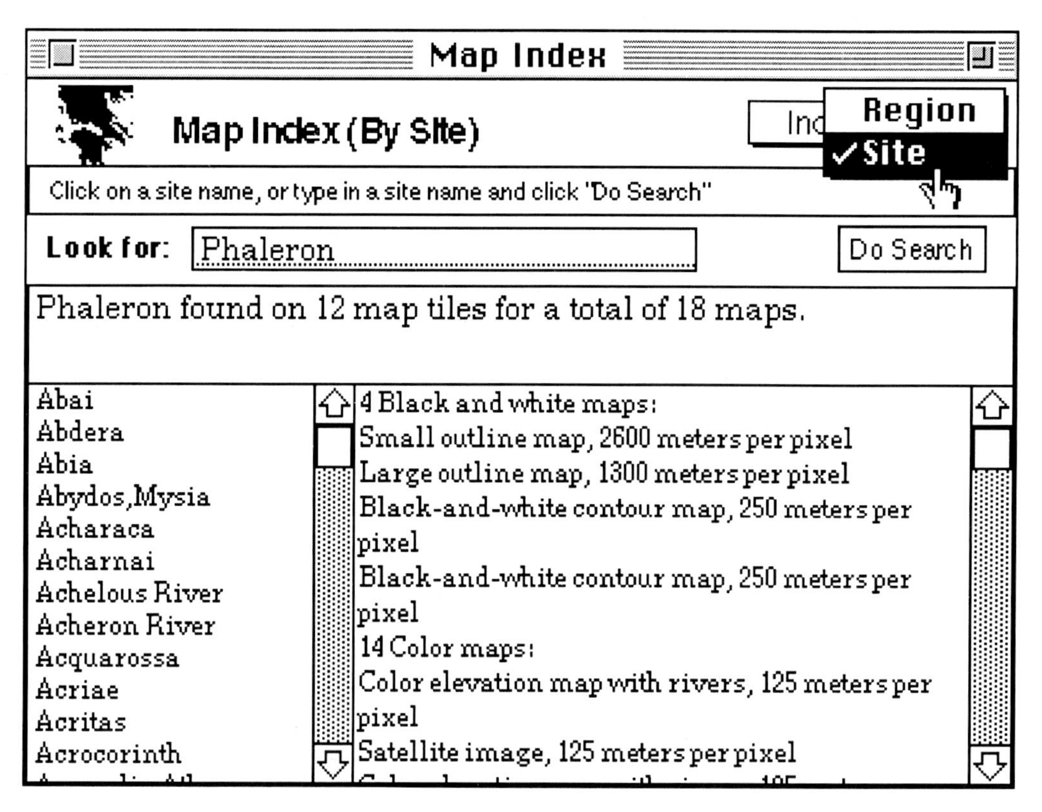

Figure 7.15 Map Index (By Site)

Map Index (By Region)

To plot sites in a region of the Greek world, choose Region from the pop-up menu Index Type, in the upper right. In the field "Look for," type the name of the region you wish to locate, and click Do Search. Or click a region from the scrolling field, in the lower left. On the right, Perseus will give you a choice of the small or large outline map. Click either one, and Perseus will plot the sites in the desired region without showing site names.

To show the site names for a plotted region, choose the option "Show site names when plotting" from the Atlas Settings.

Clear plotted sites on this map

This feature clears the current map of all plotted sites.

Plot sites in Search Saver

This feature plots a list of the sites that you have stored in the Perseus Search Saver. For information about the Search Saver, see section 5.4.

To plot the mint locations for coins in Perseus from the Archaic period, follow these steps.

➤ Get a list of mint locations by making a Browser search (the Browser is described thoroughly in section 5.1). In the Browser, click the button Coins and choose the Search topic Period from the pop-up menu in the top center. The pop-up menu now reads "Period is." Further refine your search by clicking Archaic. Set the left column of results to Mint (figure 7.16). Put your results into the Search Saver by clicking its icon on the Navigator Palette.

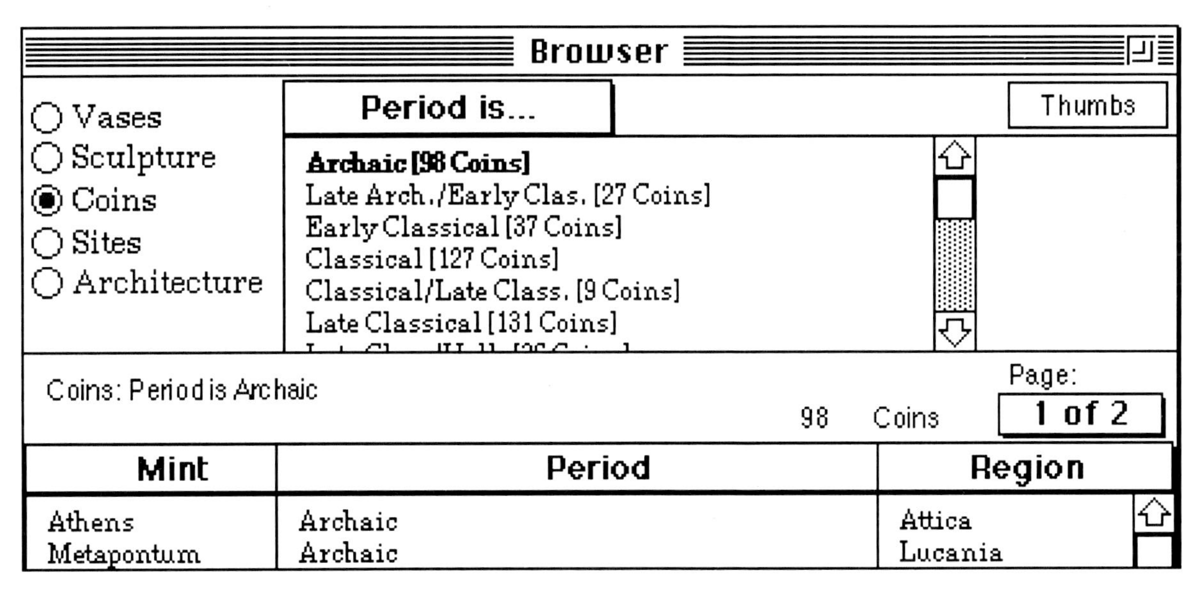

Figure 7.16 Browser search for coins of the Archaic period by mint

➤ Now bring up the small outline map by choosing Atlas from the Links menu. Choose "Plot sites in Search Saver" from the Atlas menu. Note where the sites are concentrated.

Because not all sites in the Browser are included in the Atlas database, some sites in the Search Saver may not be plotted.

Save plotted sites to notebook

This feature stores a list of sites you have plotted on a map in a Notebook card. Notebook cards can be used to keep data from session to session. To go to a site saved in the Notebook, highlight it, then choose Atlas from the Links menu. Perseus will plot this site for you in the small outline map.

7.2.4 SCROLL WINDOW

The scroll window is a floating window with a rectangle inside it. The rectangle represents the screen size of the current HyperCard stack. This tool is useful when the size of a window, such as the black-and-white line drawings in the Atlas, is larger than the current monitor size. When you place the pointer in the center of the rectangle, it changes to a hand icon. By dragging the rectangle within the constraints of the floating window, you can see the other parts of the card that were previously off the screen. You can also drag the sides of the rectangle to make the current stack wider or narrower, and you can drag the top or bottom of the rectangle to make the current stack taller or shorter.

If you need to see the scroll window in order to move around the Graphic Map Index or another black-and-white map, choose Scroll from the Go menu, or press Command-e. Press Command-e again to make the scroll window disappear. More detailed instructions for using the scroll window are presented in section 4.1.3.

7.3 BLACK-AND-WHITE ATLAS FEATURES

The Atlas uses black-and-white drawings to provide an overall glance at the geography of the Greek world and to serve as indexes to color maps.

7.3.1 OUTLINE MAPS

The small and large outline maps enclose the coastline of the Greek world, from Sicily to Western Asia Minor, and from Campania to Crete, in a black-and-white line drawing. The site list has approximately 1600 entries, which can be plotted on the outline map.

The small outline map is the default selection when you open the Atlas. Plotting sites on it is a fast way to locate sites in their geographical context.

When you are viewing the small and large outline maps, you can plot sites, plot sites within a region that you define, and compute distances between points.

7.3.2 BLACK-AND-WHITE CONTOUR MAPS

The black-and-white contour (topography) maps are offered in one scale, 250 meters per pixel. Each one shows a region approximately the size of Sicily or the Peloponnese. Lines represent topographic contours at an interval of 1000 feet.

The black-and-white topography maps cover 15 regions of roughly 200 by 300 kilometers each:

Campania
Apulia
Bruttium (Calabria)
Sicily
Epirus (Albania/Illyria)
NW Greece (Acarnania, Phocis, Aetolia, and so on)
SE Greece (Attica, Boeotia, Euboea, Thessaly, and so on)
Peloponnese, including Attica
Cyclades
Macedonia/Thrace
Marmara Sea
Troad
Ionia/Lydia
Caria/Lycia
Crete

This same division of regions is also used for the color maps.

The black-and-white contour maps are available from the Graphic Map Index only when it is set at the 260-km scale. To see a topography map, choose "Black-and-white contour map" from one of the pop-up tiles on the Graphic Map Index. To return to the Index, click "Graphic index of maps" on the Atlas Tools Navigator. To move to an adjacent topography map to the north, south, east, or west, click the directional arrows around the magnifying glass icon.

When you are viewing a topography map, you can plot sites, plot sites within a region, and compute distances between points.

7.4 THE ATLAS AND MEMORY ISSUES

Your ability to use the full features of the Atlas depends on the amount of random-access memory (RAM) in your computer and the memory partition allocated to HyperCard. Color images and color windows require more memory than textual resources and black-and-white graphics. With a color-intensive resource such as the Atlas, more RAM and a fast computer will enhance performance.

Every Macintosh with 5 MB of RAM allotted to the Perseus Player can run the basic Atlas, meaning the color and black-and-white Atlas features, although it is preferable to have at least 8 MB of RAM.

The "Compute distances" feature uses memory quickly, and users with less than 3 MB of RAM who try to compute distances will get an error message, "Not enough memory to use the Painting Tools." Consult section 2.6.2 for directions on how to increase the amount of RAM allotted to the Perseus Player.

Black-and-white outline maps are part of a HyperCard stack. Color maps are drawn on the screen in a separate window. You can click another window to bring that window to the foreground, leaving the color map in the background. When you are finished with the Atlas, you must close the color map window by clicking the close box in the upper left corner. To avoid memory shortages, however, close all color windows when you no longer need them.

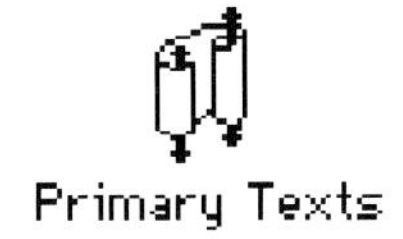

The Primary Texts resource contains works by these ancient Greek authors:

Aeschines	Diodorus Siculus	Lysias
Aeschylus	Euripides	Pausanias
Andocides	Herodotus	Pindar
Antiphon	Hesiod	Plato
Apollodorus	Homer	Plutarch
Aristophanes	Homeric Hymns	Pseudo-Xenophon
Aristotle	Hyperides	Sophocles
Bacchylides	Isaeus	Strabo
Demades	Isocrates	Thucydides
Demosthenes	Lycurgus	Xenophon
Dinarchus		

Perseus 2.0 contains selections from the works of Aristotle, Diodorus Siculus, Strabo, and Plutarch. The works of other authors are complete, but fragmentary texts are not included in this version, except in the cases of Bacchylides, the Homeric Hymns, and Hyperides.

Each Primary Text has an English translation. In many cases, the texts are accompanied by notes. Notes from the Loeb editions are given for Aeschines, Aeschylus, Andocides, Antiphon, Demades, Demosthenes, Dinarchus, Diodorus, Herodotus, Hesiod, Hyperides, Isaeus, Isocrates, Lycurgus, Lysias, Pausanias, Plato, Plutarch, Pseudo-Xenophon, and Xenophon. Although some notes are attached to the Greek text (Plato, *Symposium*, and Sophocles, *Oedipus Tyrannus*), most notes are on the English translation. Aristophanes' *Clouds, Lysistrata,* and *Acharnians* have English translations and accompanying notes by Jeffrey Henderson. Several plays by Euripides were translated and annotated by David Kovacs: *Andromache, Cyclops, Heraclides, Hippolytus,* and *Medea.* The Pindar and Bacchylides translations, both by Diane Svarlien, include her notes. Other notes are those prepared for the Loeb series by J. G. Frazer (Apollodorus), W. H. Fyfe (Aristotle, *Poetics*), J. H. Freese (Aristotle, *Rhetoric*), H. Tredennick (Aristotle, *Metaphysics*), Oldfather, Sherman, and Welles (Diodorus Siculus), and H. L. Jones (Strabo).

Primary Texts are accessible from the Primary Text Index, which is reached from the Gateway or the Links menu. Texts can also be reached from the Lookup tool (see section 4.5.1).

8.1 PRIMARY TEXTS INDEX

To go to the Primary Texts Index from the Gateway, click the Primary Texts icon. Or, from anywhere in Perseus, choose Primary Texts from the Links Menu.

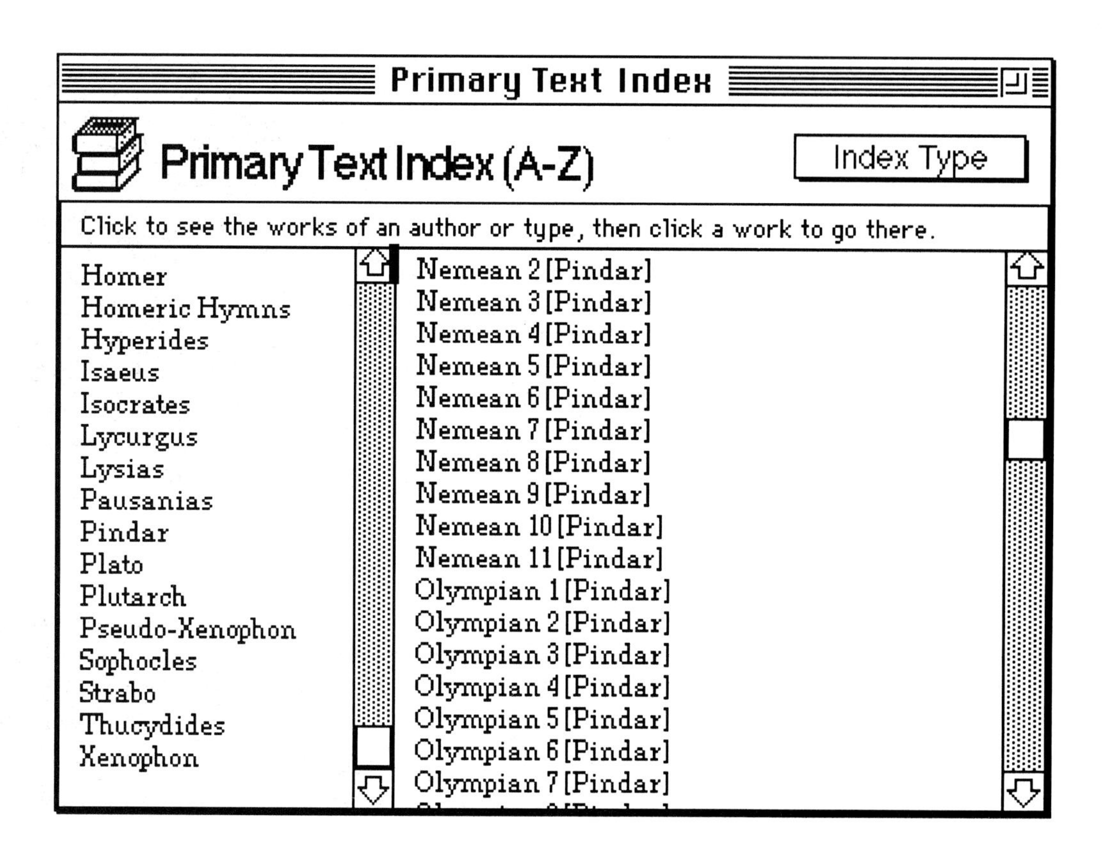

Figure 8.1 Primary Text Index, shown alphabetically by author

Choose an index from the pop-up menu Index Type. Primary Texts are indexed in the following four ways: alphabetically by author, by form (dactylic hexameter, drama, lyric meter, and prose), by genre (biography, comedy, and so on) and chronologically by date of the work. When alphabetical sort is invoked, an alphabetical list of authors appears. When an author is selected, a list of that author's works appears on the right (figure 8.1).

The following illustration of Primary Text features will use as an example the First Olympian of Pindar.

➤ From the Primary Text Index (shown alphabetically by author) scroll down and click Pindar.

A list of that author's works appears. In figure 8.1, Pindar has been selected, and the available works of Pindar appear in the list on the right.

➤ To select a work, click its title. In this case, click Olympian 1.

A text card appears, displaying the beginning of the work.

8.2 PRIMARY TEXTS DISPLAY

The default display of a Primary Text is in two columns, Greek on the left and the translation on the right. Figure 8.2 shows an example of a Primary Text display.

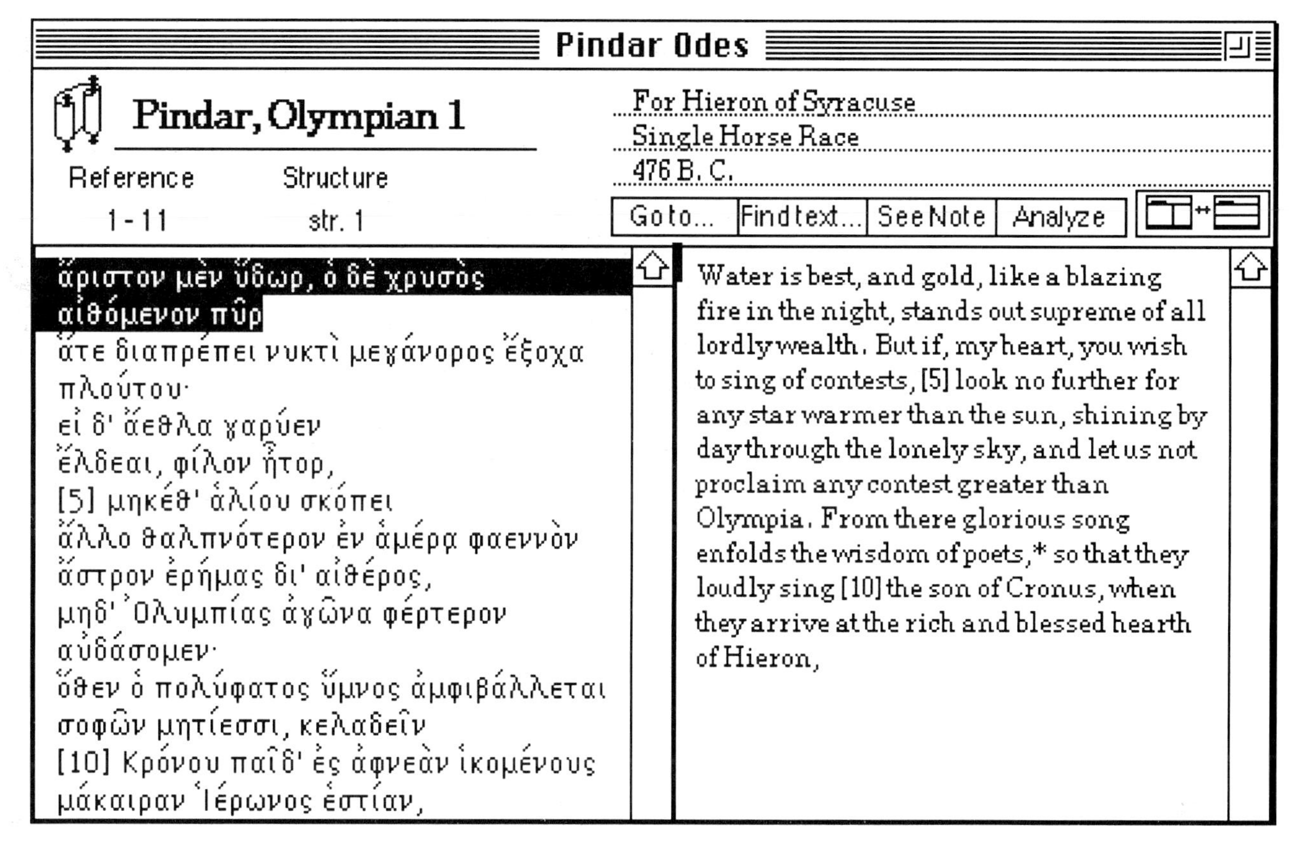

Figure 8.2 Primary Text display

Several utilities are displayed on the Primary Text card, and a Text menu also appears when a Primary Text is displayed. These features are described in the following sections.

8.2.1 TITLE

The title of the work appears at the top of each Primary Text card. Additional title information is displayed in the upper right, if appropriate.

8.2.2 TEXT REFERENCE

The chapter and section or line reference in the current work is shown at the left of the utility bar.

8.2.3 METER OR STRUCTURE

If the current text is in verse, metrical or strophe information is shown in the area next to the text reference.

Note that the structure of the First Olympian is given, with current strophe, epode, and antistrophe appearing in this area. An entire structural unit has been made to fit on one text card whenever practical.

If the text is a forensic speech, this area may display information about its structure. If the text is a prose work, nothing appears in this location.

8.2.4 UTILITY BAR

The utility bar has five buttons that allow you to access the text, analyze it, and modify the text interface (figure 8.3).

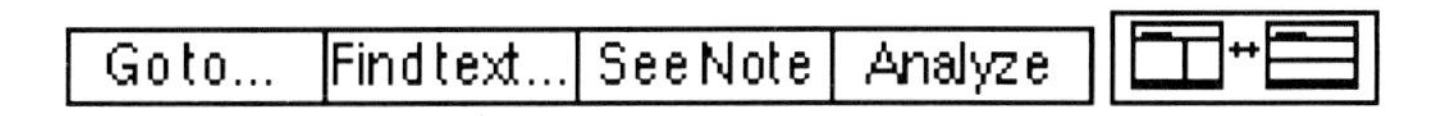

Figure 8.3 Utility bar

Go to...

This utility allows you to go to a specific reference in the current text. The location is identified by chapter and section or by line, depending on the canonical reference system for the work. The title of the current work is shown at the top of each Primary Text display.

You may use the "Go to" feature to move to different references within the current work. You may also use "Go to" to move around in works of such authors as Herodotus and Homer, whose many books are located on several stacks. You cannot use the "Go to" feature to move to a location in a different work when that work is in a different stack, however, nor can you use it to go to a work by a different author.

➤ Go to another line in the First Olympian.

When you click "Go to," a dialog box appears for you to type in the chapter and section or line that you want to see (figure 8.4). Click the Go button to see the passage you selected. (Or simply press Return.)

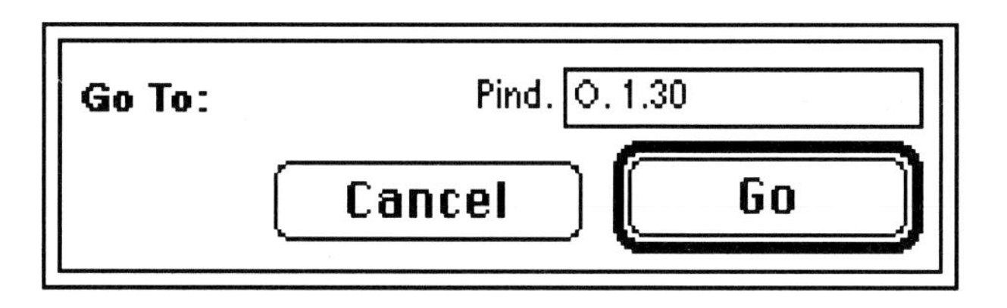

Figure 8.4 Using the "Go to" feature

The syntax for entering chapter, section, and line numbers varies depending on the canonical reference system for the work. For example, to use the "Go to" feature in Herodotus, type 3.2.1 to go to Book 3, chapter 2, section 1. If you wish, simply type 3 (with no section or line number) to go to the beginning of Book 3. To take another example, if you are in the text of *The Libation Bearers* by Aeschylus, type 45 in the Go To box to go to line 45.

Note that the Go To dialog box shows the canonical abbreviation for this author and work that is required by the Lookup tool when you use it as a shortcut. Canonical abbreviations are found in Online Help under the topic "Canonical Abbreviations for Primary Texts."

When you bring up the Go To dialog box, it contains your current location in the text expressed as a canonical reference, that is, in the correct syntax for Perseus to look up the passage.

You cannot go to the text of another author using the "Go to" feature. Use the Lookup tool in the Links menu to go directly to another text reference.

Find text...

"Find text" allows you to search for a phrase, a word, or part of a word in the current work. You can search for Greek or English text. This search utility is limited to the work of the author you have selected. The Browser and the Philological Tools provide more complex search utilities.

When you click "Find text," a dialog box appears for you to enter the text that you want to find. The dialog box also has a pop-up menu allowing you to search for either Greek or English text (figure 8.5).

In the following example, you will find other instances of words beginning with χρυσ- in Pindar's First Olympian.

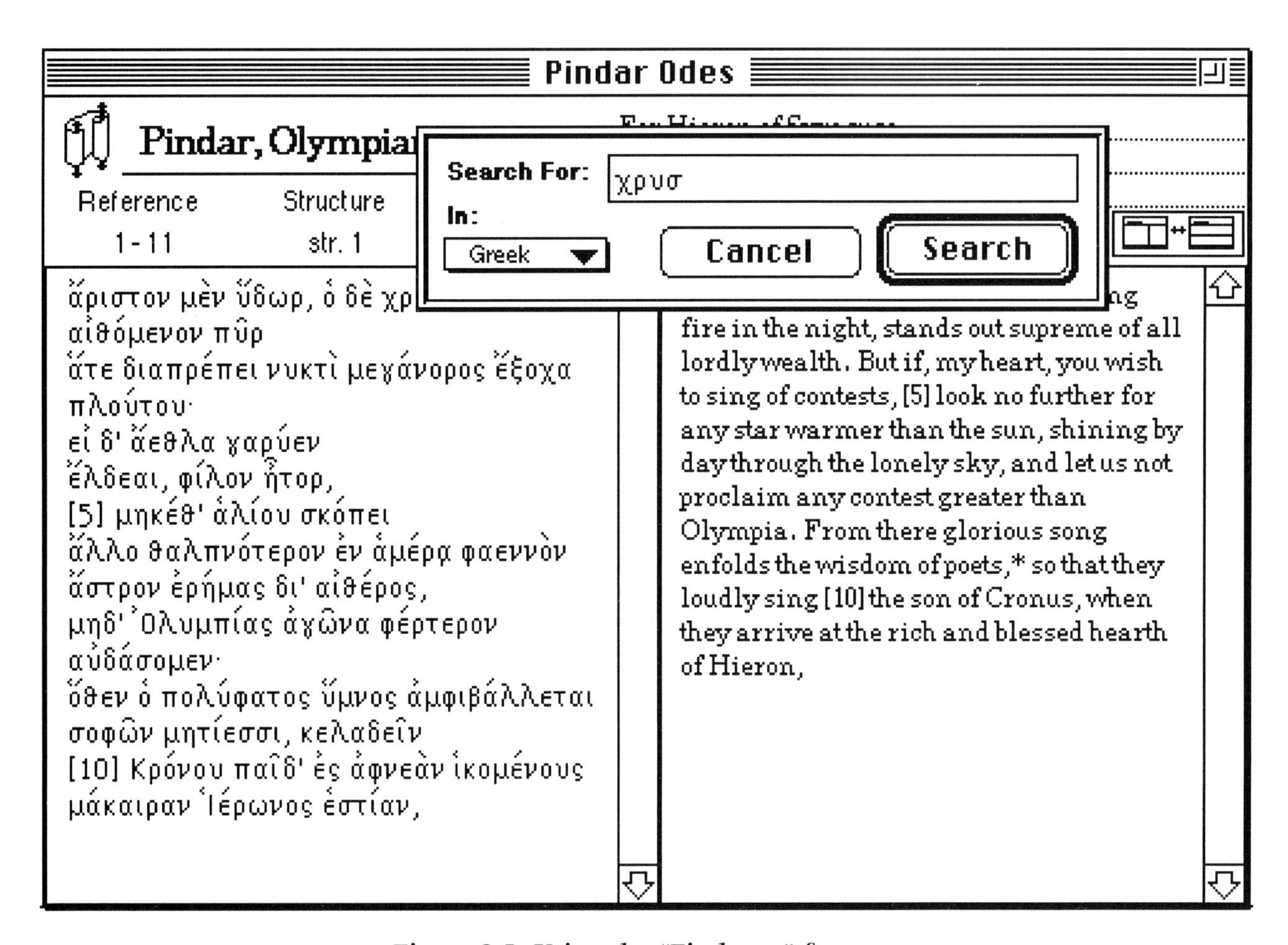

Figure 8.5 Using the "Find text" feature

➤ Highlight χρυσ from χρυσός in line 1 of the First Olympian. Click the button "Find text." A dialog window appears with χρυσ in the Search For box. Click Search. The next occurrence of the text string is highlighted in the Primary Text display. (Strings are discussed in section 8.4.1.) Click "Find text" again to repeat the search.

> To type accented Greek into the Search For box, you must have GreekKeys 7.0 installed in your system. See "A note on typing Greek" in section 8.4.1.

To search for an English word or string of letters, choose English from the pop-up menu in the lower left. Type the desired string into the Search For box and click Search.

> NOTE: Usual Macintosh procedure is to double-click the mouse to select a word. The accents do not allow this action in the Greek font, however. You must highlight a whole Greek word, instead of double-clicking it.

When all occurrences of the word or string in this work have been found and the search cycle begins to repeat itself, a dialog box informs you that the first piece of text has been found again.

For more powerful searches, use the Greek Word Search to look for all instances of a Greek word in Primary Texts. Use the English Index to look for instances of an English word.

See Note

Almost all the texts are accompanied by notes on the translation. (Notes based on the Greek text are discussed later in this section.) The notes vary in their scope and length and are indicated by asterisks in the text.

➤ To go to Svarlien's note on lines 8-11 of Pindar's First Olympian, select the asterisk following the line "enfolds the wisdom of poets" in the English text. Click the button See Note. The note appears in a new window. To display the Notes window and the text window simultaneously, hold down the shift key when you click See Note (figure 8.6).You can page through the notes using the right and left arrows on the Navigator Palette. Click "See Note in Text" to return to the annotated passage. If the Notes window is still visible, you can close it by clicking the box in the upper left.

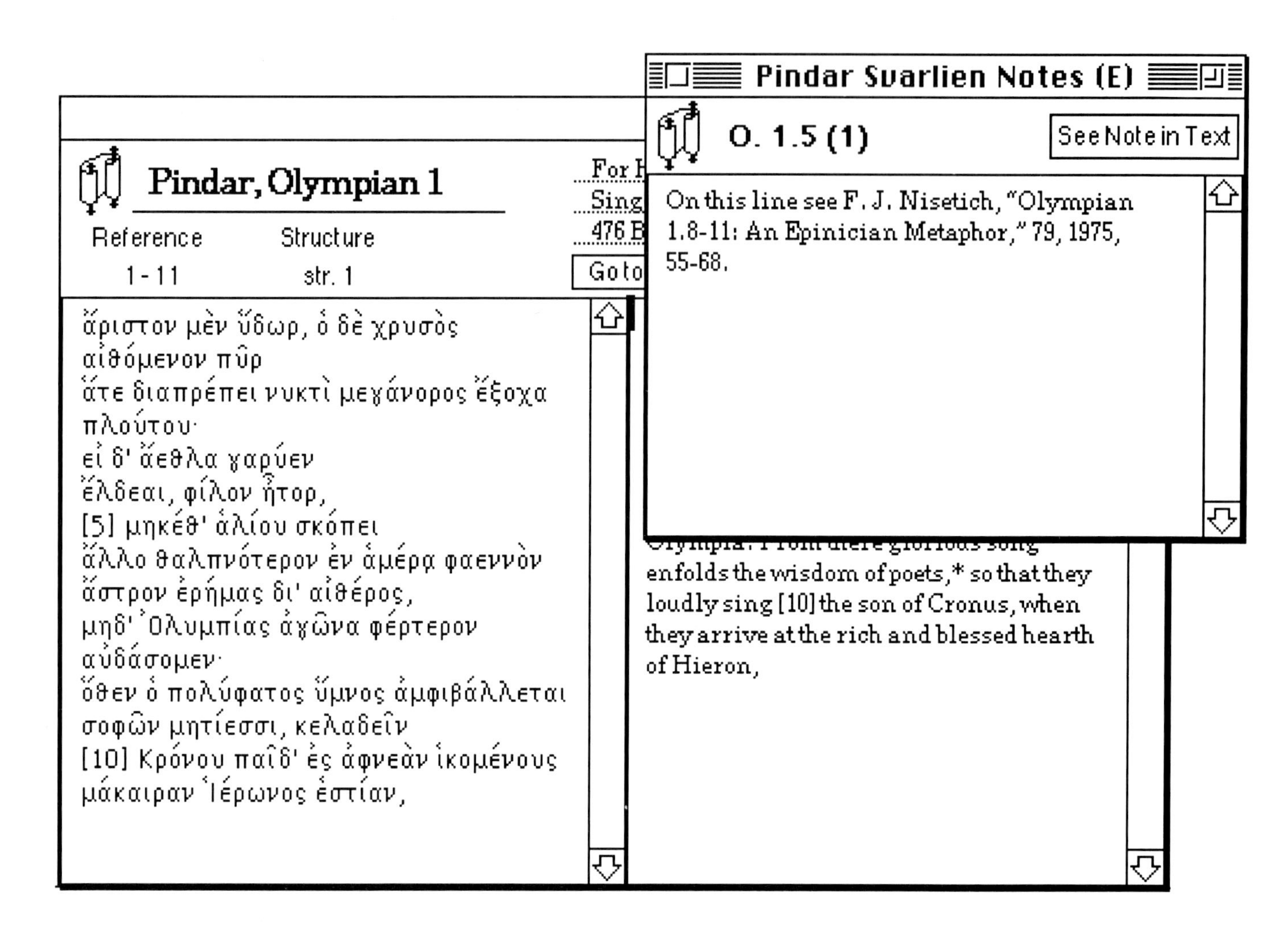

Figure 8.6 Note to the English text of Pindar's First Olympian

The Notes feature does not demand a precise selection of the asterisk. If you select a portion of the text preceding and following the asterisk, the correct note will still appear. If the text you select is keyed to more than one note, a list of possible notes will appear, and you can select one from the list.

Two works have notes keyed to the Greek text. Sophocles' *Oedipus Tyrannus* has notes by Sir Richard Jebb, and Plato's *Symposium* has extensive notes by Gilbert Rose, from the Bryn Mawr Classical Commentary (the English text of the *Symposium* contains the Loeb notes as well). Notes in the Greek text are not signaled by asterisks. To bring up the notes, select some Greek text within the line (figure 8.7). Click See Note. A dialog box will appear. In figure 8.7, there are three notes to line

1 of the OT. Click the note you wish to see, then click Go There. The note appears in a new window and behaves just like the notes to English texts, described earlier in this section.

> Remember to hold down the Shift key when clicking Go There in order to keep the text window open.

See section 8.3 for information on how to access Greek and English notes from the Text menu.

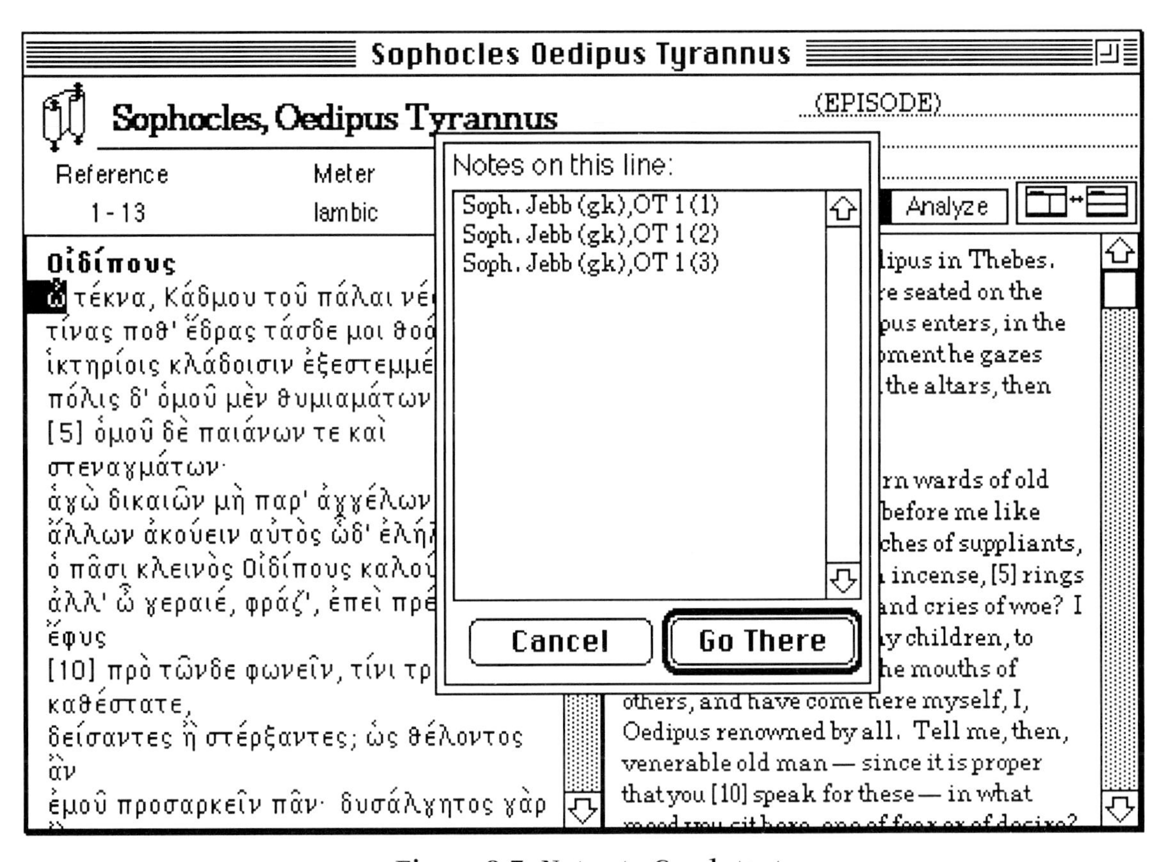

Figure 8.7 Notes to Greek text

The note stacks are titled according to their source (in the example shown in figure 8.6, Pindar Svarlien Notes [E]). The title of the note is a numerical reference that indicates the relevant section of the Primary Text or translation and a note number. For example, "Soph. Jebb (gk),OT 1 (1)" in figure 8.7 indicates Sophocles, Jebb note on Greek text of *Oedipus Tyrannus*, line 1, first of three notes on that line.

Some notes have references to other ancient texts. When these works are part of Perseus, the citation is underlined. You can select the reference and choose Lookup from the Links menu to access it directly.

Analyze

The Analyze button provides access to the Morphological Analysis tool, which parses Greek words to their dictionary form. Again, Pindar's First Olympian will be used as an example.

In the following example, you will analyze the form of a Greek verb.

➤ Select ἔλδεαι from line 4 of the First Olympian. Click Analyze. Perseus analyzes ἔλδεαι on a Morphological Analysis card, showing the dictionary form of the word, and its parse (figure 8.8). You can then use the dictionary form of the word to conduct further searches in selected authors and works. See section 8.4 for more information on the Philological Tools.

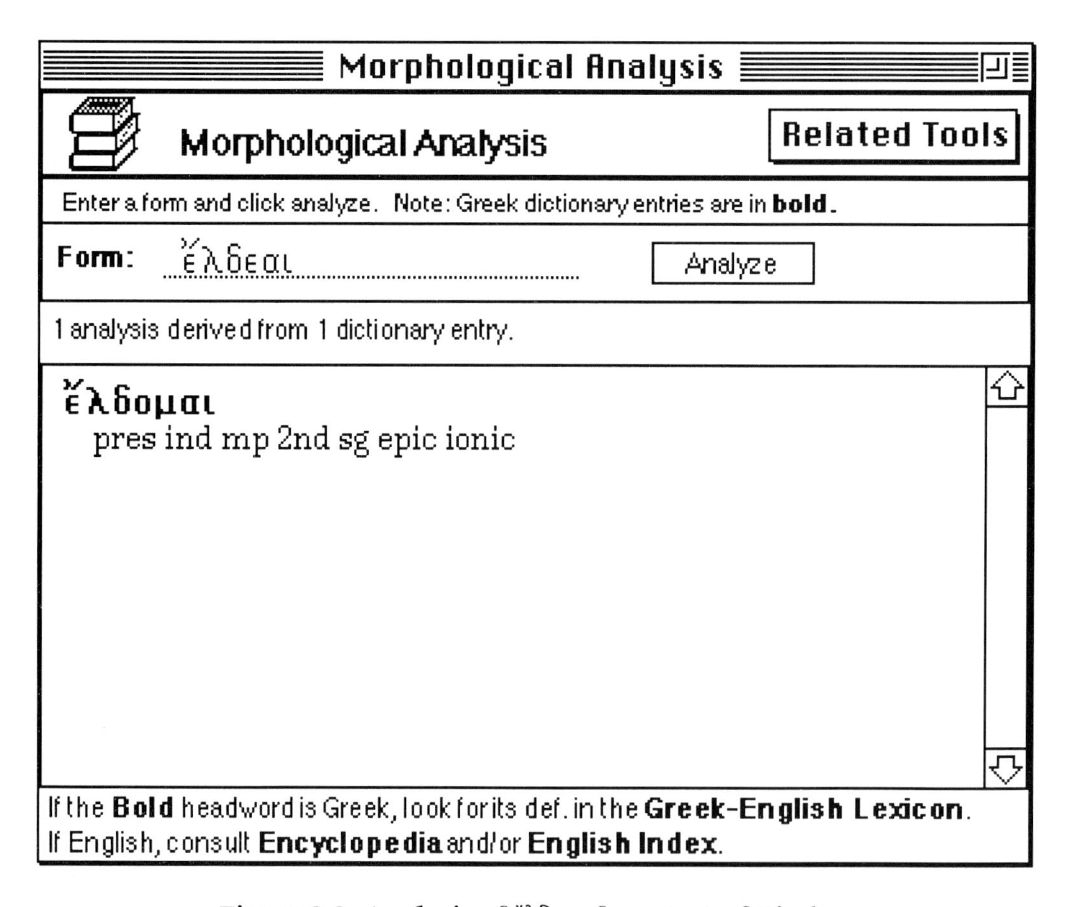

Figure 8.8 Analysis of ἔλδεαι from text of Pindar

Even if you have placed a word in the "Find text" field, you must highlight it using standard Macintosh techniques before using Analyze.

The parse "pres ind mp 2nd sg epic ionic" is explained in Online Help for the Morphological Analysis Philological Tool. For more information on Online Help, see section 3.3.

Primary Text Display

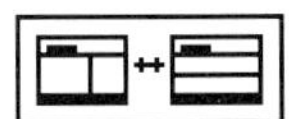

Primary Texts can be displayed in two columns (Greek on the left, English on the right) or two rows (Greek on the top, English on the bottom). The Primary Text display is controlled by a button at the right of the screen, below the additional title information. The Primary Text display button shows two outlines of the display choices. You can also change the width of the columns or height of the rows to see more of the Greek or English text at one time. The default Primary Text display is two equal columns.

➤ Click the right half of the Primary Text display button to change the format of the text to rows rather than columns.

The Primary Text is now displayed in two rows.

➤ Click the left half of the Primary Text display button to return the format of the text to columns.

Note that the vertical dividing line between the columns has a dark, wide marker at its top. This marker can be dragged to the left or right to change the width of the columns.

➤ Point the cursor over the dark, wide marker at the top of the column dividing line.

When the cursor is over the marker, the cursor becomes a vertical bar with arrows on either side (indicating the field-expander mode).

➤ Drag the marker to the left. Point the cursor over the marker again and drag it to the far right.

Note how the widths of the columns change according to the place where you released the mouse button. If you switch the display to rows, change the height of the rows by finding the marker at the left of the horizontal dividing line.

The effect of changing the display and enlarging the area containing the Greek text is particularly effective when working with poetry (figure 8.9).

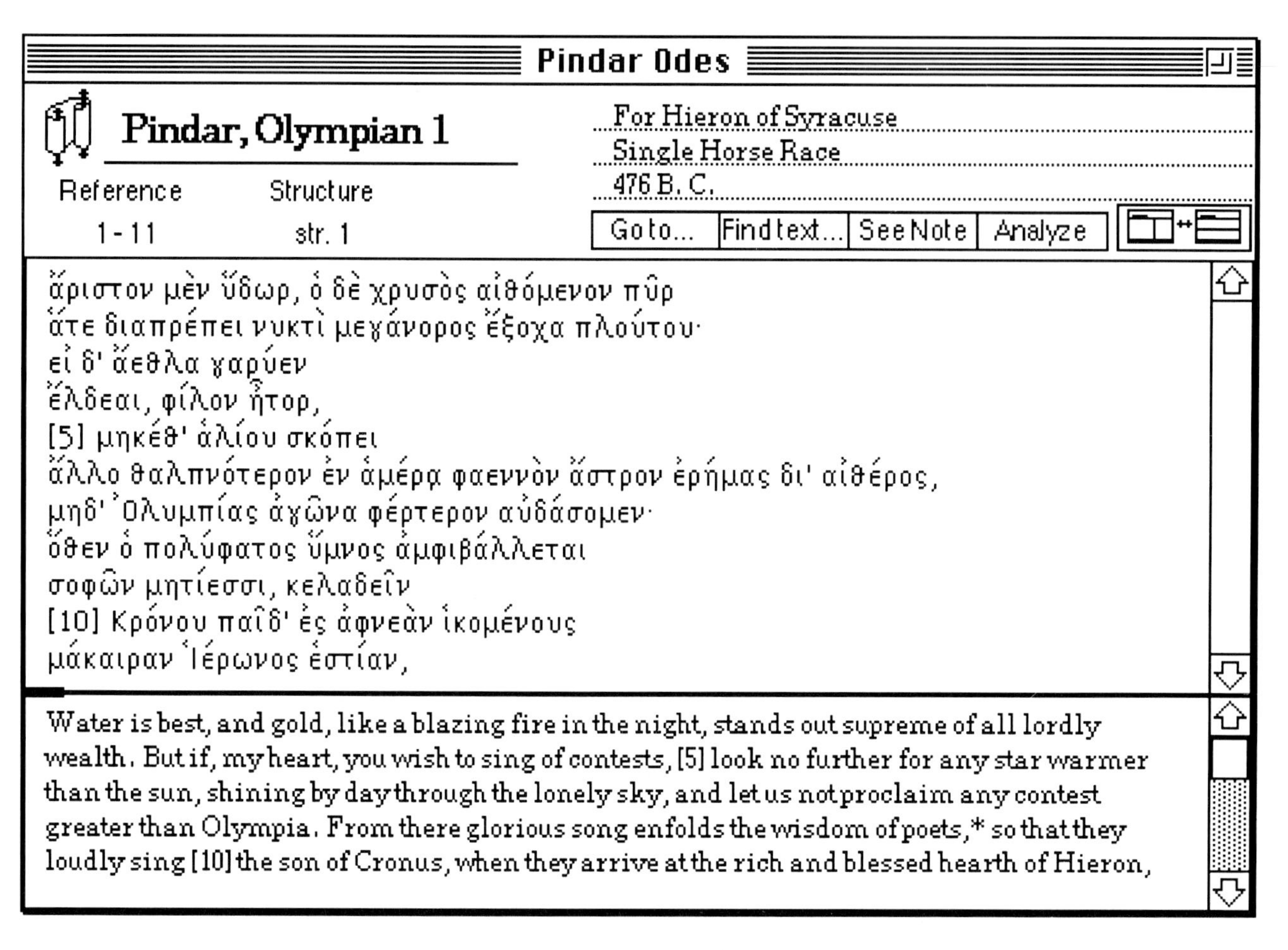

Figure 8.9 Text card with display changed

The changed text display settings will remain in effect for all Text cards throughout your Perseus session but will not be saved after you quit HyperCard.

8.3 TEXT MENU

The Text menu (figure 8.10) enables you to discover what notes and other information, if any, are available for the current card. It also lists four font sizes for the display of the Primary Text: 10 point, 12 point, 14 point, and display (large) size.

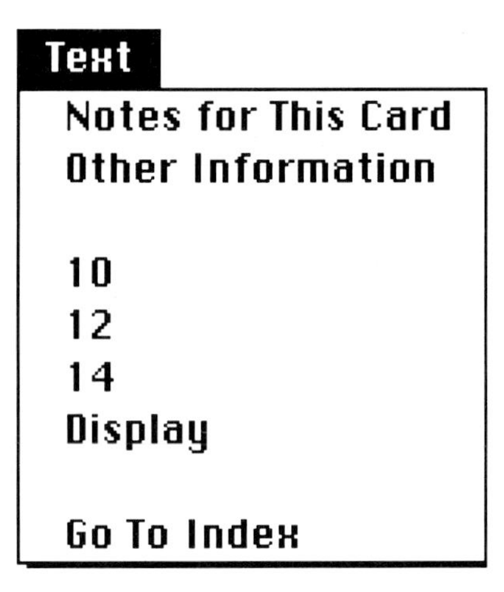

Figure 8.10 Text menu

Notes for this card

When you choose "Notes for This Card" from the Text menu, a dialog box appears, showing a complete list of the notes to the text on the current card. The list does not show all notes for the current text, only for the section of the work currently viewed on the screen. When the list appears, choose a text note and click Go There.

This feature is especially useful in the two texts where the notes are not marked by asterisks: Plato's *Symposium* and Sophocles' *Oedipus Tyrannus.*

Other information

When you choose Other Information from the Text menu, a dialog box appears, showing a list of information available in Perseus about the current text (figure 8.11).

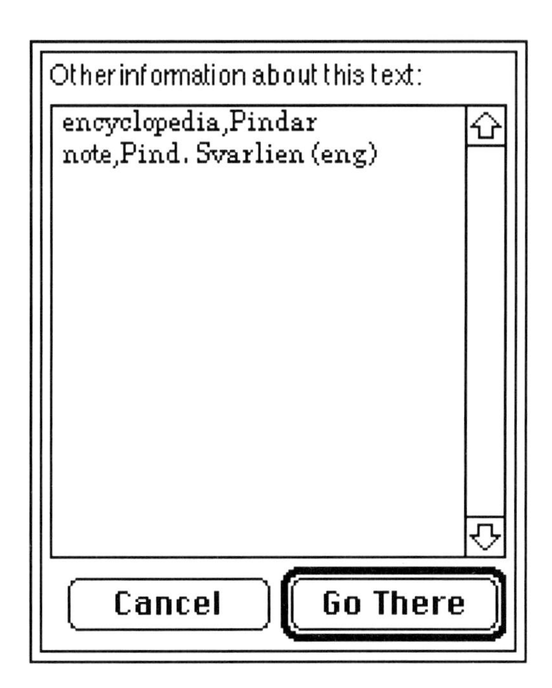

Figure 8.11 Other Information in Perseus about the current text

For most texts, the list includes a biography of the author in the Encyclopedia and a reference to any stack with notes for this text.

When the list appears, choose a resource and click Go There.

Font settings: 10, 12, 14, Display

When you choose 10, 12, 14, or Display from the Text menu, the font size of the Greek and English text changes to the selected display size.

8.4 PHILOLOGICAL TOOLS

Eight Philological Tools are available to explore the vocabulary, grammar, syntax, usage, and word frequencies in ancient Greek. They are:

Morphological Analysis
Greek-English Lexicon
Greek Word Search
Greek Words in Proximity
English-Greek Word Search
Greek Dictionary Entry Search
Greek Word Frequencies—Overview
Greek Word Frequencies—By Author

8.4.1 KEY TERMS: WORDS, STRINGS, FORMS, AND DICTIONARY ENTRIES

The Philological Tools provide support for quite powerful and sophisticated analysis of the sources in Perseus. Before you use these tools, it is important to distinguish between several different kinds of "word."

This paragraph contains 132 words. If you read through it from start to finish, counting each word as you read it, you would end up with a total of 132. In some contexts, however, we could say that the entire paragraph contains only 82 "unique" words: that is, the English word "the" would count only once, no matter how often it showed up in the text. Again, we must take account of grammatically inflected forms. Do "went," "gone," and "going" all count as unique words, or only as forms of the verb "to go"? In Perseus, word-count frequencies are a total of all words in the text, repeated and inflected. Words in the lexical tools are reached via the form given in their dictionary entry headings, rather than their inflected forms.

The following definitions will be useful:

Strings: Any collection of letters strung together is a "string." A string can be a full word (such as "philological") or a word fragment ("philol-", "-ologic-", "-ical") or both ("logic" is both a word in its own right and a *sub*string of "philological"). Virtually all the tools developed for searching Greek texts (and many of those for English as well) search not for words but for strings embedded in words. Thus "go" will retrieve "goes" and "gone" but not "went," and there is no convenient way to locate all forms of an irregular word (such as "is," "was," "be," and so on). This problem may be a nuisance in English (which retains relatively few endings), but in such a highly inflected language as classical Greek, string-based searching can be especially frustrating. The remedy for this is Perseus's morphological database, which has the ability to trace the irregular forms to their dictionary entry.

Inflected Forms and Dictionary Entries: The forms "goes," "going," and "gone" are all inflected forms that belong to the same word, "go." The Philological Tools distinguish between inflected forms and their dictionary entries. One of the major achievements of the Perseus database is that it allows users to deal not only with strings and inflected forms but with dictionary entries as well: thus you can perform the Greek equivalent of asking for "go" and retrieve "goes," "gone," and "went."

A note on typing Greek: Although cutting and pasting Greek text into a field may serve in most cases, you will find that the ability to type correctly accented Greek is indispensable in making the most efficient use of the Philological Tools. Perseus supports the SMK GreekKeys font, which must be installed in your system. Information on ordering GreekKeys may be found in section 2.1.2. The

Greek characters generally correspond to the Roman ones, with θ = y, ξ = j, σ = s, ς = w, ψ = c, and ω = v. The accents are found "under" the numbers and are typed in combination with the Option key before the vowel is typed. The Greek alphabet, its transliteration into Latin characters, and its GreekKeys equivalents may be found in Online Help under the stack topic "The Greek Alphabet."

8.4.2 DESCRIPTION AND LIMITATIONS OF THE PHILOLOGICAL TOOLS

Underlying the Philological Tools is a morphological database that was created by parsing every Greek word in the Perseus Primary Texts and storing the results. In it there are 3.4 million words but only 260,000 unique strings—in other words, each inflected form shows up, on average, 13 times. Each of these forms has been processed by the morphological analysis system developed by the Perseus Project. Its tables of nominal and verbal stems are based on those in the Liddell-Scott *Intermediate Greek-English Lexicon.* Although we have added many words to our morphological database that are not in Liddell-Scott, morphological analysis is still not available for some words in Perseus 2.0. This will change in coming years as we extract morphological information from the larger Greek lexicon, the ninth edition of Liddell-Scott-Jones. The table below shows the success rate for analyzing all forms in Perseus.

	Proper Names	Other Forms	Total
Total	31,518	227,461	258,979
Analyzed	21,742	223,919	245,661
Success	69%	98%	95%

Table 8.1 Success Rate for Analyzing Forms in Perseus

The database provides a foundation for the Philological Tools and allows you to perform two strategic functions. First, you can analyze any word in a text (except 31 percent of proper nouns), and second, you can investigate all instances of a Greek word across the range of texts. Together, these two strategies allow you to investigate Greek words in Perseus texts with greater precision than has been possible heretofore, even with electronic tools.

The Morphological Analysis tool can recognize only forms. It is not aware of the syntax of a sentence. If a form has more than one possible analysis, the only thing that the morphological analyzer can do is to list all applicable parses. It is not able to identify the syntactically correct form. Therefore, several of the Philological Tools display two sets of statistical results: one that takes into account only unambiguous forms with one possible parse, and another that includes all forms, ambiguous and unambiguous. Thus, faced with such a form as αἰσχύνῃ, the Morphological Analysis tool simply reports that this could be *either* the dative singular of the noun αἰσχύνη, "shame," *or* one of several forms of the verb αἰσχύνω, "to cause shame." The English equivalent is to recognize "fly" as either a noun or a verb but to leave it to the user to sort out the ambiguity between these two choices. (For more information on this, see the discussion of the Morphological Analysis tool in section 8.4.5.)

All the Philological Tools allow you to enter your own word or string, in Greek or English (as appropriate). They are primarily used, however, by selecting text within another Perseus resource (Greek or English text, depending on the tool to be activated), then choosing the desired tool from the Links menu. If any text is selected when a tool is activated, that tool will try to act on the selected text. To type accented Greek text, you must have SMK GreekKeys 7.0 installed in your system (information on ordering GreekKeys is in section 2.1.2). You must be precise in typing accents and diacritical marks in order for the morphological tools to recognize the word (unless otherwise specified).

8.4.3 CALCULATING FREQUENCIES

Because the length of texts varies, a dictionary entry whose forms appear 100 times in Demosthenes and 30 times in Lysias is actually *more common* in Lysias, because our corpus of Demosthenes is five times larger than that of Lysias (about 300,000 versus 60,000 words). For this reason, Perseus reports, wherever possible, not only the *instances* of a word (that is, the absolute frequency of the word—how many times a dictionary entry appears in the work of a given author, or 100 for Demosthenes and 30 for Lysias in the previous example) but also the relative frequency (frequency per 10,000 words). In other words, we take into consideration the differing sizes of the texts in Perseus 2.0 so that you can compare the frequency of words more effectively. For each dictionary entry in each text, we determine the rate at which it appears for every 10,000 words in a given text. Thus, in the previous example, the frequencies per 10,000 words would be 3.33 for Demosthenes and 5 for Lysias.

Some inflected forms are, however, "lexically ambiguous," that is, they can come from more than one dictionary entry (for example, Greek αἰσχύνῃ can be an inflected form of either the noun αἰσχύνη, "shame," or the verb αἰσχύνω, "to cause shame"). Each frequency thus has both a maximum and a minimum. The *maximum* "instances" and "freqs/10,000 words" assumes that all possible inflected forms of a dictionary entry really do belong to that entry (if you are searching for the verb αἰσχύνω, assume that αἰσχύνῃ is a verbal form). The *minimum* figure assumes that none of the lexically ambiguous inflected forms belong to the dictionary entry (if you are searching for the verb αἰσχύνω, assume that αἰσχύνη is not an inflected form of this verb). If the maximum and minimum frequencies are the same, then all the possible forms of the dictionary entry are lexically unambiguous. If the maximum and minimum frequencies are different, however, then you will have to use your judgment to determine the true frequency of the dictionary entry.

8.4.4 RELATED TOOLS BUTTON

Because the eight Philological Tools are all in the Links menu, they are available anywhere in Perseus. Some of these Philological Tools are, however, particularly useful in different positions, and each of the eight Philological Tools contains a Related Tools pop-up menu in the upper-right corner of the screen. The Related Tools menu lists other Philological Tools that are particularly relevant to the tool you are currently using.

8.4.5 OVERVIEW OF THE PHILOLOGICAL TOOLS

The Philological Tools are functionally linked to each other for maximum flexibility.

The eight Philological Tools are described briefly in this section. They divide into four basic groups:

Morphological Analysis and Greek-English Lexicon: When working with a text, you can use the Morphological Analysis tool to find out the grammatical function of a form and the Greek-English Lexicon to find out its meaning.

Greek Word Search and Greek Words in Proximity: These tools allow you to locate passages in which one or more particular dictionary entries appear.

English-Greek Word Search and Greek Dictionary Entry Search: These tools allow you to locate Greek words (or groups of Greek words) for further study.

Greek Word Freqs—Overview and Greek Word Freqs—by Author: These tools allow you to explore quantitative differences in usage between different authors, genres, and periods.

Morphological Analysis

Enter an inflected Greek form to find out its possible morphological analyses and what dictionary entries it might come from.

Not only will beginning and intermediate students of the Greek language find the morphological analysis helpful, but advanced students also will find this tool indispensable in determining the precise dictionary entry for a form: you can find out quickly whether Liddell-Scott-Jones list the words under καταπλήσσω or καταπλήττω, κατάπλοος or κατάπλους, or ῥωπεῖον or ῥωπήιον.

If you select English text or proper nouns, you will see a message that no analysis is offered for this word.

Greek-English Lexicon

Enter a Greek word in its dictionary form to find its definitions. The Perseus Greek-English Lexicon is based on the Liddell-Scott *Intermediate Greek-English Lexicon*.

You must provide the exact spelling to locate an entry. You can use the Morphological Analysis tool or the Greek Dictionary Entry Search tool to help locate the right spelling.

If you look for an English word or an inflected Greek form in the Greek-English Lexicon, you will see a message that the selected text is not in the dictionary.

Greek Word Search

Enter a dictionary entry or a string to find the texts containing it in Perseus. Greek Word Search gives the citations for each word and links you directly with the passage. You can, for example, search for φέρω and retrieve οἴσω and ἤνεγκον, or you can search for -πεμπ- and retrieve πέμπομεν, ἔπεμπε, ἀποπέμπει, and so on.

If you search for English text, you will see a message that the lemma is not used in the selected author's works.

Greek Words in Proximity

With this tool, you can make two lists of dictionary entries and identify all passages in which any possible form from list 1 appears within a given number of words of any possible form from list 2.

English-Greek Word Search

This tool allows you to search for words within a semantic category. For example, suppose you are interested in Greek words for "money" or "ship" or "statue." You can use this tool to locate probable equivalents and convert the Liddell-Scott *Intermediate Greek-English Lexicon* into a rough, but powerful, English-Greek lexicon.

The English-Greek Word Search searches in the Greek lexicon for words whose definition contains the selected word. Any italicized text in a dictionary entry from the Liddell-Scott *Intermediate Greek-English Lexicon* is treated as a definition, and in using this tool you are, in effect, consulting an index of English words from this lexicon.

Greek Dictionary Entry Search

You can use the Greek Dictionary Entry Search to locate individual dictionary entries or groups of dictionary entries. Use the Greek Dictionary Entry Search to find out precisely how a Greek dictionary entry is spelled (-σσ- or -ττ-, -ια or -ιη, for example). Again, you can locate all dictionary entries that contain a certain string: those ending in -φρων or -σις, or those that contain the string -ολβ- (such as ἀνολβία and εὔολβος), or -πεμπ- (such as ἀντεκπέμπω, διαπέμπω, and δύσπεμπτος). Finally, if you want to do a Greek Word Search but lack a convenient way of typing accents because you do not have SMK GreekKeys installed, you can obtain the form with the Greek Dictionary Entry Search.

You can go from the Greek Dictionary Entry Search tool to any of the other Philological Tools.

Greek Word Frequencies—Overview

The Greek Word Frequencies tool displays the statistical frequencies with which a particular Greek word is used among all the Greek works in Perseus. This tool will provide you with the totals for a list of words, often with interesting results: A search in the Greek Word Frequencies—Overview for αἴλουρος, "cat," produces seven instances for all Greek texts within Perseus. Perhaps not unsurprisingly, six fall in Herodotus 2, a book devoted to Egypt. The seventh is in Aristophanes; in what context will αἴλουρος appear?

Greek Word Frequencies—by Author

The Greek-Word Frequencies—by Author allows you to compose a list of words and then see which of these words occur in the works of a particular author, and how often. Because Perseus keeps the word list in its memory, the query can be repeated for each author in the database.

8.4.6 MORPHOLOGICAL ANALYSIS TOOL

The Morphological Analysis tool parses Greek word forms, showing the dictionary form (lemma) and related analysis. The Morphological Analysis tool is available directly from Primary Text displays through the Analyze button, from the Links menu, and from the Gateway via the Tools & References icon.

This tool retrieves a morphological analysis, not a syntactic analysis, of the Greek word. If the form you are analyzing could be formed from more than one word, the Morphological Analysis tool will display all possible lemmas and analyses. It does not indicate which one is correct for the particular form you selected.

If you have chosen Morphological Analysis from the Tools & References Index or the Links menu, you must enter a word to analyze. If you are in a Primary Text and want to analyze a word, highlight it and click the Analyze button. The tool will automatically parse that word.

The examples in this section will trace the analysis of words selected from a Primary Text and from Philological Tools.

➤ To analyze forms from Pindar's *First Olympian Ode,* go to Pindar First Olympian in the Primary Texts by choosing Lookup from the Links menu. Type "Pind. O. 1.1" into the box and press Return.

➤ Highlight the Greek word γαρύεν.

➤ Click the button Analyze, upper right. The Morphological Analysis card appears with the form γαρύεν above, the lemma (dictionary form) in boldface type in the middle, and the grammatical analysis below (figure 8.12).

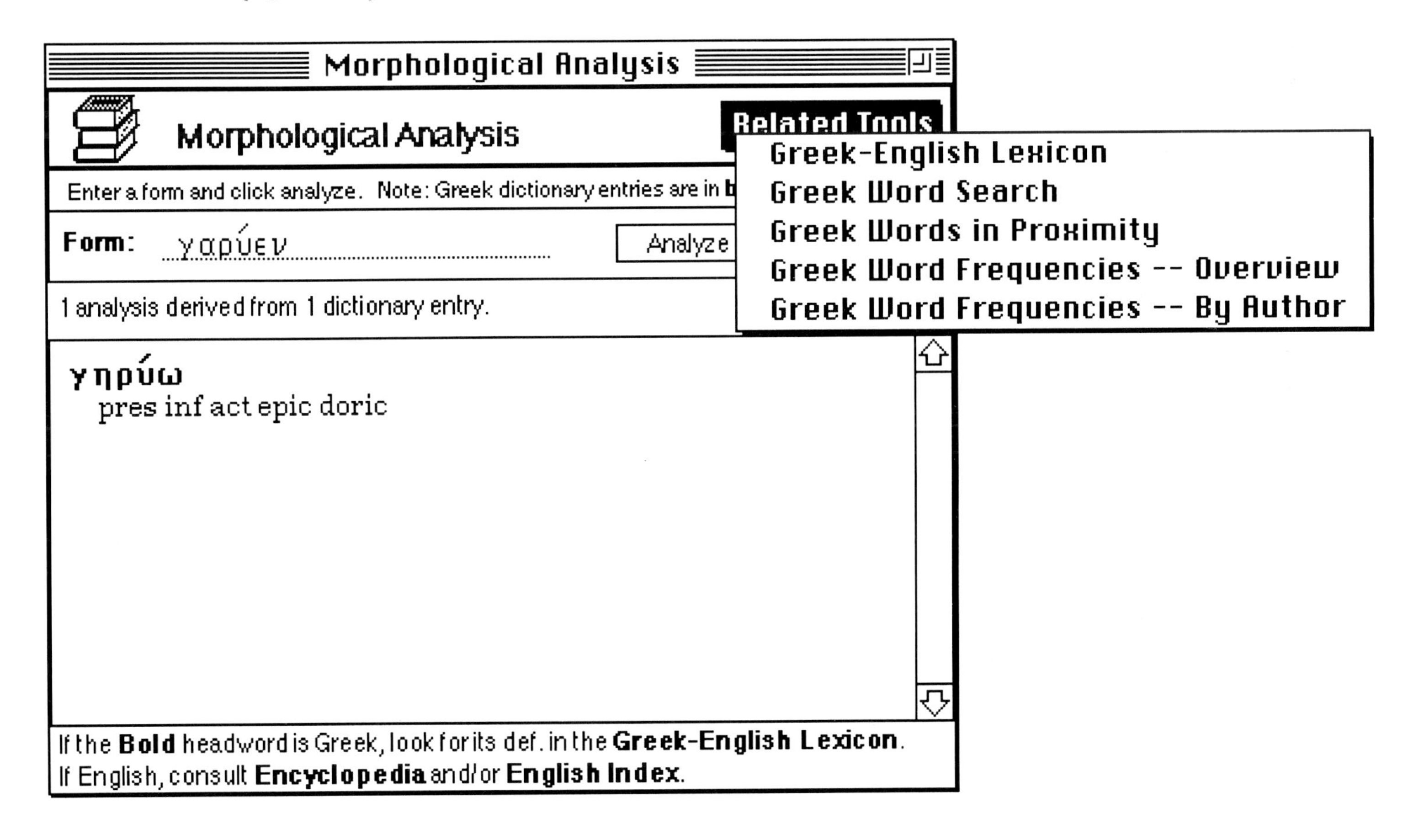

Figure 8.12 Morphological Analysis, showing Related Tools pop-up menu

Explanation of the parse abbreviation "pres inf act epic doric" is given in Online Help for Morphological Analysis.

To find the meaning of γηρύω, highlight it. Then choose Greek-English Lexicon from the pop-up menu Related Tools. (You may also go to the other Philological Tools under the Related Tools pop-up menu, described later in this section. These include Greek Word Search, Greek Word Frequencies—Overview and Greek Word Frequencies—by Author.)

To return to the text of Pindar, click the Go Back arrow on the Navigator Palette.

➤ To analyze a form directly from the Morphological Analysis card, type βόα into the Form field and click Analyze to parse the word (figure 8.13).

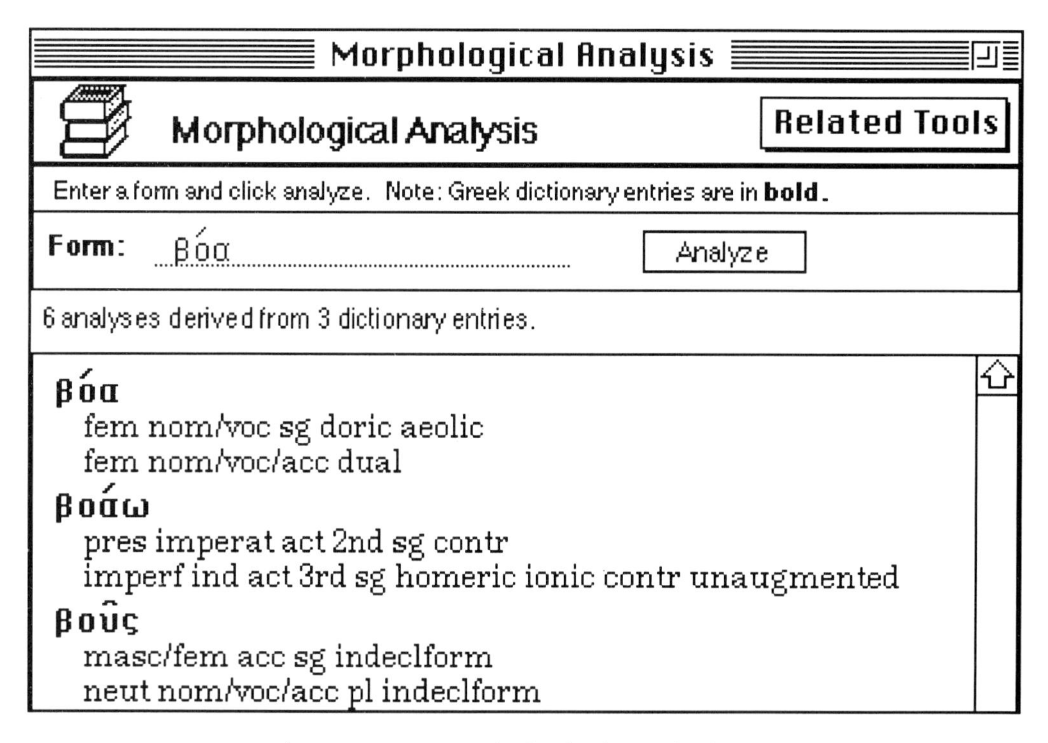

Figure 8.13 Morphological Analysis tool

To type Greek text, you must have SMK GreekKeys installed in your system. You must be precise in typing accents and diacritical marks using SMK GreekKeys.

In this case the word analysis results in three lemmas.

Related Tools

The Related Tools button in the upper-right corner relates the Morphological Analysis tool to other Philological Tools. If you select text from the Morphological Analysis before choosing another tool, the new tool will apply itself to the selection. Figure 8.12 illustrates the choices available here.

The four related tools are those that work with one or more dictionary entries. In the example using βόα, if you select one of the three lemmas (dictionary entries) and then call up one of these four related tools, Perseus will automatically paste the selected dictionary entry into the selected tool.

If you do not select anything before you call up the Greek-English Lexicon or the Greek Word Search tools, nothing will be pasted into them. Greek Word Frequency tools, however, will look up all lemmas listed—in this case, all three—if you do not select one of the lemmas.

Limitations

1. The Morphological Analysis tool is not context sensitive.

   It makes no attempt to determine whether such a form as αἰσχύνῃ is a substantive or a verb.

   If it sees such a form as πέμπετε, it recognizes this as a possible present indicative or imperative, but it also reports that this could be an unaugmented Epic or Ionic. Even if you are reading an Attic author such as Demosthenes, it still reports the possible Epic and Ionic interpretation, because you may, for example, be looking at a form from a piece of quoted poetry.

2. The Morphological Analysis tool seeks every possible morphological analysis for every form that it examines. With 30,000 stems, 10,000 inflections, and rules for coping with several Greek dialects, some of the morphological analyses can be surprising.

3. The Morphological Analysis tool does not systematically cover proper names. It can recognize 22,000 of the 32,000 proper names in Perseus 2.0—a success rate of 69 percent.

   Our morphological database is based on the morphological information from the Liddell-Scott *Intermediate Greek-English Lexicon*, a reference tool that covers only a small number of proper names. We have added morphological information for more than 10,000 additional words, and we continue to add proper names systematically.

4. The Morphological Analysis tool has been programmed to recognize many words that are not in the *Intermediate Greek-English Lexicon*, but it still is not complete. It can recognize 223,000 out of the 228,000 unique strings in Perseus 2.0—a success rate of 98 percent.

8.4.7 GREEK-ENGLISH LEXICON

The Greek-English Lexicon contains the Greek and English definitions from the Liddell-Scott *Intermediate Greek-English Lexicon*. The Greek-English Lexicon is entered from the Links menu, from the Gateway via the Tools & References icon, and from the Related Tools pop-up menu in the various Philological Tools.

Figure 8.14 Greek-English Lexicon

➤ To look up the meaning of αὐδάω in Pindar's First Olympian, go to Pindar's First Olympian in the Primary Texts by choosing Lookup from the Links menu. Type "Pind. O. 1.1" into the box and press Return.

➤ Highlight the Greek word αὐδάσομεν in line 7. Click Analyze. On the Morphological Analysis card, highlight the lemma αὐδάω, then choose Greek-English Lexicon from the Related Tools pop-up menu.

Alternatively, you can look up lemmas by typing them directly into the Entry field if you have SMK GreekKeys 7.0 installed in your system. Click the Entry field to make the insertion point appear.

Then click Look Up to see a definition of the word. You can paste in a Greek word (in its dictionary form).

The Greek-English Lexicon displays the entry for a word as it appears in the Liddell-Scott *Intermediate Greek-English Lexicon* (figure 8.14). The first field lists the definitions.

The buttons See Previous Entry and See Following Entry allow you to move backward and forward in the Lexicon.

The "Derived from" field lists explicit cross-references between dictionary entries. In practice, any word or brief phrase enclosed in parentheses at the beginning of a dictionary article in the lexicon will be placed in the Derived From entry. Thus, in the Liddell-Scott entry

αὐδάω, impf. ηὔδων: . . . (αὐδή): I. c. acc. rei, 1. *to utter sounds, speak,* Il., Eur.

(αὐδή) appears in Perseus thus (figure 8.15):

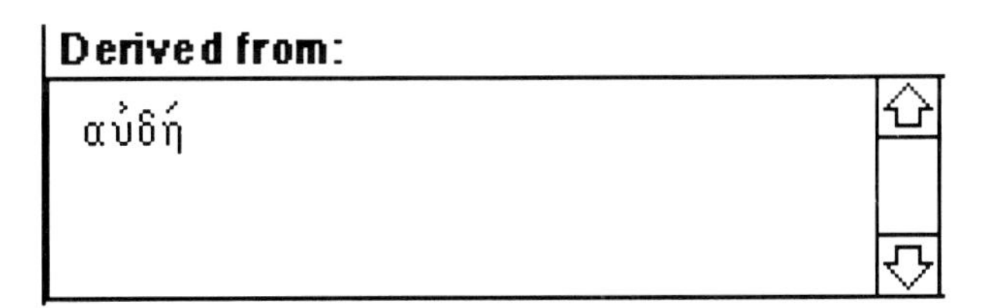

Figure 8.15 The "Derived from" field

Note that the Greek-English lexicon does not always include derivations in this parenthetical information. Consider, for example, the following entry in the print dictionary:

κυνάω, = κυνίζω, *to play the Cynic,* Luc.

This entry defines a homonymous relationship, that is, the verb κυνάω has the same meaning as κυνίζω. In Perseus, the "= κυνίζω" reference also appears in the "Derived from" field.

The other three fields on this card include information derived from, but not explicit in, the print version of the lexicon. These fields provide machine-generated indexes to help you make connections between words.

The "Source for" field lists words produced by the Entry word. In the previous example, the "Derived from" field indicates that αὐδάω is derived from αὐδή. If you call up the entry for αὐδή (by selecting the word and choosing Look Up), you will find αὐδάω in the "Source for" field, along with ἄναυδος, αὐδάζομαι, and αὐδήεις—other words produced by αὐδή (figure 8.16).

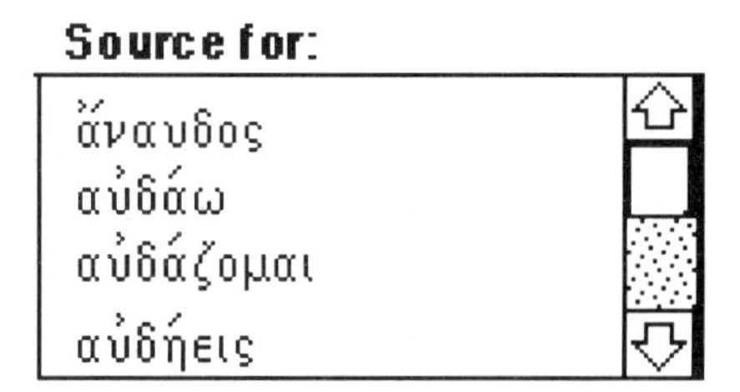

Figure 8.16 The "Source for" field

The field in the bottom left lists other possible forms of this dictionary entry that show up in other dictionary articles. Thus for αὐδή, the other possible forms are αὐδάν, αὐδή, and αὐδήν (figure 8.17). Click αὐδάν, and the forms αὔω and προφέρω are displayed in the "appears in" field, in the lower right. This means that the form αὐδάν appears in the definitions, and is used in an idiomatic citation, in the Greek-English Lexicon entries for αὔω and προφέρω. Figure 8.17 shows the results of clicking αὐδή in the field "Other possible forms in the lexicon": the forms φροῦδος, ὀμφή, and ῥέω are displayed in the field "appears in," in the lower right. To go to the dictionary entry, click a word from the "appears in" field, then click the button Look Up.

Other possible forms in the lexicon.	αὐδή appears in...
αὐδάν †	φροῦδος
αὐδή †	ὀμφή
αὐδήν †	ῥέω

Figure 8.17 Other possible forms from the lemma αὐδή that appear in the definitions of other dictionary entries

In the next example, you will find a citation for αὐδήν in the definition for the entry χέω.

➤ From the Greek-English Lexicon entry for αὐδή, click αὐδήν in the field "Other possible forms in the lexicon," bottom left. Click χέω, then click Look Up. Perseus will highlight αὐδήν in the definition for χέω (figure 8.18).

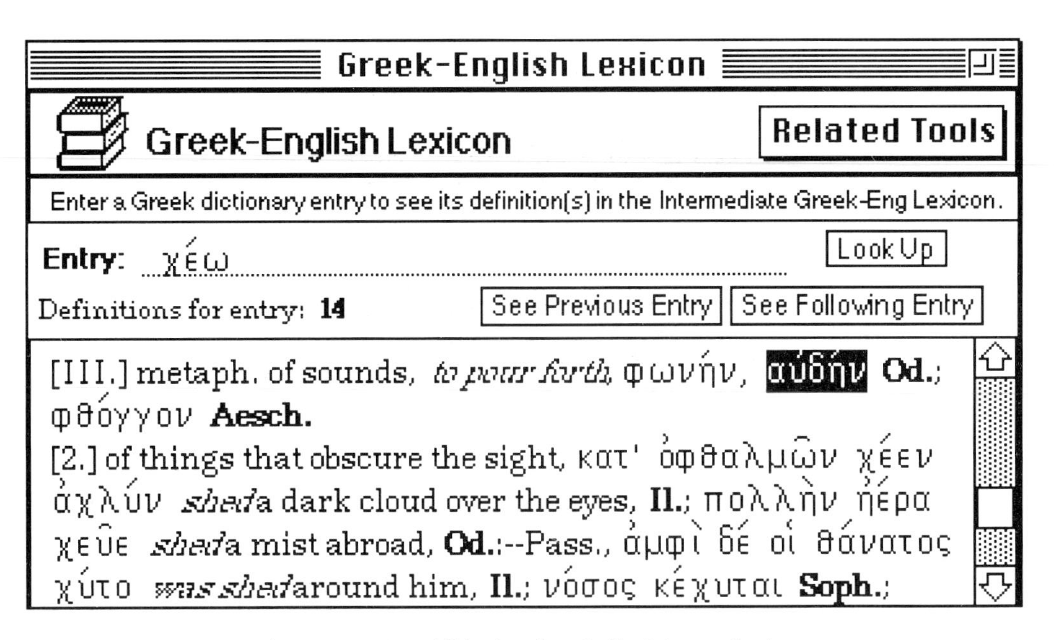

Figure 8.18 αὐδήν **in the definition of** χέω

The computer is able to create a link between the entry for αὐδή and the appropriate citation in the article for χέω, and the user can thus study an idiomatic usage of αὐδή cited in another entry of the lexicon.

Related Tools

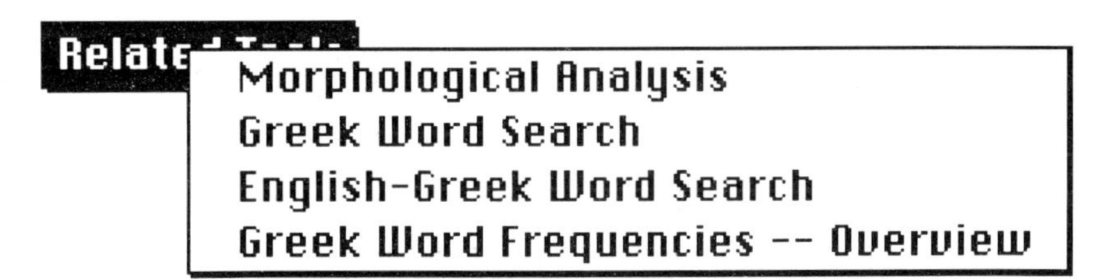

Figure 8.19 Related Tools in the Greek-English Lexicon

The Related Tools menu suggests the following options: (1) You can call up the Morphological Analysis tool to get the analysis for an inflected form in one of the definitions, (2) you can select an English word and use the English-Greek Word Search to see which other Greek dictionary articles contain this word in their definitions, and (3) you can search for, or see the frequencies of, a given dictionary entry in the works of Perseus authors.

Limitations

The Greek-English Lexicon is based on the Liddell-Scott *Intermediate Greek-English Lexicon*. We have definitions for about 35,000 words, but the *Intermediate Greek-English Lexicon* is not exhaustive, and thus there are a number of words in Perseus for which the Greek-English Lexicon has no definitions.

8.4.8 GREEK WORD SEARCH

The Greek Word Search tool allows you to search for Greek words in Perseus texts. Its features represent a significant improvement over the basic string searching to which classicists have become accustomed. Because it draws on the morphological database it can provide all inflected forms in the results, even those from a different stem. (For a definition of "strings," see section 8.4.1.)

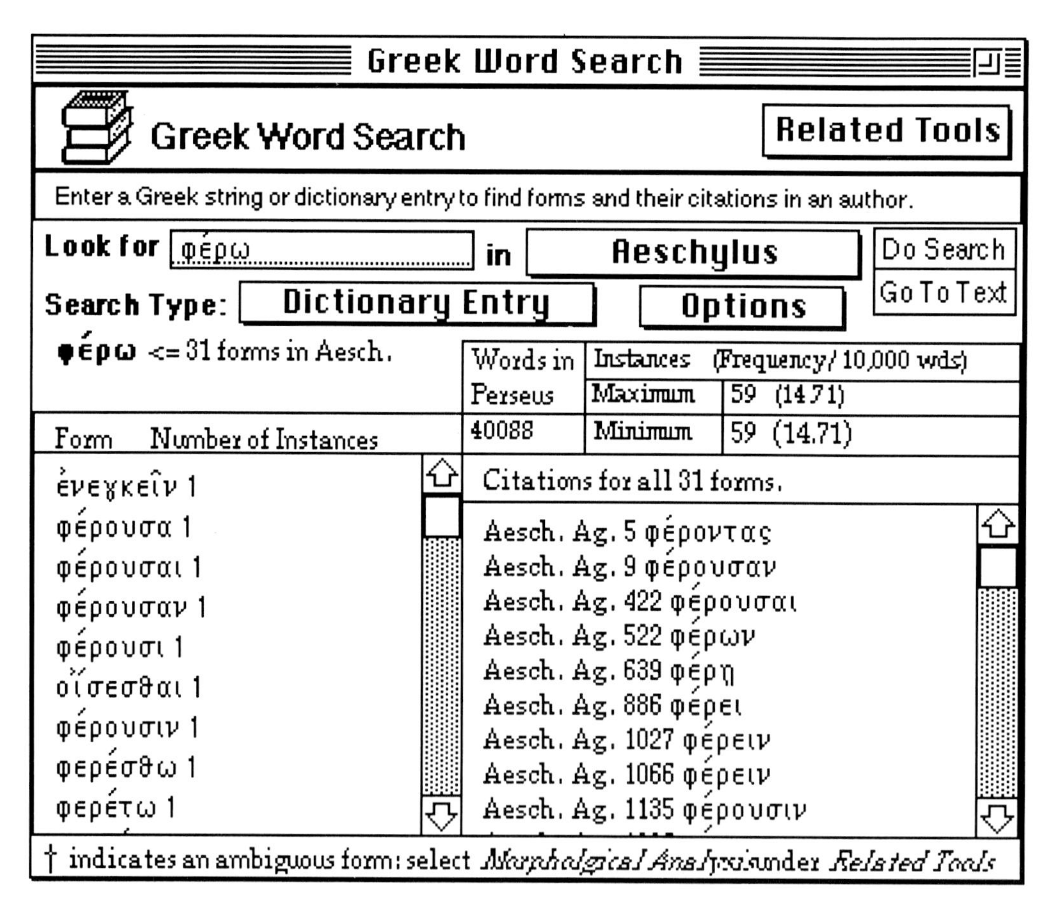

Figure 8.20 Greek Word Search: φέρω in Aeschylus

The Greek Word Search (figure 8.20) displays citations for all forms of the selected Greek word in a particular author's works—in this case, φέρω in Aeschylus. Note that forms from the future and aorist stems appear in the results field, on the left.

➤ In the field "Look for," paste—or type (if you have SMK GreekKeys installed)—a Greek word or string of characters to search for.

➤ Choose an author from the pop-up menu to determine whose works to search (figure 8.21).

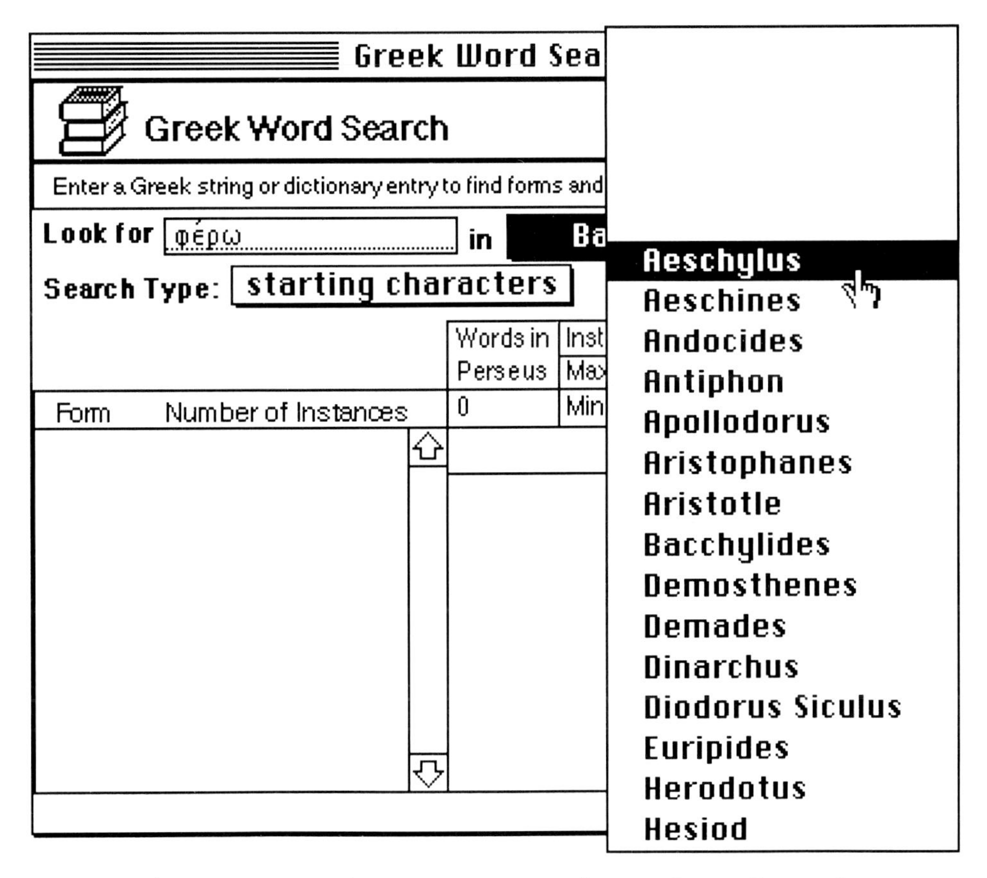

Figure 8.21 Author pop-up menu in Greek Word Search

Search Type

Several options for performing searches are available from the pop-up menu Search Type (figure 8.22). If you choose "All forms from a Dictionary Entry," which shows up by default as "Dictionary Entry," you can search for all forms of a word in the works of an author. The items "Forms with these starting characters" and "Forms with these ending characters" allow you to perform searches for words with beginning or ending strings that match the search string. With the item "Forms with this substring," you can search for words sharing the matching string in any position in the word.

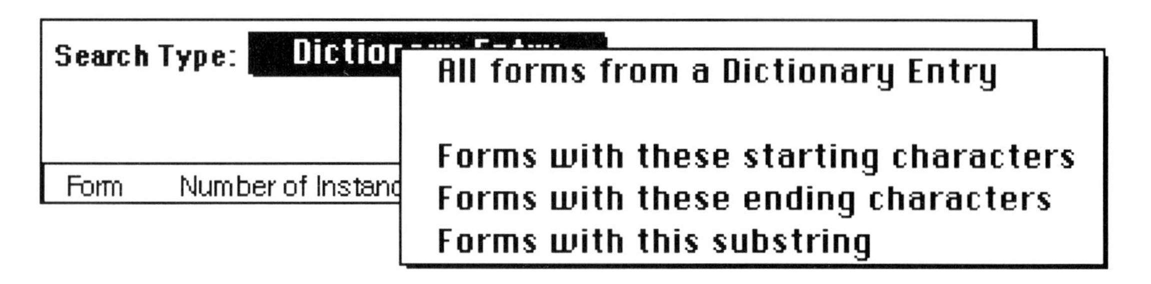

Figure 8.22 Search Type pop-up menu

➤ To perform the search, click the button Do Search.

Options

When the search is complete, the Options pop-up menu will appear, presenting you with a variety of ways to sort and classify the search results and author citations (figure 8.23).

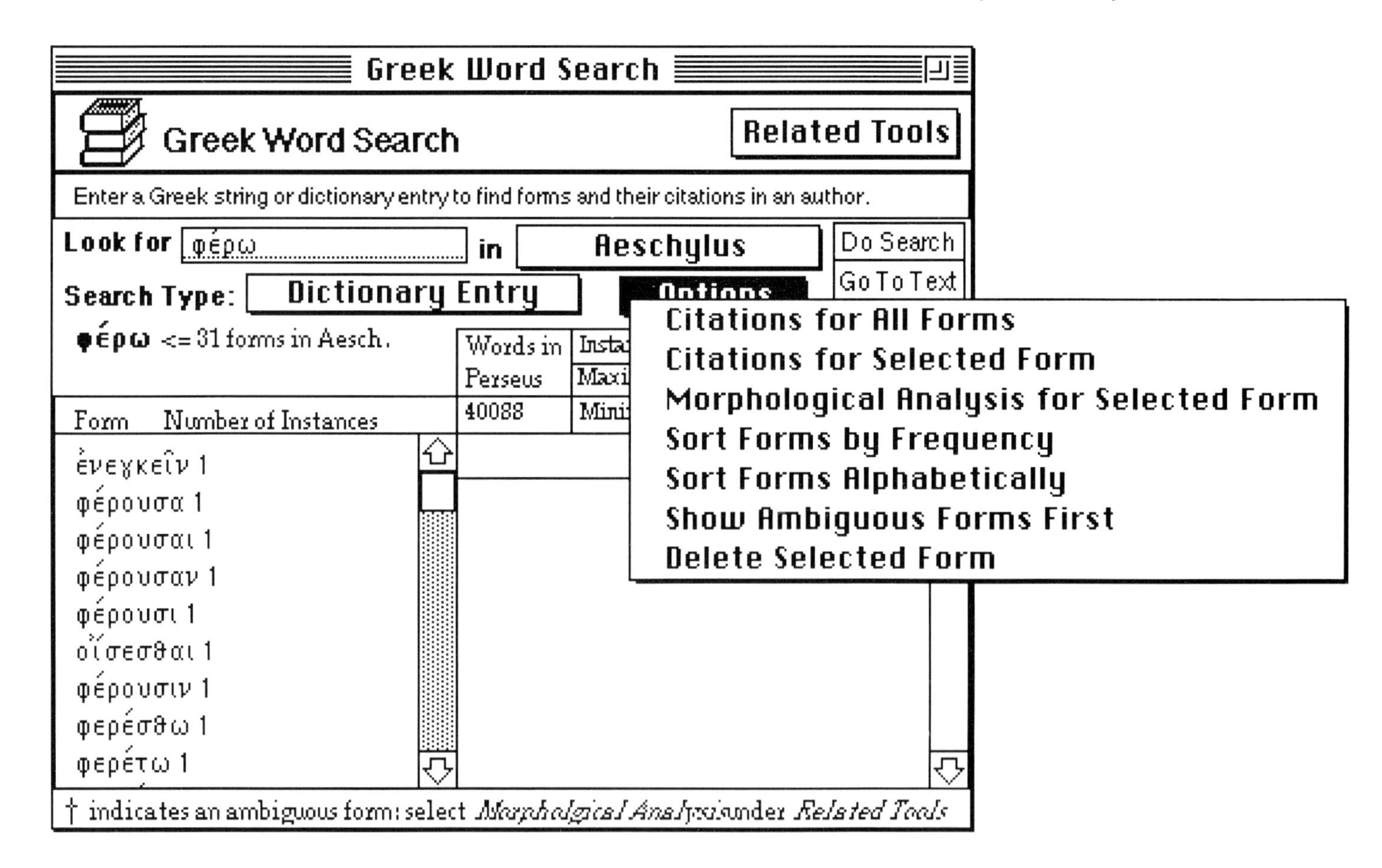

Figure 8.23 Options pop-up menu in Greek Word Search

The item "Citations for All Forms" brings up a list of all citations in Perseus for the targeted word. To go to one of the cited passages, select it and click the button Go To Text, in the upper right.

To retrieve citations for just one form, select it and choose "Citations for Selected Form" from the Options pop-up menu. To go to one of the cited passages, select it and click the button Go To Text, in the upper right.

To parse a form, select it and choose "Morphological Analysis for Selected Form" from the Options pop-up menu. To return to Greek Word Search, click the Go Back arrow on the Navigator Palette.

The list of forms can be sorted alphabetically, by frequency or with the ambiguous forms at the top. Choose "Sort Forms by Frequency," "Sort Forms Alphabetically," or "Show Ambiguous Forms First."

To discard one of the forms from the list of results, select it and choose Delete Selected Form.

Statistical Information

When a search has been performed, the Greek Word Search produces a line of statistics about the instances and frequency of the dictionary form of the word in the selected author's works. Figure 8.24 shows the statistics for φέρω in Aeschylus.

φέρω <= 31 forms in Aesch.

Words in Perseus	Instances	(Frequency/10,000 wds)
	Maximum	59 (14.71)
40088	Minimum	59 (14.71)

Figure 8.24 Greek Word Search statistics

Thirty-one forms are derived from φέρω in the works of Aeschylus. "Words in Perseus" represents the total number of words in Aeschylus in the Perseus database, 40,088. "Maximum Instances" is the number of forms of φέρω including ambiguous forms. "Minimum Instances" is the number of forms of φέρω without ambiguous forms. (In figure 8.24, both are 59 because there are no ambiguous forms.) "Frequency" is the number of instances per 10,000 words, 14.71.

To see statistics of this type for a particular word in the works of all the Primary Text authors, use the tool Greek Word Frequencies—Overview, available under the pop-up menu Related Tools, in the upper right.

Related Tools

The Greek Word Search is linked with the other Philological Tools via the Related Tools pop-up menu in the upper right. If you select Greek text from the Greek Word Search, then choose Morphological Analysis, Greek-English Lexicon, or Greek Word Frequencies—Overview from the Related Tools pop-up menu. The new tool will apply itself to the selection.

Limitations

1. A search for a word in the works of *all* Perseus authors (global search) would often produce results far beyond the capabilities of HyperCard. Until the software is developed, we suggest that you use the Greek Word Frequencies—Overview feature to see which authors use a word, then use Greek Word Search, proceeding author by author.

2. Some of the most common words in Greek are not indexed.

   Neither Greek Word Search nor Greek Words in Proximity searches Greek texts directly. Instead, these tools rely on indexes of the Perseus texts. To limit the size of the indexes, some of the most common words have not been included (table 8.2). If you wish to study these words, you must use Pandora or some other search tool for the *Thesaurus Linguae Graecae.*

ἄν	ἔτι	καί	οὐδέ	τι
ἀλλ'	ἐκ	κατά	οὐκ	τις
ἀλλά	ἐν	μέν	περί	τό
ἀπό	ἐπί	μετά	πρός	τόν
αὐτός	εἰ	μή	τά	τούς
δ'	εἰς	ὁ	τε	τοῦ
δέ	γάρ	ὅ	τήν	τῶν
δή	ἡ	οἱ	τῆς	τῷ
διά	ἤ	οὐ	τῇ	ὡς

Table 8.2 Forms Not Indexed, and Thus Not Searchable, in Perseus

   Pandora 2.5.2 is available from Scholars' Press Software, c/o Professional Book Distributors, P.O. Box 6996, Alpharetta, GA 30239-6996, telephone 1-800-437-6692 or 404-442-8633, FAX 404-442-9742.

   For information on the TLG CD-ROM, contact Theodore F. Brunner, Director; Thesaurus Linguae Graecae; University of California, Irvine; Irvine, CA 92717-5550 USA; telephone 714-824-7031; FAX 714-824-8434; e-mail tbrunner@uci.edu.

3. Lexical ambiguity.

   Remember that Perseus makes no attempt to determine whether such a form as αἰσχύνῃ is from the noun αἰσχύνη or the verb αἰσχύνω. Thus, the form αἰσχύνῃ will show up in searches for both the noun αἰσχύνη and the verb αἰσχύνω.

8.4.9 GREEK WORDS IN PROXIMITY

This tool allows you to locate passages in which any form from one list of dictionary entries appears within a given distance (in number of words) of a form from a second list of dictionary entries.

The "Greek Words in Proximity" tool is available from the Links menu and by clicking the Tools & References icon in the Gateway. The tool itself is constructed on two cards: the card appearing first (figure 8.25) contains the author lists, operating buttons, and results fields; the second card (figure 8.26) contains fields for entering and editing search lists.

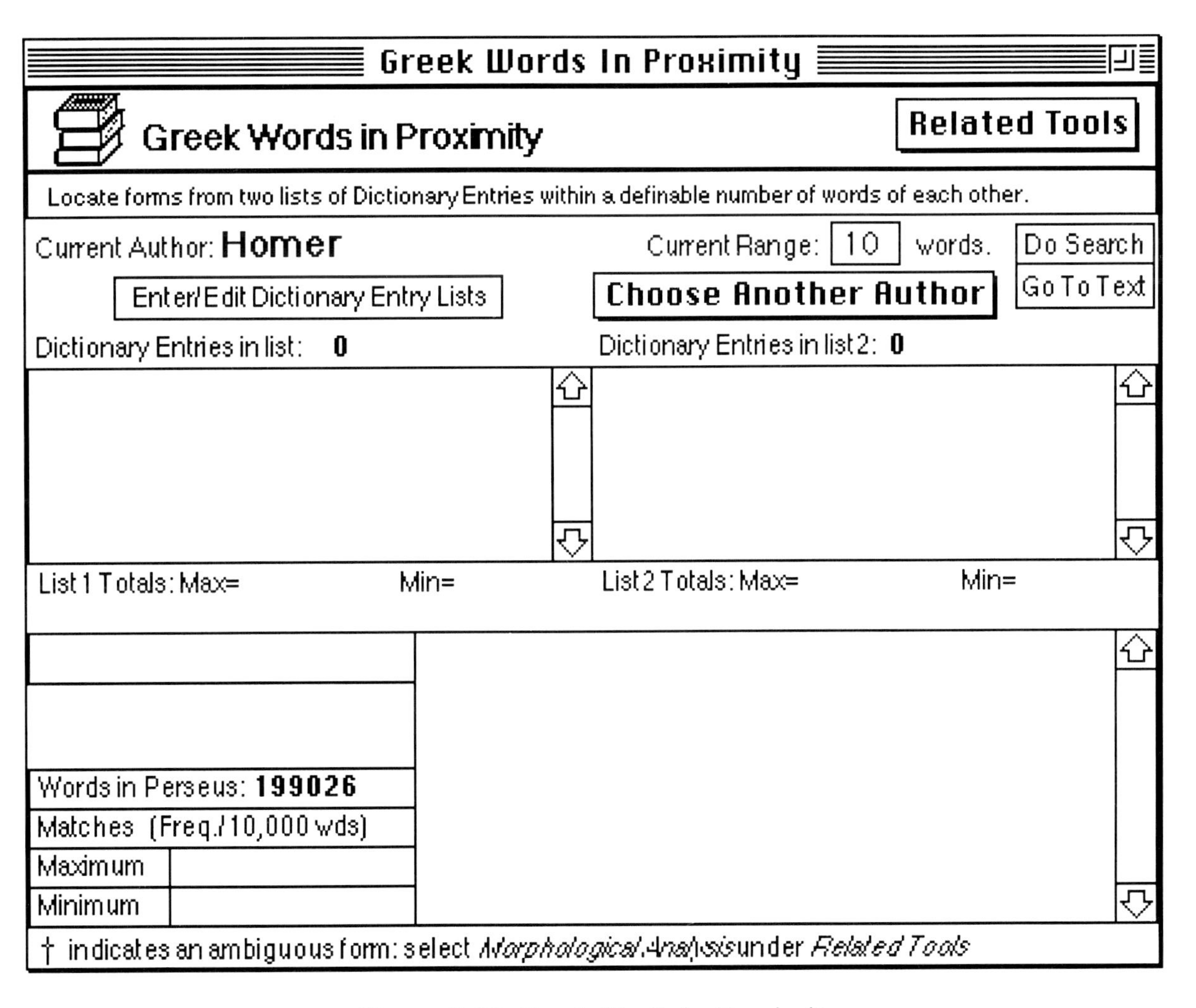

Figure 8.25 Greek Words in Proximity

An overview of how to use the "Greek Words in Proximity" tool is given in this paragraph. Examples of searches are given later in this section. From the first card, go to the Edit Lists card by clicking the button Enter/Edit Dictionary Entry Lists. Type or paste in your choices into lists 1 and 2 (figure 8.26) and return to the first card by clicking Done, in the upper right.

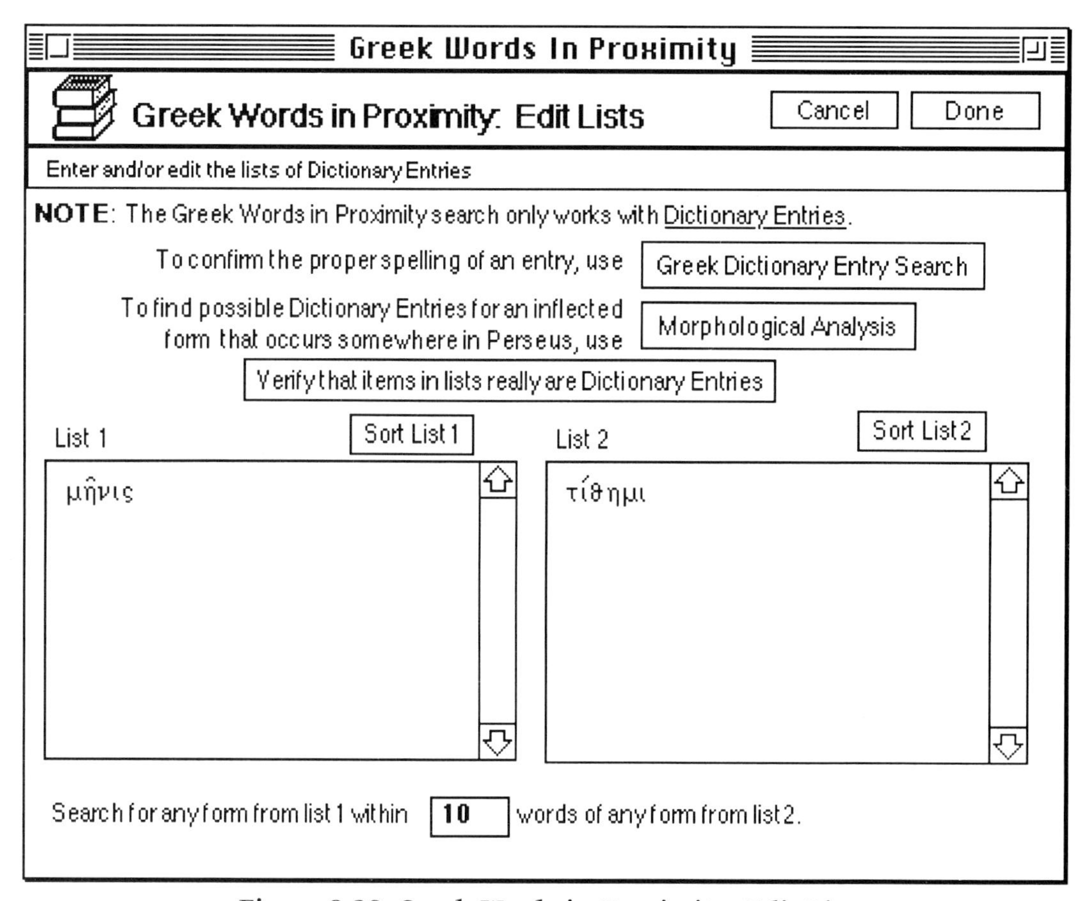

Figure 8.26 Greek Words in Proximity: Edit Lists

Now choose an author from the author list on the first card. To perform the search, click Do Search. Results appear in the field below, along with statistics. To go to a citation, select it and click the button Go To Text.

To find the words μῆνις and τίθημι in Homer within a proximity of ten words, follow these steps.

➤ Go to the "Greek Words in Proximity" tool by choosing this item from the Links menu. Or, from the Gateway, click the Tools & References icon, then click "Greek Words in Proximity" under the topic Philological Tools.

- ➤ To bring up the Edit Lists card, click the button Enter/Edit Dictionary Entry Lists. If Lists 1 and 2 contain words from a previous search, click the buttons Clear List 1 and Clear List 2.
- ➤ If you are equipped to type accented Greek, type μῆνις in the field of List 1, then type τίθημι in the field of List 2. Enter the numbers of words in proximity of which the search will take place (10) in the box at the bottom. Click Done.

Note that this tool will work only with the properly accented dictionary entry (lemma) of the words to be searched. If you cannot type accented Greek, or if you are unsure of the proper accent and spelling, click the button Greek Dictionary Entry Search. In the Look Up field, type μηνισ (no accents, no final sigma), and in the adjacent pop-up menu choose to search by "Words with this Substring" (figure 8.27).

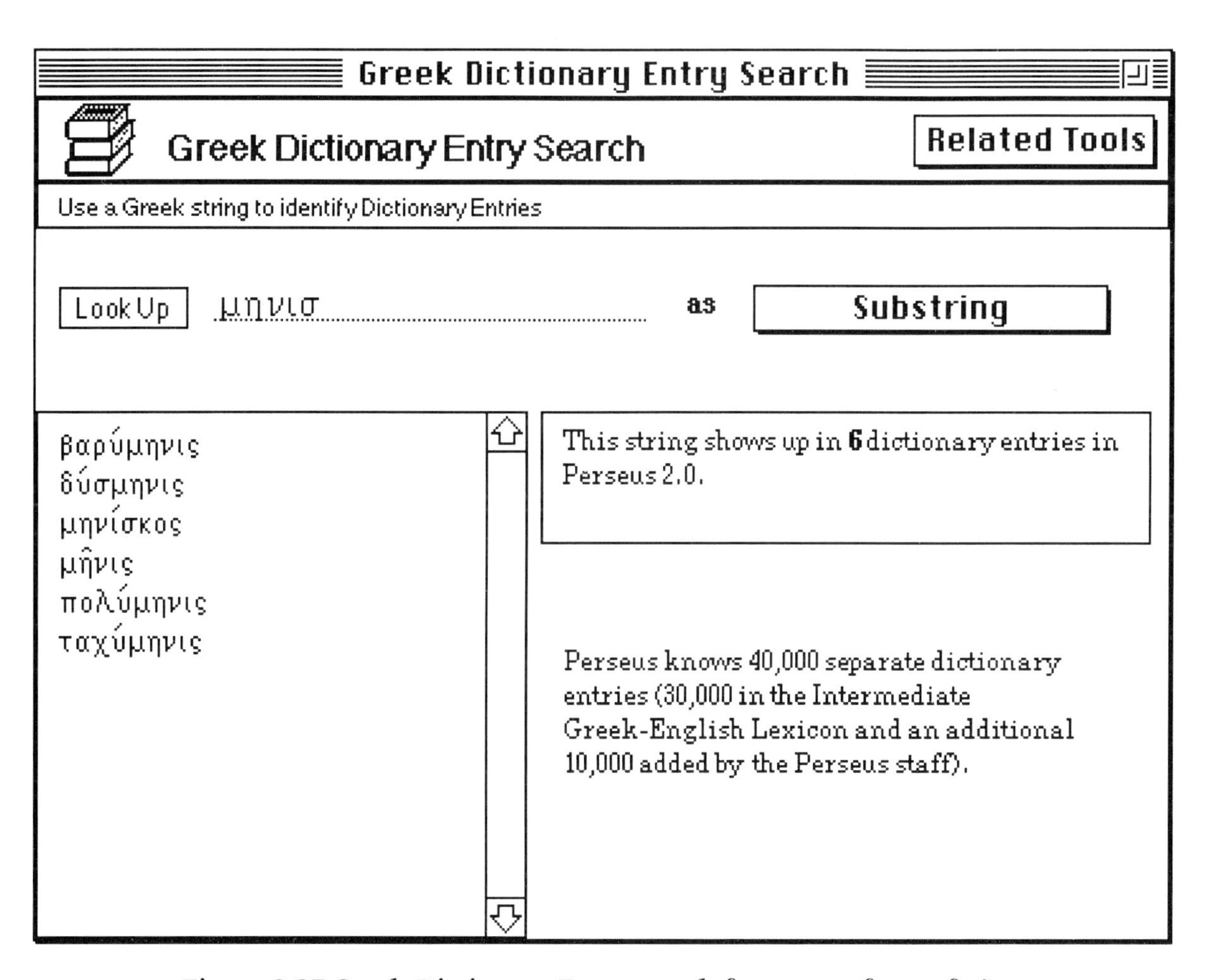

Figure 8.27 Greek Dictionary Entry search for proper form of μῆνις

➤ Now select μῆνις in the results field below and choose "Greek Words in Proximity" from the pop-up menu Related Tools, in the upper right. A dialog box will ask which list you want μῆνις entered into (figure 8.28). Click "list1." If you wish to cancel the request, click "neither." A further dialog box may appear, asking whether to add or replace your selection to the list. In this case, click Replace; if you wish to accumulate a longer list for Perseus to search, click Add.

If you have just completed the task of accumulating a long list of words from all over Perseus, you can now alphabetize your list by clicking the buttons Sort List 1 and Sort List 2.

Figure 8.28 Dialog box with query for word list

μῆνις will now be entered in List 1. Follow the same procedure for τίθημι in List 2.

Another way to obtain the lemma for a word is to use the Morphological Analysis tool. If you are viewing one of the Primary Texts in Perseus and wish to obtain the lemma for μῆνιν, for example, click the button Analyze, in the upper right of the Primary Text card. When the lemma (μῆνις) appears, highlight it and choose "Greek Words in Proximity" from the pop-up menu Related Tools. As in the previous example, a dialog box will ask which list you wish to add the word to. Make the choice and Perseus will return you to the Edit Lists card.

Now that your list of search words is complete, type the number of words in proximity, 10, into the box at the bottom. Click Done to return to the first card. Alternatively, click Cancel to return to the first card without making any changes.

μῆνις and τίθημι will now be displayed in the fields "Dictionary Entries in list."

➤ Choose Homer from the Choose Another Author pop-up menu. To perform the search, click the button Do Search. Perseus will find two citations for μῆνις in proximity with τίθημι in Homer:

Hom. Il. 1.1 μῆνιν,ἔθηκε range=10
Hom. Il. 21.523 μῆνις,ἔθηκε range=4

In the first citation, a form of μῆνις occurs within ten words of the form of τίθημι; in the second citation, the two forms are within a range of four words. To go to one of the cited passages, select it and click Go To Text.

In addition to the citations, Perseus displays a variety of statistics. In Greek, inflected forms may be ambiguous, deriving from one lemma or another (for example, the form μήνης could come from either μῆνις or the Ionic word μήνη, "moon"). Accordingly, the numbers 22 and 16 following μῆνις mean that forms of that word appear in Homer a maximum of 22 times (that is, counting ambiguities) and a minimum of 16 times (eliminating ambiguous forms).

To find a list of Greek words associated with the concept "revolt" and a list of words associated with the concept "persuade" within a proximity of ten words in Thucydides, follow these steps.

➤ From the first card of "Greek Words in Proximity," go to the Edit Lists card by clicking the button Enter/ Edit Dictionary Entry Lists. If words from a previous search are displayed in the fields, click Clear List 1 and Clear List 2. (A dialog box may ask you to confirm this command.)

➤ You will now use the English-Greek Word Search feature to generate lists of words to search. (This tool is described in greater detail in the next section.) Choose English-Greek Word Search from the Links menu. Be sure to choose the option "This word only" from the pop-up menu to the right of the Look Up field. Type "revolt" into the Look Up field and click the button Look Up, in the upper left. Choose the item "Greek Words in Proximity" from the Related Tools pop-up menu. A dialog box will ask you which list you want the "revolt" words entered into (figure 8.29). Click "list1." (If you wish to cancel the request, click "neither.") A further dialog box may appear, asking whether to add or replace your selection to the list. In this case, click Replace.

➤ Follow the same procedure for the English-Greek Word List for "persuade," and enter the list of "persuade" words into List 2.

> The Greek words in the two lists are drawn from entries in the Lexicon containing the English words "revolt" and "persuade" in their definitions. Words on the list may not always closely correspond with the targeted meaning. In some cases, you may want to edit your lists.

Your Edit Lists card should now look like figure 8.29.

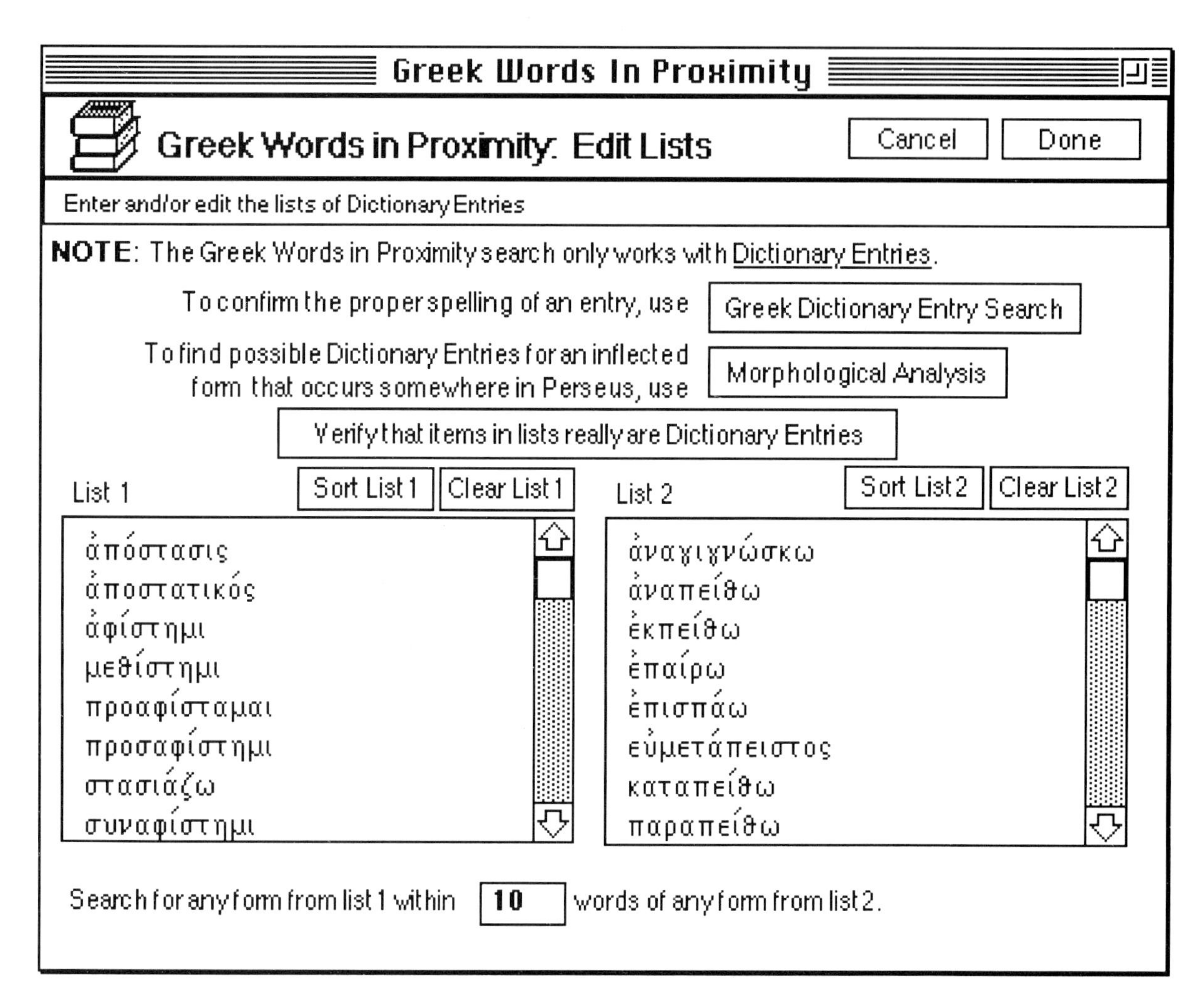

Figure 8.29 Edit Lists card, showing lists of words related to the concepts "revolt" and "persuade"

Set the span of words to be searched to 10 in the box at the bottom, and click Done to return to the first "Greek Words in Proximity" card. Choose Thucydides from the pop-up menu Choose Another Author, and click Do Search. Ten citations will appear in the field below, each of which you can move to by selecting it and clicking Go To Text.

Statistics

Statistics for the search just described are shown in figure 8.30. For List 1, there were 10 entries associated with "revolt." The asterisk to the right of the first word in List 1 directs you to the key explaining the format of the entry, which appears below the List 1 Totals.

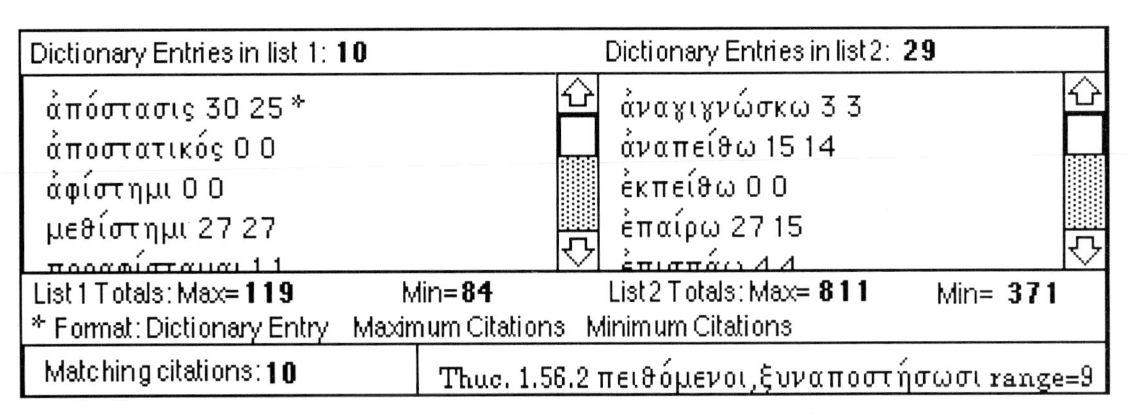

Figure 8.30 Greek Words in Proximity statistics

Accordingly, ἀπόστασις is a lemma (dictionary entry) and not an oblique form. The maximum number of occurrences of this word in Thucydides (including ambiguous forms) is 30, and 25 is the minimum number of occurrences of this word in Thucydides (subtracting ambiguous forms).

For List 1 Totals, Max = 119 means that for the 10 words associated with "revolt," the maximum number of forms found in Thucydides is 119 (including ambiguous forms), and Min = 84 means that for the same list, the minimum number of forms is 84 (subtracting ambiguous forms).

Further statistics are in the lower left. "Words in Perseus" means that there are 150,116 words in the database for the author Thucydides. For the matches in this search, the maximum number of occurrences is 4 (including ambiguous forms), and the minimum is 2 (subtracting ambiguous forms).

Sometimes Perseus will count ambiguous forms twice, forward and backward, falsely increasing the number of matching citations. If, for example, "Thuc. 2.67.1 +πεῖσαι,μεταστάντα range=5" appears four times in the list of results, you must count out the extra citations.

Options

When the search is completed, an Options pop-up menu appears in the lower left (figure 8.31), listing various ways to sort the search results.

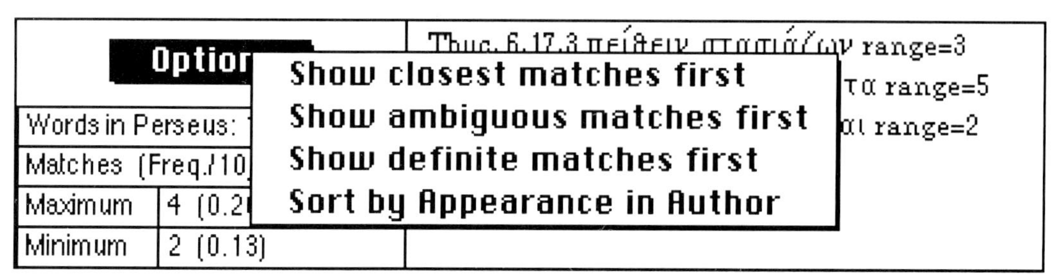

Figure 8.31 Greek Words in Proximity Options

"Show closest matches first" will display the citations starting with those whose words are closest in proximity. "Show ambiguous matches first" will display the citations starting with those containing ambiguous forms. "Show definite matches first" will display the citations starting with those that are not ambiguous. "Sort by Appearance in Author" will display the citations by line, book, or section from first to last in the works of the author.

Note that search results are limited to 30,000 characters by the HyperCard software. Thus a search for words ending in -σις within a range of five words of those ending with -άω (each suffix is found in more than 600 words) will produce an error message.

Some of the most frequently occurring words in Greek have not been indexed. Thus the "Greek Words in Proximity" tool will not work with such words as καί and ἀλλά. For a list of these words, see table 8.2.

8.4.10 ENGLISH-GREEK WORD SEARCH

The English-Greek Word Search (figure 8.32) is designed to search the Greek lexicon for words whose definitions contain a selected word or string. (Strings are defined in section 8.4.1.) Because you can use this tool to find Greek terms for English concepts, it in effect converts the Greek-English Lexicon into a rough but very powerful English-Greek lexicon. The tool is based on the entries in the Liddell-Scott *Intermediate Greek-English Lexicon*.

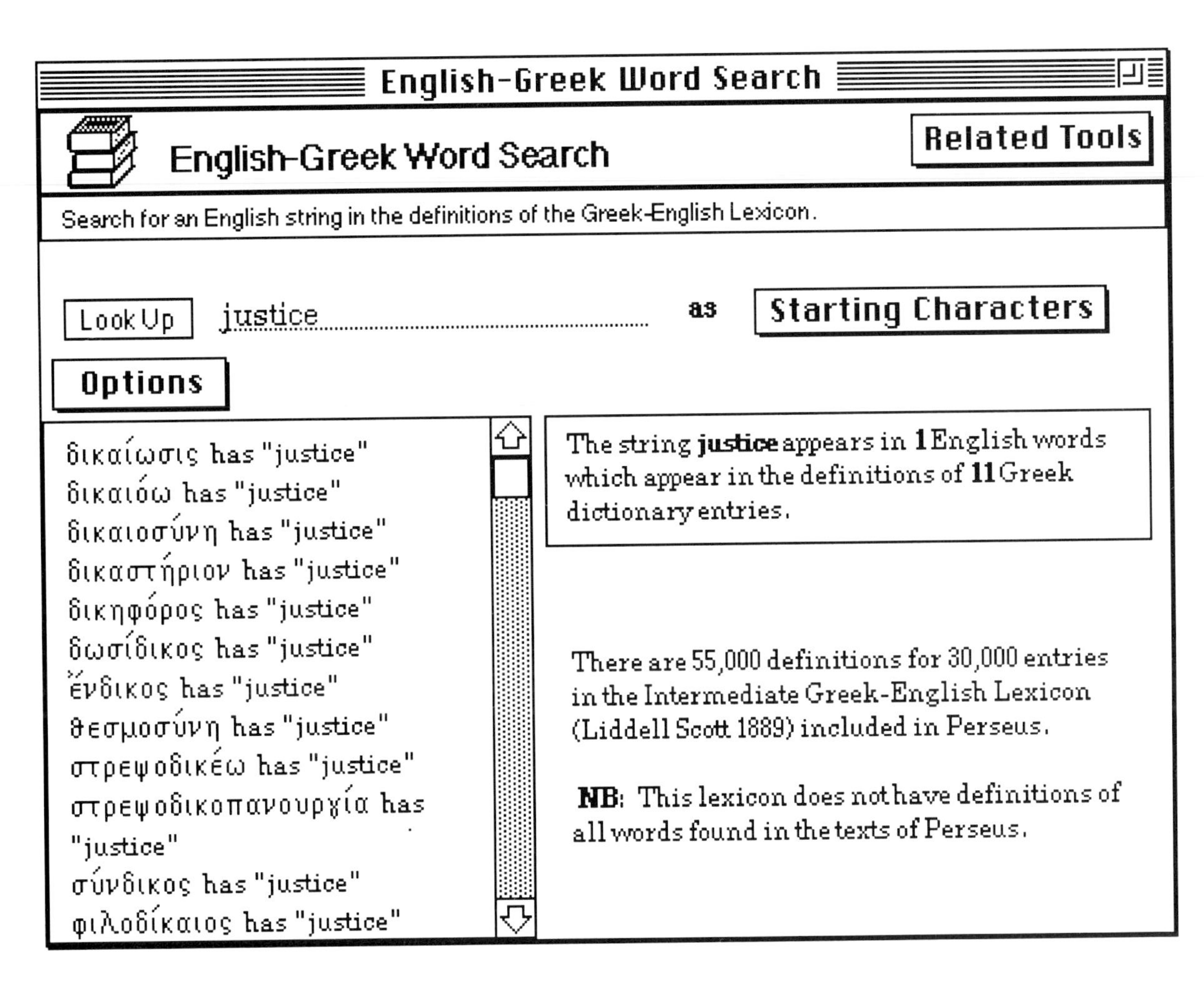

Figure 8.32 English-Greek Word Search

Not every English word in each dictionary entry has been indexed. The English-Greek Word Search will find words only in the actual English definition—words that are italicized in the print dictionary.

If you choose the English-Greek Word Search via the Tools & References Index from the Gateway or via the Links menu, you must enter a search string when the tool appears. If you choose the English-Greek Word Search via the Related Tools pop-up menu within another Philological Tool and have already selected a word, that word will automatically activate the English-Greek Word Search.

Look Up field

Use the field next to the Look Up button to enter the English word or string. If the English-Greek Word Search is showing previous results, they will be cleared with the new search. Click Look Up to perform the search.

The string or word you type must not include any spaces. The English-Greek Word Search tool will look up only one-word strings.

Search Type

Items in the pop-up menu to the right of the Look Up field define the string

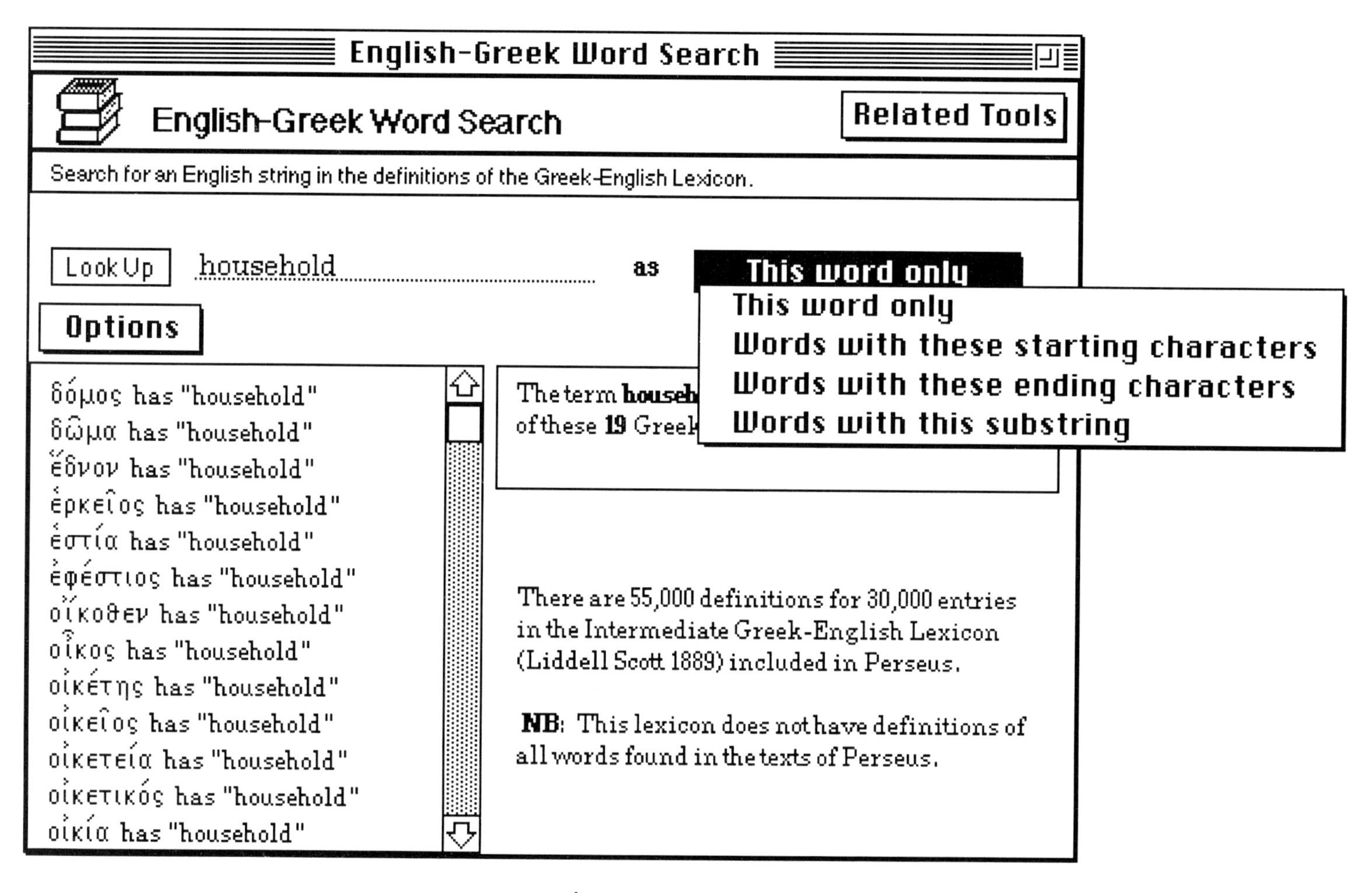

Figure 8.33 Search Type pop-up menu

to be searched. "This word only" searches for words that are identical to the string you typed (for example, "household"). "Words with these starting characters" searches for words that begin with a given string (such as "house-"). "Words with these ending characters" searches for words that end with a given string (such as "-hold"). "Words with this substring" searches for words that contain an embedded string (such as "-use-").

In the following example, you will look up several kinds of strings with the English-Greek Word Search tool.

➤ Type "household" in the Look Up field (if you haven't already done this). Choose "This word only" from the Search Type pop-up menu, then click Look Up (or just press Return). The result of the search is displayed in the text field on the lower left of the screen. The word "household" appears in the definitions of 19 Greek words, which appear in the left column. The search does not find text that is a direct translation of the selected word; instead, the search identifies Greek words that contain the selected English text in their definitions.

➤ Now try using the English-Greek Word Search to search for the string "house" (do not include a hyphen) with the search type set to "Words with these starting characters." The starting characters "house-" begin 12 English words, which occur in 187 dictionary entries.

➤ Try searches for the ending string "-hold" and the string "-use-."

Searches for extremely common English strings will take longer. On a Macintosh Performa 636CD running Perseus at 5 MB the search for -use- takes 53 seconds.

Options

When the search is completed, an Options pop-up menu appears (figure 8.34).

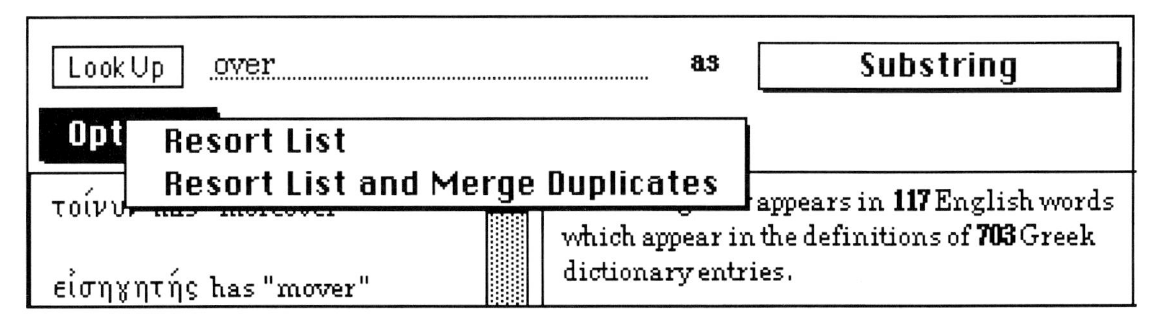

Figure 8.34 Options pop-up menu

➤ Choose Resort List from the Options pop-up menu to put the list in Greek alphabetical order.

➤ To condense the list, choose "Resort List and Merge Duplicates."

These options will take a long time to sort lists containing many hundreds of words.

You can eliminate less interesting entries by editing the results. Because you can select dictionary entries and call up their English definitions from the Greek-English Lexicon, you can use this tool even if you have little or no knowledge of Greek.

Related Tools

The Related Tools pop-up menu provides links with several other Philological Tools (figure 8.35).

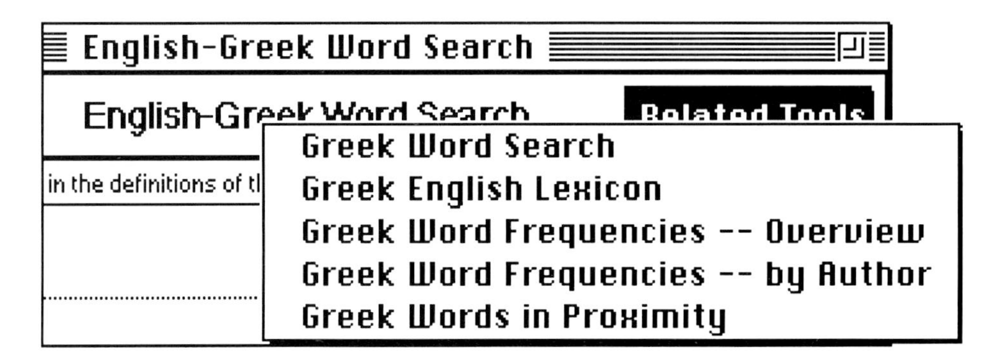

Figure 8.35 Related Tools in the English-Greek Word Search

The English-Greek Word Search generates a list of Greek dictionary entries. From the Related Tools menu, you can access the definitions of individual Greek dictionary entries by selecting them and then calling up the Greek-English Lexicon, or you can find author-by-author citations with the Greek Word Search tool.

You can also work directly with the entire list of dictionary entries that you have generated. By going to either of the two Greek Word Frequencies tools, you can see how often all the "household" words appear in works of several authors. You could thus examine whether this concept seems to be more or less common in works of different authors. (Words associated with "household" are twice as frequent in Aeschylus as in Sophocles, and 2 ⅓ times as frequent in Euripides as in Sophocles.)

If you use the Related Tools to call up the "Greek Words in Proximity" search, you can add the entire list of dictionary entries for "household" to one of the two lists (see the example in section 8.4.9). You could thus use the English-Greek Word Search to set up a search for dictionary entries that contain "household" in their definition within five words of dictionary entries that contain "guest" in their definition.

8.4.11 GREEK DICTIONARY ENTRY SEARCH

The Greek Dictionary Entry Search (figure 8.36) searches the entry headers of the Greek-English Lexicon for occurrences of a Greek character string as the starting or ending string of a word or anywhere within a word. (Strings are defined in section 8.4.1.) This tool is especially helpful in ascertaining the correct dictionary spelling and accentuation of a Greek form.

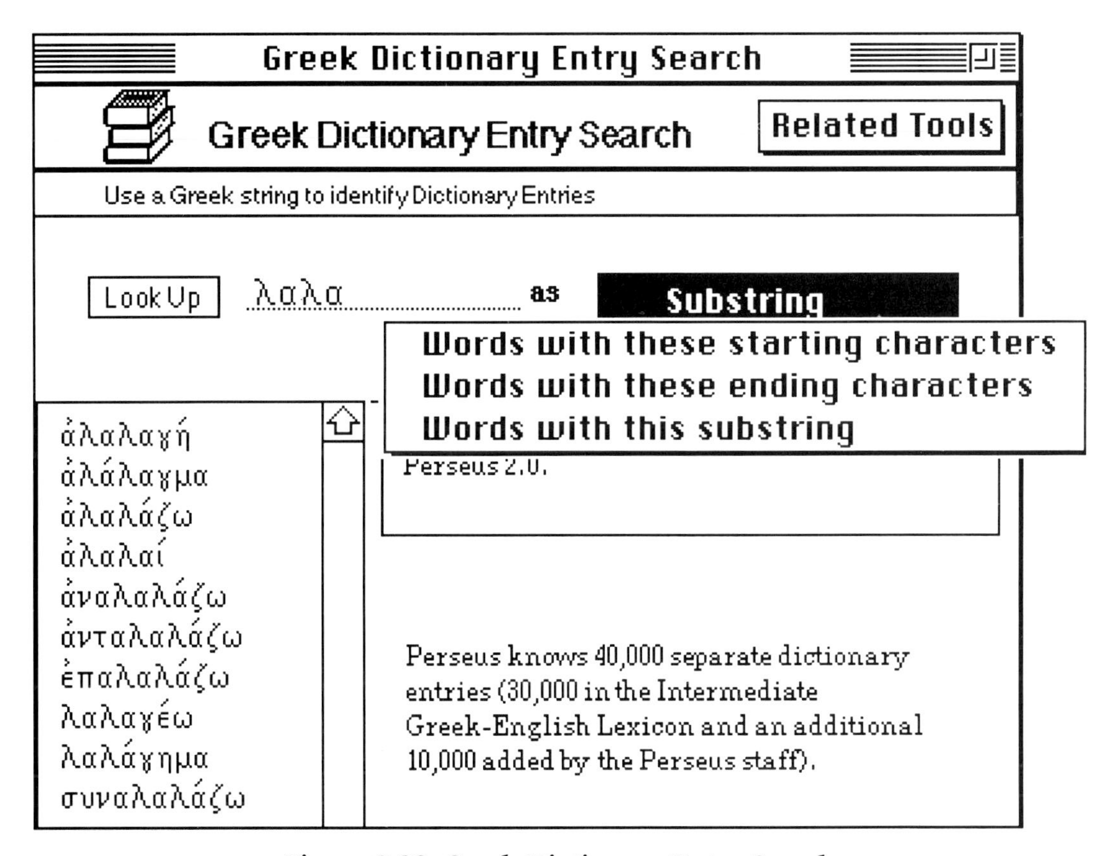

Figure 8.36 Greek Dictionary Entry Search

Look Up field and search type

➤ Enter a string to use in the Look Up field, if a word is not currently showing. (The example in figure 8.36 shows a search for the string λαλα.)

Note: it is not necessary to enter accents and breathings in order to use this tool.

➤ Click Look Up to produce the list of words.

The results appear in the field in the lower left. A dictionary entry may be selected and pasted into a field where a lemma is required (in the Greek Word Search, for example). You may also link with one of the related Philological Tools.

The pop-up menu to the right of the Look Up field gives you three ways to specify where in a word the string occurs: "Words with these starting characters," "Words with these ending characters," and "Words with this substring."

Related Tools

The Greek Dictionary Entry Search is linked with the other Philological Tools via the pop-up menu in the upper right. If you select text from the list of dictionary entries before choosing another tool, the new tool will apply itself to the selection. Thus you can copy the dictionary form of a Greek word to the following tools: Greek Word Search, Greek-English Lexicon, Greek Word Frequencies (Overview and By Author) and Greek Words in Proximity.

8.4.12 GREEK WORD FREQUENCIES

The "Greek Word Frequencies—Overview" tool displays the frequencies with which a particular Greek word, or list of words, is used among all the authors of Primary Texts. The "Greek Word Frequencies—by Author" tool displays the frequencies with which a particular Greek word, or list of words, is used in the works of one author. Both tools are accessed from the Links menu, from the Tools & Resources icon in the Gateway, and from the Related Tools pop-up menu on the other Philological Tools. If you have opened this tool from another Philological Tool, the current list of Greek words is placed in a scrolling field at the left. Each Greek Word Frequencies tool applies itself to the words in this list.

Greek Word Frequencies—Overview

The Greek Word Frequencies—Overview tool is shown with a list of words associated with "horse" (figure 8.37).

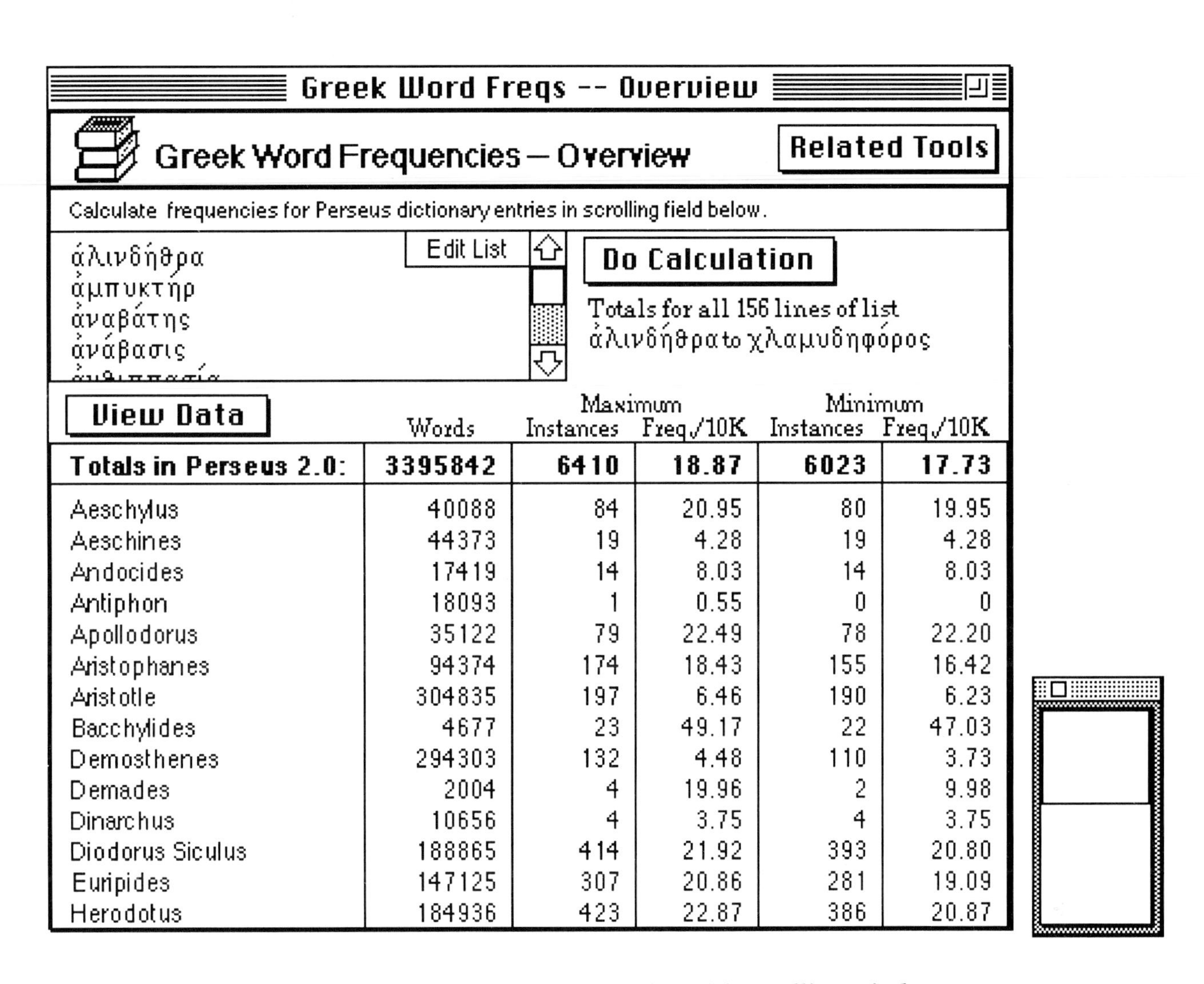

	Words	Maximum Instances	Maximum Freq./10K	Minimum Instances	Minimum Freq./10K
Totals in Perseus 2.0:	**3395842**	**6410**	**18.87**	**6023**	**17.73**
Aeschylus	40088	84	20.95	80	19.95
Aeschines	44373	19	4.28	19	4.28
Andocides	17419	14	8.03	14	8.03
Antiphon	18093	1	0.55	0	0
Apollodorus	35122	79	22.49	78	22.20
Aristophanes	94374	174	18.43	155	16.42
Aristotle	304835	197	6.46	190	6.23
Bacchylides	4677	23	49.17	22	47.03
Demosthenes	294303	132	4.48	110	3.73
Demades	2004	4	19.96	2	9.98
Dinarchus	10656	4	3.75	4	3.75
Diodorus Siculus	188865	414	21.92	393	20.80
Euripides	147125	307	20.86	281	19.09
Herodotus	184936	423	22.87	386	20.87

Figure 8.37 Greek Word Frequencies with scrolling window

The list of words was produced by the English-Greek Word Search tool; for this procedure, see section 8.4.10. Use the scrolling window to move up or down the list (use of the scrolling window is described in section 4.1.3). Edit this list (or generate your own) by clicking the button Edit List in the upper right corner of the word list field. A card labeled "Edit List of Dictionary Entries" appears (figure 8.38).

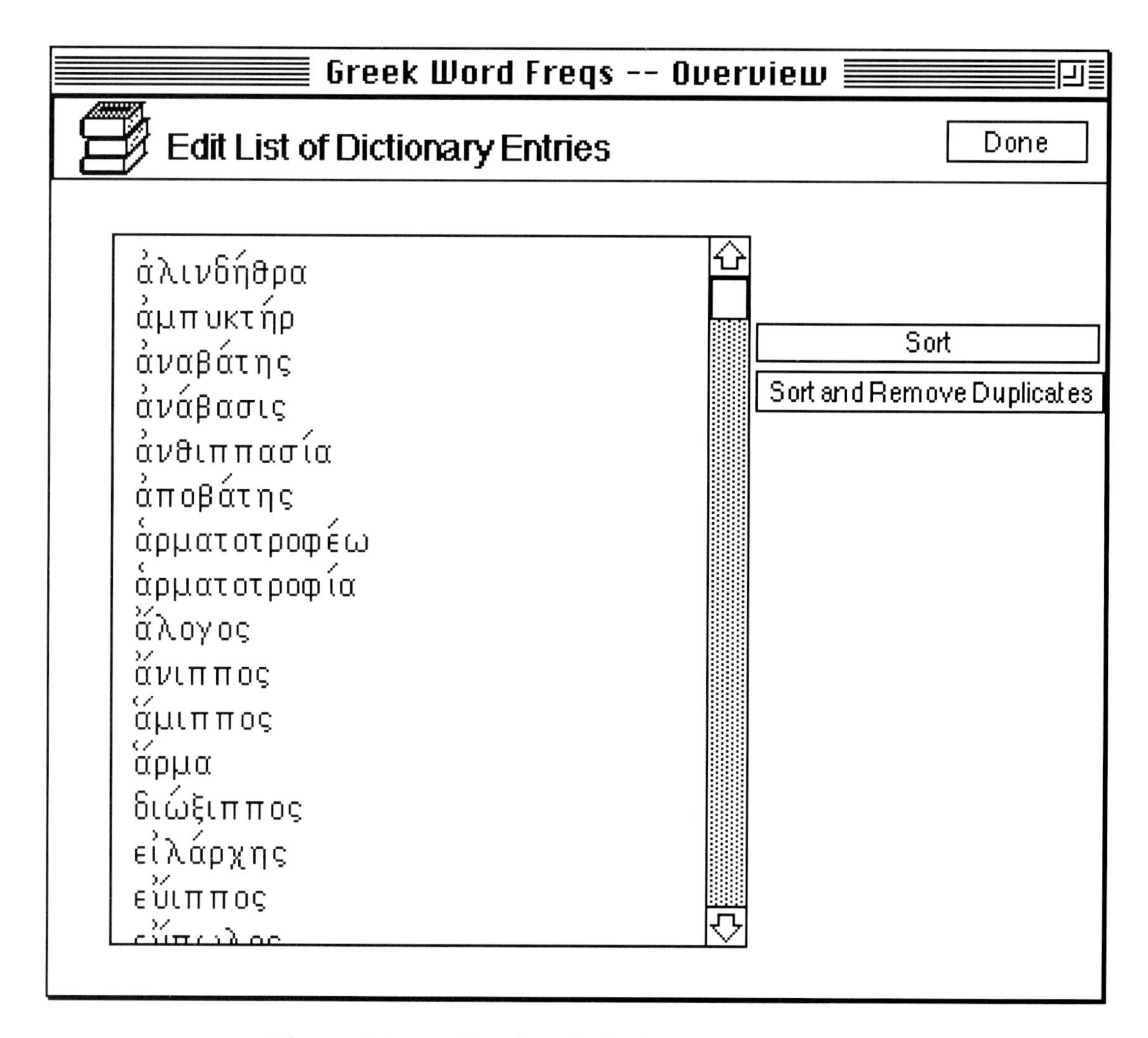

Figure 8.38 "Edit List of Dictionary Entries" card

From the Edit List card you may type in your own dictionary entries (with correct accents and breathings) or paste in entries from elsewhere in Perseus. You can find the dictionary entry with the Greek Dictionary Entry Search tool, described in section 8.4.11. Sort the list alphabetically by clicking the Sort button; sort the list alphabetically and remove duplicates by clicking the button "Sort and Remove Duplicates." When you are through editing your list, click Done.

Do Calculation

You can calculate frequencies for the whole list by choosing the item "Calculate for All Entries in List" from the pop-up menu Do Calculation. Calculate frequencies for a single word by choosing "Calculate for Selected Entry."

View Data

The pop-up menu View Data (figure 8.39) offers three ways in which to organize your results. The option Sort Authors Alphabetically is the default.

Figure 8.39 View Data pop-up menu

To group authors by literary type (Tragedy, Comedy, History, and so on), choose "Sort Authors By Type of Literature." To see results chronologically by author, choose "Sort Authors By Author Date."

Statistical information

The information for each author includes the total words in all works of the author cataloged in Perseus and the statistical reports for any possible use of the word (Maximum) and all definite uses of the word (Minimum). Instances are the number of times the word is used throughout the author's work. Frequency is the number of instances a word is used per 10,000 words.

Related Tools

The Greek Word Frequencies—Overview tool is linked with the other Philological Tools via the Related Tools pop-up menu, in the upper right. If you select text from the word list before choosing another tool, the new tool will apply itself to the selection. Select a word for which frequencies are displayed and choose Greek Word Search to see citations in the works of an author, and use Greek-English Lexicon to see the definition. For Greek Word Frequencies—by Author (described later in this section), select a word or group of words to search them; if no selection is made, Perseus will copy the entire list to Greek Word Frequencies—by Author.

Greek Word Frequencies—by Author

The description of the "Greek Word Frequencies—by Author" tool continues with the example of a list of words associated with "horse" (figure 8.40).

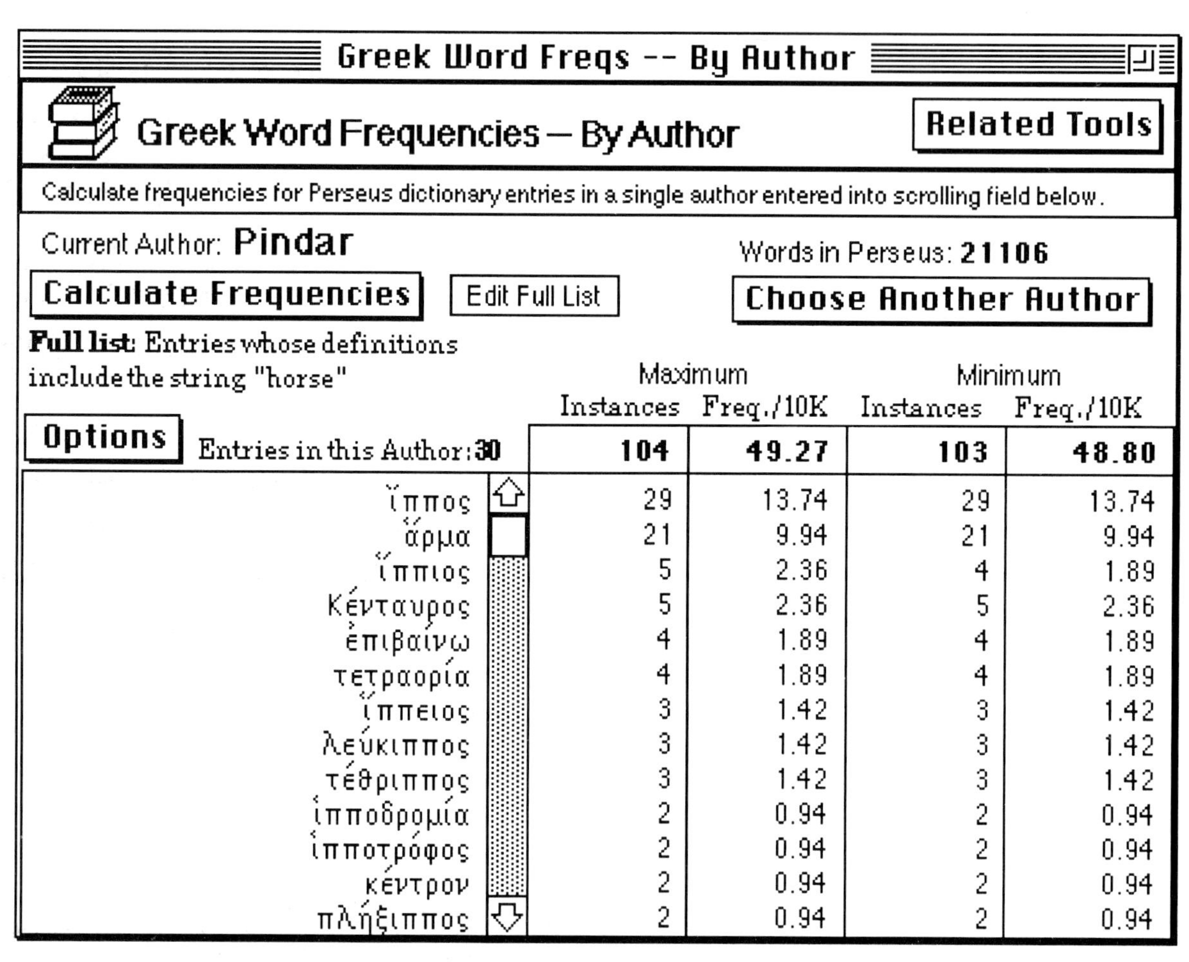

Figure 8.40 Greek Word Frequencies—by Author

You can copy a list of Greek words associated with an English word (in this case, "horse") from the English-Greek Word Search into "Greek Word Frequencies—by Author" by choosing this item from the Related Tools pop-up menu. For details on this procedure, see section 8.4.10. Edit this list (or generate your own) by clicking the button Edit Full List, to the right of the Calculate Frequencies pop-up menu. A card labeled "Edit List of Dictionary Entries" appears (figure 8.41).

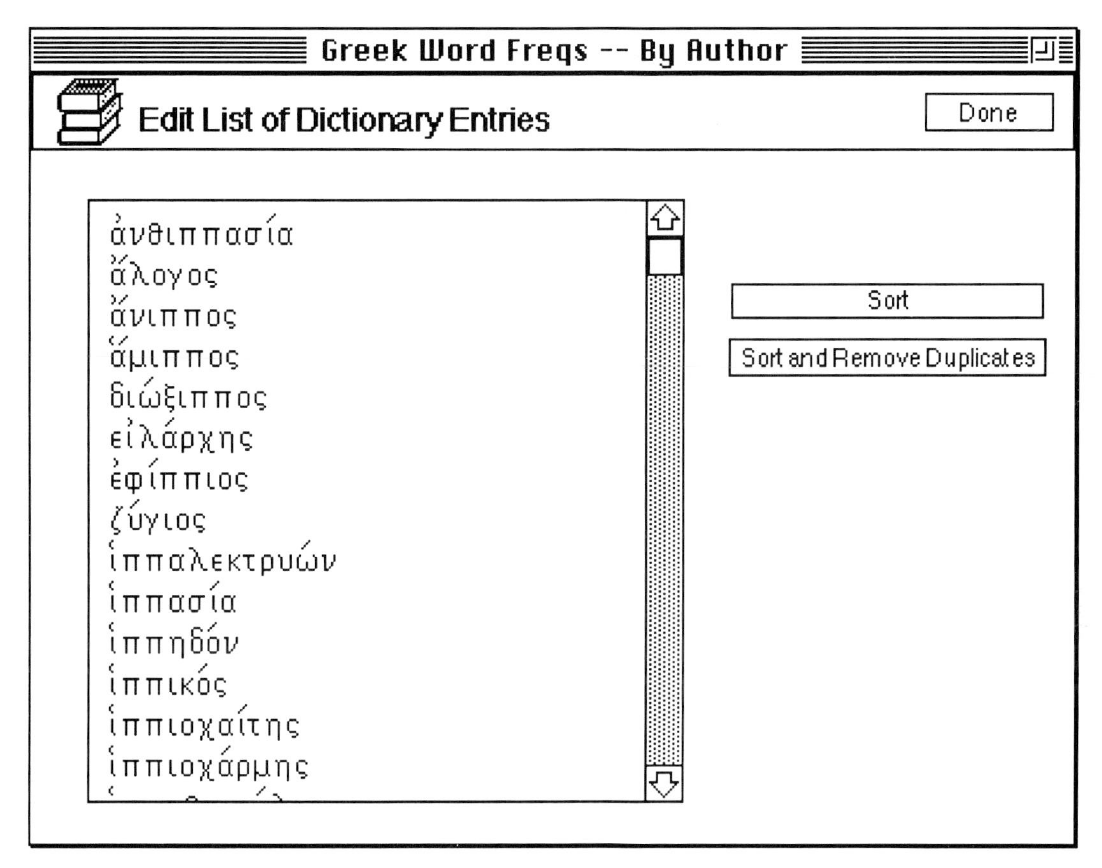

Figure 8.41 "Edit List of Dictionary Entries" card, Greek Word Frequencies—by Author

You can edit this list or type in a list of your own with correct accents and breathings. Sort alphabetically by clicking the button Sort. Remove duplicates by clicking the button Sort and Remove Duplicates. When you are through editing the list, click Done to return to the "Greek Word Frequencies—by Author" card.

The current author is displayed in the upper left. Change authors by choosing an author from the list in the pop-up menu Choose Another Author. The example will continue with words associated with "horse" in Demosthenes. (The orators as a group have a low frequency rate of "horse" words.)

Calculate Frequencies

There are three ways to calculate word frequencies in the works of an author. To see a list of only those words associated with "horse" that Demosthenes uses, choose the item "Show Frequencies for Entries in this Author" from the Calculate Frequencies pop-up menu (figure 8.42).

Figure 8.42 Ways to calculate word frequencies by author

The results of the calculation are shown in figure 8.43. The choice "Show Frequencies for all Entries in Full List" will include words from your list that are not used by Demosthenes. Choose "Precalculate frequencies for all authors" if you wish Perseus to work out the calculations for all authors in the database. (Results are displayed in backward alphabetical order, because the data for Xenophon are the last that the computer operates on.) Go from author to author via the Choose Another Author pop-up menu, or use the right and left arrows on the Navigator Palette.

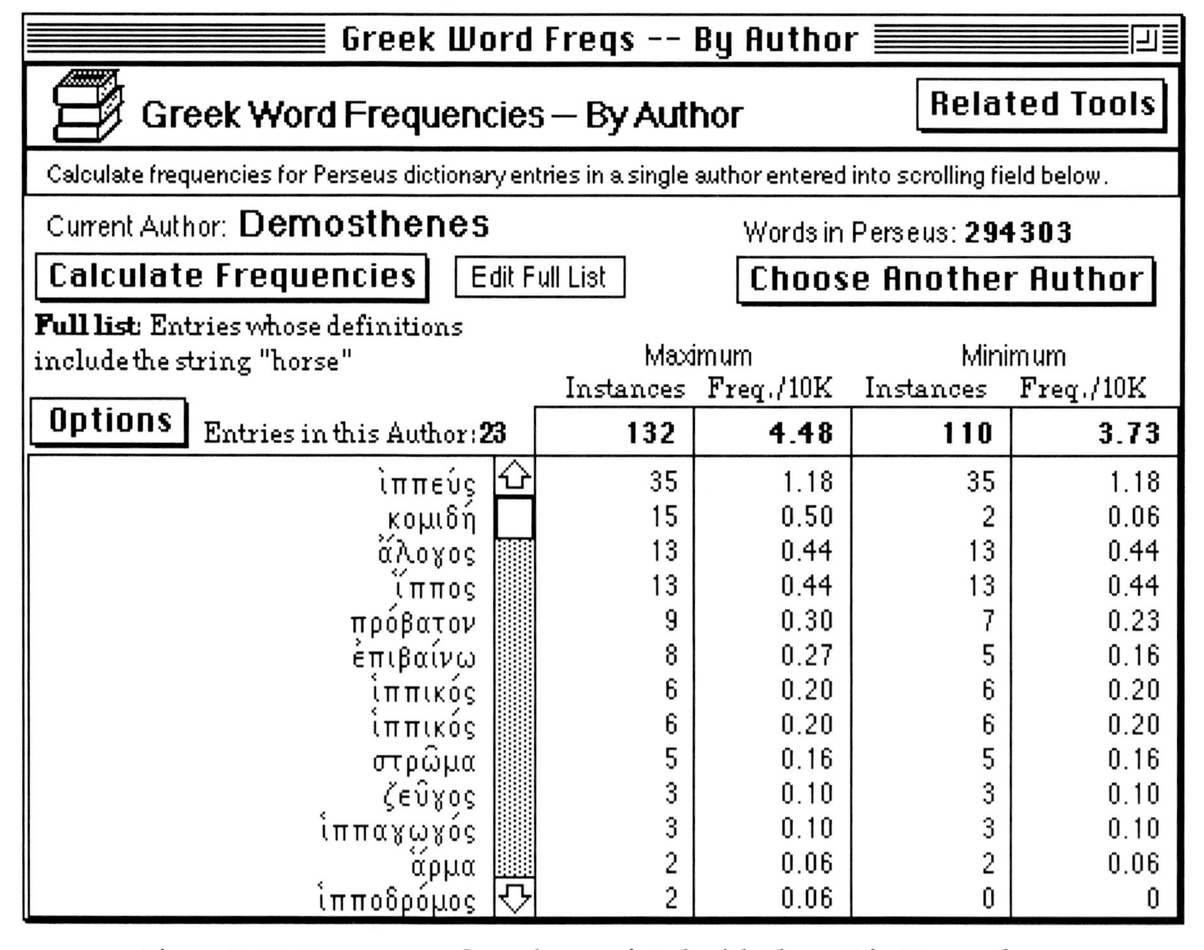

Figure 8.43 Frequency of words associated with "horse" in Demosthenes

Options

Four ways of sorting your results appear under the Options pop-up menu (figure 8.44).

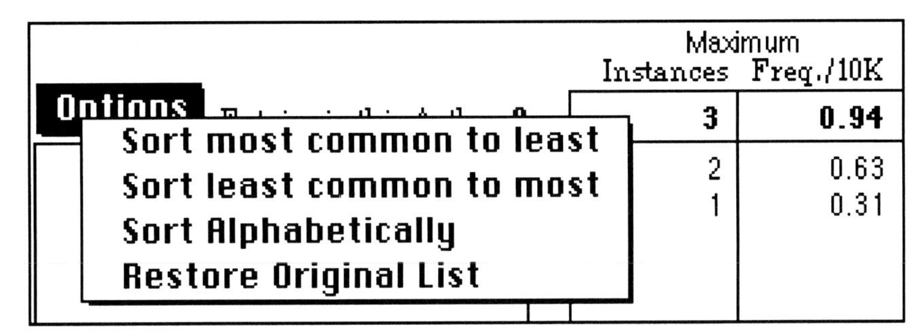

Figure 8.44 Options pop-up menu

To display the results in order from the most commonly used words to the least, choose "Sort most common to least." To reverse this order, choose "Sort least common to most." To display the results alphabetically, choose Sort Alphabetically. To bring back the original list *but remove the results of the search,* choose Restore Original List.

Related Tools

The "Greek Word Frequencies—by Author" tool is linked with the other Philological Tools via the Related Tools pop-up menu, in the upper right. If you select text from the word list before choosing another tool, the new tool will apply itself to the selection. Select a word from the list and choose Greek Word Search to see citations in the works of an author and choose Greek English Lexicon for the definition. If you make no selection and choose Greek Word Frequencies—Overview, Perseus will copy the full list to it.

Tools to search the Perseus database include the Browser and English Index (described in chapter 5) and Philological Tools for working with the Greek language (described in chapter 8). References include the Encyclopedia and Bibliography. These are the utilities and secondary resources that Perseus provides to find and analyze information.

9.1 TOOLS & REFERENCES INDEX

The Tools & References Index (figure 9.1) displays the names of tools and references in Perseus and provides access to them. As with other Perseus indexes, the main categories are shown in boldface, with subcategories shown beneath each main category.

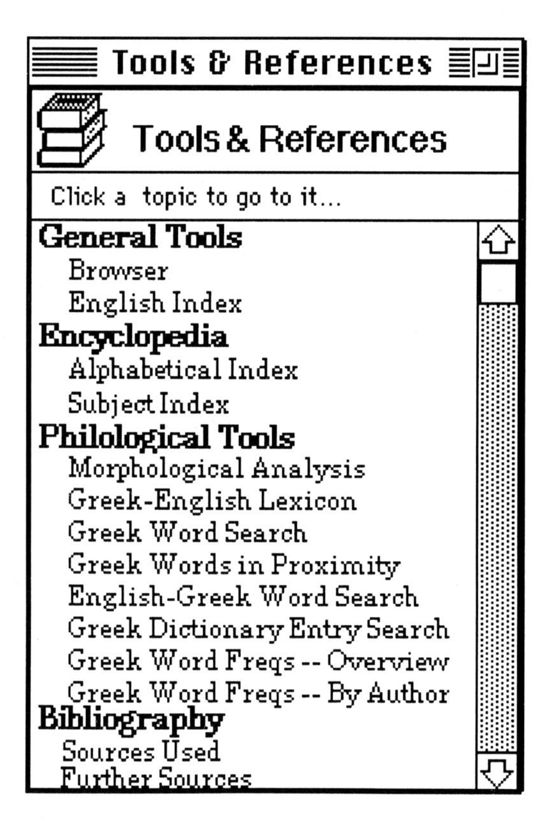

Figure 9.1 Tools & References Index

➤ Click a subcategory to use that tool or reference.

Try clicking a subcategory under each main topic. Then click the Go Back icon on the Navigator Palette to return to the Tools & References Index.

9.2 ENCYCLOPEDIA

The Encyclopedia is composed of short articles and glosses concerning Classical civilization, art, and architecture. The articles and glosses are based on several sources, and some articles are accompanied by views or illustrations. Approximately three hundred articles were written expressly for the Perseus Project. They provide descriptions of regions of Greece, biographies of ancient authors, terminology for art and architecture, and explanations of musical instruments. These articles may also be accessed from the Essays & Catalogs icon on the Gateway.

The remaining entries (approximately 3500) are derived from the indexes to the Loeb Classical Library editions of Herodotus and Apollodorus and the Frazer edition of Pausanias, and are so marked. These entries are useful primarily because they contain explanatory glosses of the encyclopedia entry. In addition, it is possible to use the references to Herodotus, Apollodorus, and Pausanias to go directly into the appropriate text.

These gloss-type entries, however, are restricted to these three authors and may not include other citations in Perseus. To find other citations, use the English Word Search or the Lookup tool.

From the Gateway, go to the Encyclopedia by clicking the Tools & References icon, then choose either Alphabetical Index or Subject Index, under the heading Encyclopedia. Or, from anywhere within Perseus, choose the item Encyclopedia from the Links menu (the Alphabetical Index is the default point of entry). The Subject Index lists only the articles written for Perseus and not the entries derived from the Loeb indexes (figure 9.2). The Alphabetical Index lists both types of Encyclopedia entries (figure 9.3).

9.2.1 SUBJECT INDEX

➤ Click Subject Index on the Tools & References Index to see the list of encyclopedia entries listed by subject.

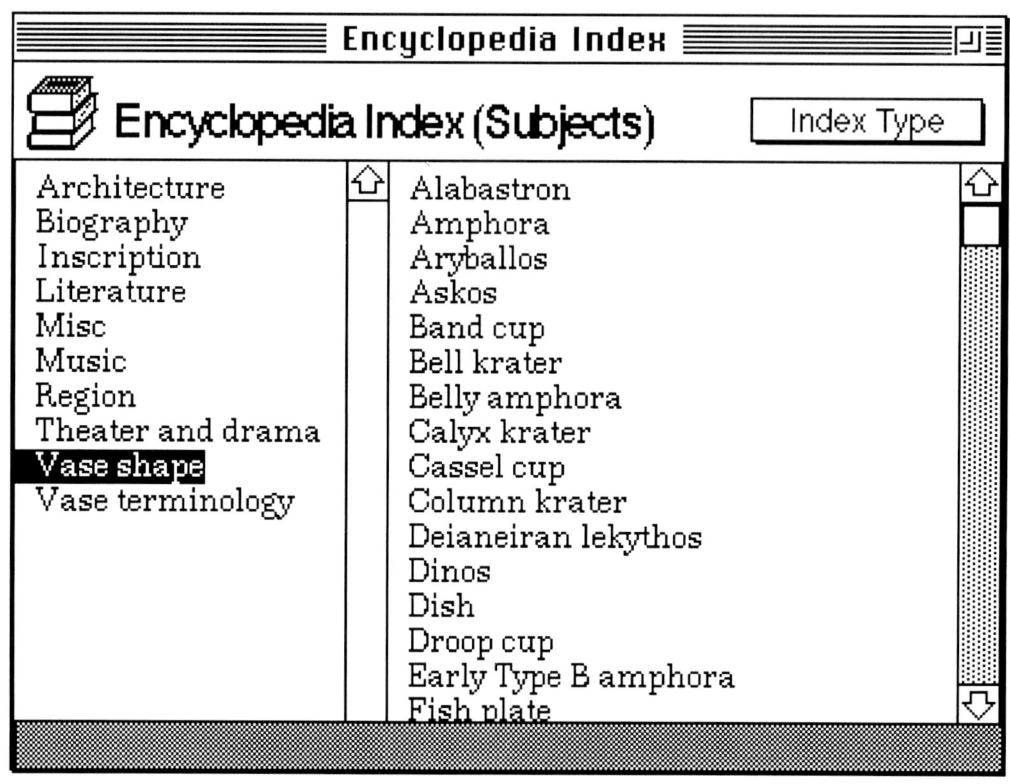

Figure 9.2 Subject Index of Encyclopedia articles

➤ Click a subject to see the list of articles on that topic.

➤ Click an entry in the right-hand column to see that article.

Try clicking the subject Vase shape and then the entry Amphora, to follow the example shown in section 9.2.3 and illustrated in figure 9.2.

9.2.2 ALPHABETICAL INDEX

To go to the Alphabetical Index, click Alphabetical Index on the Tools & References Index. Or, from anywhere within Perseus, choose Encyclopedia from the Links menu. You will then see the list of Encyclopedia entries in alphabetical order.

To go from the Alphabetical Index to the Subject Index, choose Subject from the Index Type pop-up menu, in the upper right.

➤ Click a letter at the bottom to see the list of articles beginning with that letter. Scroll down and click an entry in the right-hand column to go to that article (figure 9.3).

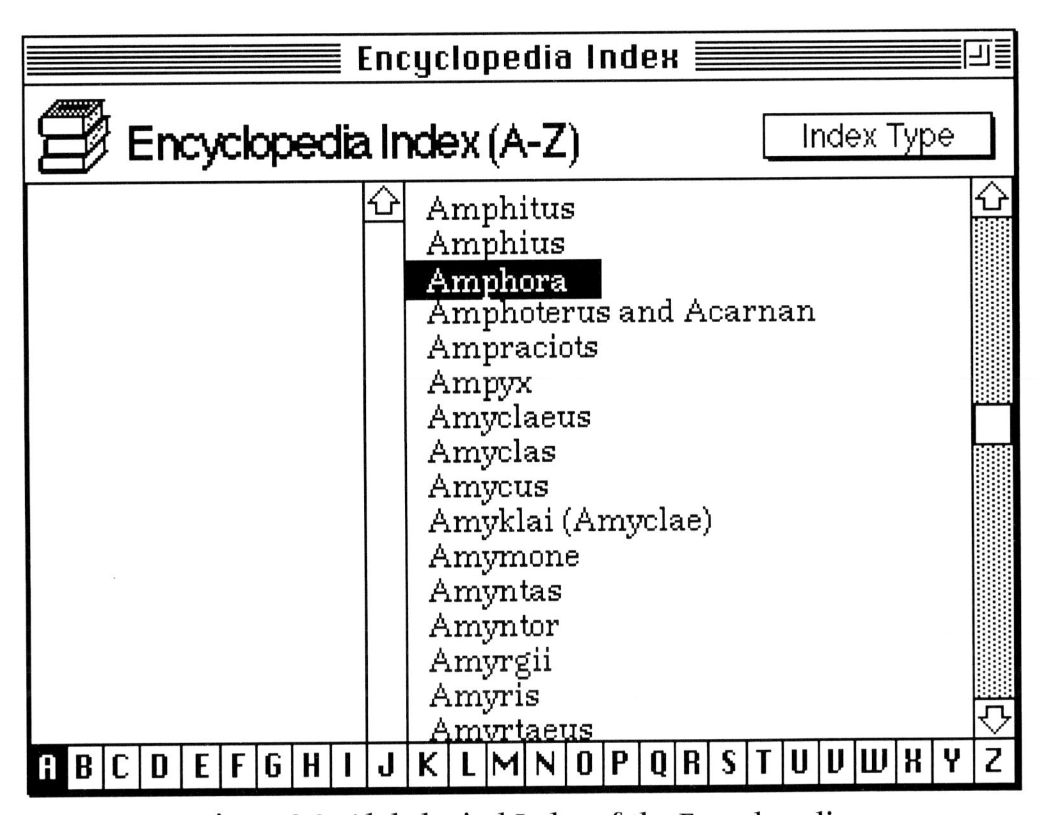

Figure 9.3 Alphabetical Index of the Encyclopedia

The example in the next section uses the article for Amphora.

9.2.3 ENCYCLOPEDIA ARTICLE

Each article in the Encyclopedia consists of the text of the article, a bibliography of primary sources, and a list of related topics in the Encyclopedia. A typical article is depicted in figure 9.4.

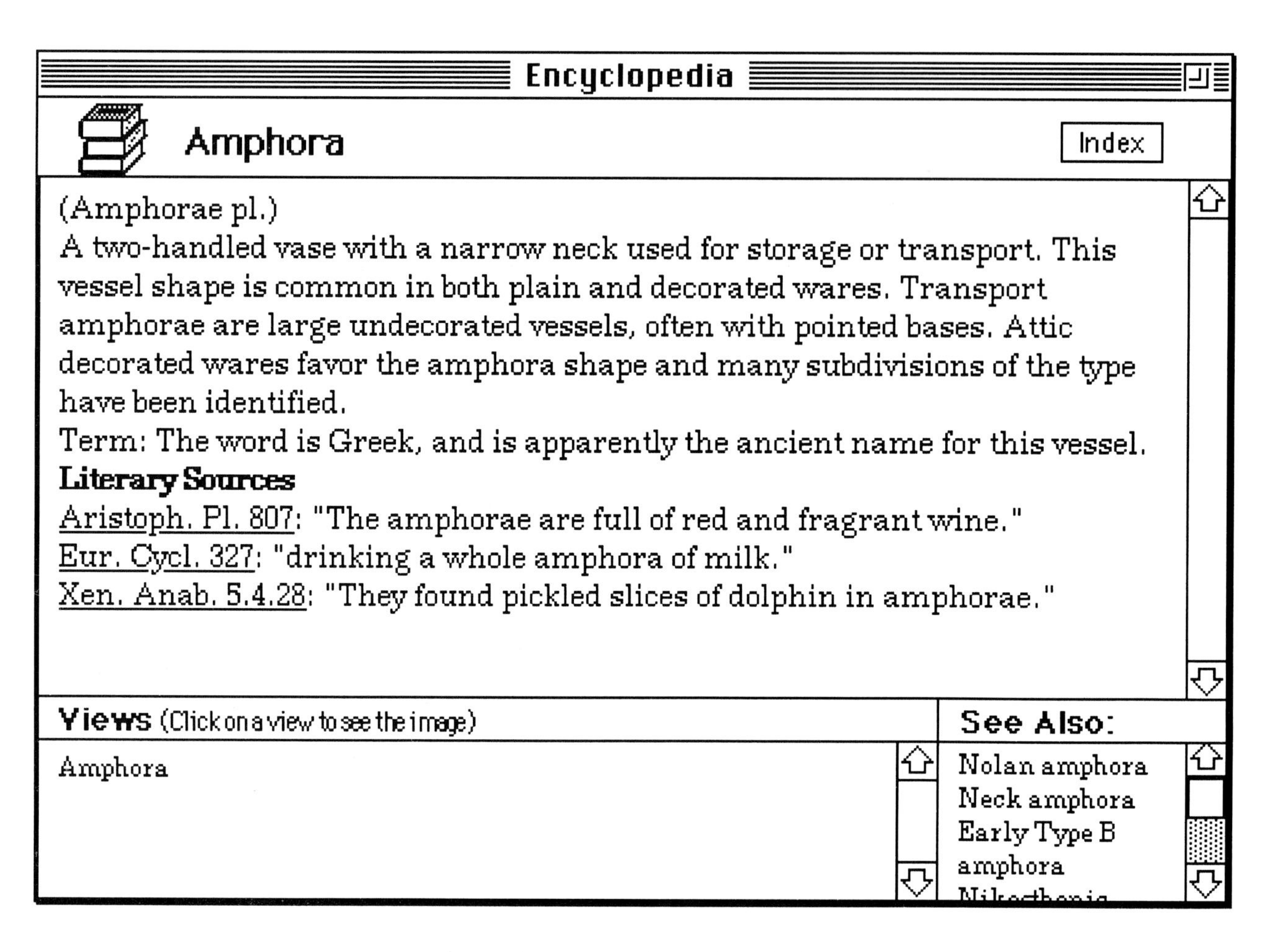

Figure 9.4 Encyclopedia article

The Tools & References icon is at the top left of the article, followed by the name of the entry. On the top right is the Index button. The text of the article appears in a scrolling text field. Literary Sources are listed at the end of this field. References to texts in Perseus are underlined and shown in their abbreviated canonical syntax.

Below the text of the article are two fields: Views and See Also. Views is a list of any illustrations and photographs related to the topic of the article. See Also lists any cross-references to related articles in the Encyclopedia.

Index

➤ Click Index to return to the Alphabetical Index of the Encyclopedia.

Literary Sources

Literary Sources for the encyclopedia article, if applicable, are shown at the end of the article.

➤ Highlight a reference from this field and choose Primary Texts from the Links menu to go directly to the reference.

To return to the encyclopedia article, click the Go Back arrow on the Navigator Palette.

Views

➤ Click a line in the list of views to see an illustration or a photograph.

If no views are available, this area will be empty.

Views are of two types: illustrations and photographs. Both types appear in an additional window. When a view is displayed, drawing or photography credits also appear in a small floating window that can be closed or repositioned on the screen.

> NOTE: The illustrations and photographs are not stored in HyperCard and therefore their treatment should be different from that of other Perseus elements. In particular, you must click the close box to remove an illustration. If the window is not active, click the title bar. If you use the Navigator while an illustration window is open, Perseus will respond, but you will be unable to see the response if the image window is covering the active HyperCard window.

See Also

➤ Click a related topic in the See Also field to see that article in the Encyclopedia.

9.3 BIBLIOGRAPHY

The Perseus Bibliography is divided into two sections, Sources Used and Further Sources. Sources Used contains citations from secondary works used to compile the Perseus database. Further Sources lists sources of information external to Perseus that are pertinent to the study of ancient Greek language, culture, and art.

9.3.1 SOURCES USED

The Sources Used resource has more than 2500 entries of materials used in the development of Perseus. It is designed to be used primarily as an interactive bibliography that you can call on whenever you see a source attribution in narrative, catalog descriptions, or notes.

To access the Sources Used Index (figure 9.5) from the Gateway, click the Tools & Resources icon, then click Sources Used, under the heading Bibliography. Or, from anywhere within Perseus, choose Sources Used from the Links menu.

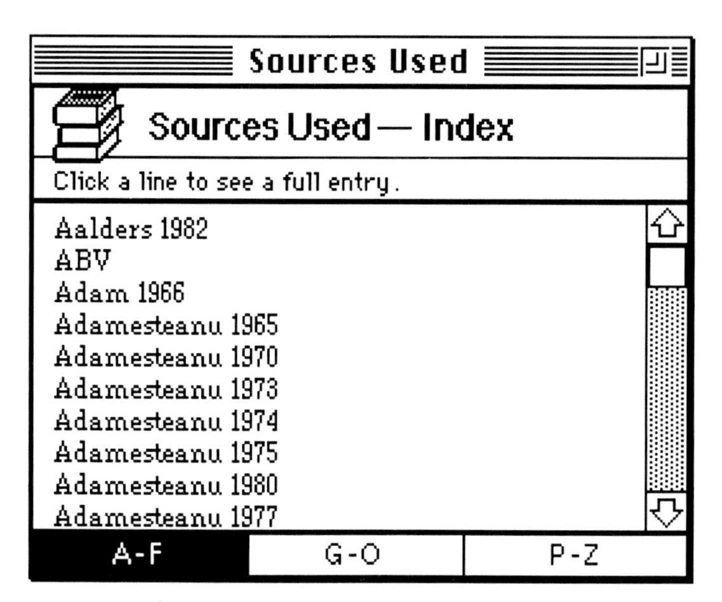

Figure 9.5 Sources Used Index

The three buttons on the bottom take you to short entry headings beginning with the letters A through F, G through O, and P through Z. Click an item in the Sources Used Index to go to the full entry. Figure 9.6 shows the full entry for the item Aalders 1982.

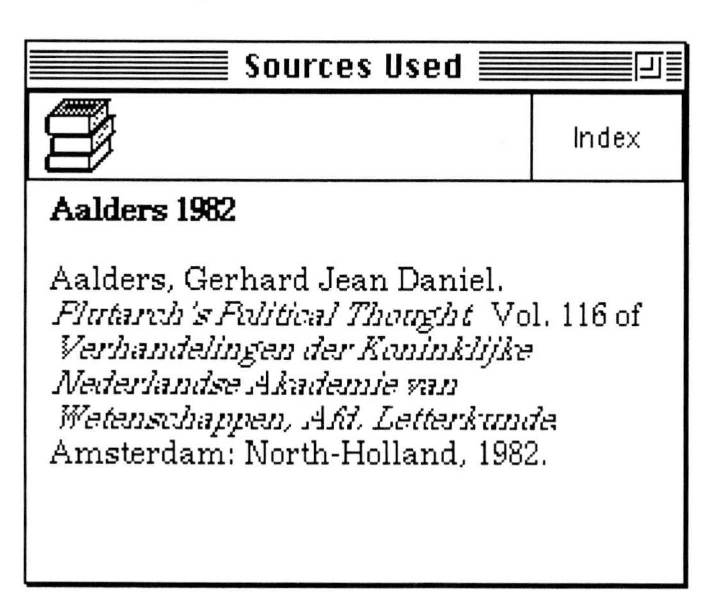

Figure 9.6 Sources Used, full entry

➤ Click the button Index, in the upper right, to return to the Sources Used Index.

To link with Sources Used from a Perseus citation, follow these steps.

The Pottery descriptions in the Art & Archaeology resource display the various sources used to compile the information in the descriptions. To follow this example, use the Lookup tool to go directly to the vase Boston 98.894.

➤ Choose Lookup from the Links menu, type "Boston 98.894" in the floating window, and press Return. Then click "in Vase Catalog" in the right column of results.

➤ When you see the Catalog Summary card for this object, click the Description button in the upper right. Scroll to the end of the description.

➤ At the bottom of the description, highlight the first source attribution, Fairbanks 1928.

Note that the selection must be exact, that is, you must not highlight the spaces before or after Fairbanks 1928.

➤ Choose Sources Used from the Links menu. (Hold the Shift key down to open the Sources Used stack in a new window.)

The Sources Used resource opens to the full citation for Fairbanks 1928. Use the Index button to see an alphabetical list of citations. Although you can page through the Sources Used information by clicking the right and left arrows on the Navigator Palette, you will be unable to relate the citations to a specific Perseus item.

9.3.2 FURTHER SOURCES

Further Sources are further bibliographic references for the interested reader. Despite the abundance of its texts, images, and reference materials, Perseus contains only a small part of the resources available to students of Classical Greece. Further Sources lists a number of books, some very old, others less so, some of interest primarily to beginners, some to specialists. These books are useful supplements to Perseus and are profitably used in conjunction with it.

The list of further sources includes grammars and dictionaries, general reference works, and specific references for history, literature, religion, myth, geography, culture, architecture, and art.

➤ To go to Further Sources, click the Tools & References icon on the Gateway, then click Further Sources under the heading Bibliography (figure 9.7).

You cannot access Further Sources via the Links menu.

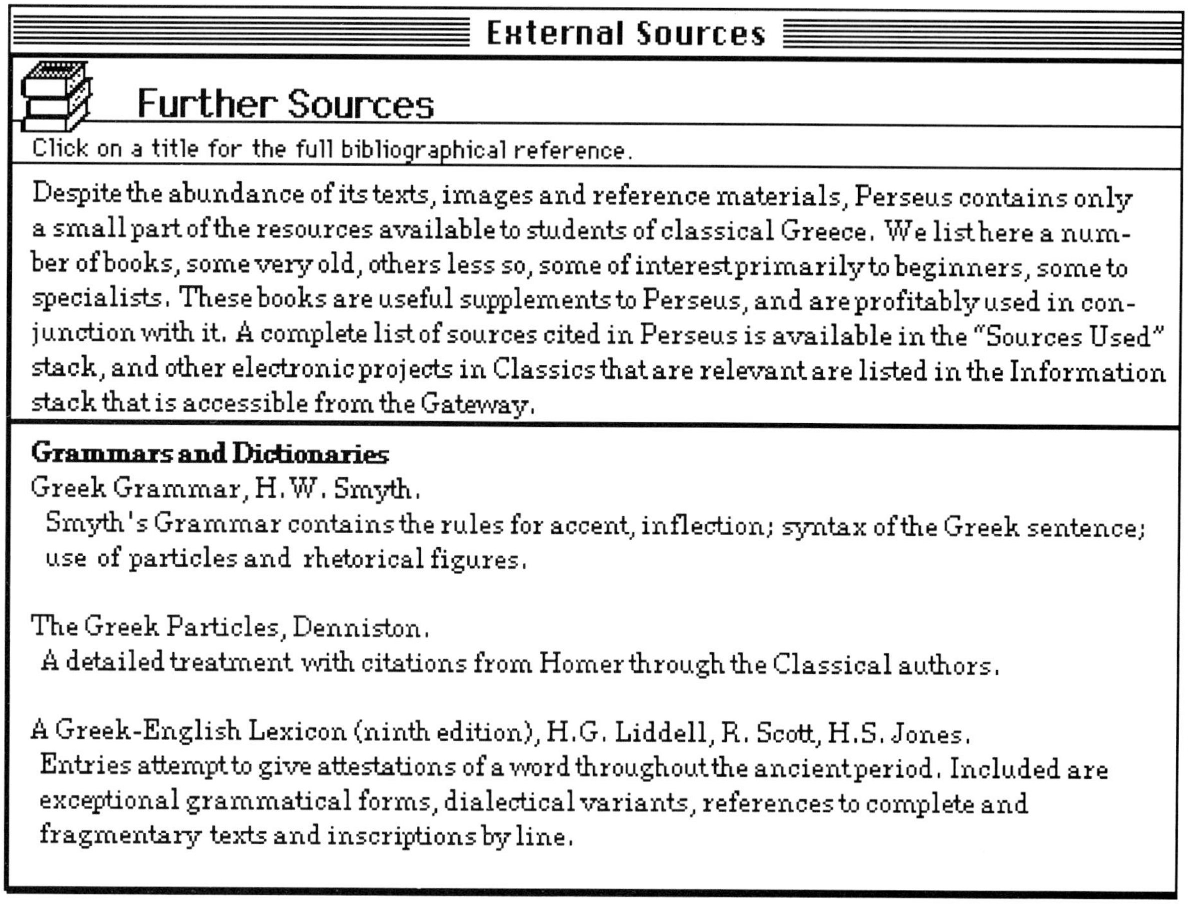

External Sources
Further Sources
Click on a title for the full bibliographical reference.
Despite the abundance of its texts, images and reference materials, Perseus contains only a small part of the resources available to students of classical Greece. We list here a number of books, some very old, others less so, some of interest primarily to beginners, some to specialists. These books are useful supplements to Perseus, and are profitably used in conjunction with it. A complete list of sources cited in Perseus is available in the "Sources Used" stack, and other electronic projects in Classics that are relevant are listed in the Information stack that is accessible from the Gateway.
Grammars and Dictionaries
Greek Grammar, H.W. Smyth.
Smyth's Grammar contains the rules for accent, inflection; syntax of the Greek sentence; use of particles and rhetorical figures.
The Greek Particles, Denniston.
A detailed treatment with citations from Homer through the Classical authors.
A Greek-English Lexicon (ninth edition), H.G. Liddell, R. Scott, H.S. Jones.
Entries attempt to give attestations of a word throughout the ancient period. Included are exceptional grammatical forms, dialectical variants, references to complete and fragmentary texts and inscriptions by line.

Figure 9.7 Further Sources

When using the Further Sources resource, you can obtain a full citation by clicking a line in the entry (figure 9.8).

Grammars and Dictionaries
Greek Grammar, H.W. Smyth.
Smyth's Grammar contains the rules
use of particles and rhetorical figure:
Sources Used
Index
Smyth 1956
Smyth, H. W., revised by G. M. Messing. Greek Grammar. Cambridge, MA: Harvard University Press, 1956.

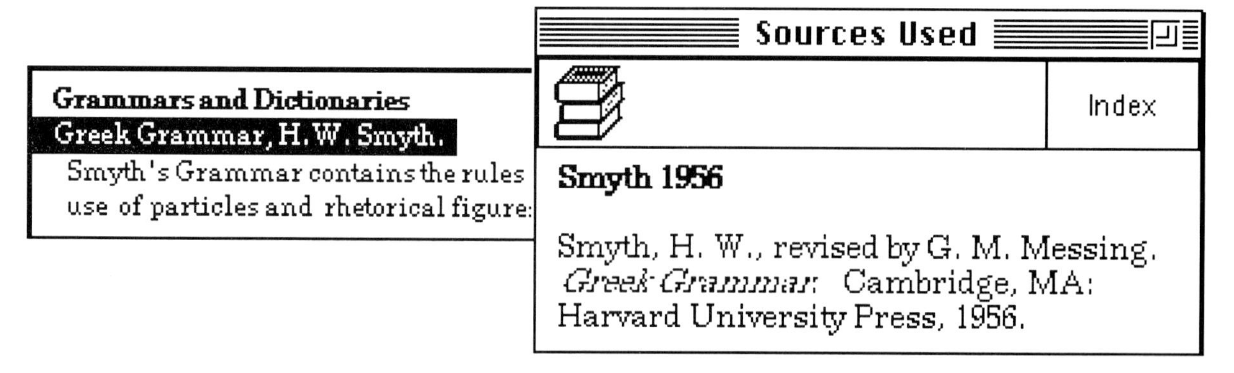

Figure 9.8 Full entry in Sources Used for a Further Sources citation

➤ To return to Further Sources, click the Go Back arrow on the Navigator Palette.

Several specialized stacks and utilities allow you to customize your use of Perseus. Use the Paths utility to create and follow Paths through Perseus. The Notebook utility records your notes and searches, or annotates Perseus resources for others. The CD Swapper is a personal stack; it stores a number of image requests until you are ready to swap the current CD-ROM. Current Assignment is also a personal stack, in which Perseus assignments, messages of the day, or other information for a group of users can be posted. All four of these utilities can be reached from the Perseus menu. Perseus Settings (overview in section 4.2.2, described in detail in section 10.5) and Atlas Settings (described in section 7.2.3) are reached from the Settings icon on the Gateway. Atlas Settings are also reached from the Atlas menu. You can configure the display of Primary Texts, in both Greek and English, by using the controls on the utility bar and the Text menu within Primary Texts (described in sections 8.2 and 8.3).

10.1 PERSONALIZING STACKS

Certain stacks—the Path, Notebook, and CD Swapper stacks—may be duplicated and renamed for your personal use.

➤ To duplicate a stack, go to the Finder, select a stack by single-clicking it, and choose the item Duplicate from the File menu. Rename the stack as you would any Macintosh file. We suggest a name identifying stack function and user (if several people share a workstation), for example, "Elli's Paths," or "Hdt. Notebook." Instructions for loading personalized stacks into Perseus are given in section 10.5, on Settings. New Notebook and CD Swapper stacks will be blank. You must delete the factory-installed Paths from a new Path stack.

A stack cannot be duplicated while it is active, that is, currently in use by Perseus.

10.2 PATHS

A Path is a sequence of Locations in Perseus. Any Perseus card or selection on a Perseus card can be considered a Location. A Path card (figure 10.1) shows all the Locations in a given Path, in sequential order, reading from left to right; the first Location is in the upper left-hand corner of the card, the last in the lower right. Each Path Location is represented by an icon indicating the Perseus resource in which that Location is found. In figure 10.1 the vase icon indicates that the objects are in the Perseus vase collection.

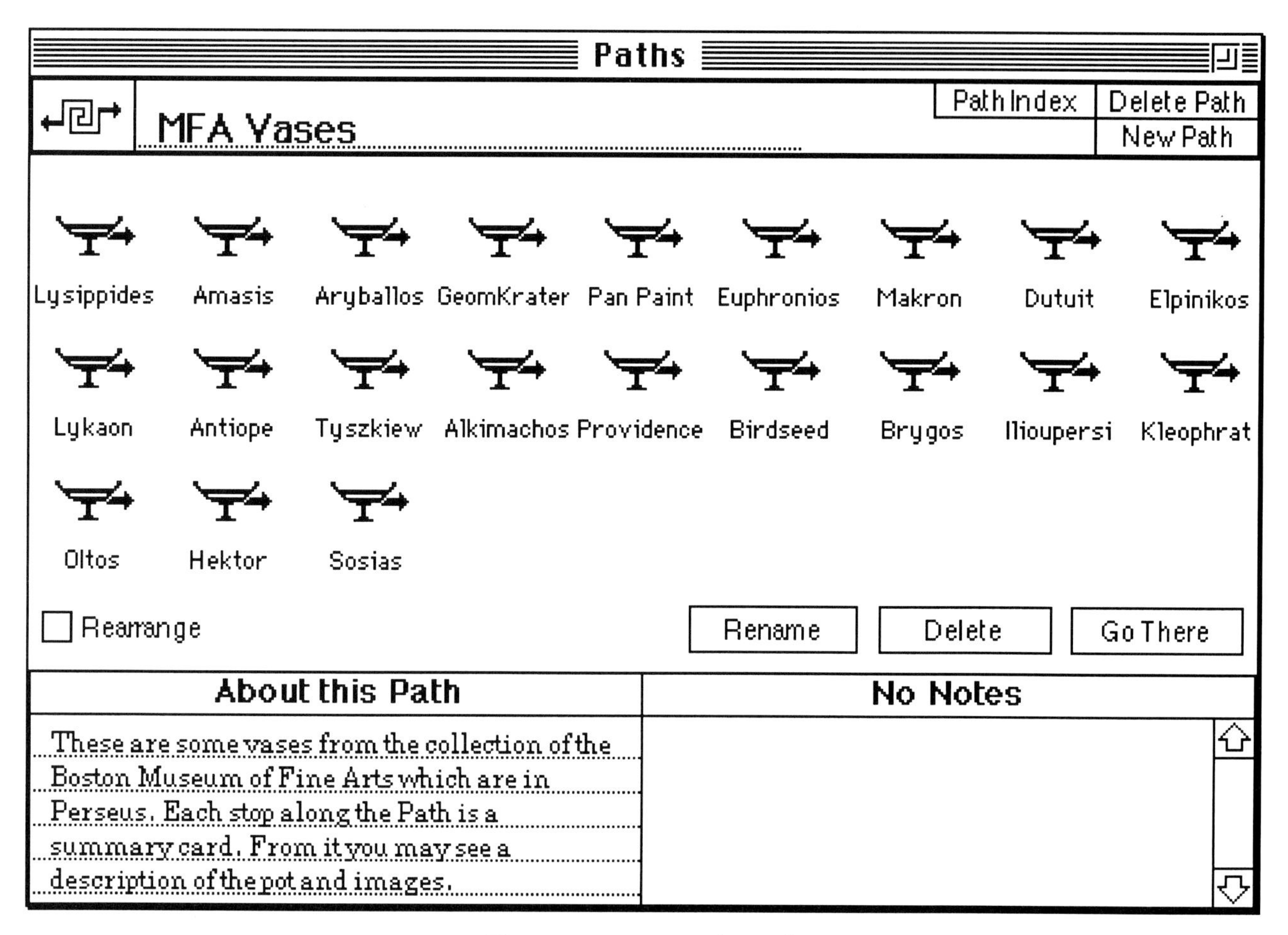

Figure 10.1 A Path card

10.2.1 CURRENT PATH STACK

A Path stack is made up of a Path Index and a number of Path cards. The Perseus Path stack is designed so that each user can create and save new Paths as well as follow previously created Paths. You can keep any number of Path stacks in the Perseus folder on your hard disk. Path stacks may contain the Paths originally distributed with Perseus 2.0 or Paths created by yourself and others.

> It is essential that the Path stacks be on your hard drive, not on the CD-ROM, for any changes to be recorded.

The current Path stack is the one in effect during your Perseus session.

➤ To choose the current Path stack, go to the Gateway and click the Settings icon. The Settings card will appear (figure 10.2).

Perseus Gateway (2.0)

Perseus Settings Card

Click on these fields and buttons to customize your version of Perseus.

Select Player Type: None

Use Video Images
Use Digital Images
Indexed Color

Path Stack: Elli's Hard Disk:Perseus 2.0:Local Stacks:Paths
Notebook Stack: Elli's Hard Disk:Perseus 2.0:Local Stacks:Notebo
CD Swapper: Elli's Hard Disk:Perseus 2.0:Local Stacks: CD Sw

Window Control: Go to cards in new window
Go to cards in same window

(Remember, holding down the shift key temporarily reverses the choice.)

Figure 10.2 Settings card

➤ Click the Path Stack button.

If there is no current Path stack, no stack name will be displayed; the name of the current Path stack will appear only if one was chosen in a previous Perseus session. Figure 10.2 shows a current stack Paths in a folder Local Stacks in a folder Perseus 2.0 in the hard disk Elli's Hard Disk. The Path stack that you select under Settings will remain the current Path stack until you change it through the Settings utility.

When you click the Path Stack button, a directory dialog box appears (figure 10.3).

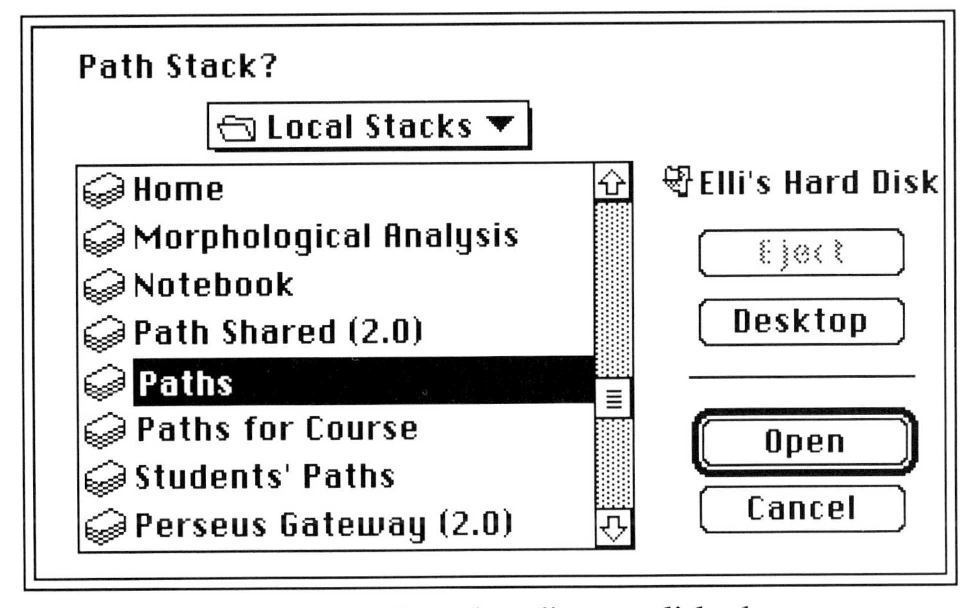

Figure 10.3 Path Settings directory dialog box

➤ Go to the folder containing the desired stack (if necessary), select the stack, click Open, and this choice will remain the current Path stack until another one is chosen.

The stack simply named "Paths" contains the Guided Tours and other Paths that are distributed with Perseus 2.0.

If you wish to follow a Path contained on a floppy disk, we suggest that you first copy the Path stack to your Local Stacks folder.

10.2.2 PATH INDEX

The Path Index (figure 10.4) lists the names of all the Paths in your current Path stack.

➤ To go to the Path Index, click the Paths icon on the Gateway. Or, from anywhere within Perseus, choose Path Index from the Perseus menu. You can choose a Path to follow from this Index. You can also create new Paths, edit a Path, or import Paths from another Path stack.

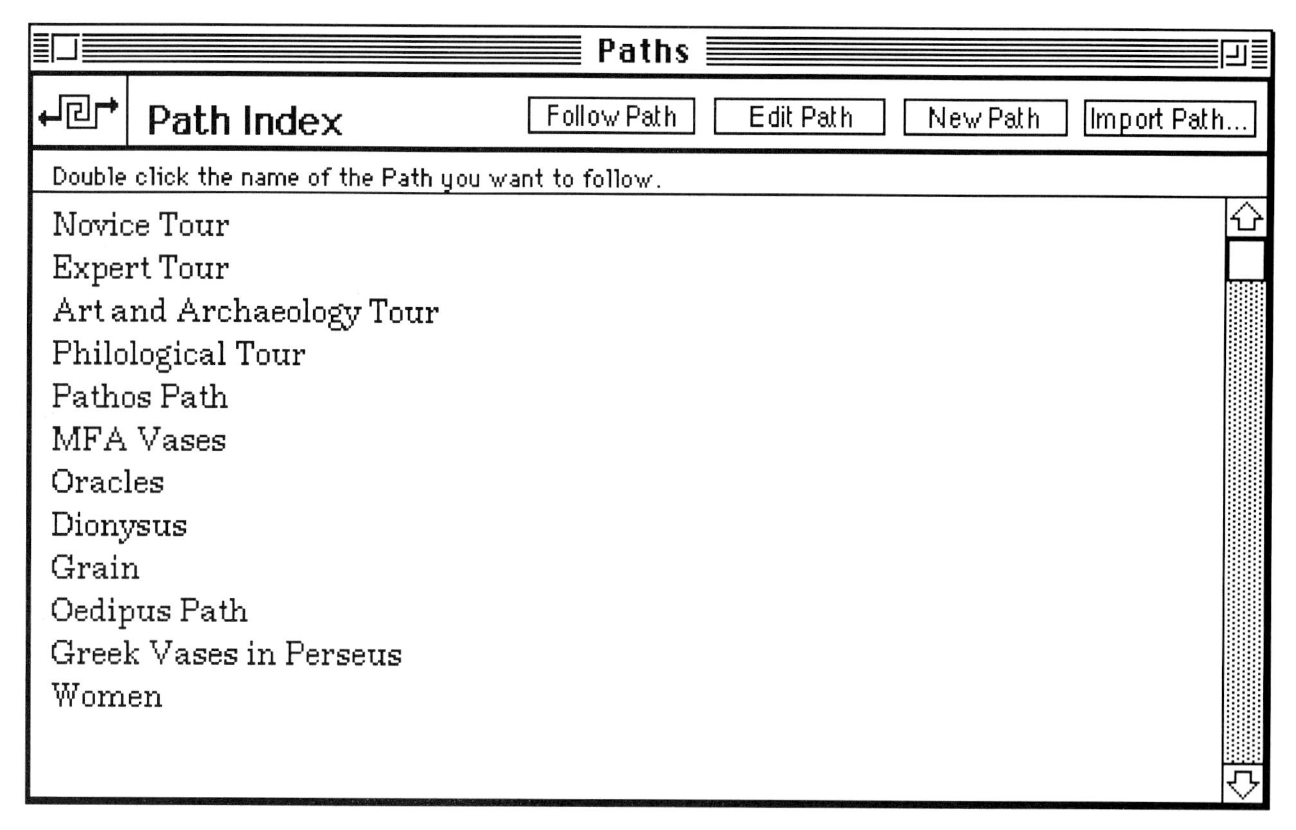

Figure 10.4 Path Index, listing the ready-made Paths distributed with Perseus 2.0

➤ To start following a Path, double-click it.

The buttons at the upper right-hand corner of the Path Index provide four utilities: Follow Path, Edit Path, New Path, and Import Path.

Follow Path

➤ Single-click a Path to select it, then click the button Follow Path. Perseus will take you to the beginning of the Path. More detailed instructions are given in section 10.2.3.

Edit Path

➤ Single-click a Path to select it, then click Edit Path. Perseus will take you to the current Path card, from which you can arrange, edit, and annotate the Path. See section 10.2.5.

New Path

➤ Click New Path. You should now be looking at a new Path card whose name is Path, followed by the time and date the new card was created. You can change the name to indicate its contents simply by typing a new name. See section 10.2.4.

Import Path

➤ To import a Path from another Path stack to the current Path stack, click the button Import Path. A dialog box appears, asking you to select the Path stack you wish to import from. Select the appropriate stack and click Open. A new dialog box appears, asking you which Path you wish to import. Select the desired Path and click OK. If you decide not to import a Path, click Cancel. If you have chosen to import a Path, Perseus will display the newly imported Path card. Click Path Index to return to the Path Index.

Do not follow this procedure to import Paths from Perseus 1.0. Conversion of Paths from version 1.0 is described in section 10.2.7.

10.2.3 FOLLOW A PATH

From the Perseus Gateway, you are always three clicks from the start of a Path. Click the Paths icon to bring up the Path Index. Select the Path you wish to follow by clicking it once. Click the button Follow Path. (Alternatively, you may double-click the Path you wish to follow.) Detailed instructions are given in this section.

➤ Choose a Path to follow from the Path Index. (To go to the Path Index, click the Paths icon on the Gateway or choose Path Index from the Perseus menu.) Select a Path and click the button Follow Path (or double-click the Path you wish to follow). Perseus will take you to the first Location on the Path.

The control used to go forward and backward along a Path, and to create new Locations on the Path, is the Path Navigator on the Navigator Palette. The active points on the Path Navigator icon are depicted below (figure 10.5).

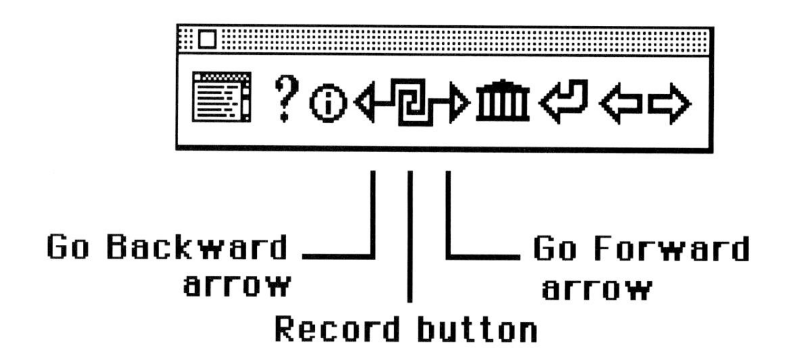

Figure 10.5 Path Navigator icon on the Navigator Palette

You can move forward and back on a Path by using the arrows on the Path Navigator icon. When you are walking a Path, click the right arrow on the Path Navigator icon to go to the next Path Location. Click the left arrow on the Path Navigator icon to go to the previous Path Location. You can also add a Location to a Path by clicking the center of the Path Navigator icon. For further details on adding Locations, see section 10.2.4.

As you follow a Path, you may choose at any time to leave your Location on the Path to investigate something else. If you decide to add the new Location to the Path, follow the instructions in the next section. If you wish to return to the Path, choose Current Path Location from the Perseus menu. If you wish to continue on the Path, click the right arrow on the Path Navigator to go to the next Location.

Feel free to leave the Path at any time to explore the Perseus environment on your own. To rejoin the Path where you left it, choose Current Path Location from the Perseus menu. If you quit Perseus, however, you must again choose a Path to follow, according to the instructions in this section.

10.2.4 CREATE A PATH

You can create your own Paths by setting up and naming a new Path card, then adding Locations to the Path, from anywhere within Perseus, with the Path Navigator.

➤ To create a Path, go to the Path Index by clicking the Paths icon on the Gateway (or, from anywhere within Perseus, choose Path Index from the Perseus menu).

The Path Index appears (see figure 10.4).

➤ Click the button New Path, in the upper right.

A blank Path card appears (figure 10.6).

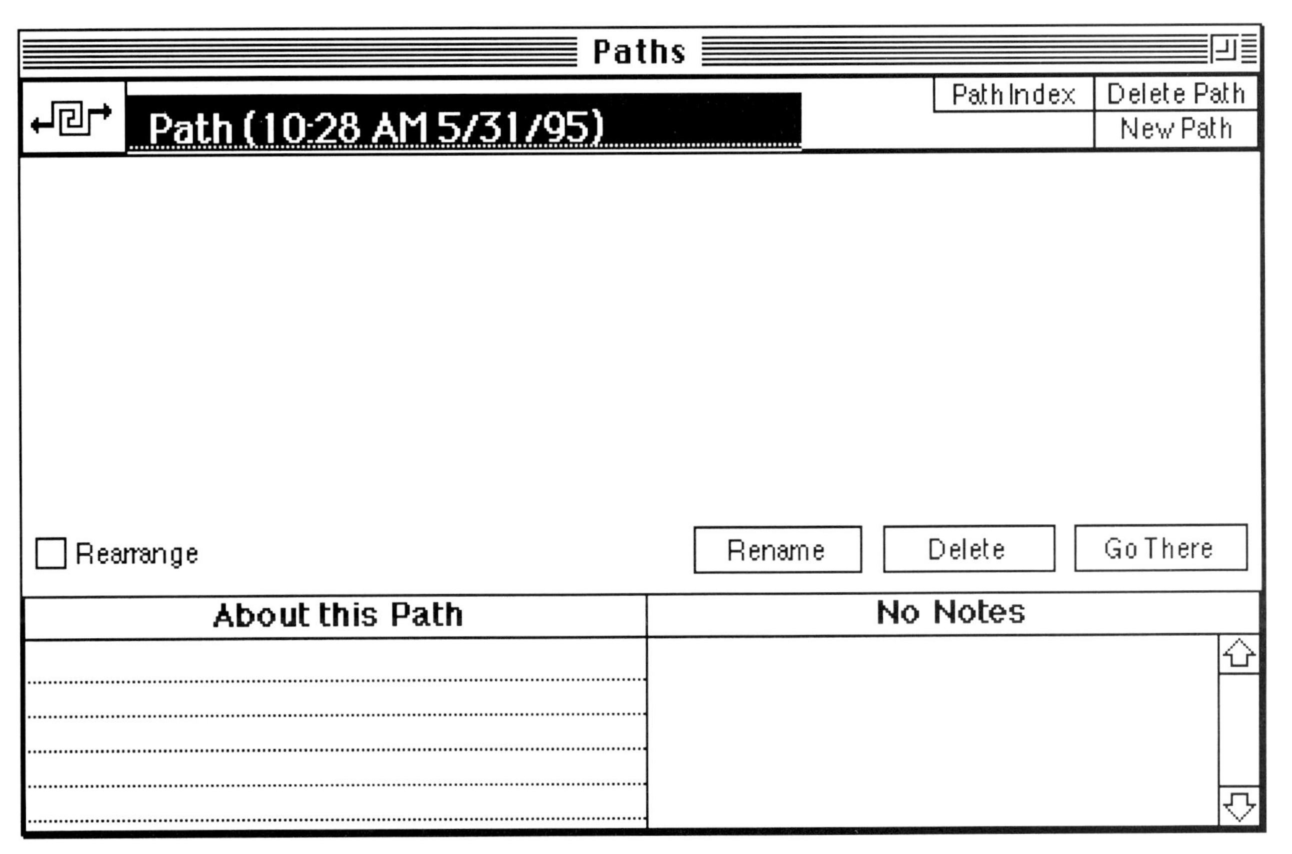

Figure 10.6 New Path card

- Give your Path a new name by typing it into the name field, in the upper left. Your new Path card becomes the current Path and is now listed in the Path Index.
- As you travel around in Perseus, you can add Locations to your Path by clicking the center of the Path Navigator icon. In response, a dialog box appears, asking you to select a Path (figure 10.7).

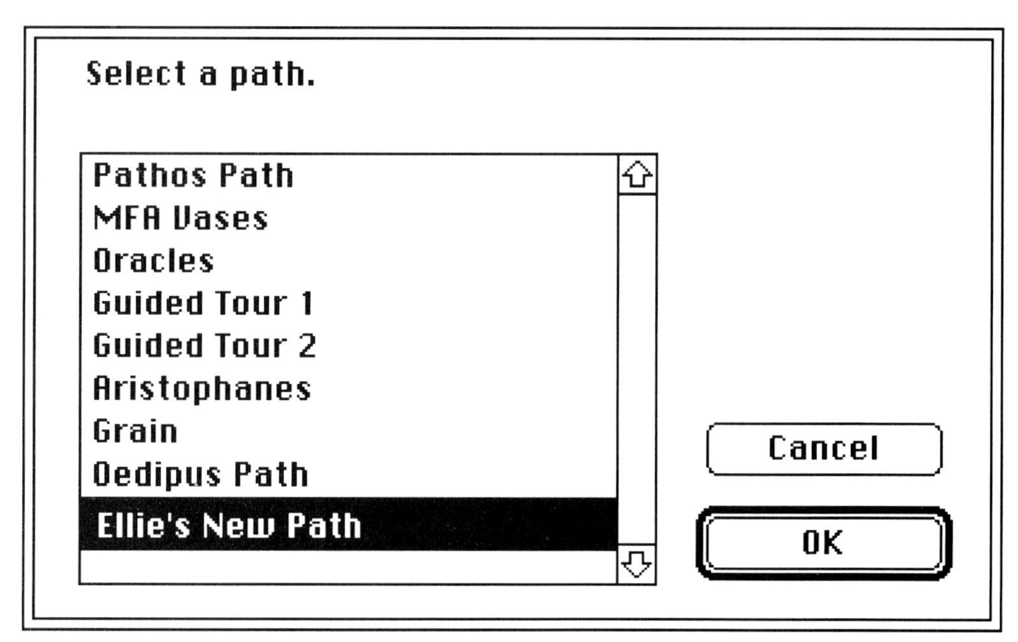

Figure 10.7 Dialog box for adding a Location to a Path

By default, the current Path has been selected, but you can add the Location to any other Path on the Path Index by selecting one and clicking OK. A Path may have as many as 27 Locations.

A second dialog box appears, asking you to name the Path Location (figure 10.8).

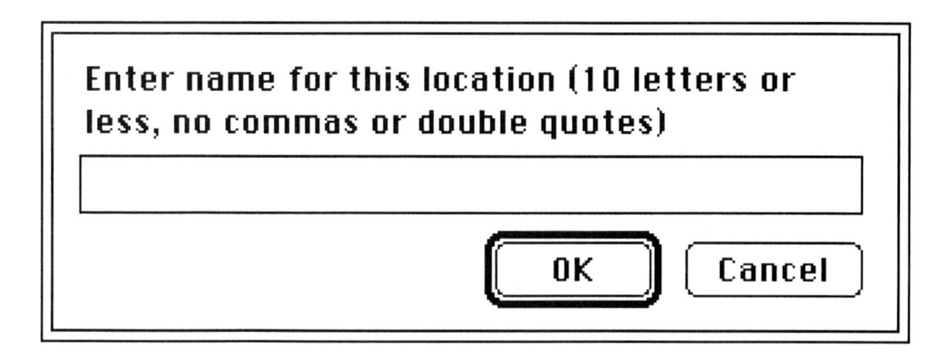

Figure 10.8 Dialog box for naming a Path Location

➤ Type a name and click OK. Please be sure that your name is ten characters or less and contains no commas or double quotation marks.

To learn how to edit and annotate your Path, read section 10.2.5.

Almost every location in Perseus can be made into a Path Location. Exceptions are the Thumbnail Browser, the Sources Used Index, and the Tools & References Index.

10.2.5 PATH CARD

Paths are stored and edited on a Path card. To edit your Path, you may rename, delete, annotate, and rearrange Path Locations.

A typical Path card is depicted in figure 10.9. Each Path card can contain as many as 27 Locations. The Locations are shown by icons indicating the Perseus resource in which they are located—for example, Primary Texts or Atlas. A note describing the Path may be added in the lower left, and notes for each stop may be added in the lower right.

➤ To go to a Path card, choose a Path from the Path Index and click Edit Path, in the upper right.

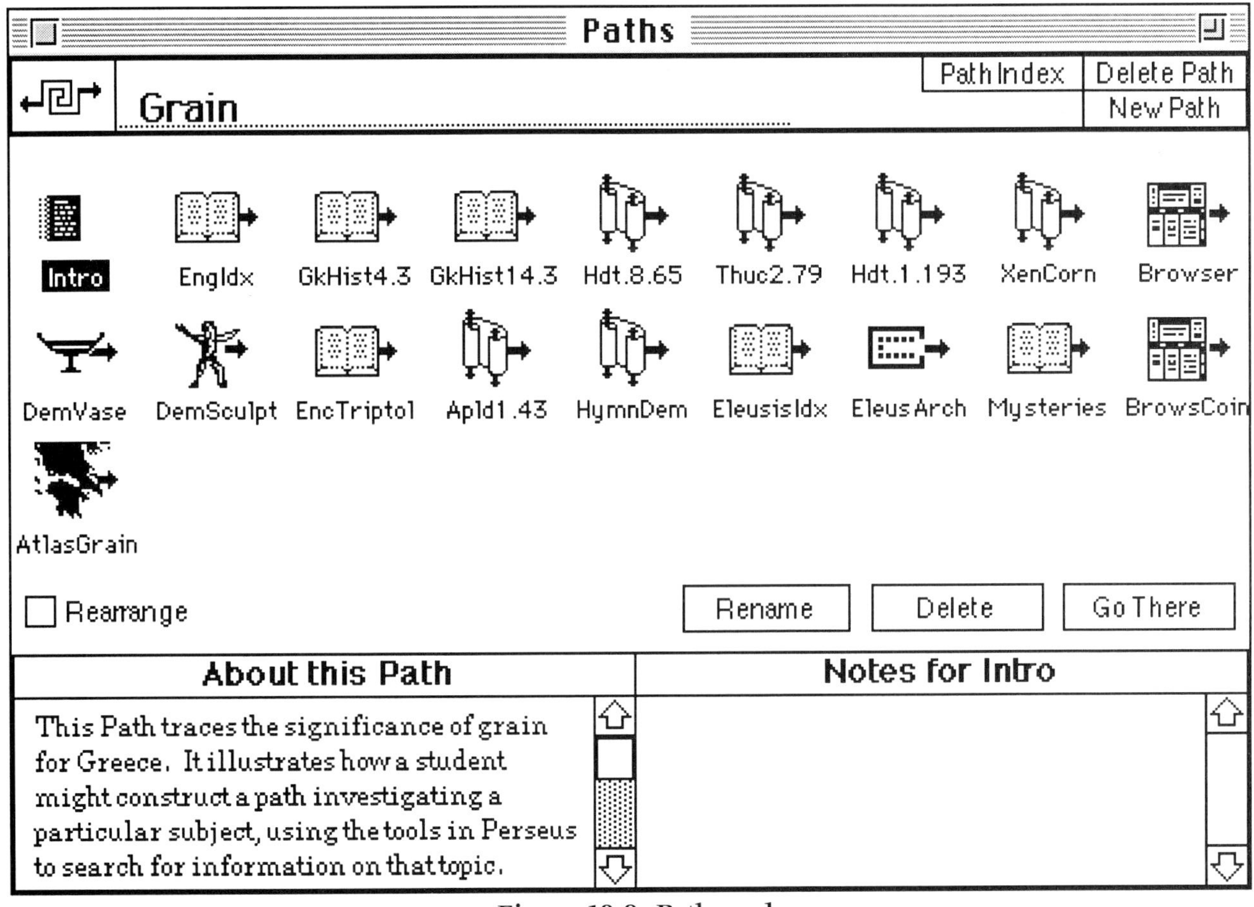

Figure 10.9 Path card

The three buttons in the upper right affect the Path card, and the three buttons in the middle right affect the Path Locations.

Path Index

➤ To return to the Path Index, click the button Path Index.

Delete Path

➤ Click Delete Path.

A dialog box appears, requesting you to confirm the deletion of this Path.

➤ Click Delete if you wish to delete the Path. If you have changed your mind or made a mistake, click Don't Delete.

A protection mechanism in Perseus prevents you from deleting a Path if it is the only remaining Path in the current stack. If you attempt to delete this Path, a dialog box appears with the message "Can't delete last card of protected background."

New Path

➤ Click New Path. You should now be looking at a new card whose name is Path, followed by the time and date this card was created.

The name of the Path is selected when you first see the card. You can change the name to indicate its contents simply by typing a new name.

Rename

The button Rename allows you to change the name of a Location.

➤ Click a Location icon to select it, then click Rename. A dialog box appears, asking you to enter a new name for the Location. Type the new name for this Location and click OK.

The Rename feature is available only when Rearrange mode (see below) is off.

Delete

Delete allows you to delete a Location.

➤ Click a Location icon to select it. Click Delete. A dialog box appears asking you to confirm the deletion of the Location. Click Delete if you wish to delete it. If you have changed your mind, click Don't Delete.

The Delete feature is available only when Rearrange mode (see below) is off.

Go There

Go There allows you to go directly to a Location.

➤ Click a Location icon to select it, then click Go There. You should now be at the Perseus card for the selected Location.

The Go There feature is available only when Rearrange mode (see below) is off.

Rearrange

After you create a number of Locations, you may wish to rearrange them in a different order on the Path card.

➤ Click the button Rearrange, in the middle left, to put the Path card into Rearrange mode. An *X* appears in the check box next to Rearrange, and the three buttons to the right—Rename, Delete, Go There—disappear. In Rearrange mode, each Location icon can be dragged around the Path card.

➤ Drag the Locations into a new arrangement just as you would drag any Macintosh icon.

You do not have to drag the icons to the exact positions where you want them to end up. Positions are relative. If you drag an icon below or to the left of the rest of the icons, it becomes the last one. When you leave Rearrange mode, the icons realign.

➤ Click the Rearrange box a second time to save the Locations in the new arrangement. The *X* will disappear.

You must click the Rearrange box to deselect it before you can do anything else to the Path. If you decide to leave the Path card or perform other functions, the Path card will take a minute to finish the rearrangement automatically, displaying a dialog box with the message "Have to finish rearranging."

Change the Path name

➤ To change the name of a Path, highlight the name in the field at the top of the card, and type in a new name.

Names may not exceed 24 characters.

Annotate the Path card

About this Path

The text in the "About this Path" field in the lower left of the Path card can be annotated with comments that are relevant to the entire Path.

➤ Click the "About this Path" field to make the insertion point appear, and type comments or instructions into the box.

Individual Location annotations

A note is attached to each Location in a Path. The annotation box in the lower right-hand corner of the Path card allows you to annotate individual Locations. When you first open a Path card, this field is titled "No Notes" and is empty.

When you click a Location, the title of this field changes to "Notes for," followed by the name of the selected Location. Any pre-existing notes for that Location appear in the field.

The annotations for a Location also appear when you are following a Path. When you arrive at a Location, its note appears in a floating window that can be closed or repositioned on the screen.

➤ You may create or edit the annotation for a Location by typing in the Notes field at the lower right-hand corner of the card, or by editing the annotation when it appears in a floating window as you are following a Path. Be careful not to edit the first line of the annotation appearing in the floating window, which lists the Path name and Location number.

You can copy and paste annotations into the Path Note field or window from a word-processing application outside of HyperCard. Be aware, however, that any text formatting (tabs, italics, and so on) will be lost—the note will show up as plain text in Perseus.

10.2.6 USE THE PATH ITEMS FROM THE PERSEUS MENU

The five Path items on the Perseus menu provide another way to use the Path features (figure 10.10).

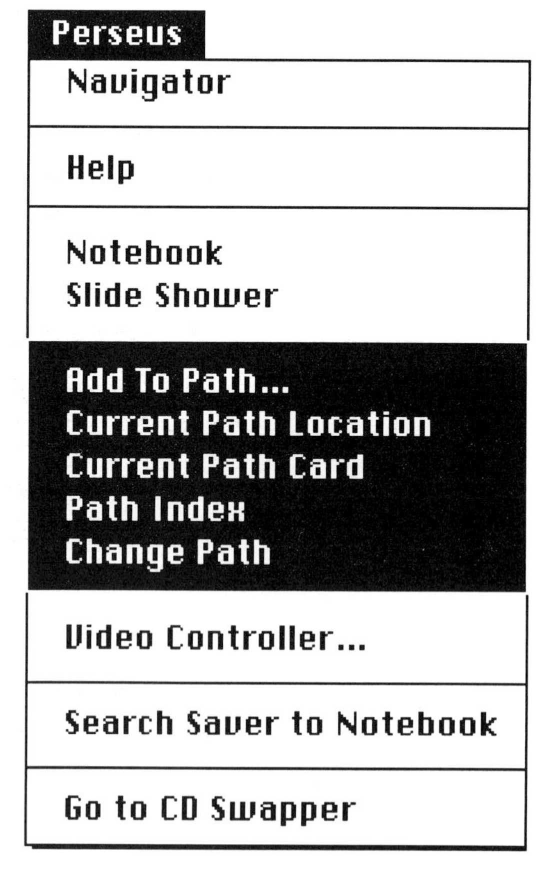

Figure 10.10 Path items in Perseus menu

Add to Path

➤ Choose "Add to Path" from the Perseus menu to add a new Location to a Path. Two dialog boxes will appear, asking you to name the Location (no more than ten characters) and to select the Path you wish the Location to be added to.

Current Path Location

➤ Choose the item Current Path Location to return to a Path you are already following. If you wish to follow a different Path, choose Path Index or Change Path.

Current Path Card

➤ In order to edit and annotate the Path you are following, go to the current Path card by choosing Current Path Card from the Perseus menu. If no Path is in effect, a dialog box saying "No current Path" will appear. In this case, click OK and select a Path from the Path Index.

Path Index

➤ Go to the Path Index by choosing Path Index from the Perseus menu. From the Path Index you may follow another Path or create a new one.

Change Path

This menu item bypasses the Path Index. When you choose it, a dialog box appears that lists the Paths in your current Path stack.

➤ Click the name of the Path you wish to follow.

10.2.7 CONVERT PATHS FROM PERSEUS 1.0 TO VERSION 2.0

Paths created with Perseus 1.0 must be converted in order to be compatible with version 2.0.

For the conversion to be successful, Perseus 1.0 and HyperCard 2.0 or better must be properly installed on your computer. Refer to the documentation for Perseus 1.0.

➤ To convert a version 1.0 Path, copy the folder Path Converter from the Perseus 2.0 CD-ROM Disk 1 to your hard disk. You may find it convenient to copy the Path Converter folder into the Perseus 1.0 Install Me folder.

➤ Quit Perseus 2.0 (if you have it running), load the Perseus 1.0 CD-ROM, and launch Perseus 1.0 by double-clicking the version 1.0 Gateway.

➤ You will now be opening a new HyperCard stack from the Perseus 1.0 Gateway. Choose the item Open Stack from the File menu. A directory dialog box appears (figure 10.11).

Figure 10.11 Open Stack directory dialog box

➤ Select the folder Path Converter and click Open; then select the stack Path Converter and again click Open. The Stack Converter will appear (figure 10.12).

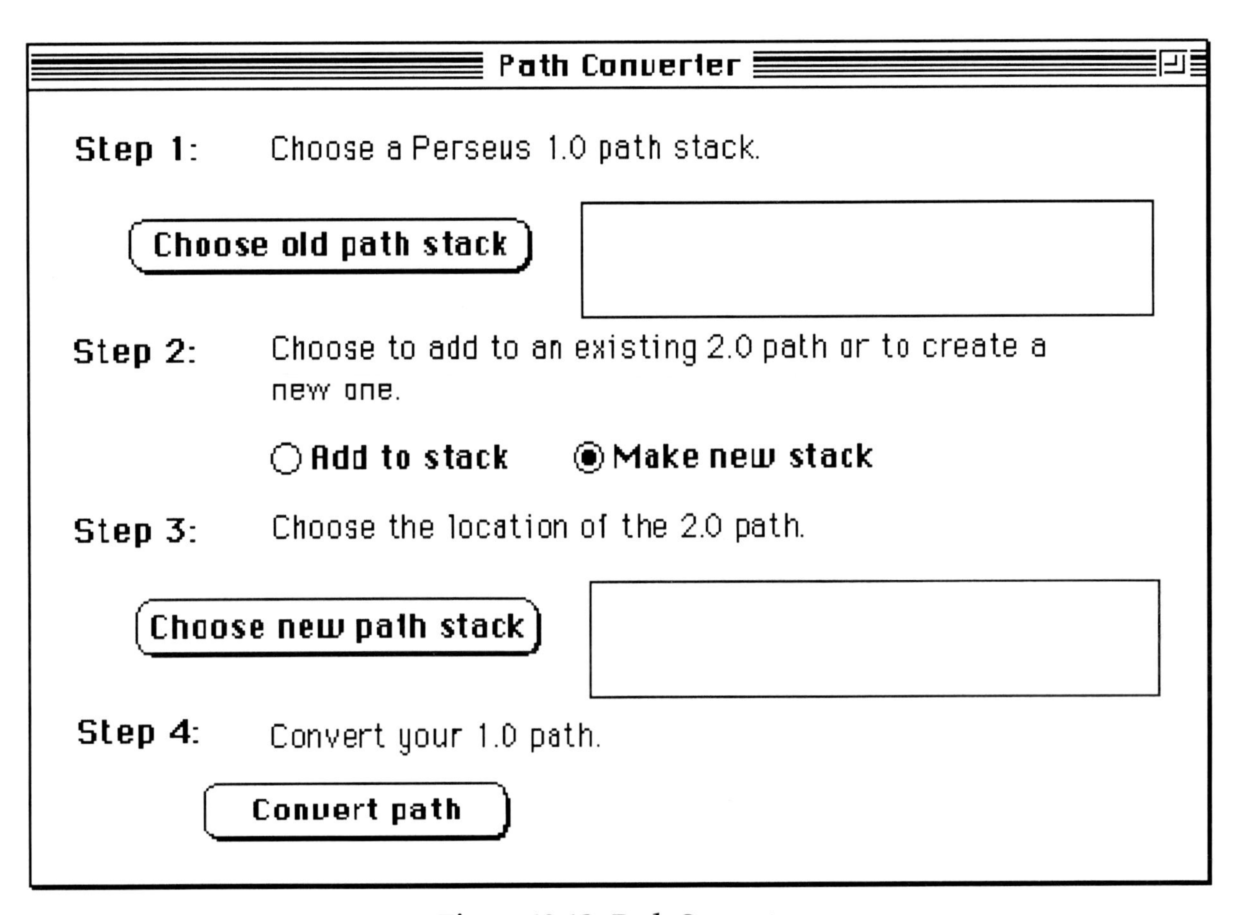

Figure 10.12 Path Converter

The four steps to Path conversion are as follows:

➤ To choose the Path from version 1.0 that you wish to convert, click the button "Choose old path stack." From the directory dialog box, select the stack you wish to convert, and click Open. In figure 10.13 the stack Paths, containing the two Guided Tours, has been selected. The name of the stack will appear in the field to the right of the button "Choose old path stack."

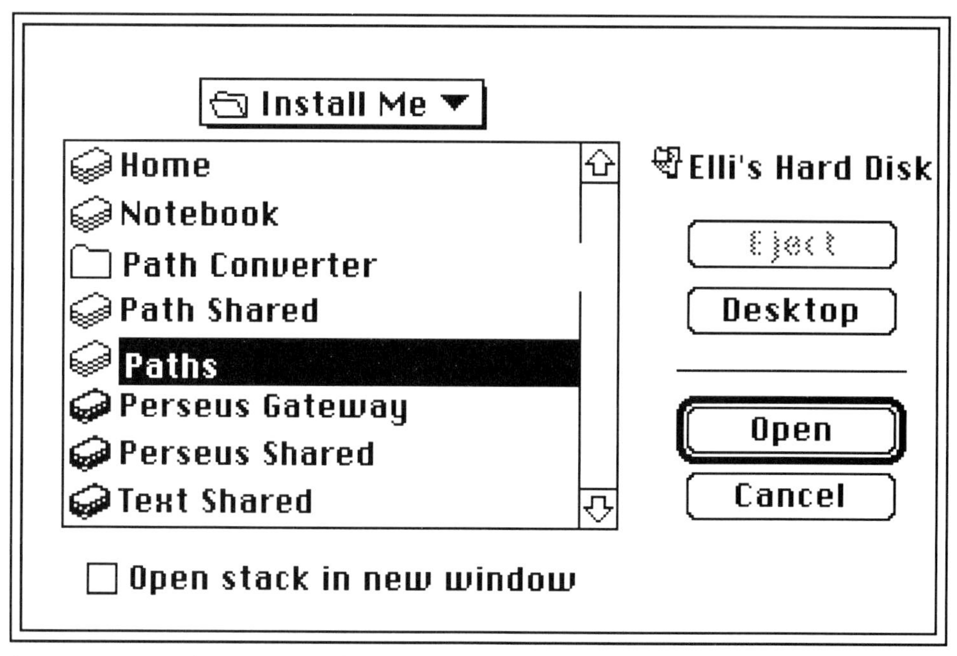

Figure 10.13 Directory dialog box from the button "Choose old path stack"

- ➤ To append the converted stack to an already existing stack in version 2.0, click the button "Add to stack." To convert the 1.0 stack into a new 2.0 stack, click the button "Make new stack."
- ➤ To choose the location of the converted Path stack, click "Choose new path stack." You may find it convenient to choose the folder Local Stacks, which contains other Perseus 2.0 stacks.
- ➤ To begin the conversion, click "Convert path."

You may now convert another Path, or quit HyperCard.

Because of the limitations of HyperCard, some Locations on the old Path may not convert, for example, Keywords in the Browser.

10.3 NOTEBOOK

The Notebook is a HyperCard stack for taking notes while browsing through Perseus. It also can be used to store the results of searches that you have saved temporarily in the Search Saver. Data you store in a Notebook stack will be saved even after you quit Perseus. We suggest that you copy and paste your material into a word-processing application in order to format, edit, and print it. Anything written with the Greek font will be changed to a Latin font in the transition; you must have SMK GreekKeys installed in your system in order to restore the properly accented Greek characters.

Read section 10.1 for directions on personalizing your Notebook stack.

The Notebook stack consists of a Notebook Index that lists the several Note cards in that Notebook. Like any other Perseus card, Note cards can be added to a Path.

10.3.1 NOTEBOOK INDEX

➤ To go to the Notebook Index (figure 10.14), choose the item Notebook from the Perseus menu. Or, from a Note card, click the button Notebook Index, in the upper right.

The Notebook Index contains a list of the names of all Note cards in your Notebook stack. Figure 10.14 shows the Note card distributed with Perseus 2.0.

From the Notebook Index, you can create new notes, rename notes, or delete notes. The buttons at the upper right-hand corner of the Notebook Index provide access to four utilities: Rename Note, Delete Note, Go to Note, and New Note.

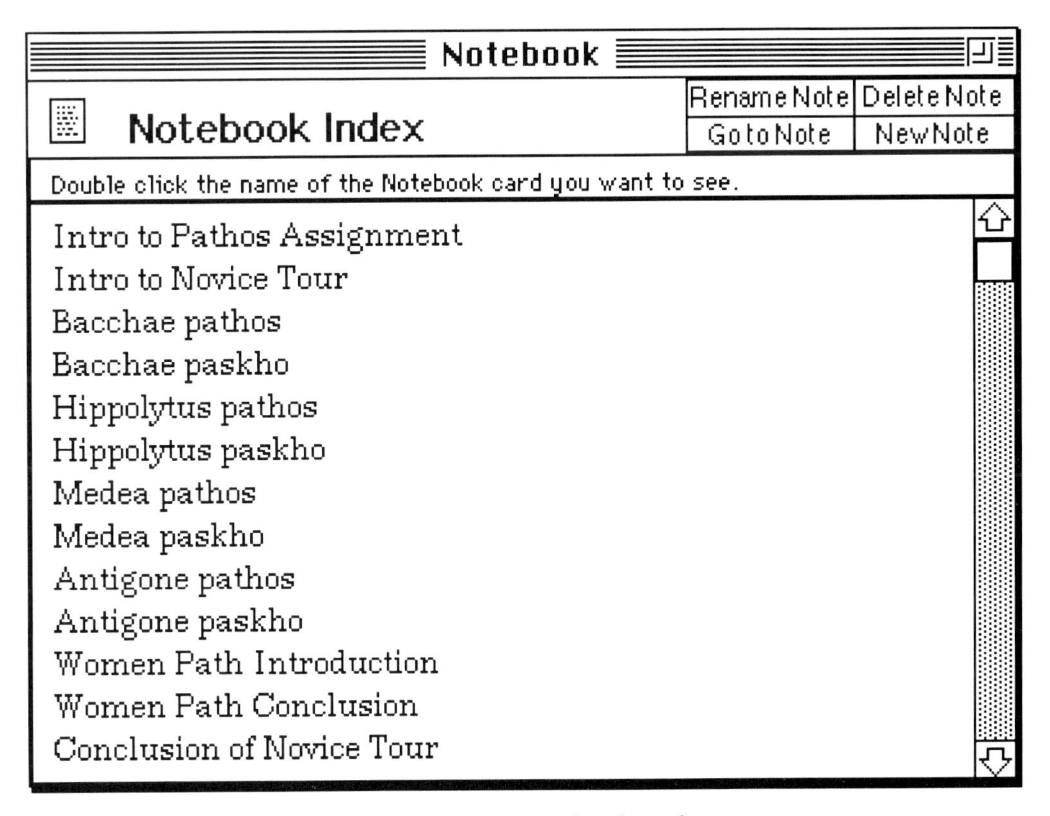

Figure 10.14 Notebook Index

The first time you choose Notebook from the Perseus menu, the Notebook Index appears. Thereafter, when you choose Notebook, the current Note card appears.

Go to Note

- Click a Note to select it, then click "Go to Note." You can also go directly to a note by double-clicking it.

New Note

- Click New Note. You will see a new card whose name is Note, followed by the time and date this card was created. You can change the name to indicate its contents simply by typing a new name. You can also rename a Note from the Notebook Index (see below).

Rename Note

- Click once on a Note to select it, then click Rename Note. A dialog box appears, requesting you to name the Note. Type a new name for the note and click OK.

Delete Note

- Click a Note to select it, then click Delete Note. A dialog box appears requesting you to confirm the deletion of the Note.

- Click Delete if you wish to delete the note. If you have changed your mind or made a mistake, click Don't Delete.

10.3.2 NOTE CARD

The Note card depicted in figure 10.15 is the first Location on a Path entitled "Women." A Note card can contain up to approximately 350 words. Three utilities are available in the upper right-hand corner: Note Index, New Note, and Delete Note. These utilities and other features of the Note card are described in this section.

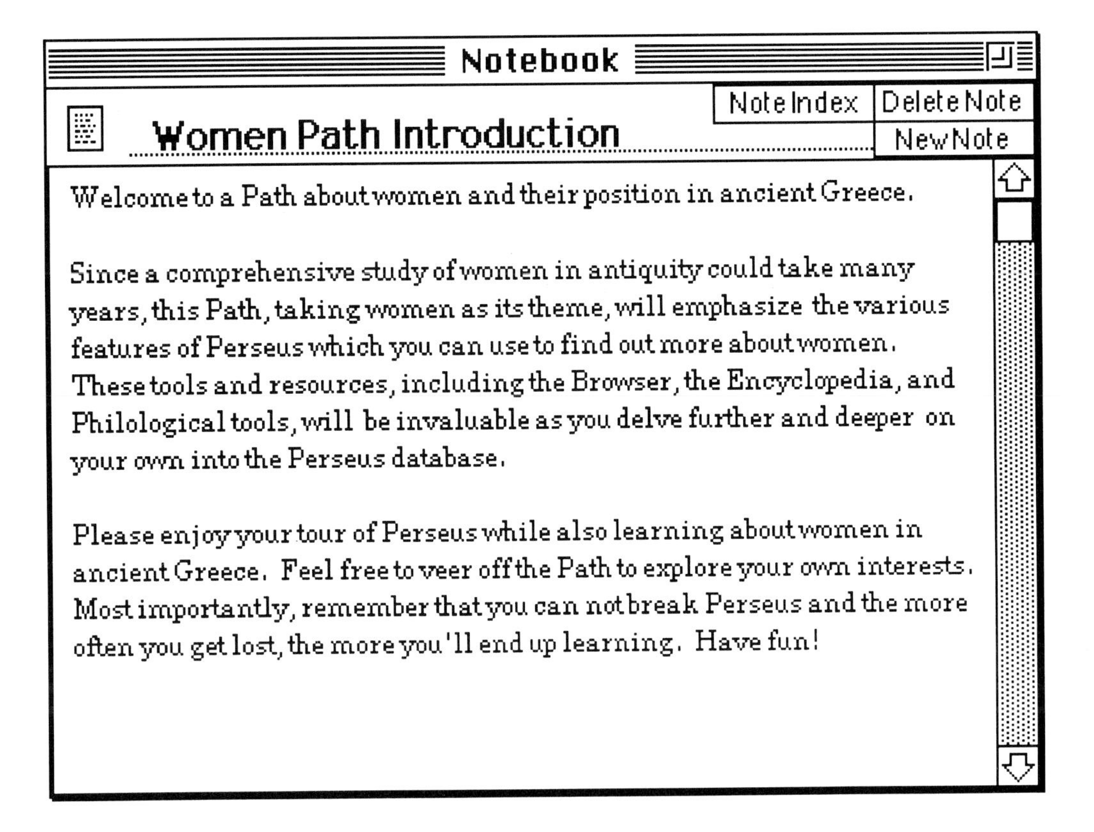

Figure 10.15 Note card

Note Index

➤ Click Note Index to return to the Notebook Index.

New Note

➤ Click New Note. You will now see a new card whose name is Note, followed by the time and date this card was created.

➤ The name of the Note is selected when you first see the card. You can change the name of the card to indicate its contents simply by typing a new name.

Delete Note

➤ Click Delete Note. A dialog box appears, requesting you to confirm the deletion of this Note.

➤ Click Delete if you wish to delete the Note. If you have changed your mind or made a mistake, click Don't Delete.

Change the Note name

➤ Select the name of the Note by highlighting it, and type in a new name.

Names may not exceed 24 characters. Notes may also be renamed from the Notebook Index.

Add or change the Note text

➤ Click the text field below the Note name to make the insertion point appear. Type your notes.

You may cut, copy, and move text on a Note card using the tools in the Edit menu.

Modify text style and font

➤ To change the text display, select a chunk of text. Choose the font and style you desire from the Font and Style menus.

Note that HyperCard is not intended for use as a word-processing application. The Tab key does not indent in HyperCard but selects fields. Formatting (italics, fonts, and so on) is not saved when text is copied from HyperCard into a word-processing application.

10.3.3 SEARCH SAVER TO NOTEBOOK

Results stored temporarily in the Search Saver may be piped directly to a new Notebook card and kept for as long as you want. Figure 10.16 shows the Site Index, with its alphabetical list of all Sites copied to the Search Saver.

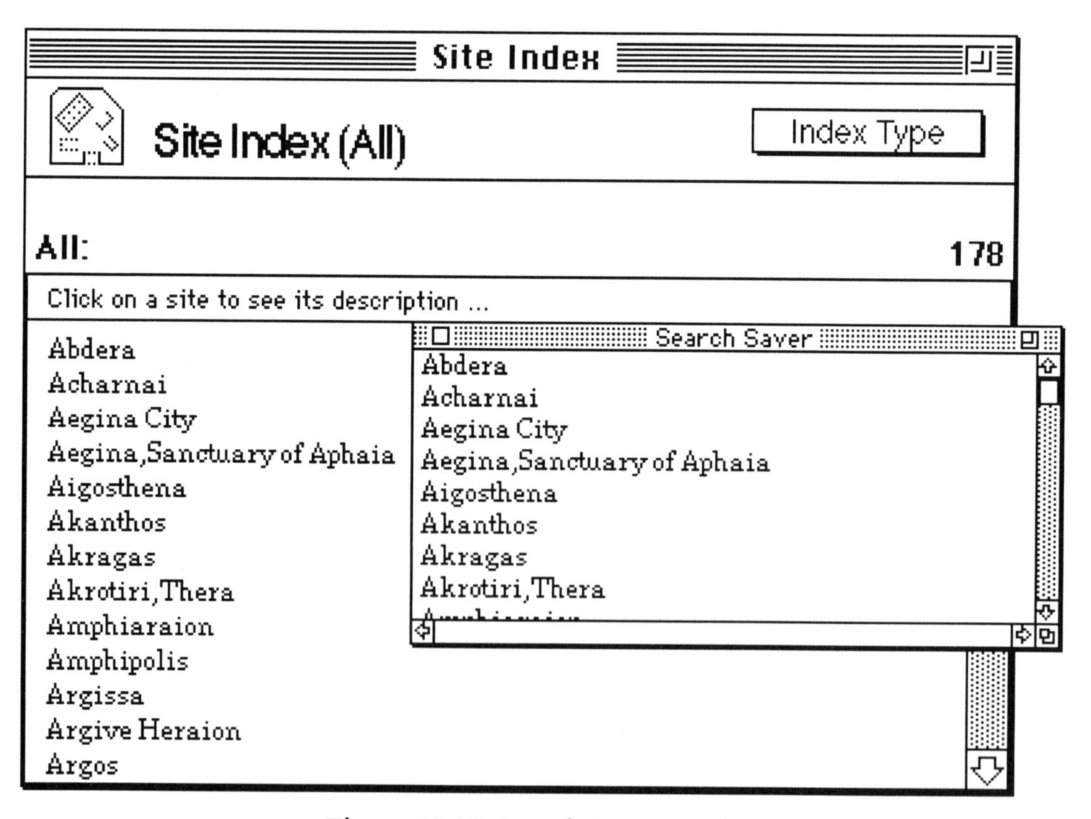

Figure 10.16 Search Saver results

➤ To save these results to a new Note card, choose the item "Search Saver to Notebook" from the Perseus menu. Perseus will create a new Note card, give the card a title, and copy the data into the text field (figure 10.17).

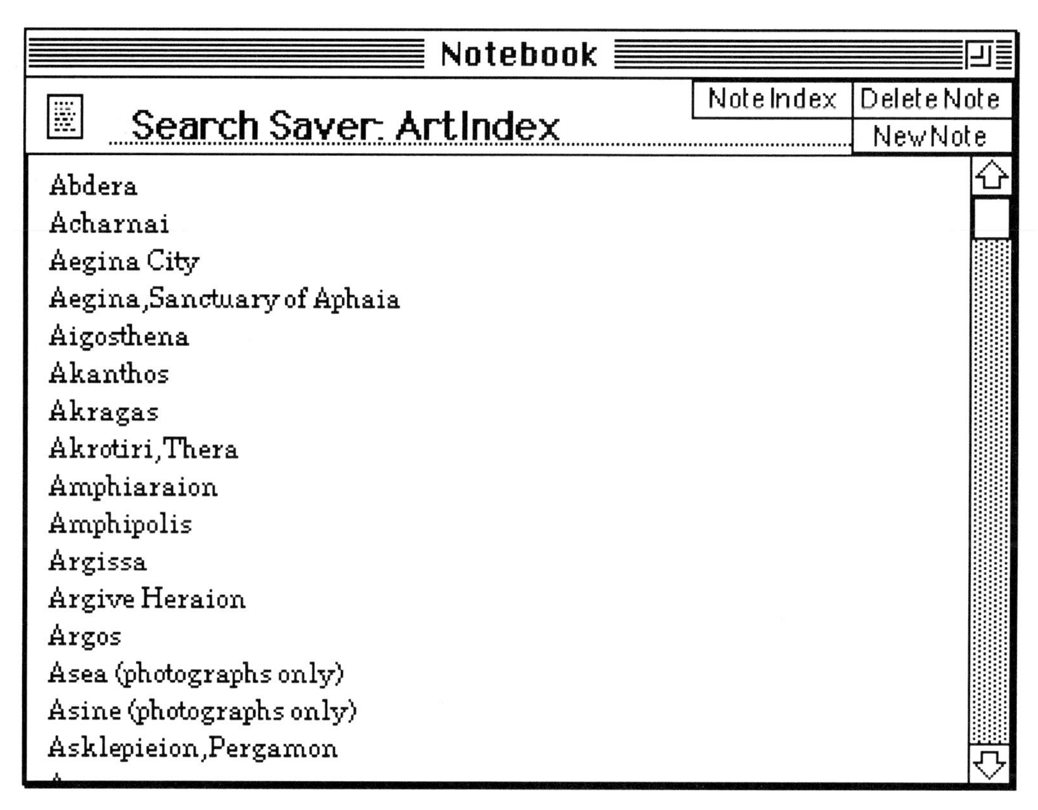

Figure 10.17 Search Saver to Notebook

When you review your results, you can select one of the sites, and then go to its Site card by choosing Sites from the Links menu. You can rename the Note card according to the procedure explained earlier. For more information on the Search Saver, see section 5.4.

10.3.4 LOCK NOTEBOOK STACK

➤ You can make your Notebook stack somewhat tamper resistant (though not hacker resistant) by going to the Finder, highlighting the Notebook stack by single-clicking its icon in your Local Stacks folder, and then choosing Get Info from the File menu. Click the Lock box.

When the stack is locked, an *X* appears in the Lock box. This means that your Note cards are read-only and cannot be deleted.

10.4 THE CD SWAPPER

Because the thousands of images in Perseus take up a great deal of space, it has been necessary to publish the Comprehensive Edition on four CD-ROMs. When you use Perseus from a CD-ROM drive and request an image, text, or map to be displayed, it may not be on the current CD-ROM. Perseus offers you the choice of swapping the current CD-ROM with the one that has the requested image, canceling the request, or storing the request until a more convenient time. The CD Swapper is the utility with which image requests are stored (figure 10.18).

If you will be swapping CD-ROMs, be sure to turn off File Sharing in the Control Panels of your Macintosh. Otherwise the Macintosh will not eject the CD.

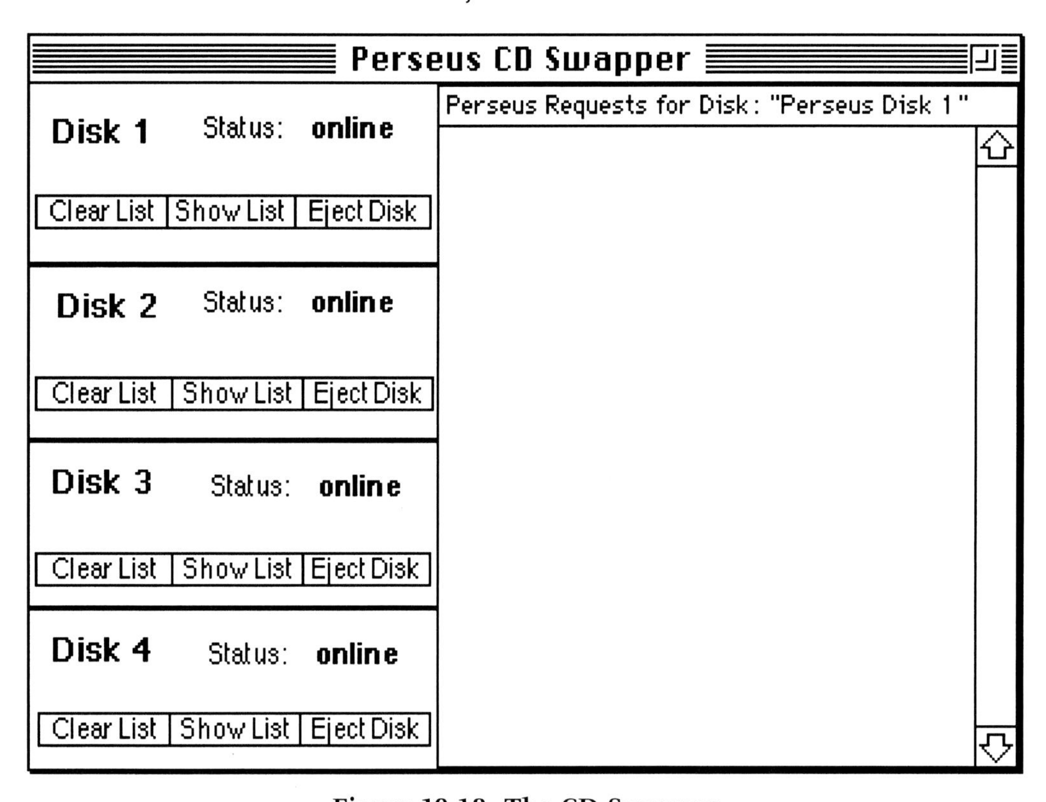

Figure 10.18 The CD Swapper

Approximately 2500 images are common to all four CD-ROMs. These so-called universal images include all images from the Museum of Fine Arts, Boston; the Encyclopedia; the Vase Painter Essays; Large Site Plans; and the Historical Overview. Other resources, however, reside on particular discs. Primary Texts, the Atlas, and full-size Sculpture images (except the Olympia Sculpture) are stored on Perseus Disk 1; the Olympia Sculpture and full-size Architecture and Site images are stored on Disk 2; full-size Vase images from collections listed in the Perseus Vase Index under A–M are stored on Disk 3; and full-size Vase images from collections listed in the Perseus Vase Index under N–Z and Coins are stored on Disk 4. All else (universal images, Catalogs and Site plans, Essays, the Encyclopedia, Sources Used, Thumbnail images, the Browser, and the English Index) is common to all four disks.

Thus, for example, if you are looking at a vase from the Yale University Art Gallery on Disk 3, you must swap CD-ROMs if you want to link with the text of the *Odyssey* on Disk 1. Alternatively, you may choose to store or cancel your request.

With the CD Swapper, requests are stored and recalled by disc number. For example, if Perseus Disk 1 is currently in the CD-ROM drive, and you have stored a number of image requests in the CD Swapper stack, you can open the CD Swapper at a convenient time to recall the image requests and insert the appropriate CD-ROM.

The CD Swapper stack, like the Paths and Notebook stacks, is a stack that can be privately maintained by the user—an advantage in a setting where Perseus is shared with other users. By maintaining your own CD Swapper stack, you can store and recall image requests in different work sessions without mixing up your requests with those of other Perseus users.

Owners of the Concise Edition of Perseus 2.0 will still be prompted by the CD Swapper dialog box if the requested image is not on the disc. If you have access to the Comprehensive Edition (at your university, for example), you can put your CD Swapper stack on a floppy disk for later research.

The images on the CD-ROMs are organized in folders according to image numbers. Each folder contains a set of related images. See section A.1 of the appendix for the contents of the folders.

NOTE: If you are using Perseus on a network or have stored all of Perseus on a gigabyte-sized hard drive, the CD Swapper will not be necessary, because all images will be available.

10.4.1 SWAPPING CD-ROMS

When you request an image that is not on the current CD-ROM, you see a dialog box that asks whether you want to swap CD-ROMs now, cancel the request, or store the request (figure 10.19).

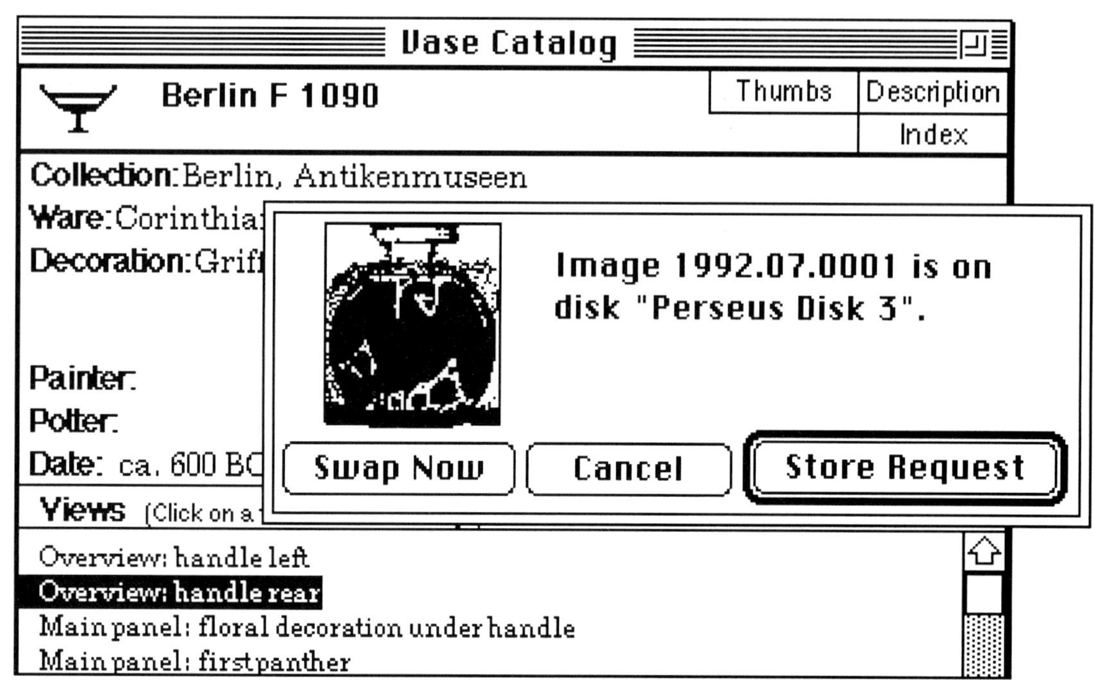

Figure 10.19 CD Swapper dialog box

The dialog box shows a thumbnail of the requested image and indicates the CD-ROM on which the full image is located.

If you choose to swap CD-ROMs now, the current CD-ROM will be ejected from the drive. You must insert the appropriate CD-ROM in the drive, then click the item you desire to link with from the list of requests in the CD Swapper.

10.4.2 STORING AND RECALLING REQUESTS

If you choose to store the request for an image that is not on the current CD-ROM, the image number and a brief description will be stored in a list in the CD Swapper stack (see figure 10.18).

➤ To find a stored image request for an offline CD-ROM, you must previously have stored an image request. For example, with Disk 1 in the CD-ROM drive, choose Vases from the Links menu. Bring up the Vase Index by Collection. Click "Berlin,Antikenmuseen," then click "Berlin F 1090," on the right. Select an image from the Vase Catalog card, and the CD Swapper dialog window will appear. Click Store Request.

➤ Open the CD Swapper by choosing it from the Perseus menu. Perseus will ask you to choose the current CD Swapper stack.

The four discs are listed at the left. At right is a list of stored image requests for one of the CD-ROMs.

Each CD-ROM shows a status of being offline or online. There are also three buttons, Eject Disk, Show List, and Clear List. Eject Disk causes the appropriate CD-ROM to eject from the drive. Show List displays the list of stored image requests for the selected CD-ROM. Clear List deletes the stored image requests for the selected CD-ROM.

➤ Click the Eject Disk button below the number of the current disk to eject the disk, and insert the disk containing the image you wish to see. Then click a line in the list of image requests, and the image will appear. If you request to see an image before changing disks, a dialog box will ask you to insert the appropriate disk. Once you do so, you will have to click the image request again.

➤ You can personalize your CD Swapper stack by duplicating and renaming it (see section 10.1).

10.5 SETTINGS

Detailed configuration settings are accessible from the main Settings utility, reached by clicking the Settings icon on the Perseus Gateway. The Settings utility enables you to choose which stack Perseus will use as the current Path stack, Notebook stack, or CD Swapper stack. The Settings utility offers a choice of using video images from the videodisc or digital images from the CD-ROM volumes. You can use one or both types of images, if your hardware configuration includes a videodisc player. The Settings utility also lets you identify the videodisc player in your configuration.

If you will be using the digitized CD-ROM images, you no longer have to use the Settings utility when you first install Perseus. The Path stack, Notebook stack, and CD Swapper stack distributed with Perseus 2.0 are by default the current stacks on startup, and they will remain so until you change them. The configurations offered by the Settings utility for dealing with images are, for the most part, optional. You must change the current Settings only if you wish to change the configuration of your computer and monitor.

The Perseus Gateway is an unlocked stack (a locked stack is indicated by a small Lock icon at the far right of the menu bar). Therefore, any user may change the Settings. A troubleshooting tip is to check the Settings if you share the Gateway with other users.

10.5.1 PATH, NOTEBOOK, AND CD SWAPPER SETTINGS

➤ Click the Settings icon on the Perseus Gateway. The Perseus Settings Card appears (figure 10.20).

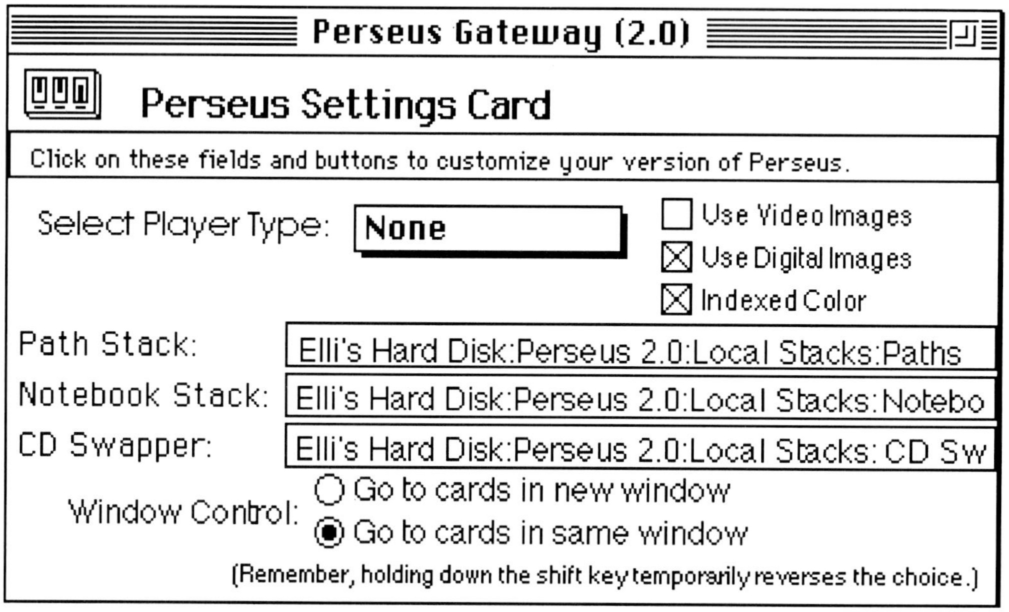

Figure 10.20 Perseus Settings Card

You can customize your configuration by establishing specific locations for user Paths and user Notebooks. (The Notebook and Path utilities are described earlier in this chapter.)

In figure 10.20, the Path Stack specification instructs Perseus to look for the Path stack called Paths, in the folder Local Stacks on Elli's Hard Disk. Similar specifications are shown for the Notebook Stack and the CD Swapper stack.

When you first install Perseus, the default Path and Notebook and CD Swapper stacks are those distributed with the Perseus CD.

➤ To change the Path stack, click the box to the right of Path Stack. A directory dialog box appears for you to identify the file location of the Path stack you wish to make current. Select the desired stack and click Open. Repeat the procedure to change the Notebook and CD Swapper stacks.

You may wish to copy and rename the Path, Notebook, and CD Swapper stacks to create custom stacks. By renaming these stacks, you can distinguish your Paths and Notebooks from those of other users. If several people are using Perseus at one time (on a network), a stack being used by more than one person cannot be changed. Being able to change and annotate the Path and Notebook stacks is very important if you use these features. Copy and rename these stacks as part of your software installation (do this on the Macintosh desktop). See section 2.4, "Detailed Installation and Startup Procedures."

10.5.2 CHOOSE IMAGE TYPE

Perseus offers two types of photographic images. One set of images has been digitized from the Perseus slide archive and stored on the Perseus CD-ROM volumes. The digitized images are compressed 24-bit images that can be displayed on 24-bit, 16-bit, and 8-bit color monitors. The other set of images is on the Perseus videodisc. These require the use of a videodisc player controlled by the Macintosh. See chapter 2, "Equipment Requirements and Setup," for more information on hardware requirements for images. You may use the videodisc images, the digitized images, or both.

➤ To load the appropriate settings for your videodisc player, click the box Use Video Images. Then choose one of the player names from the pop-up menu Select Player Type. If no videodisc player is connected to the Macintosh, the pop-up menu will be inactive.

Perseus 2.0 supports the following videodisc players: Hitachi 9550, Pioneer 4200, Pioneer 6000A, Pioneer 6010A, Sony LDP 1200, Sony 1500, Sony 2000. The name of the selected player appears on the pop-up menu.

The setting below Use Digital Images is a selection for Indexed Color. Digital images are displayed according to the capacity of your monitor and the settings in the Monitors Control Panel (available by choosing Control Panels from the Apple menu). Although Perseus images are 24-bit images, they can be displayed in 8-bit color through the application of a color look-up table (CLUT), or an index of 256 colors that best represent the image in an 8-bit environment. The default setting is to have indexed color on, regardless of the color depth of your monitor. The ability to turn indexed color off simply anticipates future advances in color display technology.

10.5.3 WINDOW CONTROL

Perseus can be set up to open to cards in a new window or open to cards in the current window. Going to cards in a new window means that when you bring up a new card, your previous location in Perseus remains on the screen in a background window. You can progressively layer windows on the screen, but if you exceed the number of open windows allowed by your system's memory, a dialog box will advise you to close some of the windows.

Going to cards in the same window means that your previous location in Perseus is replaced by the card of the new location. No layering of windows occurs.

Either setting can be temporarily reversed by pressing the Shift key while clicking the mouse or choosing a menu item. For example, as you read a Primary Text, you may wish to analyze a word while keeping your Primary Text location in a background window. If the setting is to go to cards in the same window, press the Shift key when you click Analyze, and the Morphological Analysis of the selected word will appear in a new window.

10.5.4 DETAILED CONFIGURATION

The Perseus Gateway stack contains eight cards. These are:

Card 1: Gateway
Card 2: Atlas Settings. Use to save changes in the Atlas configuration.
Card 3: Settings. Discussed earlier in this section.
Card 4: Perseus Movie Settings. Discussed later in this section.
Card 5: Perseus Link Database. Do not change.
Card 6: Perseus File Database. For customized installations.
Card 7: Perseus Image Database.
Card 8: Perseus State of the World. Do not change.

From the Gateway, click the left and right arrows on the Navigator Palette to go to these cards.

Perseus will not operate with the Gateway stack locked. Thus, the data on these cards is not tamper-proof. If any of the data is lost, you can always copy a new Gateway stack from the Local Stacks folder on Perseus Disk 1.

Perseus Movie Settings

➤ To change from Small (default) to Large Thumbnail Browser, unlock the card by clicking the button Edit Settings. A dialog window appears asking if you are sure you want to make the change. If so, click Yes. If you are not sure that your computer has adequate memory for the large Thumbnail Browser, click the Advise button, and Perseus will advise you. Click the button Large Thumbnails. Be sure to click the Lock Settings button before leaving the card.

The Thumbnail images are built from so-called QuickTime movies, although there is no cinematography involved. To change the locations where QuickTime movies are kept, follow these steps. (For network administrators.)

➤ Unlock the card by clicking the button Edit Settings. A dialog window appears asking if you are sure you want to make the change. If so, click Yes.

➤ Type the file path for the movie location in the field provided. Be sure to click the Lock Settings button before leaving the card.

10.6 CURRENT ASSIGNMENT

You may find it useful to create a new HyperCard stack named Current Assignment, on which to post class assignments, messages of the day, or other information useful to a group of users.

You can name any stack in the Local Stacks folder Current Assignment. On the next startup of Perseus, that stack will appear as an item in the Perseus menu. If there is no stack named Current Assignment, no such item will appear in the menu.

> Because the user level under the Perseus Player is set to Read Only, you cannot create a new stack unless you do it under the HyperCard application set at user level 5. From the Finder, you can always rename any already existing stack Current Assignment.

You can make your Current Assignment stack somewhat tamper resistant (though not hacker resistant) by locking the stack from the Get Info box in the Finder (see section 10.3.4 for more detailed instructions). When the stack is locked, its cards are read-only and cannot be deleted.

A.1 CONTENTS OF IMAGE FOLDERS

Contents of image folders on Perseus Disk 1

1987.02: Sculpture from the British Museum, London

1987.03: Reconstructions of the Acropolis from the Royal Ontario Museum, Toronto

1987.04: Sculpture from the Harvard University Art Museums, Cambridge, MA

1987.06: Sculpture from the Martin-von-Wagner-Museum, Würzburg

1987.07: Sculpture from the National Museum, Copenhagen

1990.10: Sculpture from the National Archaeological Museum, Athens

1990.11: Sculpture from the Delphi Museum

1990.13: Sculpture from the Glyptothek, Munich

1990.14: Sculpture from the British Museum, London

1990.15: Sculpture from the Agora Museum, Athens

1990.33: Sculpture drawings by Perseus drafters

1990.36: Sculpture photographs from the Deutsches Archäologisches Institut

1991.05: Sculpture drawings by Candace Smith

1992.01: Sculpture from the Metropolitan Museum of Art, New York, NY

1992.04: Sculpture from the Musée du Louvre, Paris

1992.05: Sculpture from the Staatliche Museen (Pergamonmuseum), Berlin

1992.07: Sculpture from the Staatliche Museen (Charlottenburg Antikenmuseum), Berlin

Contents of image folders on Perseus Disk 2

1987.03: Reconstructions of the Acropolis from the Royal Ontario Museum, Toronto

1987.08: Architecture and topography slides from Thomas Martin and Ivy Sun

1987.09: Architecture and topography slides from the Weinberg collection

1989.01: Architecture and topography slides from Kimberly Patton

1989.v1: Architecture and topography video stills from Fritz Hemans

1990.12: Sculpture from the Olympia Museum

1990.13: Reconstructions of Aegina from the Glyptothek, Munich

1990.14: Reconstructions of Olympia from the British Museum, London

1990.20: Architecture and topography slides from Gregory R. Crane

1990.21: Architecture and topography slides from Maria Daniels

1990.27: Architecture and topography slides from Beth McIntosh and Sebastian Heath

1990.30: Aerial site photography by Father Schoder, S.J., from *Wings Over Hellas*

1990.33: Architectural drawings by Perseus drafters

1991.04: Architecture and topography slides from Michael Bennett

1991.09: Architecture and topography slides from Don Keller

1992.02: Architecture and topography slides from Nick Cahill

1992.12: Architecture and topography slides from Pamela J. Russell

1993.01: Architectural drawings by Candace Smith

1993.02: Architecture and topography slides from Nick Cahill

1994.01: Architecture and topography slides from Maria Daniels

Contents of image folders on Perseus Disk 3

1990.01: Vases from the Harvard University Art Museums, Cambridge, MA

1990.05: Vases from The J. Paul Getty Museum, Malibu, CA

1990.06: Vases from the Johns Hopkins University, Baltimore, MD

1990.14: Vases from the British Museum, London

1990.17: Vases from southern U.S. collections in the Shapiro catalog:

The Ackland Art Museum, University of North Carolina at Chapel Hill
Archer M. Huntington Art Gallery, University of Texas at Austin
Birmingham Museum of Art, Birmingham, AL
Cummer Museum of Art and Gardens, Jacksonville, FL
John and Mable Ringling Museum of Art, Sarasota, FL
North Carolina Museum of Art, Raleigh, NC
Tulane University Art Collection, New Orleans, LA
The University Museum, University of Arkansas, Fayetteville, AR

1990.18: Vases from midwestern U.S. museums in the Moon catalog:

Allen Memorial Art Museum, Oberlin College, Oberlin, OH
Cincinnati Art Museum, Cincinnati, OH
The Cleveland Museum of Art, Cleveland, OH
Dayton Art Institute, Dayton, OH
Frederick R. Weisman Art Museum, University of Minnesota, Minneapolis, MN
Indiana University Art Museum, Bloomington, IN
Indianapolis Museum of Art, Indianapolis, IN
Joslyn Art Museum, Omaha, NE
Kelsey Museum of Archaeology, Ann Arbor, MI
Krannert Art Museum, University of Illinois, Champaign, IL
The Minneapolis Institute of Arts, Minneapolis, MN
Museum of Art and Archaeology, University of Missouri at Columbia
The Nelson-Atkins Museum of Art, Kansas City, MO
Putnam Museum, Davenport, IA

The Saint Louis Art Museum, St. Louis, MO
The Toledo Museum of Art, Toledo, OH
Washington University Gallery of Art, St. Louis, MO
Wright Museum of Art, Beloit College, Beloit, WI

1990.19: Vases from the Wadsworth Athenaeum, Hartford, CT

1990.25: Vases from the Mount Holyoke College Art Museum, South Hadley, MA

1990.32: Vases from the University Museums of the University of Mississippi

1990.33: Vase drawings by Perseus drafters

1990.34: Vases from the Antikensammlungen, Munich

1991.01: Vases from the University Museums of the University of Mississippi

1991.02: Vase drawings from Furtwängler and Reichhold

1992.06: Vases from the Musée du Louvre, Paris

1992.07: Vases from the Staatliche Museen (Charlottenburg Antikenmuseum), Berlin

1992.08: Vases from the Staatliche Museen (Pergamonmuseum), Berlin

1993.01: Photographs of vase drawings from Furtwängler and Reichhold

Contents of image folders on Perseus Disk 4

1989.00: Coins from the Bowdoin College Museum of Art, Brunswick, ME

1989.06: Vases from the Yale University Art Gallery, New Haven, CT

1990.02: Vases from the Yale University Art Gallery, New Haven, CT

1990.03: Vases from the Rhode Island School of Design Museum, Providence, RI

1990.08: Vases from the Smith College Art Museum, Northampton, MA

1990.09: Vases from the Williams College Museum of Art, Williamstown, MA

1990.26: Coins from the Arthur S. Dewing Coin Collection

1990.29: Vases from the Worcester Art Museum, Worcester, MA

1991.07: Vases from the University Museum, University of Pennsylvania, Philadelphia, PA

1991.08: Vases from the Tampa Museum of Art, Tampa, FL

1991.10: Vases from the Toledo Museum of Art, Toledo, OH

1992.09: Vases from the Martin-von-Wagner-Museum, Würzburg

A.2 OUTSIDE SOURCES OF SLIDES IN PERSEUS

Many slides in Perseus were made especially for the project by Perseus photographers, working with collaborating museums. Some slides in Perseus were donated by or purchased from museum and other slide collections, and are used with their permission. These institutions and their addresses follow:

The Ackland Art Museum
Columbia and Franklin Streets
University of North Carolina at Chapel Hill
Chapel Hill, NC 27599

Allen Memorial Art Museum
Oberlin College
Oberlin, OH 44074

Archer M. Huntington Art Gallery
University of Texas at Austin
Art Building
23rd and San Jacinto Streets
Austin, TX 78712

Birmingham Museum of Art
2000 8th Avenue N.
Birmingham, AL 35203

The British Museum
Great Russell Street
WC1B 3DG
London, England

Cincinnati Art Museum
Eden Park
Cincinnati, OH 45202

The Cleveland Museum of Art
11150 East Boulevard at University Circle
Cleveland, OH 44106

Cummer Museum of Art and Gardens
829 Riverside Avenue
Jacksonville, FL 32204

Dayton Art Institute
456 Belmonte Park North
Dayton, OH 45405

Deutsches Archäologisches Institut
Fidiou 1
106 78 Athens, Greece

Frederick R. Weisman Art Museum
University of Minnesota, Twin Cities
333 East River Road
Minneapolis, MN 55455

Harvard University Art Museums
32 Quincy Street
Cambridge, MA 02138

Indiana University Art Museum
Indiana University
Bloomington, IN 47405

Indianapolis Museum of Art
1200 West 38th Street
Indianapolis, IN 46208

The J. Paul Getty Museum
17985 Pacific Coast Highway
Malibu, CA 90265

John and Mable Ringling Museum of Art
5401 Bay Shore Road
Sarasota, FL 34243

Joslyn Art Museum
2200 Dodge Street
Omaha, NE 68102

Kelsey Museum of Archaeology
The University of Michigan
434 South State Street
Ann Arbor, MI 48109

Krannert Art Museum
500 E. Peabody Drive
University of Illinois
Champaign, IL 61820

Martin-von-Wagner-Museum of the University of Würzburg
Antikensammlung
Tor A, Residenz
W-8700 Würzburg, Germany

The Minneapolis Institute of Arts
2400 Third Avenue South
Minneapolis, MN 55404

Museum of Art and Archaeology
University of Missouri—Columbia
Pickard Hall
Columbia, MO 65211

Museum of Fine Arts, Boston
465 Huntington Avenue
Boston, MA 02115

National Museum, Copenhagen
Prinsens Palais
Frederiksholms Kanal 12, 1220
Copenhagen, Denmark

The Nelson-Atkins Museum of Art
4525 Oak Street
Kansas City, MO 64111

North Carolina Museum of Art
2110 Blue Ridge Road
Raleigh, NC 27607

Putnam Museum
1717 W. 12th Street
Davenport, IA 52804

Service photographique
Reunion des Musées Nationaux
89 Avenue Victor Hugo
75116 Paris, France

Royal Ontario Museum
100 Queen's Park
Toronto, Ontario M5S 2C6
Canada

The Saint Louis Art Museum
One Fine Arts Drive
Forest Park
St. Louis, MO 63110

Saul S. Weinberg Slide Collection
Department of Archaeology
Boston University
675 Commonwealth Avenue
Boston, MA 02215

Schoder slides from *Wings Over Hellas*
Bolchazy-Carducci Publishers
1000 Brown Street
Wauconda, IL 60084

Staatliche Antikensammlungen und Glyptothek
Königsplatz 1 u. 3
W8000 Munich, Germany

Staatliche Museen zu Berlin—Preußicher Kulturbesitz
Bodestrasse 1-3
W-1000 Berlin 19, Germany

The Toledo Museum of Art
2445 Monroe Street
Toledo, OH 43620

The Trireme Trust U.S.A.
c/o Paul Lipke
Shipservices
4a Winslow Street
Plymouth, MA 02360

Tulane University Art Collection
Tulane University Library
7001 Freret Street
New Orleans, LA 70118

The University Museum
University of Arkansas
Museum Building Room 202
Fayetteville, AR 72701

University Museums
The University of Mississippi
University, MS 38677

Wadsworth Athenaeum
600 Main Street
Hartford, CT 06103

Washington University Gallery of Art
One Brookings Drive
St. Louis, MO 63130

Wright Museum of Art
Prospect and Bushnell
Beloit College
Beloit, WI 52511

A.3 AUTHORS, WORKS, AND THEIR CANONICAL ABBREVIATIONS

All Primary Texts, related notes, and secondary textual materials are located on Perseus Disk 1.

Aeschines Aeschin.

1 Against Timarchus
Aeschin. 1

2 The Speech on the Embassy
Aeschin. 2

3 Against Ctesiphon
Aeschin. 3

Aeschylus Aesch.

Agamemnon
Aesch. Ag.

Eumenides
Aesch. Eum.

Libation Bearers
Aesch. Lib.

Prometheus Bound
Aesch. PB

Persians
Aesch. Pers.

Seven Against Thebes
Aesch. Seven

Suppliant Maidens
Aesch. Supp.

Andocides Andoc.

1 On the Mysteries
Andoc. 1

2 On His Return
Andoc. 2

3 On the Peace with Sparta
Andoc. 3

4 Against Alcibiades
Andoc. 4

Antiphon Antiph.

1 Prosecution Of The Stepmother For Poisoning
Antiph. 1

2 The First Tetralogy: Anonymous Prosecution for Murder
Antiph. 2

3 The Second Tetralogy: Prosecution for Accidental Homicide
Antiph. 3

4 The Third Tetralogy: Prosecution for Murder Of One Who Pleads Self-Defense
Antiph. 4

5 On the Murder of Herodes
Antiph. 5

6 On the Choreutes
Antiph. 6

Apollodorus Apollod.

Book 1
Apollod. 1

Book 2
Apollod. 2

Book 3
Apollod. 3

Epitome
Apollod. E

Aristophanes Aristoph.

Acharnians
Aristoph. Ach.

Birds
Aristoph. Birds

Clouds
Aristoph. Cl.

Ecclesiazusae
Aristoph. Eccl.

Frogs
Aristoph. Frogs

Knights
Aristoph. Kn.

Lysistrata
Aristoph. Lys.

Peace
Aristoph. Peace

Plutus
Aristoph. Pl.

Thesmophoriazusae
Aristoph. Thes.

Wasps
Aristoph. Wasps

Aristotle Aristot.

Constitution of the Athenians
Aristot. Ath. Pol.

Economics
Aristot. Econ.

Eudemian Ethics
Aristot. Eud. Eth.

Metaphysics
Aristot. Met.

Nicomachean Ethics
Aristot. Nic. Eth.

Poetics
Aristot. Poet.

Politics
Aristot. Pol.

Rhetoric
Aristot. Rh.

Virtues and Vices
Aristot. Vir.

Bacchylides Bacchyl.

Ode 1
Bacchyl. 1

Ode 2
Bacchyl. 2

Ode 3
Bacchyl. 3

Ode 4
Bacchyl. 4

Ode 5
Bacchyl. 5

Ode 6
Bacchyl. 6

Ode 7
Bacchyl. 7

Ode 8
Bacchyl. 8

Ode 9
Bacchyl. 9

Ode 10
Bacchyl. 10

Ode 11
Bacchyl. 11

Ode 12
Bacchyl. 12

Ode 13
Bacchyl. 13

Ode 14
Bacchyl. 14

Ode 14b
Bacchyl. 14b

Ode 15 (Dithyrhamb 1)
Bacchyl. 15

Ode 16 (Dithyrhamb 2)
Bacchyl. 16

Ode 17 (Dithyrhamb 3)
Bacchyl. 17

Ode 18 (Dithyrhamb 4)
Bacchyl. 18

Ode 19 (Dithyrhamb 5)
Bacchyl. 19

Ode 20 (Dithyrhamb 6)
Bacchyl. 20

Demades Demad.

1 On the Twelve Years
Demad. 1

Demosthenes Dem.

1 First Olynthiac
Dem. 1

2 Second Olynthiac
Dem. 2

3 Third Olynthiac
Dem. 3

4 First Philippic
Dem. 4

5 On the Peace
Dem. 5

6 Second Philippic
Dem. 6

7 On Halonnesus
Dem. 7

8 On the Chersonese
Dem. 8

9 Third Philippic
Dem. 9

10 Fourth Philippic
Dem. 10

11 Answer to Philip's Letter
Dem. 11

12 Philip's Letter
Dem. 12

13 On Organization
Dem. 13

14 On the Navy-Boards
Dem. 14

15 For the Liberty of the Rhodians
Dem. 15

16 For the People of Megalopolis
Dem. 16

17 On the Treaty with Alexander
Dem. 17

18 On the Crown
Dem. 18

19 On the Embassy
Dem. 19

20 Against Leptines
Dem. 20

21 Against Meidias
Dem. 21

22 Against Androtion
Dem. 22

23 Against Aristocrates
Dem. 23

24 Against Timocrates
Dem. 24

25 Against Aristogeiton 1
Dem. 25

26 Against Aristogeiton 2
Dem. 26

27 Against Aphobus 1
Dem. 27

28 Against Aphobus 2
Dem. 28

29 Against Aphobus 3
Dem. 29

30 Against Onetor 1
Dem. 30

31 Against Onetor 2
Dem. 31

32 Against Zenothemis
Dem. 32

33 Against Apaturius
Dem. 33

34 Against Phormio
Dem. 34

35 Against Lacritus
Dem. 35

36 For Phormio
Dem. 36

37 Against Pantaenetus
Dem. 37

38 Against Nausimachus and Xenopeithes
Dem. 38

39 Against Boeotus 1
Dem. 39

40 Against Boeotus 2
Dem. 40

41 Against Spudias
Dem. 41

42 Against Phaenippus
Dem. 42

43 Against Macartatus
Dem. 43

44 Against Leochares
Dem. 44

45 Apollodorus Against Stephanus 1
Dem. 45

46 Apollodorus Against Stephanus 2
Dem. 46

47 Against Evergus And Mnesibulus
Dem. 47

48 Against Olympiodorus
Dem. 48

49 Apollodorus Against Timotheus
Dem. 49

50 Apollodorus Against Polycles
Dem. 50

51 On The Trierarchic Crown
Dem. 51

52 Apollodorus Against Callipus
Dem. 52

53 Apollodorus Against Nicostratus
Dem. 53

54 Against Conon
Dem. 54

55 Against Callicles
Dem. 55

56 Against Dionysodorus
Dem. 56

57 Euxitheus Against Eubulides
Dem. 57

58 Against Theocrines
Dem. 58

59 Apollodorus Against Neaera
Dem. 59

60 The Funeral Speech
Dem. 60

61 The Erotic Essay
Dem. 61

Exordia
Dem. Ex.

Letters
Dem. L.

Dinarchus Din.

1 Against Demosthenes
Din. 1

2 Against Aristogiton
Din. 2

3 Against Philocles
Din. 3

Diodorus Siculus Diod.

Book 9
Diod. 9

Book 10
Diod. 10

Book 11
Diod. 11

Book 12
Diod. 12

Book 13
Diod. 13

Book 14
Diod. 14

Book 15
Diod. 15

Book 16
Diod. 16

Book 17
Diod. 17

Euripides Eur.

Alcestis
Eur. Alc.

Andromache
Eur. Andr.

Bacchae
Eur. Ba.

Cyclops
Eur. Cycl.

Electra
Eur. El.

Hecuba
Eur. Hec.

Helen
Eur. Hel.

Heracles
Eur. Her.

Heraclidae
Eur. Heraclid.

Hippolytus
Eur. Hipp.

Iphigenia in Aulis
Eur. IA

Ion
Eur. Ion

Iphigeneia in Tauris
Eur. IT

Medea
Eur. Med.

Orestes
Eur. Orest.

Phoenician Women
Eur. Phoen.

Rhesus
Eur. Rh.

Suppliants
Eur. Supp.

Trojan Woman
Eur. Tro.

Isthmian 3
Pind. I. 3

Isthmian 4
Pind. I. 4

Isthmian 5
Pind. I. 5

Isthmian 6
Pind. I. 6

Isthmian 7
Pind. I. 7

Isthmian 8
Pind. I. 8

Nemean 1
Pind. N. 1

Nemean 2
Pind. N. 2

Nemean 3
Pind. N. 3

Nemean 4
Pind. N. 4

Nemean 5
Pind. N. 5

Nemean 6
Pind. N. 6

Nemean 7
Pind. N. 7

Nemean 8
Pind. N. 8

Nemean 9
Pind. N. 9

Nemean 10
Pind. N. 10

Nemean 11
Pind. N. 11

Olympian 1
Pind. O. 1

Olympian 2
Pind. O. 2

Olympian 3
Pind. O. 3

Olympian 4
Pind. O. 4

Olympian 5
Pind. O. 5

Olympian 6
Pind. O. 6

Olympian 7
Pind. O. 7

Olympian 8
Pind. O. 8

Olympian 9
Pind. O. 9

Olympian 10
Pind. O. 10

Olympian 11
Pind. O. 11

Olympian 12
Pind. O. 12

Olympian 13
Pind. O. 13

Olympian 14
Pind. O. 14

Pythian 1
Pind. P. 1

Pythian 2
Pind. P. 2

Pythian 3
Pind. P. 3

Pythian 4
Pind. P. 4

Pythian 5
Pind. P. 5

Pythian 6
Pind. P. 6

Pythian 7
Pind. P. 7

Pythian 8
Pind. P. 8

Pythian 9
Pind. P. 9

Pythian 10
Pind. P. 10

Pythian 11
Pind. P. 11

Pythian 12
Pind. P. 12

Plato Plat.

Alcibiades 1
Plat. Alc. 1

Alcibiades 2
Plat. Alc. 2

Apology
Plat. Apol.

Charmides
Plat. Charm.

Cleitophon
Plat. Cleit.

Cratylus
Plat. Crat.

Critias
Plat. Criti.

Crito
Plat. Crito

Epinomis
Plat. Epin.

Euthydemus
Plat. Euthyd.

Euthyphro
Plat. Euthyph.

Gorgias
Plat. Gorg.

Greater Hippias
Plat. Hipp. Maj.

Lesser Hippias
Plat. Hipp. Min.

Hipparchus
Plat. Hipparch.

Ion
Plat. Ion

Letters
Plat. L.

Laches
Plat. Lach.

Laws
Plat. Laws

Lovers
Plat. Lovers

Lysis
Plat. Lysis

Menexenus
Plat. Menex.

Meno
Plat. Meno

Minos
Plat. Minos

Parmenides
Plat. Parm.

Phaedo
Plat. Phaedo

Phaedrus
Plat. Phaedrus

Philebus
Plat. Phileb.

Protagoras
Plat. Prot.

Republic
Plat. Rep.

Sophist
Plat. Soph.

Statesman
Plat. Stat.

Symposium
Plat. Sym.

Theaetetus
Plat. Thaeat.

Theages
Plat. Theag.

Timaeus
Plat. Tim.

Plutarch Plut.

Alcibiades
Plut. Alc.

Aristides
Plut. Arist.

Cimon
Plut. Cim.

Lysander
Plut. Lys.

Nicias
Plut. Nic.

Pericles
Plut. Per.

Solon
Plut. Sol.

Themistocles
Plut. Them.

Theseus
Plut. Thes.

Pseudo-Xenophon Ps. Xen.

Constitution of the Athenians
Ps. Xen. Const. Ath.

Sophocles Soph.

Ajax
Soph. Aj.

Antigone
Soph. Ant.

Electra
Soph. El.

Oedipus at Colonus
Soph. OC

Oedipus Tyrannus
Soph. OT

Philoctetes
Soph. Phil.

Trachiniae
Soph. Trach.

Strabo Strab.

Book 6 (South Italy, Sicily)
Strab. 6

Book 7 (fragmentary)
Strab. 7

Book 8 (Macedon and Greece)
Strab. 8

Book 9 (Athens, Boeotia, Thessaly)
Strab. 9

Book 10 (Aetolia, Crete, other islands)
Strab. 10

Book 11 (Asia Minor–East)
Strab. 11

Book 12 (Asia Minor–Central South)
Strab. 12

Book 13 (Asia Minor–North)
Strab. 13

Book 14 (Asia Minor–West, Southwest, Cyprus)
Strab. 14

Thucydides Thuc.

Book 1
Thuc. 1

Book 2
Thuc. 2

Book 3
Thuc. 3

Book 4
Thuc. 4

Book 5
Thuc. 5

Book 6
Thuc. 6

Book 7
Thuc. 7

Book 8
Thuc. 8

Xenophon Xen.

Agesilaus
Xen. Ag.

Anabasis
Xen. Anab.

Apology of Socrates
Xen. Apol.

On the Cavalry Commander
Xen. Cav.

Constitution of the Lacedaemonians
Xen. Const. Lac.

Cyropaedia
Xen. Cyrop.

Economics
Xen. Ec.

Hellenica
Xen. Hell.

Hiero
Xen. Hiero

On Horsemanship
Xen. Horse.

On Hunting
Xen. Hunt.

Memorabilia
Xen. Mem.

Symposium
Xen. Sym.

Ways and Means
Xen. Ways

A.4 AUTHOR GROUPS

Authors are listed here by form and genre.

Hexameter

Homer
Hesiod

Lyric

Baccylides
Pindar

Tragedy

Aeschylus
Euripides
Sophocles

Comedy

Aristophanes

History

Herodotus
Thucydides
Xenophon

Orators

Aeschines
Andocides

Antiphon
Demosthenes
Demades
Dinarchus
Hyperides
Isaeus
Isocrates
Lycurgus
Lysias

Philosophers
Plato
Aristotle
Xenophon??

Post-Classical
Pausanias
Plutarch
Apollodorus

Licensing Agreement for

Perseus 2.0: Interactive Sources and Studies on Ancient Greece

The copyright to the enclosed CD-ROM database, *Perseus 2.0: Interactive Sources and Studies on Ancient Greece* (hereafter "the database"), is owned by the Corporation for Public Broadcasting and the President and Fellows of Harvard College and is protected by the copyright laws of the United States and the universal copyright convention. Neither Yale University Press (hereafter "the publisher") nor the President and Fellows of Harvard College nor the Corporation for Public Broadcasting represents or warrants that the information contained in the database is complete or free from error, and they do not assume, and do expressly disclaim, any liability to any person or institution for any loss or damage caused by the database, whether such errors or omissions result from negligence, accident, or any other cause. Neither the publisher nor the Corporation for Public Broadcasting nor the President and Fellows of Harvard College will be responsible for the installation or maintenance of the database. In no event will the publisher, the Corporation for Public Broadcasting, or the President and Fellows of Harvard College be liable for any damages arising from use of or inability to use the database.

No part of the database may be copied onto electronic or magnetic media or other machine-readable form except for temporary use or storage. Information retrieved from the database, whether printed, transcribed, photocopied, or downloaded, cannot be resold. In no event may the database in its entirety or in lengthy sequences be printed, transcribed, photocopied, or downloaded, for sale or conveyance of value to a third party or for any other purpose. The database cannot be used as a component of or as the basis for any derivative work, database, courseware, software program, or other work without the express written consent of the publisher. The database shall be acknowledged, with the proper copyright notice, as the source of any derivative work.